The Global Family Therapist

Integrating the Personal, Professional, and Political

Benina Berger Gould

Saybrook Institute

and

Donna Hilleboe DeMuth

University of New England School of Social Work

Allyn and Bacon

Boston London Toronto Sydney Tokyo Singapore

This book was developed under the auspices of the American Family Therapy Association (AFTA).

Editor-in-Chief, Social Sciences: Susan Badger
Composition Buyer: Linda Cox
Manufacturing Buyer: Louise Richardson
Cover Administrator: Suzanne Harbison
Cover Designer: Mike Fender
Production Administrator: Deborah Brown
Editorial-Production Service: P. M. Gordon Associates

Copyright © 1994 by Allyn and Bacon
A Division of Simon & Schuster, Inc.
160 Gould Street
Needham Heights, MA 02194

Library of Congress Cataloging-in-Publication Data

The global family therapist : integrating the personal, professional, and political /
   [edited by] Benina Berger Gould, Donna Hilleboe DeMuth.
       p. cm.
   Includes bibliographical references.
   ISBN 0–205–14107–2
   1. Family psychotherapy—Social aspects. 2. Nuclear warfare—
Psychological aspects. 3. Family psychotherapy—Political aspects.
4. Family—Mental health. I. Berger Gould, Benina. II. DeMuth,
Donna Hilleboe.
RC488.5.G56 1994
616.89′156—dc20   93–17694
                                                                              CIP

Printed in the United States of America
10 9 8 7 6 5 4 3 2 1   98 97 96 95 94 93

In memory of
Mortimer M. Berger, 1911–1988
and
Mabel Tronnes Hilleboe, 1899–1992

We dedicate this book to our children, grandchildren, and great-grandchildren.

Contents

Foreword

During the last decade, family therapy theory and practice have been influenced from two directions. One direction has encouraged the field to pay increased attention to the experience of the individual in the family system, including such issues as affect, cognition, ethics, and individual responsibility. The other direction has expanded the boundaries of our focus to include all of the larger systems that have an impact on family functioning and well-being, including medical, legal, educational, and religious systems, as well as the wider social contextual levels of culture, race, class, and gender. This book, *The Global Family Therapist: Integrating the Personal, Professional, and Political*, intricately braids these two directions in a volume that is truly systemic. Benina Berger Gould and Donna Hilleboe DeMuth and their colleagues from the American Family Therapy Academy Study Group on Family Systems Thinking and the Nuclear Dilemma have produced a unique edited volume, one that taps multiple levels of *system*, including the inner system of the individual (both client and therapist); the family; the family–larger system; and, in a meaningful expansion of all previous work, the system formed by individuals, the family, the therapist, *and* the global context. This work helps us to see a new level of system, so encompassing that one cannot delude oneself into thinking that it is possible to stand outside of it or to be "neutral."

In most edited volumes, a group of authors, many of whom may never see or speak with one another during a book's genesis, is brought together by an editor. In contrast, this book arose from a group of people who have been working together on the nuclear issue and environmental survival in an interdependent fashion. Early in the 1980s, the nuclear threat began to appear as a topic in plenary sessions and in workshops at national family therapy conferences. As quickly as this critical issue appeared, it disappeared from the public professional arena, and newer, "trendier" topics took its place. The authors of this volume, however, kept on working: they examined the effects of the nuclear threat on children and families; sought new models of research, theory, and practice sufficient to hold the magnitude of pending nuclear holocaust; and created paradigms that challenge the traditional locus of assessment and intervention. While each chapter stands on its own, the voices of the authors speaking to one another as they struggled with the most painful and perilous issues of our time come forth. As a reader, I came away with a sense of yet another system, that of professionals collaborating with both courage and vulnerability, with clear differentiation from one another and an overarching sense of connectedness, to produce an original work. Their collaboration serves as a template for the deep exploration of other issues in our field.

The chapters in this volume are written in the first person, creating yet another level of system, that of author and reader. As a reader, I came to know more than the theories of the authors. I was brought into direct contact with inner thoughts that usually do not make it to the printed page: their fears, their moments of deepest despair, and their moments of greatest hope. Courageous ventures to Russia and Nicaragua; into the closed and rarefied world of arms and defense policy analysts; into the polarized abortion debate; and into environmental concerns are brought exquisitely alive in a manner that neither allowed me to put distance between myself and the issues nor overwhelmed me with their enormity. This group of colleagues has struggled for more than a decade to understand how the global issues of nuclear and environmental threats can meaningfully be brought into the consulting room and how the usual walls of the consulting room can be torn down and refashioned to include key segments of a community, a nation, or self-defined enemies. Their expertise as well as their humbleness has generated an open-ended volume, one that requires the reader to keep working long after the reading has stopped.

In recent years, the family therapy field has been grappling with many clinical issues that were previously invisible to us, including the debilitating effects of addictions, incest, and physical abuse in families and the ignored realities of how gender, ethnicity, race, and social class shape family and therapeutic relationships. As the field has developed, it has become abundantly and sometimes painfully clear that if clients do not raise an issue, this does not mean that the issue is not critical. The present volume helps us to take the next step in breaking the silence, in opening toxic secrets, and in making the less visible more visible.

As I read *The Global Family Therapist*, I found myself reaching for a new lens for both theory and practice. I began to imagine a therapy with much less distance between therapist and client, a therapy where our connectedness as human beings was far more profound than our differences.

Evan Imber-Black

Introduction

BEGINNINGS

One of the great benefits of thinking systemically is that crisis can be seen in a more hopeful light; we know that even as crisis escalates, the forces for growth within a system may actually become more available. In this regard, global systems are no different than family systems.

In the spring of 1982, the world seemed to be rushing headlong into a nuclear confrontation that would annihilate the entire planet. Midway through his first term of office, President Ronald Reagan had escalated the arms race against the "evil empire" of the Soviet Union. Experts warned that current nuclear technology was sufficient to destroy both countries as well as to alter irrevocably the world's environmental ecosystem.

As our nation came terrifyingly close to nuclear war, however, counterforces were already beginning to mobilize. For example, in June, a rally protesting nuclear war drew 400,000 marchers to New York City; organizations such as SANE/Freeze and Physicians for Social Responsibility were being revitalized; and the International PSSR was about to receive a Nobel prize for its efforts to bring Soviet and American physicians together on behalf of world peace. Change was in the air. Yet experiencing only our individual concerns, many of us did not realize that we were taking a small part in the beginning of a historic movement.

During that same year, we, Donna and Benina, were both busy with our own families, with teaching, and with our private practices. Both of us were slightly disillusioned veterans of the civil rights movement. Later we learned that we were both feeling enraged, frightened, and helpless in the face of escalating threats to global survival. Separately we had begun to re-energize ourselves through the Despair and Empowerment concepts of Joanna Rogers Macy (1981). Family developments had intensified our sensitivity to the planetary dilemmas. Donna had recently become a grandmother; Benina's 15-year-old son felt stuck in his worry about the world's future.

Responding to a real sense of urgency, but without a clear agenda, Donna convened an Interest Group at the Annual Meeting of the American Family Therapy Association[1] (AFTA) in Boston, June 1982, to address concerns about professional responsibility vis-à-vis the perilous world situation. Benina joined the group. We viewed tapes of children discussing their fears of nuclear war and cried together for the first, but not the last, time.

Together Donna and Benina formed a partnership. We wanted to use our expertise as family therapists to find ways to intervene into the troubled global system, and we did not want to tackle this enormous task alone.

At the same meeting, in a synchronicity that no longer seems unusual, a group led by Donald Bloch from the Ackerman Institute for Family Therapy[2] called together a large number of AFTA members who were also concerned about the possibility of nuclear war. The group, named Half-Life, focused on political action. Their first step was to petition the Board of Directors of AFTA to take an official position condemning the use of nuclear weapons. In response, the Board appointed Don as chair of the first Task Force on the Nuclear Threat. In 1983, Benina was handed the mantle, and the Task Force was renamed the Study Group on Family Systems Thinking and the Nuclear Dilemma.[3] Both the Study Group and the Interest Group on Global Survival Issues continued to meet, learning, during the following years, how to exist within an organization that, until then, had been entirely devoted to clinical and research matters.[4]

This book brings together the work of some of the AFTA members who were part of these groups. It does not include all of the work done by family therapists who have been concerned about global issues, nor does it include a focus on every one of the threats to our planet. Perhaps that would be impossible. Notable omissions are concerns about acquired immunodeficiency syndrome (AIDS), overpopulation, famine, and political genocide.

Rather, this book is the story of a journey taken by a few adventurous and hardy souls with a common purpose and shared expertise. The journey began in response to our concerns as family therapists about imminent nuclear war but developed in ways that express our unique personal, professional, and political interests and styles. Most of us have met at the Annual Meeting of AFTA and discussed our work together then. This volume, however, projects strongly individuated voices weaving a central tapestry.

The world has changed a great deal since 1982 and so have we. Our work has broadened and deepened over time. Some concerns about nuclear war have been eased by the reduced tensions between the Western and Eastern blocs of nations, with the Berlin Wall crumbling down. We realize, however, that other international conflicts still are unresolved and that the proliferation of nuclear weapons runs rampant. Equally pressing for us, as we write, is the slower, more insidious threat to the fragile earth ecosystem created by a society that chooses not to control its technological excess. At the same time, our future is increasingly in jeopardy from threats of the AIDS epidemic, homelessness, and uncontrolled violence.

The authors and editors of this book believe strongly that the position of the clinician in regard to the dangers of global self-destruction has not changed. We see that most of us still treat the psychological complaints of individuals and families within the pseudosafety of our offices, while the fires of long-term devastation rage quietly and almost invisibly outside our doors (Porter, 1987). This book chooses to focus instead on how these fires affect our work and the lives of the families we see.

CHALLENGES, REWARDS, AND APPRECIATIONS

Throughout the entire book, we are interested in the personal, professional, and political challenges that emerge for the family therapist whose work broadens to a global perspective, in whatever form that work may take.

For example, there is a danger of distorted thinking or of creating simplistic solutions when knowledge gained from work with small systems is used to address issues that exist in larger and more complex systems. In addition, the therapist can step beyond the usual boundaries of objectivity in this work. We walk a fine line between the concerned citizen's zeal for activism and the clinician/researcher's commitment to thorough and accurate explorations. Finally, and perhaps most important, we can become overwhelmed by the life and death nature of the complex issues we explore. We struggle to maintain our emotional balance in this task, becoming neither paralyzed by despair nor relieved by diminishing the seriousness of the dangers.

Just as we can experience terror as we work in the context of the world's enormous problems, however, we also can experience the hope and support available because of its enormous resources. For us, Benina and Donna, the sense of resource has become more prominent than the sense of despair. We could not have done this work without these resources and would like to acknowledge them now.

First, we give credit to the American Family Therapy Academy, which gave us the first forum for our work and brought together the wonderful human beings who have authored this volume. We are grateful to Richard Schwartz and Morris Taggert, Chairs of the Publications Committee of the AFTA Board, for their encouragement and promotion of the work. We also would like to express deep appreciation to other AFTA members whose work has supported us, even though it is not directly represented in the book: Celia Falicov, Robert Garfield, Robert Jay Green, Rachel Hare-Mustin, Dennis Jaffe, David MacGill, Michelle Klaven Ritterman, Marvin Snider, and Steve Zeitlin. We also thank Susan Watson, Barbro Miles, and Sandra Blair from the AFTA central office. Susan Badger of Allyn and Bacon believed in the work immediately and, with Dana Hayes, helped us in the tedious process of bringing our manuscripts into the shape of a book. The highly respected professionals who reviewed an earlier draft of the book were tremendously helpful to us in our revisions. They are Gregory Brock, Vincent Foley, Daniel Lee, Lee Combrink-Graham, Marsha Mirkin, and Marilyn Mason. Our thanks go to each one of them.

Our gratitude swells for Marsha Pravder Mirkin. Her sensitive editing of the book *Political and Social Contexts of Family Therapy* (1990) first allowed Donna to find her written voice. Her wisdom, heart, and energy inspired us all, both during the times when she had hoped to co-edit this volume, and after she had moved on.

Special thanks go to our spiritual mentors and teachers: Joanna Rogers Macy, Virginia Satir, Susan Griffin, Wendy Roberts, Barbara Hazard, Chellis Glendinning, Susan Buffany, Ngawangthondup Narkyid, and Venerable Lama Kunga Rinpoche. We thank our parents who gave us the sense of vision as well as the tools to engage in this work. We also appreciate the many feminist scholars who have affirmed our belief in the moral value of human connections and also in the importance of nonlinear approaches to learning.

Michelle Klaven Ritterman's outspoken voice has given courage to us both, through her life and through her book, *Hope Under Siege* (1991).

Special help was given to Donna by her friend Carol Burdick's generosity, editing skill, and unfailing love. Thanks as well go to Brenda Garmon, whose infinite patience allowed, finally, a coherent typescript to emerge. The devotion, stimulation, and perspective of friends and colleagues held Donna to the course over the years: Joe Melnick, Bruce St. Thomas, Kathleen Sullivan, Denis Noonan, Mary McCann, and Bonnie Lazar from the Family Interviewing Project; Sarah Conn, Suzie Pearce, Sarah Pirtle, Kevin McVeigh, Ervin and Sylvia Staub, and Marya Bloom from Interhelp; and Johanna Schwab, Goldie Ivener, Jane Gerber, Michele Baldwin, and Anne and Bill Nerin from the Avanta Network. Finally, Peter McNelis, then Director of the University of New England School of Social Work, and Harold Johnson, Dean of the School of Social Work, University of Michigan, were invaluable in making library facilities available.

Benina was assisted by Susan Moon, her editor and friend. Her colleagues at the Center for Science and International Affairs (James Blight, Ash Carter, and Joseph Nye) as well as at the University of California, Berkeley, Center for Slavic and East European Studies trusted her always in whatever her work involved. Friends and members of her peer supervision group also stood by her: Erica Stern, Linda Leah Lund, Casi Kushel, Sarah Stearns, and Jane Ariel. Extra thanks go to her sisters, Stefani Berger Steiger and Amanda Berger Emsellem, who provided both political wisdom and babysitting when needed.

Both of us were inspired by a passionate wish that the dysfunctional planet be restored, to sustain the lives of our children Ezra, Alison, and Tenzin Lhadon Gould and Jodi, Nancy, and Michael DeMuth and Barbara DeMuth Clark. They inspire us and lead us forward. In addition, Donna's awareness of the next generation is always present in the lives of her grandchildren: Kristofer, Alia, Mischa, Emily, Caitlin, Michele, Ryan, and Kathryn.

Donna appreciates the love of her husband, Donald, over many years as well as his determination that the word processor not entirely dominate their life together.

Benina thanks her husband, Jeffrey, for being with her this time around, when the work demanded all her energy. He has supported her with love and appreciation of her courage and fortitude.

Finally:

To Donna—I thank you for your kindness and nurturance throughout. You have the traits I most associate with a highly developed human being: compassion, patience, and plenty of chutzpah.

To Benina—your chutzpah always came through when mine wavered! Most of all, I have loved the way in which you accepted and reframed all the negative energy and emotions that this work can inspire. You have helped me to feel less scared and less crazy in this scary and crazy world.

For both of us, the greatest consequence of our work together has been that we have lost much of the sense of impotence against the forces of global destruction with which we began. We have learned that we do have tools to use in the service of survival. Using them, creating this book, has left us more hopeful for the future. If we, ordinary people, can find a way to do something to help our planet survive, then perhaps so can others.

NOTES

1. The American Family Therapy Association, since renamed the American Family Therapy Academy, is an international group of teachers and researchers in family systems therapy, whose purpose is to encourage high levels of expertise in the work.
2. The Ackerman Institute is a well-known family therapy research and training center in New York City.
3. Study group members were all interested in family systems, some primarily as clinicians, some as researchers. For the purposes of clarity, we will describe them inclusively as "family therapists."
4. Organizational movement was also occurring. Six years later, the AFTA Board of Directors adopted a resolution that AFTA become involved in social policy issues (AFTA *Newsletter*, 1988).

BIBLIOGRAPHY

AFTA and social policy advocacy. (1988). AFTA *Newsletter, 32,* 6.

Macy, J. (1981). Despair work. *Evolutionary Blues—An Interhelp Quarterly, 1.*

Mirkin, M. P. (Ed.). (1990). *Political and social contexts of family therapy.* Boston: Allyn & Bacon.

Porter, K. (1987). The role of the psychotherapist in the nuclear age. In K. Porter, D. Rinzler, & P. Olsen (Eds.). *Heal or die: Psychotherapists confront nuclear annihilation.* New York: Psychohistory Press.

Ritterman, M. K. (1991). *Hope under siege: terror and family support in Chile.* Norwood, NJ: Ablex Publishing Co.

Donna Hilleboe DeMuth
Benina Berger Gould

Setting the Context
for the Global Family Therapist

The relationship between family therapy theory and practice and a global point of view may seem to be obvious, given the focus on context that systems thinkers espouse. Nonetheless, little attention has previously been paid to this issue. The three authors in this section, Donna Hilleboe DeMuth, Norbert Wetzel, and Erika Waechter, present their unique visions of this relationship.

In Chapter 1, *A Global Paradigm for Family Therapists in the 21st Century*, Donna makes a case for expanding the client/therapist contract to include the essential meaning of the planetary dilemma. She explores ways in which theory and prevailing practice can both support and impede such an approach to therapy. She argues for a new view of *distance regulation* and a new definition of self for both client and therapist that would encourage their empowerment in the face of global dangers. Her work is influenced not only by systems thinking, but also by the work of feminist psychology and the Despair/Empowerment movement.

Norbert presents a similar point of view, in Chapter 2, *Beyond the Therapy Room: Therapy and Politics in the Nuclear Age.* His approach, however, is very different from Donna's. His thinking is informed by his studies in philosophy and theology. He argues for a new epistemology in family theory that could reconcile the claims of both the individual and the system. Like Donna, he sees a new paradigm for family therapy emerging in which the best interests of the client/family would be served by a focus on healing the troubled world system. He too proposes a new model for defining self, based on the literature of philosophy and ethics.

Erika's approach is more pragmatic. In Chapter 3, *How Do Therapists Deal with Issues of Global Survival in the Therapy Hour?*, she reports on what a number of practicing therapists actually do in response to global survival issues. For example, she examines how they conceptualize these issues in relation to their clients' presenting problems and how they respond to clients' concerns about the world situation. In summarizing her study, Erika also calls for a redefinition of family systems thinking so that issues of global concern may be more readily incorporated into the therapeutic process.

Chapter 1

A Global Paradigm for Family Therapists in the 21st Century[1]

Donna Hilleboe DeMuth

As psychological habituation to war and evil spreads, the intellectual and professional community has—more than ever—a moral obligation to link its scholarly perspectives with ethical involvement. For, to know about killing—and to remain silent—is to be an accessory to that killing and to face profound moral corruption. To meet the evils of power with professional neutrality is to become a behavior technologist who helps render society holocaust-prone.

—Chatham, 1978

These strong words force me to declare a position.

No, I am not neutral. I am no longer distant from the perils of our times. I will name them as evil. The wanton destruction of trees and air is named murder. The annihilation of millions of lives in Nazi Germany, in Soviet Russia, in Cambodia, and in Chile is named genocide, the murder of the race. I name as evil the technology that gives us the possibility of destroying the entire world in 6 minutes. That evil, culturally sanctioned, is named abuse of power. Its manifestations are visible even in rural Maine, where I live, as children and women are beaten, as young people shoot each other with guns, and as desperate people anesthetize themselves with chemicals.

I know that the further I detach myself from the awareness of evil, the less I feel it personally, and the easier it is for me to go on with my daily life, which I love. But, because I do love life so much, I do not want to be a killer, or even an unwitting accomplice to killing. In the vision of Staub (1990), if I do not speak out, I will become a perpetrator of the very violence I abhor.

My skill in the world is as a therapist and healer. The consistent focus in my life, both at home and at work, is on family. Therefore, it makes sense to me to use my family therapist's knowledge to refine my rage, to understand more fully the nature of the evil, and to learn how the forces of growth can be put to use for the good of the planetary family. I will remind myself often that the lives of children, including my own, are at stake. I can do nothing else.

The threat of nuclear holocaust has been in the foreground of my own awareness as I have searched for ways to integrate my personal, professional, and political life. For the purposes of this chapter, however, I will understand *nuclear war* not only as a terrible threat in its own right, but also as a metaphor for the global disaster that is coming more slowly, quietly, and, perhaps, more insidiously from many other directions, such as the deterioration of the environment, widespread famine, and the scourge of acquired immunodeficiency syndrome (AIDS).

For the purposes of this chapter, I will define a system in terms used by Pappajohn and Spiegel (1975):

> Cultural, social, psychological, and biological events constitute a field of transacting processes in which change in one part is related to change in the others. (p. ix)

When I refer to culture, I will borrow the definition used by Kai Erikson (1976):

> [T]hose modes of thinking and knowing and doing that a people learn to regard as natural, those beliefs and attitudes that help shape a people's way of looking at themselves and the rest of the universe, those ideas and symbols that a people employ to make sense of their own everyday experience as members of society. (p. 79)

I believe that culture is the "stuff" of psychotherapy, expressed through ordinary events of the lives that clients present to us (Carter, 1990; McGoldrick, Pearce, & Giordano, 1982). Many pioneers of family therapy maintained that there is direct relationship between the problems brought by our clients to therapy and the culture in which they—and we—live (Bateson, 1987; Framo, 1972; Framo & Green, 1981; Satir, 1983). To be effective, family therapists must know a great deal about the nature of their culture. Therefore, it is absolutely necessary for us to know something about the ways in which living under the threat of apocalypse affects both our clients and ourselves.

Understanding, however, is different from intervening. If, as family therapists, we use our knowledge to offer suggestions for healing global dysfunction, we raise profound questions about our role in society. Do we have the responsibility to intervene in matters of social concern, as Framo (1972) and Charny (1982) have mandated? Do we have sufficient expertise? If so, how can we best use it?

An eloquent defense of the socially concerned family therapist comes from O'Connor (1989):

> By helping people adjust to a destructive society are we doing more harm than good? . . . The planet is dying because we are satisfied with our limited relationships in which control, denial, and abuse are tolerated . . . Healthy relationships are not an esoteric goal. [They are] a matter of our very survival and the survival of most of the life on this earth. (pp. 69, 70)

In this chapter, I will develop more fully my ideas and the ideas of others about the role of family therapists in global matters. First, I will attempt to define the problem. Next, I will present evidence to support the relevance of family therapy concepts and expertise to the understanding of and solutions to the problems of the evils that I have named. Then I will explore the need to expand our definition of family therapy in the nuclear age by redefining our current notions of therapeutic distance and of self-in-context. I will end with some pre-liminary ideas of how that redefinition might actually shape the clinical work that we do.

DEFINING THE PROBLEM

The first concern for the family therapist who intervenes in global matters is to define the problem. There is no *identified patient*. Clients rarely name their worries about world survival as part of their difficulties.

Family therapists do know that the way a problem is defined can lead either to its solution or to lack of solution. The problem of the global threats, however, is that, as Schwebel (1986) points out, they are diffuse and ambiguous. Public pronouncements of political leaders could lead us to believe either that the prob-lems of global self-destruction are unsolvable or that they do not exist. Most of us have little evidence in our immediate lives to indicate that our survival is at risk. Meanwhile, television reports emphasize the dramatic events that are polluting the environment: the *Valdez* oil spill, contaminated hypodermic needles on beaches, garbage barges adrift off the coast of New Jersey, and many other horrors. Famine overcomes Somalia; the AIDS epidemic begins to reach into larger segments of the population. As the United States and the former Soviet Union de-escalate the nuclear arms race, the existence of nuclear warheads in the Middle East and in China indicates that the danger still exists. Despite this reality, less than half of the adult respondents to recent studies (Kanovsky, 1989) believe that a nuclear war will occur in their lifetime.

There is considerable evidence that long-term, chronic stress can have impact on psychological functioning just as severely as can acute or traumatic stress (Davidson, Fleming, & Baum, 1986; Glendinning, 1990; Pilisak, 1989; Terr, 1990). Living under the threat of "the bomb" leads most people to cope by minimizing the reality of danger and by not bringing it into their awareness (Taylor, 1989; Figley & McCubbin, 1983; Lazarus & Folkman, 1984; McCubbin & Patterson, 1983). Ornstein and Ehrlich (1989) as well as Goleman (1988) believe that this response pattern is inherent in the human personality. For purposes of survival, human beings have been programmed since prehistory to respond to immediate dangers, such as a tiger approaching the cave, and to screen out dangers that do not require their immediate attention.

Even before the nuclear bomb had been dropped, in *Civilization and Its Dis-contents* (1930), Freud spoke of his concern that modern technology had created risks for human survival that contributed substantially to psychological distress. Subsequently, some of the most eloquent psychological thinkers of the century also have suggested that the average person may, indeed, not be naming his or her unrest and unhappiness correctly (Alexander, 1946; Frank, 1964; Fromm, 1974; Lifton, 1967, 1979, 1986, 1987; Lorenz, 1974; Macy, 1981, 1983, 1991; May, 1950). These scholars believe that much human malaise stems from the chronic stress of living with threats of technological disaster. To date, there has been no research evidence to support this conclusion. Yet, their intuitive truths may not be so easily dismissed.

Just as clients cannot always define their problems fully when they enter our offices, the community of humankind may also be lacking in the resources that could allow them to define their "problem" as one of global danger. Kanovsky (1989) and Goldberg (1984) point out that issues of nuclear holocaust and global deterioration do not lend themselves to easy solutions; many people believe that there is nothing they can do to change the situation. Therefore, their appraisal of the problem may require that, to be comfortable, they ignore the danger and go on with their lives. Lifton (1967) called this phenomenon *psychic numbing*, noting that, in the nuclear age, we all lead double lives.

The most significant consequence of defining the global dilemma as either nonexistent or unsolvable is that people are then left with no room for solutions to emerge. Some observers of the psychology of living under the bomb have pointed out that the greatest danger of the so-called denial of nuclear realities comes from the sense of detachment from the problem and ensuing apathy, which keeps people from investing their energy in working toward political or social safeguards against the disaster (Goldberg, 1984; Kanofsky, 1989; Macy, 1983, 1991; Lifton, 1987). It seems as if coping devices that work in the present do not serve us very well to keep us safe in the future.

I am reminded of the descriptions of community awareness of the possibilities of disaster in Buffalo Creek, West Virginia (Erikson, 1976) and Centralia, Ohio (Garula, 1989) during the years before those events. Citizens knew that there was ample potential for serious mine-related accidents to occur. Ultimately, indeed, catastrophic accidents later destroyed much of their communities. Yet, before the accidents, as both physical and social structures were deteriorating, residents chose to ignore what they saw. Both Erikson and Garula emphasize that in these communities the already existing erosion of cohesion and mutual support prevented the development of community action projects that might have prevented the disaster.

It is easy to conclude from these studies, as Lifton (1967) did from his, that an entire society could have been traumatized by unnamed nuclear terrors and fears of environmental destruction. In their review of research on the stress of living under chronically hazardous environmental conditions, Davidson, Fleming, and Baum (1986) report that

> It is likely that post-traumatic stress disorder (PTSD) like symptoms may develop following less . . . immediately threatening events that pose chronic or recurrent danger. (p. 58)

Flannery's (1990) description of the relationship of the victim of PTSD to his or her social support system brings an interesting connection to my mind:

> The traumatic event occurs, the victim's assumptive world is shattered, personal control or mastery is dislodged, and integrated social networks or caring links to other persons are disrupted. This is true in the acute, protest phases, and is more pronounced in the chronic, numbing phases. . . . [T]his loss of mastery and attachments to others is often complicated by their assumption that no other human being . . . can really be of help. (p. 593)

I do see chilling parallels between the experiences of the residents of Centralia and Buffalo Creek, those of PTSD victims, and those of the world population, who see the foundations of their planetary home crumbling. We are in the chronic, numbing phase of reaction. The damage, however, may not be as visible in terms of individual responses as it is in the dysfunction of larger social structures. If we examine some of the adjectives used by social commentators to describe contemporary problems, we can easily detect their similarity to the symptoms that are often seen in individuals suffering from PTSD.

Some of the terms used are:

Addictive (Schaef, 1987)
Narcissistic (Lasch, 1975)
Fragmented (Gergen, 1991)
Manic (Kitwood, 1990)
Detached from emotion (Caldicott, 1984)
Dangerously pseudo-reasonable (Ruddick, 1989)
Anxious (Dumont, 1991)
Disconnected (Erikson, 1976)
Distrustful (Bellah et al., 1985)
Empty of meaning (Wychsograd, 1985)
Apathetic/despairing (Macy, 1983)
Consumption driven (Ehrenrich, 1990)

Perhaps this is where the unnamed problem is to be found; it is in our culture rather than in our psyches.

This brings me to a central paradox. I have indicated elsewhere that the family has not been studied extensively in the investigations of nuclear psychology, nor have family therapists addressed global concerns in their work with families (DeMuth, 1990; see also Chapter 4).[2]

In trying to respond to this paradox, I will now address the following questions:

1. Does family systems thinking have anything to offer to our understanding of global issues?
2. How must the family therapist change his or her thinking to adopt a world view?
3. What methods could we use to create a practice of global family therapy?

IS FAMILY SYSTEMS THINKING USEFUL IN UNDERSTANDING GLOBAL SURVIVAL ISSUES?

Obviously I believe that family systems thinking can be useful in addressing our current dilemmas. Many basic family therapy concepts come to mind. We are all familiar with expanding therapeutic context from the individual to the family or community. We take for granted that the problem may not reside solely in the individual who expressed the pain and that awareness of trouble in the system may not be immediately available to the individuals within it. We are comfortable with the notion of broadening context to increase therapeutic effectiveness, for example, to bring in the spouse of a depressed patient to decrease symptom-maintaining behavior on his or her part.

Further, family systems thinking can provide a more optimistic model for approaching the psychology of global survival (DeMuth, 1990). We already work from a growth perspective. Most of us are essentially hopeful about human nature and believe that the drive for health is inherent within individuals and systems. We can also support optimism in the face of enormous struggles because we know that problems do not necessarily need to be resolved sequentially. We believe that whole systems can change with appropriate interventions at significant junctures. Most important, we already preach that the way a problem is defined leads to either its solution or its nonsolution. Our role as healers suggests that when we define the problem in a different way, effective clues to its solution will emerge.

Family therapists have techniques that may be relevant to the task. We are experts in problem solving and conflict resolution within intimate systems. It may not be grandiose to propose that, as family therapists, we know something about how to resolve the pull between personal goals and system goals, which might be useful to a civilization that is burying itself in its own greed.

HOW MUST THE FAMILY THERAPIST CHANGE HIS OR HER THINKING TO ADOPT A WORLD VIEW?

I believe that family systems thinking can be helpful in the quest both to understand and to intervene in issues involving planetary survival. Next I will look more closely at some changes we family therapists might have to make to incorporate a global view into our clinical work.

I will propose that certain common notions held by family therapists might need to shift: (1) the definition of appropriate emotional distance and (2) the definition of the optional self as highly individuated. Throughout I will suggest that both therapist and client would need to focus on the deeper meaning of life experiences and allow for intensely affective interchanges in their work.

Therapeutic Distance as a Counterforce to the World View

I believe that the stance of therapeutic distance taken by most family therapists is central to the difficulties we face in broadening context to include global issues. I propose that from this stance, difficulties can surface in three ways. First, in an attempt to achieve *clarity*, distance can lead us to diminish affect, trivialize meaning,[3] and ignore many of life's realities. Second, in an effort to achieve *omniscience*, the distance can lead us to take a hierarchical role in which we find it difficult to explore issues unless we believe that we know much more than our clients do. Third, in an attempt to achieve *efficacy*, we place emphasis on immediate objectives and measurable results at the expense of achieving more important but more difficult goals.

Distance Can Achieve Clarity at the Expense of Meaning. Many family therapists are more concerned with the structure and operational rules within a system than by the meaning of the phenomena they observe. We want to see accurately the events in the family. Therefore, we focus our attention on patterns. In doing so, we are likely to diminish the value of the direct experience of the immediate participants in the drama we observe. Himmelfarb, speaking to the National Council on the Humanities (1991), described this process as *reductionism*. She understands that, in times of great tragedy, a detached response can offer greater psychological safety. She also warns, however, that when events that have dire meanings, such as the Holocaust or nuclear bombings, are viewed from too great a distance, they can be trivialized. Unless one concentrates directly on the content of the experience, one cannot fully understand its importance. Without this immediacy, according to Himmelfarb, we cannot use history effectively to learn from the tragedies of our time.

I remember vividly how in my own training as a family therapist, I had to learn to withdraw, emotionally and sometimes physically, to understand the complex and often emotionally draining material I viewed. I do understand the need for distancing, especially when facing a horror of such magnitude as the possible destruction of our entire world. I increasingly see the dangers, however, of pulling back.

It is hard for us to give up the illusion of clarity to take on a complex subject such as global survival, which can have such an emotional impact. The role of the *bystander,* who observes from a distance and thus can see what is clearly going on, has been honored by Kantor and Lehr (1975). Both Kantor and Lehr and Staub (1990), however, view the bystander's detachment as a potential danger for a healthy system. Detachment can lead to depersonalization. Lifton (1986) has also argued that such evils as the Holocaust can occur only when the perpetrator is emotionally separated from his or her immediate experience of the oppressive act.

Feminist family therapists have illuminated this issue, pointing out that the "pure" practice of structural or strategic therapy may have done harm by ignoring the harsh nature of power imbalances within many families (Hare-Mustin,

1989; Luepnitz, 1988; McGoldrick, Anderson, & Walsh, 1989; Walters, Carter, Papp, & Silverstein, 1988). Working from an emotional distance, a focus on structure has limited many of us from seeing, and therefore addressing, issues of victimization of women and children by violent invasions.

I believe that the issues of threats to the life of our planet are equally violent and invasive to our clients but even less visible even than the threats of wife battering and child abuse. Only when we move closer to the experience does the impact of living in the nuclear age become clear. The apparent clarity we gain from emotional distance is an illusion.

Hierarchical Distance Disallows Engaging with the Unknown. A second peril for the family therapist in the global arena can also develop when the stance of distance also becomes hierarchical. As superiors, we therapists can not only believe that we see our clients more keenly than they see themselves, but also that we are in a position to make exquisitely accurate moves to disrupt dysfunctional patterns. We are led to believe that we know more about how to solve their problems than they do. Such grandiosity leads us to making enormous errors, by avoiding elements of experience that we do not understand. A very familiar example of such an error is when a therapist, taking a strongly directive position, persists in focusing on an assigned task when the family is silently struggling with issues of dying. The therapist may not feel comfortable with leadership when death is the issue and may unwittingly be unwilling to relinquish control of a more manageable topic.

As therapists, we are as vulnerable as our clients in our feelings of helplessness about the global crisis. Most of us find it difficult to face situations for which there are no easy solutions. If we face the meaning of global realities in our lives and those of our clients, we can no longer seem to know more than they. We open ourselves up to the possibilities of confusion and lack of direction, a difficult position for a healer to take.

Understanding human nature in its cultural/historical/global context requires more intellectual breadth and depth than does understanding the dynamics of self or of family. Most of us will find this expansion taxing, even if we were enriched by a broadly based training or are blessed (and cursed) with an inquiring mind.

We are in the same place as our clients. We can believe that admitting our need to open our horizons to planetary realities could be beneficial. There may not seem to be as much reward for so doing as there is in retaining our false sense of omniscience. My own experience, however, has been that when a family member tentatively opens up his or her terror for the global future, the leadership I take simply to join with that terror becomes empowering to us all. I do not, myself, need to understand. I need only to say, "I feel that way too, sometimes," and allow room then for family members to talk together about their feelings. I lead then, in not allowing any of us to deflect from the shared concern we have, even as I support those members who are not ready for such a discussion.

Distance Allows for Undue Emphasis on Results.   The distance taken by many family therapists leads us to a third dilemma as we contemplate working from a global frame. Products of our culture, we are behaviorally focused and goal oriented. We look for results. Without them, unless we are sustained with a sense of deeper purpose, we are at risk for disappointment and burnout. We feel successful when we can set achievable goals, work with observable behavior changes, and come to effective solutions with our clients.

The challenge of working slowly, without immediate reward, expecting change to come in small increments, is familiar to those rare family therapists who work with chronically disadvantaged families. A special mind set is required to sustain the long haul.

I work with parents of Head Start children, many of whom have been bruised by public and parental authority figures. The teachers and I know that it may take an entire year simply to get a mother to talk openly with one of us when she comes to pick up her child. We assume that we will get to know her gradually, over the preschool years of several of her children, before we will gain her trust and can help her to make changes in her life. We believe that she and her children are worth this kind of patience.

Those of us who are challenged by global issues must develop a similar belief system about the long-range value of our work. A different kind of distance is required for therapists who take this route. We must release ourselves from the demands of quick success and look ahead to the future. At the same time, we will find ourselves focusing more intensely on the meaning of our direct experience and on its affective impact.

Redefining the Place of Affect and Meaning.   Thus, we see that the emotional distance that has allowed the family therapist to develop a sense of clarity, superior knowledge, and efficacy has made it more difficult for him or her to take a world view.

It occurs to me that we must now reassess the discomfort with affect that many of us share. Looking at the possibility of the death of the planet can evoke tremendously powerful images for therapist and client alike. Conn, Greenspan, Surrey, Watkins, and Yeomans (1991), like Macy (1983); Porter, Rinzler, and Olsen (1987); and O'Connor (1989), believe that unless we face our reactions directly, we cannot actively heal either our personal concerns or those of the planet at large. Many family therapists would find it uncomfortable to take this position. The tools of the new paradigm may come more easily to other kinds of practitioners who stress the importance of working with affect.

Is it possible that the psychodynamic therapist, who focuses on internal experience, could be better equipped to deal with feelings of despair and helplessness about the world? Has he or she profited from being trained in the slow process of letting meaning unfold and from experiencing inner pain in a supportive context? Porter (1987), Giegerich (1987), Kitwood (1982), and Charny (1982) answer in the affirmative.

Needless to say, I am oversimplifying. No systems thinker looks *only* outward or works *only* from a distance. Whitaker and Bumberry (1988), Boszormenyi-Nagy and Sparks (1973), Satir (1983) and Kantor and Lehr (1975) have maintained that exploring the individual's direct experiences and looking at the meaning of family interactions are crucial for healing. Also, we know that family therapists do not hold a monopoly on maintaining therapeutic distance. Many psychodynamic practitioners are uncomfortable with direct, affective experience. Many also take a hierarchical and goal-oriented position in relation to their clients. All of us, regardless of orientation, will need to find a stance with clients that will enable us to handle the discouragement and despair that will occur as we face global realities in our practice.

Recent developments in family therapy theory and practice, reflected in the work of O'Hara and Anderson (1991), Doherty (1991), Maturana (1991), Hoffman (1990), support my suggestions for redefining the place of affect and meaning in clinical work. The "postmodern" theory supports a less rigid definition of objective truth and deplores a hierarchical stance taken by the therapist. According to Hoffman, the new epistemology places importance on the need to use the clients' language and culture. It assumes that there is always a political and social agenda, whether it is open or hidden. It suggests that therapists do not need to know a great deal more about life than do their clients, so long as their mutual dialogue has meaning.

I believe that current definitions of therapeutic distance in family therapy have impeded us from including a global perspective. I also believe that those definitions are beginning to change. Next we shall look at some current definitions of self, which I maintain also must be changed if the global paradigm is to take hold.

A New Definition of Self for the Family Therapist[4]

I believe that to create a therapeutic milieu that incorporates concern for the planet, the family therapist needs to redefine the prevailing view of the self as a bounded, separate entity. It would seem as if family systems thinkers would have already taken this view. In practice, however, it appears to me that most of us support a notion of self that overly prizes individuation and autonomy, subtly rewards clients who differentiate most completely from family and community, and does not even contemplate self in relation to the whole planet.

The global paradigm, reflecting both current scientific and ancient Buddhist wisdom, sees the individual not as a separate entity but as an open channel to the larger world around him or her. Both problems and solutions come from this connection.

Most family therapists, despite understanding the relationship between individual and context, have a definition of *individual* that is narrower than that which the global perspective requires. Differentiation of self from others is seen as a primary goal of development and the epitome of healthy emotional functioning (Bowen, 1978; Minuchin, 1974). Until recently, we have found little support from mainstream family therapists of the notion that, especially for women, self is more appropriately defined in terms of its connectedness to others (Gilligan, 1982; Jordan, Kaplan, Miller, Stivers, & Surrey, 1991).

Differention of self is, indeed, a primary goal only when viewed in terms of Western culture, whose basic focus is on the individual. In fact, I believe that such notions of individuation are not core tenets of systems thinking. They reflect the frustrations that Himmelfarb (1991) referred to in dealing with complexity. These notions are also based on a patriarchal model that assumes that sharing with others almost inevitably diminishes the self.

With the Western notion of the separate self prevailing, we are apt to see that including global concerns in our work with clients would be an additional burden to their already stressed lives as well as to our own (Simon, 1990). Others see the issue differently. Conn (1990a, 1990b, 1991) states that therpy is actually enriched by broadening the context from individual to global. Family therapist O'Connor (1989) and psychodynamic therapist Mack (1990) agree. The change in focus can help clients deal effectively with self-blame and allow them to feel connected to others; no one is ever alone in his or her suffering once the context broadens. A powerful example of this notion comes from the client advocacy movement, in which empowerment comes from allying oneself to a community of others struggling with the same concerns.

In my work with groups of parents and professionals concerned about helping children deal with nuclear anxiety, I found that the first task was for us to talk together about our own fears for the planet (DeMuth, 1990). Like Macy (1981, 1983, 1991) and Conn (1990b), I discovered that this experience was empowering for most of us. Following these discussions many participants volunteered "Now I don't feel so alone." A sense of strength was enhanced by linking our concerns not only to each other, but also to a community of other concerned people around the world. Our single selves had not been enough to help us face global uncertainties.

CREATING THE PRACTICE OF GLOBAL FAMILY THERAPY

> Powerlessness, self-estrangement, and the other subjective forms of alienation are not "just in your mind." They are realistic perceptions of objective social conditions. They are the link between social conditions and emotional well-being or distress. (Mirowsky & Ross, 1989, p. 12)

It may take only a small leap of faith for family systems thinkers to include the pressures of living in a culturally dangerous society as part of our definition of all presenting problems. Our own experience of concern for the world can link us to an awareness that the system we are "treating" is also in danger. We allow ourselves to become the *identified patient* to support our knowledge that threats of pollution, AIDS, famine, and nuclear war in the entire ecosystem must be dealt with for each of us to feel truly healthy and empowered.

I move now to the question of what clinical tools are needed to create a family therapy that includes such global awareness. We are just beginning to develop such a practice. Some techniques are borrowed from our usual repertoire; some will need to be developed. The following suggestions come both from my own experience and from my discussions with others who are exploring the new paradigm.

Modeling

At the very least, we can demonstrate our values to our clients by taking an activist position regarding our concerns for the world. We can show that planetary survival really matters to us by making public comments and by leaving appropriate literature in our waiting rooms but mostly by taking action. We can work for causes that we believe will make a positive difference to the world and therefore demonstrate to our clients that we care about their future.

I once worked with a couple in which the husband was a well-known activist for a conservative political organization that believed that world peace was best achieved through military strength. The wife was clearly uncomfortable with a poster in my office that showed a woman holding a baby in one arm and a globe in the other. It was labeled "Children Ask the World of Us—Women's Action for Nuclear Disarmament." Her values of politeness constrained her at first from more than oblique comments about the poster. As I encouraged her to develop her thoughts more fully, however, she began to engage with me in a shared concern for the future of our grandchildren. The husband, at first silent, joined with conventional political rhetoric. The wife then, energized by her own strong feelings, moved to a discussion with him that constructively individuated their feelings about politics. Not only was this exchange helpful in the couple system, but also my therapeutic alliance was strengthened by my own ability to understand their political views more fully and by our eventual agreement to agree about concerns and goals but to disagree about methods.

Reframing

Therapists can reframe almost any issue brought up by clients to make a connection between the individual problem and the problem of the family or community. We can learn to make the same connections between the personal and the global, and we can, I believe, easily do this without imposing an undue burden on either the client or ourselves.

For example, when a couple is deadlocked in a power struggle, we can make an analogy to the deadlock of nations struggling over power in the Middle East. We do not need to pursue the issue further but simply make it clear that the personal problem exists not only in itself, but also as a microcosm of the events in the larger world. If it seems appropriate, a next move might be to suggest that conflict resolution techniques might be more helpful than all-out war in both the personal and the global situations. We are simply developing a point of view that enlarges the context.

Allowing the Deeper Meanings to Emerge

Global concerns may not surface immediately for us and for our clients. We already know, however, that important issues of meaning often are hard to get at. We learn to ask sensitive, nonintrusive questions, which validate for clients that their unspoken concerns are legitimate, even if they are not ready to be articulated. For example, most of us are comfortable with asking depressed clients about how they view themselves in the future. It would not be invasive, in my opinion, to ask this client about other ideas of the future that might concern him or her. We assume, by *not* asking, that the despair is strictly a personal one, and thus prevent clients from expressing a more wide-ranging angst, if this is indeed their experience.

Children who draw pictures of bombs may not only be revealing fears about their own aggression or about wars within the family. We have ample data to assure us that children, from the age of four, have gathered from the media considerable information about the horrors of war. We know that for most children, anxieties about war are both substantial and unexpressed. As sensitive therapists, we might help these children by supporting their parents to encourage discussions about war or about other global concerns. Focus on the immediate context might not reach the heart of the children's worries.

Demonstrate a Positive, Problem-Solving Stance

We can do much more than explore and empathize with clients' concerns for the planet. We can, as we do with personal or family issues, engage in a process of problem solving. We need not lecture or exhort. Merely asking people, especially children, to talk about their ideas about solving world problems can be remarkably energizing for them. The discussion can also inspire the questioner, as I have learned over the past seven years, while observing families discuss together their thoughts and feelings about nuclear war.[5]

I remember the relief expressed by a ten-year-old girl and her mother, who had never before discussed their mutual concern about nuclear war. The discussion began with the daughter's drawing of a mushroom cloud. The mother had felt guilty because she was politically inactive. The daughter had had nightmares about nuclear bombs but had been afraid to tell her mother about them. After their talk, both said they felt less afraid and better understood. Yet I could easily have focused on the personal aggression revealed by the daughter in the drawing.

A therapist friend told me of the following incident. Her client, when asked in a couple session what he would say to his wife if he were able to talk freely to her, responded "I would tell her how profoundly I feel about the danger to this planet's environment." When asked why he could not reveal these thoughts to her, he replied "She would not take me seriously." The wife, unready to engage so directly with her spouse, did try to minimize with easy reassurance. Rather than moving the exchange into the area of the couple's interpersonal dynamics, my friend continued to support her to talk about her own fears for the world future, first to herself, then to her husband. She focused on the meanings expressed and joined the couple with a brief statement of her own concerns. The distance between the couple lessened, and the interpersonal work could then begin.

It interested me that the husband also revealed that he had wanted to tell a previous individual therapist how much he worried about the future of the earth but had also held back, fearing that the first therapist would see his concern only as a sign of personal weakness. My friend's validation of her client's thoughts was important, far beyond the level of transferential process.

Caveats

Of course, it is risky to allow the presence of global concerns into the consulting room. In my view, it is, in the long run, riskier *not* to allow them. It might be helpful, however, to look at some cautionary notions.

When we allow for less distance between client and therapist as we explore global concerns together, we must never lose touch with the *third eye*, which allows us to observe the process as we experience it. We must, ethically, always be more concerned with the client's pain than with our own, even as we share a common anguish.

Exploring planetary concerns must be done with total respect for clients' differences from ourselves—they may be more or they may be less concerned; they may be concerned about different issues or need not be concerned at all; they may have different ideas for political solutions. The existence of those differences does not demand that we be silent, any more than when the differences are personal. The same therapeutic ethic still exists; namely, we must not *impose* those differences on clients.

Redefining self-boundaries as open to the planet or universe does *not* mean, in Minuchin's (1974) terms, that those boundaries need to be diffuse. Instead they need to be permeable, open to receive information from outside and to respond back to outside events, in a circular loop that can change when circumstances demand. The self needs to be an open system (Kantor & Lehr, 1975), which can negotiate and adapt as it needs to. There will always be times when therapeutic or real life focus needs to be clearly on self, on family, or on the immediate community.

In other words, the global paradigm may not work well for family therapists who are either new to the work or so old that they are burned out, for those who are in personal or professional crisis, or for those whose personality structure or professional training does not operate well within an open therapeutic system. In all cases, a focus on global issues cannot work well for family therapists who work in isolation from one another. It is too new and too demanding.

REDEFINING THERAPEUTIC CONTEXT

By now, it should be clear that I am proposing that we bring the realities of global fragility into our role as healers. A therapy could then develop that dares to submit itself to uncertainty and to intellectual and affective challenges that are not easily resolved. In such a therapy, less attention would be paid to surface issues. Meaning would be defined in Kantor and Lehr's (1975) terms:

> [S]ome kind of philosophical framework that provides us with explanations of reality . . . so that we glean a sense of who and what we are, and perhaps even who and what man is. (p. 37)

The goals of global family therapy would fit with the postmodernist views of Doherty (1991):

> [T]o enable clients to find new meanings in their life situations and to restorying their problems in ways that free them from the mesmerizing power of the dominant culture. (p. 38)

This therapy would reflect as well the concerns of Schwartz (1991) who views the work as:

> [A] kind of detoxifying enterprise focused not only on removing symptoms but also on helping clients examine the cost of pursuing the American dream. (p. 66)

The new paradigm for family therapists would dare to include the value of preserving life on the planet as part of its basic premises and would create an expanded framework to deal with the culture of danger we all live in. We would re-examine our values so that we would not perpetuate destruction, violence, or abuse of power either in our personal lives or in the life of the planet.

Hoffman (1990) maintains that the therapist should be constantly aware of his or her own values and use his or her subjective experiences as a major part of the healing process. I, too, believe that the therapist is stronger when he or she openly declares values. For example, in my own practice, I found that I needed to tell couples that I strongly believed in working hard to maintain a long-term relationship. The declaration did not change my work substantially; I could still support couples for whom my own belief system would have been inappropriate. I found, however, that my honesty allowed me to be more comfortable and more effective. It occurred to me that my values had been expressed as much by what I did not say as by what I had openly stated. In not declaring a position, I was at risk of seeming to support practices that I do not indeed value.

Declaring my belief in the importance of planetary survival seems to be not very different from declaring my belief about relationships. Other therapists have presented opposing views. Porter et al. (1987) and O'Connor (1989) believe in a therapist's obligation to raise issues of such importance with clients, whereas Zur (1990) and Riskin (see Chapter 6) maintain that such interventions intrude unethically into clients' rights. I maintain, however, that healers who do not mention their awareness of planetary danger are as much at risk of influencing families as those who do.

My own concern, echoing that of O'Connor, is that by our silence about global issues, we continue to reinforce for our clients the notion that nothing can be done to save the world from destruction. We are tacitly approving mass suicide, in the same way as the Berlin Psychoanalytical Association, by refusing to take a stand against Nazi ideology, supported mass genocide (Staub, 1990).

Few of us yet have a solid enough conceptual base for the paradigm shift. Further, we need the support of community as we develop the new forms. For many of us, this will include a greater awareness of the spiritual meaning of our work. We also need connection to others who will encourage us, ask questions to help expand our thinking, remind us not to grow impatient at the slowness of our task, help us to laugh and cry. They will provide what human families, at their best, are able to do. We also need connection to a sense of higher purpose, to the universe, to whatever each of us in our own way would call divine.

This work is not to be done alone. I believe that we who think systemically can contribute in a substantial way to the psychology of global awareness and survival. To do so, we will need to risk modifying our stance of therapeutic distance, bring issues of affect and meaning into our work, and borrow from the new notions of self-in-context. We will need to develop new techniques and take the risks of declaring ourselves to have values about the importance of the whole planet.

We will expand our vision, create new therapeutic tools, and form a solid, supportive community to aid in the quest. It is an exciting and challenging time. I hope those of us who have begun the journey will be joined by other family therapists who care as much as we do about the planet's survival but have not yet found a way to express their concern.

> Meaning emerges . . . and becomes process, and it derives in part from attending seriously to the world and one's connections to it, not merely from personal gratification, goal oriented activity, and feeling good. There is pain in it and beauty in it—and that is, finally, what our psychotherapies have lacked. (Olsen, 1987, p. 46)

NOTES

1. Sarah Conn and Mary Jane Ferrier gave me great help with an earlier version of this paper.
2. Please see reviews of the literature in Chapter 4 of this book and in DeMuth (1990).

3. I am indebted to the work of David Kantor in exploring the concept of meaning (values and purpose) in family therapy and practice.
4. The work of Sarah Conn and her group and of Joanna Macy has been both inspirational and influential to me as I developed the concepts of the self openly bounded to the planet.
5. This project is reported on in Chapter 7.

BIBLIOGRAPHY

Alexander, F. (1946). Mental hygiene in the atomic age. *Mental Hygiene, 30,* 529–534.

Bateson, G. (1987). *Steps to an ecology of mind.* New York: W.W. Norton.

Bellah, R. N., Madsen, R., Sullivan, W. M., Swidler, A. & Tipton, S. M. (1985). *Habits of the Heart: Individualism and commitment in American life.* Berkeley and Los Angeles: University of California Press.

Bowen, M. (1978). *Family therapy in clinical practice.* New York: Jason Aronson.

Caldicott, H. (1984). *Missile Envy.* New York: Morrow.

Carter, B. (1990, March). *Gender, class and culture.* Paper presented at the Family Networker Conference. Washington, DC.

Charny, I. W. (1982). *How can we commit the unthinkable?: Genocide, the human cancer.* Boulder, CO: Westview Press, p. 362.

Chatham, C. S. (1987). The beginning, not the end of the age of genocide: A psychoanalyst's encounter with the slaughter of Paraguayan Indians. In R. Aren (Ed.), *Genocide in Paraguay.* Philadelphia: Temple University Press, p. 362.

Conn, S. (1990a). *Protest and thrive: The relationship between social responsibility and personal empowerment.* Cambridge, MA: Center for Psychological Studies in the Nuclear Age.

Conn, S. (1990b). The self-world connection: Implications for mental health and psychotherapy. *Woman of Power, 20,* 71–76.

Conn, S., Greenspan, S., Surrey, J., Watkins, M., & Yeomans, A. (1991, May). Toward a new model of psychotherapy: Connecting the personal and the global. Symposium delivered at the Massachusetts School of Professional Psychology, Dedham, MA.

Davidson, L. M., Fleming, I., & Baum, A. (1986). Post traumatic stress as a function of chronic stress and toxic exposure. In C. R. Figley (Ed.), *Trauma and its wake. Vol II: Traumatic stress theory, research and intervention.* New York: Brunner/Mazel.

DeMuth, D. H. (1990). Some implications of the threat of nuclear war for families and family therapists. In M. Mirkin (Ed.), *The social and political contexts of family therapy.* Boston: Allyn & Bacon, pp. 355–82.

Doherty, W. J. (1991). Family therapy goes post modern. *Family Therapy Networker, Sept/Oct 15*(5), 37–42.

Dumont, M. (1991). A Gedanken experiment. Part II: Anxiety as a social disease. *Readings: A Journal of Reviews and Commentary in Mental Health, June,* 16–18.

Ehrenrich, B. (1990). *Fear of falling: The inner life of the middle class.* New York: Harper Perennial.

Erikson, K. T. (1976). *Everything in its path.* New York: Simon & Schuster.

Figley, C. R., & McCubbin, H. I. (Eds.) (1983). *Stress and the family. Vol II: Coping with catastrophe.* New York: Brunner/Mazel.

Flannery, R. B. (1990). Social support and psychological trauma: A methodological review. *Journal of Traumatic Stress, 3*(4), 593–609.

Framo, J. L. (Ed.) (1972). *Family interaction: A dialogue between family researchers and family therapists.* New York: Springer.

Framo, J. L., & Green, R. J. (Eds.) (1981). *Family therapy: Major contributions.* New York: International Universities Press.

Frank, J. D. (1964). *Sanity and survival.* New York: Random House.

Freud, S. (1930). *Civilization and its discontents.* (J. Riviere, Trans.) New York: J. Cape & H. Smith.

Fromm, E. (1974). *The anatomy of human destructiveness.* New York: Holt, Rinehart, & Winston.

Garula, C. (1989, April). *Psychological effects of man-made disasters.* Paper presented at the American Orthopsychiatric Association, New York.

Gergen, K. (1991). The saturated family. *Family Therapy Networker, 15*(5), 27–35.

Giegerich, W. (1987). Saving the nuclear bomb. In V. Andrews, R. Bosnak, and K. W. Goodwin (Eds.), *Facing Apocalypse*. Dallas, TX: Spring Publications.

Gilligan, C. (1986). *In a different voice: Psychological theory and women's development*. Cambridge, MA: Harvard University Press.

Glendinning, C. (1990). *When technology wounds: The human consequences of progress*. New York: Morrow.

Goldberg, G. S. (1984). Adding the arms race to the psychosocial equation. *Social Work, Sept/Oct*, 481–483.

Goleman, D. (1988, October). *The social trance: Collective self deception*. Cambridge, MA: Center for Psychological Studies of the Nuclear Age.

Hare-Mustin, R. (1989). The problem of gender in family therapy theory. In M. McGoldrick, C. M. Anderson, and F. Walsh (Eds.), *Women in families: A framework for family therapy*. New York: W.W. Norton.

Himmelfarb, G. (1991, May). *Of heroes, villains, and valets*. Paper presented at the 20th Jefferson Lecture, National Endowment for the Humanities, New York.

Hoffman, L. (1990). Constructing realities: An art of lenses. *Family Process, 29(1)*, 1–12.

Jordan, J. V., Kaplan, A. G., Miller, J. B., Stiver, J. P., & Surrey, J. L. (1991). *Women's growth in connection: Writings from the Stone Center*. New York: Guilford.

Kanofsky, S. (1989). *The possibility of nuclear war: Appraisal, coping and emotional response*. Unpublished doctoral dissertation, California School of Professional Psychology, Berkeley/Alameda.

Kantor, D., & Lehr, W. (1975). *Inside the family: Towards a theory of family process*. New York: Harper Colophon.

Kitwood, T. M. (1990). *Concern for others: A new psychology of conscience and morality*. New York: Routledge, Chapman and Hall.

Lazarus, R. S., & Folkman, S. (1984). *Stress, appraisal and coping*. New York: Springer.

Lasch, C. (1975). *The culture of narcissism*. New York: Norton.

Lifton, R. J. (1967). *Death in life: Survivors of Hiroshima*. New York: Simon & Schuster.

Lifton, R. J. (1979). *The broken connection*. New York: Simon & Schuster.

Lifton, R. J. (1986). *The Nazi doctors*. New York: Basic Books.

Lifton, R. J. (1987). *The future of immortality and other essays for a nuclear age*. New York: Basic Books.

Lorenz, K. (1974). *Civilized man's eight deadly sins*. New York: Harcourt-Brace-Jovanovich.

Luepnitz, D. A. (1988). *Feminist theory in clinical practice*. New York: Basic Books.

Mack, J. (1990). *Changing models of psychotherapy, from psychological conflict to human empowerment*. Cambridge, MA: Center for Psychological Studies in the Nuclear Age.

Macy, J. (1983). *Despair and personal power in the nuclear age*. Philadelphia: New Society.

Macy, J. (1991). *World as lover, world as self*. Berkeley, CA: Parallax Press.

Macy, J. R. (1981). Despair work. *Evolutionary Blues—An Interhelp Quarterly, 1*.

Maturana, H. R. (1991). Science and daily life: The ontology of scientific explanations. In F. Steier (Ed.), *Research and reflexivity*. Newbury Park, CA: Sage.

May, R. (1950). *The meaning of anxiety*. New York: Ronald Press.

McCubbin, H. I., & Patterson, J. M. (1983). The family stress process: The double ABCX model of adjustment and adaptation. *Marriage and Family Review, 6*, 7–37.

McGoldrick, M., Anderson, C. M., & Walsh, F. (1989). *Women in families: A framework for family therapy*. New York: W.W. Norton.

McGoldrick, M., Pearce, J. K., & Giordano, J. (Eds.) (1982). *Ethnicity and family therapy*. New York: Guilford.

Minuchin, S. (1974). *Families and family therapy*. Cambridge, MA: Harvard University Press.

Mirowsky, J., & Ross, C. (1989). *Social causes of psychological distress*. New York: Aldine de Gruyter.

O'Connor, T. (1989). Therapy for a dying planet. *Family Therapy Networker, Sept/Oct*, 69–72.

O'Hara, M., & Anderson, W. T. (1991). Welcome to the postmodern world. *Family Therapy Networker, 15(5)*, 19–25.

Olsen, P. (1987). Meditations on Godot: Nuclear therapy, death, and the maiden. In K. Porter, D. Rinzler, P. Olsen (Eds.), *Heal or die: Psychotherapists confront nuclear annhilation*. New York: Psychohistory Press.

Ornstein, R., & Ehrlich, P. (1989). *New world, new mind: Moving toward conscious evolution*. New York: Doubleday.

Pappajohn, J., & Spiegel, J. (1975). *Transactions in families*. San Francisco: Jossey-Bass.

Pilisak, M. (1989). Living downwind. *Readings, 4(1)*, 16–19.

Porter, K., Rinzler, D., & Olsen, P. (Eds.), (1987). *Heal or die: Psychotherapists confront nuclear annhilation*. New York: Psychohistory Press.

Ruddick, S. (1989). *Maternal thinking: Toward a politics of peace*. New York: Ballantine.

Satir, V. (1983). *Conjoint family therapy* (3rd ed.). Palo Alto, CA: Science & Behavior.

Schaef, A. W. (1987). *When society becomes an addict*. San Francisco: Harper and Row.

Schwartz, R. (1991). The American nightmare. *Family Therapy Networker, 15(2)*, 64–68.

Simon, R. (1990). Does nuclear war have a place in family therapy? In M. P. Mirkin, (Ed.), *Social and political contexts of family therapy*. Boston: Allyn & Bacon.

Staub, E. (1990). *The roots of evil: The origins of genocide and other group violence*. Cambridge, MA: Cambridge University Press.

Taylor, S. (1989). *Positive illusions*. New York: Basic Books.

Terr, L. (1990). *Too scared to cry*. New York: Harper & Row.

Walters, M., Carter, B., Papp, P., & Silverstein, S. (1988). *The invisible web: Gender patterns in family relationships*. New York: Guilford.

Whitaker, C. A., & Bumberry, W. M. (1988). *Dancing with the family: A symbolic experiential approach*. New York: Brunner/Mazel.

Wychsograd, E. (1985). *Spirit in ashes: Hegel, Heidigger, and man-made mass death*. New Haven: Yale University Press.

Zur, O. (1990). On nuclear attitudes and psychic numbing: Overview and critique. *Contemporary Social Psychology, 14(2)*, 96–110.

Chapter 2

Beyond the Therapy Room: Therapy and Politics in the Nuclear Age*†

Norbert A. Wetzel

Psychotherapy today has to consider the complex forces outside the therapy room that co-determine the therapeutic process inside between an individual, a couple, a family, and the therapist. The concept of the individual existing like Leibniz' "monad" separated or "absolutely independent" (Flew, 1979, p. 236) from his or her societal context is no longer useful to us in guiding our thinking about therapy. The locus of therapeutic interaction and experience is no longer shielded by high walls like a medieval castle but rather resembles a tent that is open on all sides.

*To the memory of Ignacio Martín Baró, murdered in San Salvador, November 16, 1989.

†The text of this chapter is based on plenary presentations during the First and Second International Family Therapy Congress in Prague (1987) and Budapest (1989) and on discussion papers for a workshop and a seminar that I gave at the International Congress, "The End of Grand Designs and the Flowering of Systemic Practice" (Heidelberg, April 3–7, 1991). I am particularly grateful for discussions with Alma Menn and Dick Auerswald, with whom I conducted the workshop and seminar. I have presented similar ideas as a lecturer during the annual meeting of the German Association for Family Therapy (DAF) in Berlin on October 5, 1991.

TWO CHALLENGES TO FAMILY THERAPY TODAY

Professional Engagement on Societal Level

This insight is valid for any form of psychotherapy, but it is particularly true and relevant for systemic couples and family therapy. From the beginning of their work, it was important for family therapists to reflect and consider the context of their therapeutic activities. They understood that they could no longer practice therapy in a vacuum isolated from societal reality. Guided by their sensitivity to the context within therapy, they began to look beyond the therapy room and to pay attention to what is going on in the context surrounding a family (Stierlin, Rücker-Embden, Wetzel, & Wirsching, 1980).

Now we have to take another step and consider what appears to me to be the *first challenge to family therapy* today: Our concern for the well-being of our client families leads us to participate directly in the transformation of the societal context in which families live. Our professional responsibility for the mental and psychological health of our clients demands interventions not only on the intra-familial level, but also on a societal level. We are challenged by the very nature of the therapeutic process to take positions and to act politically because it is no longer possible to isolate the family context from the surrounding society, not even on a conceptual level.

The initial focus of our work as systemic therapists is certainly the web of relational structures inside a family or a couple. Individuals, couples, or families, however, should not simply have to return after therapy to an unchanged social environment that is hostile and destructive to life and families. We have to help families overcome their widespread powerlessness in the face of larger social institutions. We have to cooperate with other citizens toward a balance of power and interests between families and society so that it is possible for individuals, couples, families, and larger social institutions to preserve and develop their own identity without destroying the others' identity in the process. In this societal context of family therapy, power emerges as a central theme. Balancing the vital interests of individuals, of families, and of larger institutions has to do with power and with management of conflict and requires among other things a set of guiding principles that are fundamentally ethical in nature.

Psychotherapy in general, therefore, and family therapy in particular, is confronted with the challenge not only to *study* the societal context in which therapy happens. It requires a *direct engagement* for the well-being of families; that is, it requires direct political action, participation in the societal reconciliation of powerful conflicting interests and in the search for principles guiding this process.

This challenge in turn compels us to examine a number of difficult *questions.* What ideas, insights, and experiences, specifically, can family therapists contribute with professional legitimacy to the societal discourse about the future? What have they learned using a systems perspective in their work with couples and families that may be useful when applied to political action? Which basic ethical assumptions will give guidance and orientation in a societal context in which power and conflict are the central themes?[1]

A Personal Reflection

Having grown up in post–World War II Germany, I have vivid memories of gradually becoming aware of the immediate history of my country. With the awareness grew the realization of and the bafflement about my parents' generation's silence about the atrocities committed by the Nazis. (During one of my conferences about the psychosocial consequences of the nuclear threat, a German physician in the audience compared being silent about the nuclear threat now with the blindness of the German [mental] health community during the Nazi era.) I could no longer see therapy as a process unfolding in a societal vacuum. Not only the nuclear threat, but also all other issues of power, violence, and obstruction of human life within the larger societal context of our clients had to be addressed as part of the professional responsibility of a therapist.

Epistemological Foundation for Family Therapy

Any attempt at addressing these questions leads us on a more abstract level of reflection to a *second challenge* family therapy finds itself confronted with today. The task of developing a philosophical/epistemological foundation for family therapy has not yet been resolved satisfactorily despite all endeavors since the early days of the application of systems theory to clinical work with families. Constructivism and more recent systemic paradigms (such as Maturana's "autopoetic" model), now prevalent in the field, have helped to raise the theoretical discourse in family theory to the epistemological level but have not provided us with a coherent framework for our thinking about family therapy.[2]

In my view, we are confronted with the challenge to reformulate the balance between subject and totality, between the individual and the entire system in family theory. We have to examine the usefulness of the system or context paradigm itself, particularly regarding the question of whether it can present the theoretical basis for a balance of power and justice between all individuals within the family context. Eventually we will encounter the unavoidable inquiry into the foundation for our experience of being subjects defined by our relatedness to others.

The proposed revision of the theoretical and conceptual basis for family therapy is, of course, part of the rapid societal transformation that we are currently witnessing and in which we all participate as actors. The traditional constructions of the relationship between subject and totality on the societal level, that is, individualistic capitalism and collective communism, have broken down. We have become more aware of the power of the institutional contexts in which families live and develop. Within the family system, we take more seriously the complexity of the relationship between the individual and the entire system.

What emerges on all levels of systemic organization is the necessity for a new theoretical definition of the relationship between subject and totality and of the implied questions of power and ethics in relational systems.

Both Challenges are Interconnected

Both challenges mentioned here are interconnected. They demand from the family theorist as well as from the family clinician a similar capacity of reconciling complex polarizations. We see, then, a multifaceted process unfold: thinking about family contexts inside and outside the therapy room, reflecting on possible contributions from the field of family therapy toward making societal systems more human, committing oneself toward the political implementation of such contributions, *and* thinking about the epistemological foundation of family therapy and of social systems in general. All these processes mutually influence each other.

The question, therefore, that I would like to pursue in this chapter can be formulated in its most general form like this: What can family therapists contribute for family systems and societal systems to become or to remain human? In this question, I see therapy and politics interconnected. Both require constant reflection on systems as systems of people and direct and often public engagement and intervention. I believe that pursuing this question, making it part of the therapeutic as well as global discourse, and intervening in family and societal systems according to our answers are part of our professional responsibility.

In my attempt to respond to this question, I would first like to remind us of the importance and the extent of systemic *power* and *violence* within the life context of families. I will then pursue further the reflections regarding the relationship between *subject* and *totality* and would like to point out an alternative approach. Third, I will present some thoughts about the *process of change* in families and larger systems. From there follow questions about the *vision*, the *utopia*, toward which families and larger systems could progress. Finally, I would like to introduce a *symbol:* the figure of the *stranger* who will pose some questions to us.

THE POWER OF SYSTEMS OR SYSTEMS OF POWER

Family Systems Therapy and the Reality of Systemic Power and Violence

We have learned during the recent decades to appreciate better the power of family systems over individual family members. We are more attentive to contexts of chronic exploitation and oppression within families. We are quicker to notice not only the first indications of intrafamiliar *terrorism* (Stierlin et al., 1980), but also of sexual abuse and physical violence. Recent studies by feminists alerted us to injustices toward women that are firmly established in systemic structures.

Family therapists now take serious the long underestimated familial hierarchy of men over women all too often manufactured through male physical violence. Subtle forms of violence are less often clinically minimized.

Within the larger societal context, we recognize similar realities, especially during times of breakdown of political systems large and small. We see more clearly the power plays and the violence to which entire families are exposed by societal institutions, such as hospitals, the army, and schools. Families get destroyed by bureaucracies that were originally created and intended for the support of families (Elizur & Minuchin, 1989; Minuchin, 1991).

More important, the context of our treatment families is determined by economic dependency and powerlessness interconnected with drug use, illness, homelessness, unemployment, or general impoverishment and crime. The rich are getting richer, and the poor are getting poorer. The worldwide economic system presently supported by the affluent Western countries under the leadership of the United States will continue to produce war, hunger, ecological disasters, and demoralization through powerlessness. The families, women, men, and children, who come apart in these societal contexts are not the authors of their own history. They are confronted with real systemic power and physical violence. They live in societal contexts that are in part or in their totality destructive to humans. My point is, these oppressive realities directly influence the mental health of our clients. At the same time, they pose an epistemological challenge to the currently prevalent models of family theory. Violently destructive forces in the societal environment of families are not products of subjective constructs by the people in question. They defy the usual conceptual definitions within a systemic or constructivist framework of thinking.

The nuclear war context is, of course, the ultimate in power, violence, and potential destruction. Even now, after the end of the cold war, this suicidal threat has hardly diminished. The conversion needed here goes far beyond the conversion of factories to a peace economy. We need an epistemological and conceptual transformation that can support the required structural, economic and political systems changes.

As systems thinkers and constructivists, we are here faced with basic questions that we cannot escape. How can we comprehend and conceptually define these societal phenomena so that we can deduce orienting guidelines for our daily behavior as citizens and as therapists? How does our clinical reflection and practice need to change for us to do justice to the phenomena of sexual and physical abuse, pervasive systemic violence, and destruction? How do we as therapists actively intervene on a societal level so that the therapeutic process with families can be effective?

We Live in a Global Village (McLuhan & Powers, 1989)

These problems have become considerably more pressing through the epochal change that has taken place since August of 1945. The contextual background on which the psychotherapeutic drama unfolds and the social framework within which we have to engage ourselves as speakers for our clients have become *global.*

The release of two nuclear bombs on Hiroshima and Nagasaki ushered in the possibility for the human race to annihilate itself and all life on our planet (Wetzel & Winawer, 1986). This event transformed the already existing but invisible unity of humanity into a globally effective context that expressed itself in many fields and on many levels. Not only the nuclear reality, but also other phenomena have changed epochally the context in which we lead our daily lives. I am thinking here of phenomena such as the worldwide effects of ecological disasters, the rapid electronic networks (the "electronic village"), the increasing integration of national economies into one global economic system, the world hegemony of the United States after the breakup of the Soviet Union, the omnipresence of the media in our living rooms during the Gulf War, and many other factors.

It is, therefore, no longer sufficient to conceptualize a family's context in a rather narrow way or to fight for the interests of families only locally. To engage politically in a global context has become our professional and ethical duty as therapists because our survival and that of our clients are threatened on a global level.

THE INDIVIDUAL IN THE GLOBAL VILLAGE OR SUBJECT AND TOTALITY

Our new appreciation for systemic power and violence both within families and in the context surrounding families shall provide us with the background for questions regarding a new formulation of the relationship between subject and totality, especially from the perspective of multigenerational family therapy.

Questions from the Practice of Family Therapy

Individual Responsibility and Systemic Totality. For the process of healing within a family, it is often crucial that individual members own up to the consequences of their behavior on others. They need to accept the burden of responsibility and acknowledge, as the case may be, that their actions violated relational justice and contributed to the pain or illness of others. Similarly, it is frequently of therapeutic significance that a family member begins to understand that he or she does not have to do penance for the "sins" of parents and does not have to punish himself or herself. In both examples, responsibility is attributed to the autonomous subject and not to the family system as a whole.

In divorce therapy or in cases of chronically or terminally ill family members, but also in the therapy with families in which adult children and parents cannot let go of each other, I see families again and again involved in conflicts that have a profound impact on the fate of relatives or of the following generations. Decisions such as to end or to continue to tolerate an unhappy marital relationship, to care for an aging or a terminally ill parent or to let him or her die, or to realize a professional career or a long coveted wish for a certain lifestyle against the interests of others within the family are not decided by the entire system but by individual members. Relational structures, motivations, and influences that are connected with the system as a whole are crucial for the understanding of these decisions, but we clearly attribute them to the irreducible uniqueness and freedom of the individual and his or her mystery.

This appears conceptually impossible, however, if the individual is defined as part of a larger system or organism with the conceptual rigor that is required by systemic thinking. According to systems theory, to be part of a whole, a totality, is not "external" to the subject (in the sense of a quality a posteriori added on to an essentially closed being), just as it is not "external" to a cell to be part of a larger organism. We are others, that is, profoundly different according to the various organisms, such as families, professional groups, or nations, to which we belong while experiencing also our sameness and identity. How can we comprehend and conceptualize both the autonomy, uniqueness, and freedom *and* the fundamental dependency, vulnerability, and exposure of human subjects that we experience both in ourselves and in our work with families?[3]

Inner and Outer Reality.   The application of the constructivist approach to family theory has without doubt been helpful to recognize the limits of a naive empiricism and to question the assumptions of the phenomenological method. We have learned to appreciate the active-creative side of cognition, and we understand how much truth is the result of a consensus about individual and social constructs. But with adopting the position of constructivism, can we relinquish or abandon precise description of observable processes or empirical research in family therapy? Or can we neglect the inner and subjective experience of our partners in the dialogue in favor of their and our constructs of meaning and truth (Bouchard & Guerette, 1991)?

Further, as I have pointed out, our clients, couples and families, are exposed to real power systems, real oppression, and real misery. These realities are not products of subjective constructions by the people involved. How can we take these facts theoretically into account as part of our reflection about the relationship between subjects (i.e., individuals, families, ethnic groups) and totalities (i.e., family systems, ghettos, the city, the ethnic majority, nations)? And how can we deduce from our theory initiatives for contextual practice and intervention in families and larger systems?

Intersubjective Empathy.   We also have not yet conceptually justified the incredibly complex phenomenon of *intersubjective understanding* (i.e., the empathic process of mutual vulnerability and recognition) that develops in front of our eyes, in our experience and through our active participation, whenever a couple or a family arrives for therapy. How are individual and collective observing, experiencing, and projecting interwoven with each other so that a dialogical relationship between partners develops that is truthful and significant? How do subjects relate more than superficially to each other? How do they form a human social system without loosing their autonomy?

Questions from the Experience of Living in the Global Village

On other levels of systemic organization, these questions return with increased complexity. In the age of an economically and electronically more and more interdependent and interconnected world, it is without question of high priority to study and clarify the relationship between individual and collective subjects (i.e., nations) and humankind as a whole.

The worldwide conversation about the conceptual reorientation and the practical restructuring within the global village has just begun and is promising. It should not break down prematurely. Family therapists are perhaps able to help because they learned something about how to prevent the familial dialogue from collapsing. Here are some questions and observations perhaps worth considering in the global discourse.

- Destructive family feuds are rooted frequently in repressed and forgotten memories of the sufferings and sacrifices of previous generations, memories of missed or hindered possibilities of living, that manifest themselves in illness and breakdown of relationships. Within the complex context of reasons preceding wars, we can also find, in my opinion, the collective memory of groups or nations of past injustice, of the misery of innumerable people in previous generations. Do we see in these memories only obstacles, prejudices, or thought constructs that need correction? Or is there a need in fact to do grief work and make *collective remembrance* possible, in order that we may find a balance of justice that can serve as a foundation for collective healing and the reconciliation of hostile ethnic or national systems (Benjamin, 1969; Peukert, 1984; Wetzel, 1980)? The current ethnic violence in the former Yugoslavia provides an example for the disastrous consequences of suppressing century-old memories of past injustice.

- From our work with family myths and from the study of the social construction of national myths, legends, and enemy images, we know how important it is for social groups and systems of any size to construct *narratives that create meaning and cohesiveness* for their unit. From what point on do these constructs become imperialistic weapons? Especially in the recent past we have experienced how after the breakdown of the "evil empire" (R. Reagan) the lack of a collective enemy led to the successful construction of a new enemy image, which then became a deciding prerequisite for the inhuman and ecologically disastrous Gulf War. What possibilities do we have on a societal level to do what we are accustomed to in family therapy: to question those constructs, to explore their roots, and to offer alternatives?

- As in our clinical work with couples and families, the survival of societies and nations within the human family depends on our moving beyond moral appeals to a conceptual demonstration, what precisely it means to be co-responsible for the fate of our planet and to reverse the current trend toward self-destruction, nuclear or otherwise (Starke, 1992). If an *ethic of "universal solidarity"* (Peukert, 1984) with the suffering of others, especially in regard to future generations, will not be left hanging in the air and remain an unfounded appeal, this ethic must be anchored in the nature of relationships. It must address the dialectic balance of subject and totality.

Dilemma of the Systemic-Constructivist Paradigm

The issues that were raised here from the point of view of the practice of couples and family therapy and from the experience of living in the global village led me to question the prevalent models of family theory. I believe that the conceptual models family theorists have transferred to therapy (e.g., systems theory, constructivism) are inadequate in their application to family theory, especially when applied to interpersonal relationships and social systems. None of the models is, in my view, able to do justice, conceptually, to the dialectical tension between subject and totality.

Process of Cognition.   The various systems paradigms as well as constructivism are stretched beyond their conceptual limits when applied to social units such as families, institutions, or nations. Interpersonal relationships are being understood and conceptualized in these paradigms according to the model of processes by which we know and perceive inanimate objects. In the *process of cognition,* the human mind transcends everything that it can conceptualize within the horizon of being. In fact, our mind appropriates everything through cognition; nonhuman objects become its possession, something that has at least the potential to be fully comprehended. Things, plants, and animals become our cognitive property, just as everything turned to gold that Midas touched.

Simply as objects in the process of cognition, other human subjects are objectified, too, through our perceiving and comprehending. They tend to become "things for me," for the comprehending mind. They would lose their mystery, their subjectivity, were it not for the fact that we experience the others also as forever eluding the comprehensive mind. In other words, cognition of other human beings by us is embedded in an ontological relation that rests on the mystery of the other and on his or her willingness to become open to us.

Systems theory and constructivism respectively appear, therefore, appropriate as epistemological paradigms for the construction of mechanical or biological systems and for the design of alternative realities according to the subjective comprehension of the objective world. This model of thinking about intersubjective processes, however, falls fundamentally short of the claim to be able to conceptualize relationships between people as autonomous subjects of freedom and self-determination. It is inadequate as an epistemology for social relationship systems because autonomy *and* relatedness do not appear to be conceptually substantiated.

Basis for Interpersonal Ethics?   The systemic paradigm[4] (in its more traditional form or in a constructivist sense) is also *unable to provide a basis for interpersonal ethics.* The joint construction of mutually acceptable models of living and world views by individuals, groups, and societies does not suffice as basis for an ethic of solidarity. Any such construct can be validated by consensus and made rational and plausible. It remains unclear in this co-construction, however, how I should be affected by the suffering of the other in the first place or why and how I should change my life in relationship to other subjects or systems. Mutuality, that is, the art of negotiating an intersubjective (or intersystemic) balance of interests, as welcome as it may be as a step in the process of reconciliation, in the final analysis serves mainly the self-assertion of the individual subject (or system). Further, interpersonal ethics must also be capable of providing a foundation for an inter-subjectivity in which the accounts of merits and debits *cannot* be balanced. Such an ethic must be able to show how suffering and death, even death for others, can be derived from the nature of the relationship.

***Autopoetic* System Model.**   In *Maturana's conceptual model* of the *structure determined* and *autopoetic* system, the subject (and in a modified sense also a family system, a nation, and so forth) remains closed in itself. Intersubjective (or intersystemic) relationships are stated but not convincingly demonstrated. They are conceptualized as externally added on to the subject (or the social system) and as supplementary to the constitution and structure of the subject (or the individual system). Instructive interaction between people that profoundly changes who they are is, therefore, a "myth" according to Maturana. Incidentally modern research into the physiology of the brain has proved Maturana's original studies of the frog's cognition to be at best of limited value. More recent research lends strong support to the assumption that on a biophysiological level, too, we are constituted through interactive exchanges with our environment, above all with other people.

If we direct our focus to the internal structure of a social system, it would follow from this model that the relational patterns of the individuals who form the system remain substantially untouched by the environment of the system. In this case, however, it is difficult to demonstrate conceptually how powerful forces outside the family group, for instance, can have the overwhelming and very real impact on their relational structure that we described earlier.

Finally, the reality of other subjects remains in this model outside the horizon of understanding or of relating, that is, finally irrelevant. Individual subjects or social systems (which are here often hypostasized to units with, in essence, a nature similar to a subject) are unable to transcend themselves toward other people or groups. Relationships are in the end illusionary. Other people, and even more so other social systems, remain constructs designed with the appearance of objectivity in the mind of the individual subject or of the human system.

Formulation of the Dilemma

The application therefore of a cognitive model of thinking to the relationship between subjects, between subjects and a totality, and between human systems results in the following unacceptable statements that express basically the same predicament.

Regarding the relationship between two or more subjects, intersubjectivity is either a form of *colonialistic* seizure of the others, who lose their strangeness and degenerate to constructs of the subject's mind, to "objects" created according to one's own image, to reproductions. In this case *relationship* appears to be preserved at the expense of the autonomy of the other. Or the subject does not relate to others as subjects at all in the process of cognition. All subjects remain in their autonomy unreachable for each other, unrelated, unconnected, and uncomprehended. The others only *seem* to be partners of a relationship. In truth, they are delusions of the self originating in the process of cognition. In this case, *autonomy* appears to be preserved at the expense of relatedness.

Regarding the relationship between subject and totality, the dilemma can be formulated similarly.

Either the totality of a system is conceptualized as a new ontological unity, much like individuals. Then the subjects making up the totality lose their uniqueness and irreducible dignity and degenerate into mere cells in a qualitatively higher organism. The whole swallows the subjects. Or the subjects preserve their uniqueness and their mystery, relating neither to each other nor to a larger whole. The totality we are talking about is only apparent; it does not exist outside of the constructing mind or a societal consensus. The subjects construct the totality as illusion.

In the terms of systems theory, the dilemma can be formulated similarly. Either the higher order of the whole destroys the individual in his or her subjectivity, or the totality is only appearance, an illusion that hides the relational isolation of the subjects.

I think it is apparent from this dilemma that the application of the cognitive epistemological model to human relationships leads to the *de(con)struction* of the other as such and of the knowing subject itself, since being a self includes relatedness.

Outlines of a Radically New Approach: The Ontology of the Other

I would like to suggest here briefly a radically new approach to the philosophical and epistemological foundation of family therapy. This new epistemology (Auerswald, 1987) is owed to the work of the French philosopher Emmanuel Levinas (Bernasconi & Critchley, 1991; Levinas, 1969, 1978, 1981, 1987, 1989).[5]

I mentioned earlier the double-faced nature of the human condition. We experience ourselves as autonomous subjects of human dignity, freedom, history, and responsibility *and* as finite beings who have not created or constructed themselves but who are to the core of their being dependent, co-determined by others and related to others. Levinas developed in his discussion of the works of Husserl and Heidegger a new approach to reconcile subjectivity with relatedness. According to this approach, the foundation of the subject as autonomous and unique, that is, as self, has to be seen precisely in his or her relatedness to and responsibility for the other logically before the process of cognition, in which the other becomes an object of the subject's comprehension. In his phenomenological analyses and in his basic studies, Levinas emphasizes and details the fundamental orientation of the subject toward the other and the ontological openness toward the experience of the other subject as such. That centeredness of the subject in the other can then serve as a basis for an initial understanding of the other and for a co-construction of the relationship.

This basic philosophical approach can be illustrated with an example from our day-to-day experience. Parents are constituted as parents through their responsibility for their children. They become parents through their children. They are duty bound to their children before their own decision to accept this role. The parents' relationship and their vulnerability to their children constitute, confirm, and validate them as parents and, in a more basic sense, as autonomous subjects.

In Levinas' philosophy, which we cannot describe here in detail, the subjectivity of the subject and the identity of the individual as a human being is preserved, even constituted through and within a system of related individuals. At the same time, the others remain others; they stay strangers, mysterious and beyond the complete grasp of the cognitive act of the subject's mind.

The importance of Levinas' *ontology of the other* becomes more apparent when one realizes that it precedes logically any epistemology (in Auerswald's [1987] definition) as its foundation.[6] At the same time, Levinas' philosophy yields also a foundation for a postmodern ethic, that is, one that is not particularistic and does not need to deduce magically from somewhere "eternal" ethical values.

PROCESS OF CHANGE IN FAMILIES AND SOCIETAL SYSTEMS

I have discussed earlier the professional duty of therapists, not only to accompany the process of change within the context of therapy with families, but also to promote this process within a global context through their engagement and participation as mental health professionals. I would like now to suggest some communalities in the process of change in families and in larger societal systems that can be useful for therapeutic and political work.

Process of Change

In families or larger social systems, change is initiated and implemented through cognitive dissonances, relational conflicts, and contextual breaks within the system or between the system and the larger environment. These *tectonic faults* are in turn triggered by "unidentified guests" (Eliot, 1950), by "strangers" (Kristeva, 1990), by those who do not "belong," who remain puzzling in one way or another.

In families, these strangers are rebellious teenagers, disenchanted spouses, acting-out children, psychotic relatives, and, yes, therapists. Within the magnetic field of the therapeutic context, the therapist is a stranger, often making the family uneasy. The therapist is someone who asks unexpected questions and has surprising responses to the dilemma of the family. Similar to the index patient in a family, therapists also bring "unfamiliar" viewpoints and alternative life options into the conversation. And so gradually a change process begins to evolve on the level of relational structures.

On the global level of the world family, the frequently stagnant, partially mad, and, since August 1945, potentially self-destructive ecosystem earth has no challengers from outside because it is global and there is no context "outside" of it. It also cannot easily be moved toward change from inside, certainly not by those who are fully integrated into the system.

The global ecosystem can be changed only by people who themselves became strangers, who have not fully adapted and do not fit into the system. The *innovative* impulse toward a new vision originates in those who have learned a new way of thinking, just as we have attempted to learn a *holistic* view as therapists in the family system.

For the process of continuous self-change, therefore, on which the survival of social systems, from the family to the ecosystem earth, is dependent, it is of crucial significance that there is room in the communicational structure of the system as well as in our conceptual reflection for innovative breakthroughs. Social systems of whatever order need the creative initiatives of individuals and have to rely on challenges by strangers, especially on those that shift the balance between subject and totality in the direction of more human dignity and justice.

Resources for Change

What are the resources, however, from which this process of continuing innovation and transformation can be nurtured and guided if, different from family systems, there is no supervisor for the planet earth behind the one-way mirror of world history? Neither a "Greek chorus" nor a "reflecting team" is available to consult with the disturbed planetary system humankind; to reorient it; or, even more important, to urge it on, to speed up the global discourse about its own future in a serious manner.

In families, a new future is often created from the dialogue with the past. More precisely, it is most often the past as repressed, forgotten, misunderstood origin of a family that blocks the path into the future. Vice versa, listening to the voices from the past and accepting the burden, the challenges, and the wisdom of past generations opens new perspectives and unlocks new opportunities for living.

Similarly, on a planetary level, it is of utmost importance to refer back to the history of humankind and to be in dialogue with it. The forgotten voices of prophetic men and women, the lost and silenced in the official historiography of the victors, and the repressed advocates of a more human way of life could become for us at the beginning of the planetary age the indispensable and inexhaustible choir that challenges us to a continuous transformation of our thinking. In the planetary society, therapists as agents of change in the family context could devote part of their energy to the task of guiding and influencing the dialogue with history, of lending their ear to the voices of the past, and of helping them get expressed in the global conversation.

In addition, the transformation process on a world level and the development of more human systems will depend on whether or not we succeed in maintaining the global discourse that has already started. As therapists, we know of the almost insurmountable obstacles that obstruct a global exchange about alternative possibilities of social interaction and communication with each other that is unconstrained by power and domination (Peukert, 1989). We also have ideas about factors that will keep clients' conversation about the structure of their relationship more or less free of disturbances and focused. I think therefore that it is possible to contribute from the experience of family therapy to the debate over the future in the global village. We can specifically address the task of keeping the communicational structures free from suffocating interventions or destructive domination.

VISIONS OF CHANGE

Instead of outlining here yet another visionary design, I would like to add a few remarks that have to do with the process and the continuation of the global discourse and with the role of family therapists in it.

The Basis: Levinas' Ontology of the Other

I am beginning with the fundamental orientation toward the other that, according to Levinas, constitutes the individual as an autonomous and unique subject. Each of us is logically before his or her inter-connectedness with a context or a social system so solicited by the powerlessness and vulnerability of the other human being that this responsibility for the other's well-being creates the basis for the subject as a self, as the carrier of absolute dignity and humanity. This centeredness of our inner being in the other makes it possible for us to reconcile conceptually autonomous subjectivity and fundamental relatedness.

The subject's relatedness to the other is in Levinas' philosophy ontologically defined. The other is always *every* other, in a spatial and temporal sense universal. This basic quality manifests itself in the encounter with the face of a specific other. Through the experience of the humanity of this one specific other, the encounter refers to all others who participate in the humanity of the one. In other words, the experience of the global village brings into our explicit reflection what constitutes the essence of human beings as subjects already: his and her and their relatedness to the others in a global sense. The epochal step toward the modern experience of the essential unity of humankind is, therefore, only phenomeno-logically catching up with something that was already given with the existence of humanity as a whole. From this basic approach, a number of aspects become evident that I would like to mention briefly.

Global Epistemological Transformation

The *ontology of the other* originating in the work of Levinas and the experience of the unity of humankind require and enable an *epistemological transformation on a global level.* Many studies that were influential in the development of family therapy prepared us for this step (the work of Bateson, von Foerster, von Glaser-feld, Prigogine, Maturana, for instance, extensively discussed in Simon, Stierlin & Wynne, 1985, and in Auerswald, 1985, 1987, 1991). The transformation of our thinking from the mechanistic world view of Descartes and Newton toward an *ecosystemic epistemology* (Auerswald, 1991) is in no field of human knowledge more crucial than in the transformation of world society and its innumerable subsystems in the direction toward a more human systemic organization. Because family therapists start from the same new model of thinking, they are able to participate with legitimacy in the debate over the future configuration of the global relational and communicative structures.[7]

Ethic of Universal Solidarity

With the dawn of the universality of our experience as inhabitants of the global village, it is also immediately clear that *any ethic,* no matter what the content, has to be valid in a *universal* way. A particularistic ethic, referring to ethnic or nationalistic groups or the rich countries of the Western world, that is, any ethic that is context specific or system immanent, does not deserve that name.

How do we find a foundation for a universal ethic? Levinas' ontology of the other, it seems to me, implies basic assumptions for an *ethic of universal solidarity,* assumptions that we can also find in fragmentary form in the work of other contemporary authors. I would like to point out, however, one crucial aspect for an inquiry into possible foundations of an ethic of universal solidarity. The thrust of Levinas' entire philosophical position is that ethics and ontology are identical; that is, ethical principles are no longer deduced from a more basic philosophical doctrine or agreed on in a societal consensus; instead they are the essence of the intersubjective relationship.

Global Discourse

One of the themes to which family therapists have a particular access through their professional work is the *discourse about justice.* This discourse, through which subsystems of the planetary human system (i.e., ethnic groups, nations, social classes, institutions) can come to agreements about a balance of conflicting interests and claims, will decisively determine the coming decades, economically, politically, and ecologically. It will have features that are similar to those that characterize the dialogic process between members of a family about a balance of interests, merits, and debits. From a family therapy perspective, we could contribute specific rules and guidelines that originate in the practice of conflict exploration and resolution in families, particularly in regard to those factors that could prevent the breakdown of the global discourse.

Information and Control

Finally, I would like to indicate another aspect that stems from working with families. Family systems frequently keep important information secret, individual members "administer" and protect the family memory like a treasure, and many important details can be uncovered only through direct exploration. Opening the access to the family's memories and stories often proves to be crucial to effective reconciliation and to the creation of more health-promoting family system structures.

In the global village of the human family, survival is increasingly dependent on who controls the stream of information, how information is divided and processed, and whether or not the individual citizen of the world society has access to *alternative sources of information*. In the conversation among individuals, groups, nations, and parts of the global society, much will depend on whether enough individuals will be guided by an imperative toward a more comprehensive understanding of the other, whether enough groups can find a more sophisticated view of the "facts," against the prejudices of the world media, and whether in the long run we can create world-based information channels that express and make accessible alternative options for living and alternative viewpoints. The electronic possibilities in the global village are already in existence.

STRANGER IN THE FAMILY—IN THE GLOBAL VILLAGE

I would like to illustrate the central thesis of this chapter with the figure of the stranger as a symbol. It is not by accident that recently the questions regarding the fate of the refugees and of the applicants for asylum and immigration have triggered such passionate debates in Europe.

The Stranger

Strangers, guests, and migrants have to trust the benevolence, the sense of justice, and the respect of the citizens, the indigenous. Vice versa, it is the duty of the host, of the citizens, to be concerned with the well-being of their guests, the strangers; they experience themselves as responsible. Both guest and host, or stranger and citizen, are related to each other. Their existence centers around the other but in a way that is not mutual. The well-being of the other, the stranger, is the center of concern of the host, not the other way around. The host, the citizen, is constituted as such by being related to the guest, the stranger.

In all of this, the strangers remain mysterious, just as the others in our general reflection on the process of intersubjective cognition. As others, they are removed from our complete comprehension, from our total understanding, and it is as others that they are part of the social system.

In this perspective, the relations between myself and the others, between therapist and clients, between those that are at home in the global village and those that have immigrated are similar to the laws regulating relations between the guest and the host, to the sanctuary laws or to the laws regarding pilgrims. Since ancient times, these laws had sacred dimensions; guests and people requesting asylum were untouchable. The vulnerability of the guests or of the applicants for asylum or of the pilgrims was the basis for a relationship of responsibility, at least within a limited realm. In the therapeutic context, an interpersonal relationship is created that is characterized by professional responsibility and the therapist's concern for the others. I am proposing here to see the challenge of family therapy in the *global* character of this concern and to see in Levinas' ontology of the other a foundation for basic structures of intersubjectivity.

The Questions

I would like to end with three questions addressed to mental health professionals and to the citizens of the global village. They were originally formulated at the time of the Gulf War (Wetzel, 1992).

1. Can we become or remain strangers, or "unidentified guests" in our society who voice dissent in the context of a partly destructive or mad system? Our professional knowledge does not allow us to be blind to the horrendous physical and emotional damage that is inflicted day in and day out on children and families abroad and here by wars and by the contexts that produce wars, especially economic exploitation, racial violence, and systemic oppression. Are we willing to shoulder the burden of not fitting in with everyone else in our society, so that we can remain faithful to our professional mission even beyond the boundaries of the therapy room?
2. Can we speak up for the strangers in the global village, for the migrants, for those without a voice (Martín-Baró, 1991)? Can we transcend a context-limited, national-, ethnic-, or class-specific ethic toward an ethic of universal solidarity? Antagonistic and irreconcilably hostile family, group, or nation systems can have deadly consequences for those people who are considered the others, as we observe these days again. The others in warring contexts become strangers and then enemies that need not be understood anymore and can, even should be, eliminated. Can we produce the same sensitivity that we have for the suffering of the others in a family system also for those suffering in the world system and advocate for them? Can we be hosts in the global village for the strangers and migrants?
3. Can we allow ourselves to be lured into embarking on a cognitive and emotional journey into an unknown future that parallels our ontological relatedness to the other and will lead us away from the traditional Cartesian world

view of intellectual analysis, mechanistic conquests, and dualistic thinking? The direction points toward an ecological and systemic epistemology that includes interpersonal responsiveness, global participatory conversation, and mutually supportive co-evolution between people who are strangers to each other yet share the same humanity.

Frequently we challenge families to this journey in the process of helping them overcome long-lasting family strife and suffering. Why should we not ourselves begin this journey and invite others from the global village to join us? In my opinion, our survival as human family on the planet earth depends on the answer we give.

NOTES

1. How specific and definite the challenge to family therapy for political and societal engagement in the interest of client families has to be formulated can be seen from an official position paper of the Commission for Professional Ethical Affairs of the American Psychological Association: "Reducing the likelihood of nuclear conflict must take precedence over the ordinary scientific and professional concerns of the American Psychological Association that bear on human welfare in more limited ways" (APA, Board of Social and Ethical Responsibility for Psychology, May 1982; in Nelson, 1985, p. 549).
2. I have chosen not to give extensive bibliographical data in this chapter. The theories and the authors mentioned here can be found either in Simon, Stierlin, & Wynne (1985) or in Gurman & Kniskern (1981 & 1991).
3. Systemic family theorists, like Paul Dell and others, attempted repeatedly to define more precisely the qualitative differences between mechanical systems, biological organisms, and social, i.e., human, systems. Such a definition has not been presented convincingly so far in my view as part of the conceptualization of systems theory as a foundation for family therapy.
4. I am following here Auerswald's distinction of the concepts epistemology, paradigm, theory, model (Auerswald, 1987).
5. The following outline of Levinas' approach assumes that systems theory and constructivism will continue to have significance for family therapy as paradigms and as models (Auerswald, 1987), but not in the fundamental sense of being the epistemological basis for family therapy.
6. An extensive discussion of the philosophy of Levinas in its application for a theoretical foundation of family therapy is reserved for a later publication.
7. While I am finishing this chapter, the suffering in Somalia (and other parts of Africa) and the ethnic violence in what was Yugoslavia have reached horrible proportions. The world watches apparently unable to intervene effectively. What could demonstrate more powerfully the need for an epistemological transformation! The time has come to create global structures and institutions that could deal successfully with ecological disasters, regional breakdowns of authority structures, and ethnic and tribal antagonisms that victimize millions of "others."

BIBLIOGRAPHY

Auerswald, E. H. (1985). Thinking about thinking in family therapy. *Family Process, 24,* 1–12.

Auerswald, E. H. (1987). Epistemological confusion in family therapy research. *Family Process, 26,* 317–330.

Auerswald, E. H. (1991). *Ecopoiesis and family well-being.* Unpublished manuscript.

Benjamin, W. (1969). *Illuminations.* New York: Schocken.

Bernasconi, R., & Critchley, S. (Eds.) (1991). *Re-Reading Levinas.* Bloomington, IN: Indiana University Press.

Bouchard, M.-A., & Guerette, L. (1991). Psychotherapy as a hermeneutical experience. *Psychotherapy, 28(3),* 385–394.

Eliot, T. S. (1950). *The cocktail party.* London: Faber & Faber Ltd. (1976 edition.)

Elizur, J., & Minuchin, S. (1989). *Institutionalizing madness. Families, therapy and society.* New York: Basic Books.

Flew, A. (Ed.) (1979). *A dictionary of philosophy* (2nd ed.). New York: St. Martin's Press.

Gurman, A., & Kniskern, D. (Eds.) (1981 & 1991), *Handbook of family therapy* (Vols. I & II). New York: Brunner/Mazel.

Kristeva, J. (1990). *Etrangers à nous-mêmes.* Paris: Librairie Artheme Fayard.

Levinas, E. (1969). *Totality and infinity. An essay on exteriority.* (A. Lingis, Trans.). Pittsburgh: Duquesnes University Press.

Levinas, E. (1978). *Existence and existents.* (A. Lingis, Trans.) The Hague: M. Nijheff.

Levinas, E. (1981). *Otherwise than being. Or beyond essence.* (A. Lingis, Trans.) The Hague: M. Nijheff.

Levinas, E. (1987). *Collected philosophical papers.* (A. Lingis, Trans.) Boston: M. Nijheff.

Levinas, E. (1989). *The Levinas reader.* (A. Hand, Trans.). New York: B. Blackwell.

Martín-Baró, I. (1991). Towards a liberation psychology. In J. Hasset & H. Lacey (Eds.). *Towards a society that serves its people: The intellectual contribution of El Salvador's murdered Jesuits.* Washington, DC: Georgetown University Press.

McLuhan, M., & Powers, B. R. (1989). *The global village: Transformations in world life and the media in the 21st century.* New York: Oxford University Press.

Minuchin, S. (1991). The seductions of constructivism. *The Networker, 15(5),* 47–50.

Nelson, A. (1985). Psychological equivalence. Awareness and response-ability in our nuclear age. *American Psychologist, 40,* 549.

Peukert, H. (1984). *Science, action, and fundamental theology. Toward a theology of communicative action.* Cambridge, MA: The MIT Press.

Peukert, H. (1989). *Communicative action, systems of power accumulation and the unfinished projects of enlightenment and theology.* Unpublished manuscript.

Simon, F. B., Stierlin, H., & Wynne, L. C. (1985). *The language of family therapy. A systematic vocabulary and source book.* New York: Family Process Press.

Starke, L. (Ed.) (1992). *State of the world 1992. A Worldwatch Institute report on progress toward a sustainable society.* New York: W.W. Norton.

Stierlin, H., Rücker-Embden, I., Wetzel, N., & Wirsching, M. (1980). *The first interview with the family.* New York: Brunner/Mazel.

Wetzel, N. (1980). *Solidarität mit den Toten. Zum Umgang mit den Toten im Familiensystem und zur Trauerarbeit in der Familientherapie.* [Solidarity with the dead. Relating to the dead in the family system and mourning in family therapy.] In Duss-von Werdt, J., & Enderlin, R. (Eds.) *Der Familienmensch. System und Handeln in der Familientherapie.* Stuttgart: Klett-Cotta.

Wetzel, N. (1992). Beyond the therapy room: Therapy and politics. A family therapist's reflections. *New Jersey Psychologist, 42(1),* 20–21.

Wetzel, N. A., & Winawer, H. (1986). The psychological consequences of the nuclear threat from a family systems perspective. *International Journal of Mental Health, 15,* 298–313.

Chapter 3

How Do Therapists Deal with Issues of Global Survival in Therapy?

Erika Waechter

In my 25 years of experience as a clinician, I have never had clients come into the office expressing concerns regarding global survival. I had never had discussions with colleagues about this topic or gone to a conference where it was a major focus. The one exception has been the American Family Therapy Association (AFTA) Interest Group and Task Force on Nuclear Issues, which was the motivating force behind my participation in this publication.

I tried to take some responsibility in regard to my concerns by faithfully attending the AFTA meetings. Others did more than just attend meetings—they did research, talked to groups, and wrote about their experiences and findings. After each meeting, my efforts to do something never left the planning stages. I planned with great resolve, year after year. Once I offered a community college class for families to discuss how issues of global threat were affecting the family. One person signed up. I felt stuck. I decided that perhaps I was not skilled enough to offer help to the general public; the next year, I decided to talk with other therapists about their feelings and those of their own families regarding global survival issues. Other than announcing my intentions to a few colleagues, however, I did nothing. I never exactly understood what stopped me besides a busy schedule. I was definitely feeling hesitant. I couldn't take initiative. Would they think I was wasting their time, and was it too personal?

I remained lethargically inactive until the 1990 AFTA meeting, when this book was taking shape. There my friends and colleagues convinced me that since I had always wanted to do something, my opportunity had arrived. No one yet was addressing the question of what actually happens in the therapy room around global survival issues. This was a new perspective for me, a new vantage point from which to pursue the issues that I believed needed talking about.

I work together with seven other therapists in a private practice group, and global survival issues were seldom, if ever, talked about in my sessions nor in my colleagues' sessions. Why should this be? Psychotherapy, after all, deals with issues that cause emotional distress and consequent dysfunction. Why wouldn't the threat of annihilation be an issue that causes emotional distress?

I did not feel as constrained about addressing therapists about their work. Initial questions to ask came quickly to mind. Taking on the challenge to gain some understanding, I designed a list of questions and interviewed 18 therapists. In this chapter, I will begin with a brief description of my survey subjects. The bulk of the chapter will be examples, summary statements of and some discussion about the answers given to each question. The final section will be some thoughts about how to understand the answers that the subjects gave to this survey.

SUBJECT RECRUITMENT

My original thought was simply to talk to every therapist that I knew about the questions I had. Indeed, I began with some of my office colleagues. I then realized that I would not be able to interview everyone and that I should interview people I didn't know, or know so well, people who also might have different points of view. I tried to get some balance, in my sample of 18 subjects, in terms of gender, discipline, and theoretical orientation.

There was no resistance to being interviewed when I called up these therapists and said that I was collecting information for a book on global survival issues and had four questions that I wished to ask them. Some people were excited about the survey, and others were puzzled about what I might ask and whether they had anything to say about this subject. Interviews ranged in time from 20 minutes to an hour.

The majority of the subjects have a general practice, but one therapist works almost exclusively with women, one primarily with medically related problems, one primarily with children; several spend more of their professional lives teaching and writing and have small practices. Of the 15 with full-time practices, only three describe themselves as family therapists, and there were no very psychoanalytically oriented subjects. Most say they are systemically oriented. The age range is between mid-thirties and early fifties. There are 12 women and 6 men: five social workers, two counselors, one psychiatrist, and 10 psychologists (a mix of Ph.D. and Master's degrees). All but four live in cities of about 150,000 population. The other four live in large urban centers.

RESPONSES TO THE SURVEY

1. Does the Peril that the World Is in Come Up in Your Clinical Work? If So, How?

It was interesting that the immediate response to my first question was "yes" from only six of the 18 therapists, and of the six, one qualified with "yes, indirectly," and another said, "only with nonadult clients." The others answered "not frequently," "comes up sometimes," "very little as a specific focus," "rarely," "if you define the question broadly, then yes," and "can't think of a specific time it has come up." One therapist answered "never."

With the exception of the therapist who answered "never" to question #1, however, most had quite a bit to say in the course of the survey. Some of those that had little to say tended—as they were responding—to wonder why that was.

2. What Is Coming Up in Therapy that Has to Do with (a) War Stories? (b) Environmental Destruction? (c) General Worry about the World? (d) Nuclear Threat? (e) Global Survival Awareness?

In answering the five parts to question #2, some therapists gave the same answers to two of the five parts. Generally, however, there were definite patterns in the answers to each of the five parts.

Responses to the question about war stories were quite uniformly related to personal events. Most frequently this had to do with Vietnam War experiences or in some cases the legacy that that war had left in the society. Some examples are:

"I've seen Vietnam vets so I've certainly heard some pretty disturbing stories from them."

"I have never talked to a Vietnam vet who didn't have post-traumatic stress symptoms—somatic, sleep problems, real heavy guilt issues around being involved in killing."

"In my case load what's coming up now has mostly to do with unfinished business left over from the Vietnam War. The agony about not being better integrated in the society."

"I do have one case currently where the father of two teenage kids is a Vietnam vet and apparently had very traumatic experiences in Vietnam. There is a lot of confusion in the family about whether violence is right or wrong."

The question about environmental destruction produced several different themes. First, there were varying expressions of how guilt has led to action. For example, one therapist said that she had three clients in the last year who left their line of work in large part because they didn't feel all right about what they were doing. They were experiencing some kind of occupational guilt. Another talked about clients trying to make career choices toward careers that save the environment. Another therapist talked about a client who felt she didn't deserve anything. This then translated into the client being overly conscious about the environment.

Second, there were clients who seemed less moved to action but who were discussing environmental issues. For example, I was told that one client talks about her desire to be more connected to the earth and her desire to help save the planet. She also speaks of her concern with the state of the world and feels she is personally responsible for helping people feel better. She is not active in organizations that will do that, but she's very concerned about it.

A third theme in response to this question had to do with illness. A number of examples were given having to do with existing cancer or fears of having cancer. In these cases, clients linked the fear to the polluted environment or specifically to the use of pesticides.

The question concerning general worry about the world brought responses with political overtones. It is important to note that, of all the questions, this one produced the most vivid expressions of fear, anxiety, and powerlessness.

A common response from clients who are parents is their anxiety about letting children out of their sight because the world is unsafe. Parents also expressed confusion and frustration about how their children are doing and how goal-oriented they are. Clients who were either children or adolescents were reported to have a sense of uncertainty about the future. One child therapist said that she thinks that children know something is wrong in the world and that their parents aren't doing anything about it. This therapist sees children who think it is their job to try to change the situation. Another therapist reported, "sometimes I have little kids in here—you know eight-, nine-, ten-year-olds—who are worried about hunger in Africa and things like that."

The powerlessness people can feel often comes out in mistrust. One therapist responded that clients will comment, "What's it all about anyway? We'll all be destroyed." General discouragement as well as specific angers about authorities such as big business, government, and the military were also mentioned. Another therapist said he has a client who is terrified to breathe the air. He also had two clients last year who were very active in environmental causes. They both have a tremendous amount of anger about issues because they think that they were lied to by authorities. Still another response was from a therapist who says she has some fairly radical clients, and from them she hears a great deal of expression of hopelessness. These clients see less leadership in government and decreasing quality of education. They fear that there is no way to overcome the lack of attention to progressive concerns that have occurred in the last 10 years. They also fear that a trend toward selfishness—"me" stuff—leaves a legacy that cannot be healed.

A number of respondents to general worry about the world mentioned clients' concerns about the economic condition of the world. One therapist, in my view, seemed to sum up things in her discussion as follows:

"I think that (general worry about the world) comes up in my sessions a great deal. It's the fear of violence because I work with domestic violence—rape, incest, the whole thing—destruction of the family, sexism, racism. A great many of my patients are gay and so I am very aware of discrimination against people with different sexual preference. I also hear about old women who are very worried about poverty and who have concerns about the ways people with mental illness are treated. A lot of social issues come up in my therapy."

In the discussion of the question related specifically to nuclear threat, there was remarkably little response. Not one therapist reported adult clients feeling concern about nuclear war. The therapist in my survey who works primarily with children and adolescents, however, stated that her clients have shown symptoms that, when she explored them, can be traced to fears of nuclear holocaust. Unfortunately, more information about the symptoms is not available but would be an area for further exploration. Adults did express to therapists some concern about nuclear reactors, nuclear waste, and safety from radiation and nuclear plants but not about nuclear bombs. Occasionally some less direct expression of hopelessness was reported, such as "Why bother? The world is going to blow up...," and the clients expressed feelings that there isn't anything they can do about it anyway.

My question having to do with global survival was less specific, and, indeed, the answers were more general. The following is a sampling of these responses:

"I guess it comes up with AIDS HIV people in terms of the epidemic. They're the only people who seem to talk about it."

"They talk about needing to live in a more cooperative way."

"Some people have a panic and a real obsession about the world ending. But it's linked also to God and evil and the devil and how we'll be punished... an internalized horrible fear."

"Global survival—environmental survival? Again I hear a lot of expression of fear that there are more and more people who have less and less and that the gap between them and the few who have more and more is increasing and that's contributing to malaise and chaos. Somebody made the connection the other day about their view of the move towards democracy all over the world, saying that the pull away from communism wasn't necessarily a good sign. Indeed, it might be a reflection of incredible desperation; there was more global evidence that things were falling apart economically."

"You know it's kind of hard. I feel like I'm giving you kind of an awareness of things... because I don't think the survival of the planet has been what I think is the main therapeutic issue. It's not like a presenting problem that we've worked on. But one of the ways that it's come up is by comparison... in other words... maybe some kind of guilt stuff... like, well I should be thankful for what we have in this country... at least we are not starving."

"I think where that comes up most is when I'm working with parents who have been politically aware and politically active. Now with young children, they are trying to make some peace with the more radical views that they themselves may have had as college students and in their twenties. They are raising children now and using disposable diapers and wanting a third child and things like that. They're feeling a lot of stress around those conflicts . . . feeling as if they are betraying certain ideals and values that they not only held but fought for."

3. What Do You Do When This Happens?

The third question that I asked had to do with the therapist's response to these issues when in the session. The majority of respondents said they support their client's expression of concerns and try to be validating. Many described trying to understand the concerns, see what meaning the concerns have to their clients, link them to more deep-seated fears, and bring out the feelings clients are having about the issues.

Beyond this general approach, I noticed that half the therapists fell into one of two groups. One was those who have strong political positions but are concerned that discussing political issues interferes in the therapy. A subgroup of these therapists expressed confusion about how to deal with issues because of their own anxieties or their own past choices. For example, one comment was, "having done some fairly destructive environmental self-indulgent activities, I certainly have enough garbage in my back yard to not point the finger in talking about how clients make a decision." This therapist concluded that he does explore clients' ability to conceptualize, take responsibility, and accept the consequences for their choices.

Others, however, had comments like, "I personally have strong views on most of the subjects and I try to keep those out of therapy because even though the person may agree with me, I think it distracts from the work." Or "I never talk about politics. I sometimes get tempted. It feels as if the boundaries get muddied because it's so much of an issue for me." Another therapist, who actually thought global survival issues came up a lot in her work, answered this question as follows:

"For the most part I say that I'm supportive of their expression. Occasionally it makes sense to me that there is some need for validation of their reality. When I think that is fitting as a therapist, then I will validate their reality to the extent that I feel that way. If I don't think it fits in then I won't because I myself am subject to go off on political discourse . . . I have to watch out that I don't get hooked."

By contrast, the other group of therapists have strong political positions and assumed one talks about these things as one would anything else. They tended to say things like, "I take it very seriously," and described the ways they process the issues. Part of what they do is to help clients become empowered around their concerns—to join a group or otherwise take active steps to reduce their fears more effectively.

Those who were seeing children tried to get parents to help relieve their children of responsibilities that were burdensome. Therapists working with teenagers tried to help parents of these teens understand why their children's perspective of the world and their future was often so negative.

The remaining half of my survey subjects did not think that much related to these issues came up in therapy. They gave the general response reported in my first paragraph in this section. About one-fourth answered that their first concern is whether the issue is a therapeutic one or not. Others who thought global survival material came up as side issues used the concerns as a metaphor for their therapeutic focus.

4. Has a Situation Ever Come Up in a Therapy Hour that Has Led You to Believe that There Are Issues Related to Global Survival that You Have Chosen Not to Pursue? If so, Why?

To the last question of my survey, nine respondents clearly said "no." Three had some interesting extra comments:

"No, I do not ever cut off any issue with my clients ever. I had two patients where I had to really be parental and refute their horror about fearing the end of the world and create safety in this room. So I play a bit the prophet and say, 'Look, people are waking up and we will all globally work on issues.' But usually I don't minimize at all, cut it off ever. I try to touch on the inner resources, how they can deal with realistic threats and just feel some ritual safety, and even create safety in their own lives."

"No, I think if it comes up and I'm aware it comes up I'll do something with it. But I more likely than not will put things in a political context or a class background . . . understand the personal dynamics. I just remembered I had this one couple where he's working on the nuclear free zone and he's not taking care of himself or his partner. He's externalizing what he needs and is not introspective at all. He's also putting out the stand that his political work needs to be more grounded. His personal life needs to be attended to and then his political work will be even more effective. Of course people are fearful that if they start dealing with their own personal stuff they'll become apolitical . . . so I support their activity but it's from a healthier place. I mean that's an important value of mine that I make sure people hear because they're afraid that focusing on the personal will take the political away from them . . . too many of their friends have gone to therapists and have stopped being political."

"No, in fact I often look for it when it's not presenting."

There were also several interesting answers from therapists who said they chose not to pursue issues at times:

"Well I can't think of a specific vignette on this but probably the types of cases I tend to explore less with are people who are really into a sense there's no meaning in the world . . . there's no meaning in life . . . and are depressed."

"I think that every case I handle individually and there are times I don't pursue aspects of it because I'm trying to do what's best for the client . . . sometimes my own political beliefs are completely at odds with what's best for the client so there have been a number of occasions where I've chosen not to deal with it."

"I really don't remember but I would say that in some ways I might see people bringing up global concerns as a way of not talking about other specific concerns that I think they need to talk about in therapy. I am not a therapist who would necessarily focus on those concerns unless somebody brought them up specifically as concerns."

CONCLUSION

When I first looked over the results of my survey, I personally identified more with those therapists who expressed confusions, ambivalence, or ignorance about how to deal with global issues in therapy. I also identified with those who said that global concerns do not come up directly in the therapy hour.

Since I have been working on this chapter, however, my consciousness has expanded, and I now believe that more material about global survival could come up. My listening is a bit different now because I have the question of what does my client's issues have to do with global survival issues more in the forefront. Although I still have not developed a clear conceptual framework to integrate the larger issues into the more personal in an effective way, I hope to do so. I am aware that as I pursue this endeavor I need to work on becoming still more conscious about including this in my work as a first step. I do pursue questioning clients and validating concerns somewhat more firmly now.

Therefore, the small number of direct client comments on global survival in my practice has been saying more about me, I believe, than about the relevance of the topic to clients. I believe that the clients who are dealing directly with immediate survival issues—trauma, poverty, joblessness, natural disasters, family members in the military, and so forth—are more likely to bring survival as an issue into therapy. Often in such instances I see clients defining as a personal failure a situation that clearly is larger than that of their own making. In such cases, I can decide to reframe the survival issue into a larger frame to help the client see his or her own responsibility more clearly.

Much of what emerges in therapy depends on the therapist's conceptual framework. The questions the therapist asks and the data the therapist chooses to respond to help to define the content of the therapy. Despite the fact that the client brings the "problem" to the therapy, it is the therapist who helps to shape what will actually happen as the therapy process develops.

In trying to understand the results of this survey, one overriding thing stands out. For most therapists, whether they expressed the view that the issue of global survival awareness was a topic of their therapy sessions or not, the topic as part of the therapeutic work presented confusions, concerns, or pitfalls. A second point that stood out, as I reported earlier, was the viewpoint of some therapists that this topic does not exist, at least not in a significant way, in therapy. It was encouraging to learn, however, that at least several therapists of my small sample did feel comfortable relating to global survival issues as therapeutic concerns.

I think the question still remains, in terms of general practice, why isn't global survival more of a therapy focus? Caldicott (1991) says the planet has only ten years before it reaches the point of no return. Clearly the subject is a serious one. This contradiction deserves some serious thought.

Fortunately, some people have started thinking seriously. Conn[1] has discussed her position that psychotherapy needs to develop a *self-world connection*. Systems-based theories for working with clients have broadened our focus from the individual to the family and community, but this is still a very narrow focus. O'Connor (1989), in his article on "Therapy for a Dying Planet" says, "Perhaps it is time for another leap. It is time to begin to go beyond our individual families to attend to the Family of Man" (p. 70). Conn (1990) also suggests that "to encourage the massive behavioral adaptations required to protect the earth from humanity's excesses, we need to broaden our concept of self to include other groups of people and other life forms" (p. 5).

It is clear that our training as family therapists did not provide a conceptual framework for addressing global survival issues. The research data about the effects of living in a nuclear age have not been presented to the therapeutic community. Therapists still have little notion of psychological techniques to help them work with the material about planetary survival. I am reminded of the state of the art regarding the treatment of incest when I was in graduate school nearly 30 years ago. I heard about incest only as it was mentioned in one or two studies coming from the remote (at least from me) hills in the southeastern part of the United States. The message I received was that I would never need to deal with incest. I worked in large clinics for children for more than 12 years, and not once was there an identified case of incest. This would not be the case today. Now half my practice concerns itself with issues brought by adult survivors of incest.

In a book edited by Porter (1987), various therapists discuss their thoughts and experiences regarding the role of therapy in a nuclear age. One therapist, Ellen Becker, says, "We attune ourselves to hear and value what we consider to be relevant." She goes on to say:

> A clinician's unwillingness, lack of desire, or indifference to the nuclear peril may cause statements referring to the nuclear peril to be overlooked. On the other hand, it is important to recognize the danger inherent in overidentification with issues that both client and therapist think are important. (p. 31)

The people in my survey expressed the danger of overidentification without strongly expressing the danger of indifference.

We can only be in a position to attune ourselves, without overidentification, however, if we have a better way of conceptualizing global survival issues in a therapy context. If we have a framework, we know how to listen, we know what questions to ask, and we also have a way of dealing with our own issues so that they will not pollute our work with clients. Fortunately, this work, although still at a formative stage, has now begun.

I will conclude with an inspiring example of Conn's (1991) thinking about a new framework by quoting her opening paragraphs in an article for the Center for Psychological Studies in the Nuclear Age:

> "Garbage," says Ann, when speaking to her therapist about her depression. "I can't stop thinking about all the garbage that's piling up everywhere. Where is it all going to go?"
>
> In this opening scene in the movie, *Sex, Lies and Videotapes*, Ann is presented as a disempowered woman. When she talks about garbage and other issues of concern in the larger world, we in the audience laugh. These concerns are not taken seriously as expressions of Ann's need to participate in the world, but are left as statements symbolic of her inner emptiness. Instead of being taken as a sign of her connectedness with the world, they symbolize her separation from her own life, which she has given over to the role of non-working-wife-of-a-successful-lawyer-with-a-large-house-in-the-suburbs. Ann's house is empty of people, her life empty of activity or purpose, and her therapy empty of empowerment.
>
> But garbage is out in the world, not just in Ann's inner life. In fact, pollution is a global problem, which Ann was experiencing personally. Personal and global pain are not separate spheres: They are intimately related. Great potential for personal empowerment can be found in attending to our awareness of global problems and to our understanding of how they connect with each other and with our personal lives. (p. 1)

Appendix

Questionnaire

1. Does the peril that the world is in come up in your clinical work? If so, how?
2. What is coming up in therapy that has to do with
   a. war stories?
   b. environmental destruction?
   c. general worry about the world?
   d. nuclear threat?
   e. global survival awareness?
3. What do you do when this happens?
4. Has a situation ever come up in a therapy hour that has led you to believe that there are issues related to global survival that you have chosen not to pursue? If so, why?

NOTE

1. See DeMuth and Wetzel (Chapters 1 and 2) for further discussion of Conn's and others' work.

BIBLIOGRAPHY

Caldicott, H. (1991, November). *Building a healthy america.* Lecture presented to a general audience at the Hult Center, Eugene, OR.

Conn, S. (1990). *The self-world connection: Implications for mental health and psychotherapy.* Cambridge, MA: Center for Psychological Studies in the Nuclear Age.

Conn, S. (1991). *Protest and thrive: The relationship between global responsibility and personal empowerment.* Cambridge, MA: Center for Psychological Studies in the Nuclear Age.

Conn, S. (1991). *When the earth hurts, who responds?: Psychotherapy in a global, earth-centered context.* Cambridge, MA: Center for Psychological Studies in the Nuclear Age.

O'Connor, T. (1989). Therapy for a dying planet. *Networker, Sept/Oct,* 69–70.

Becker, E. (1987). Addressing the nuclear issue in the psychotherapy hour: a clinical and personal perspective. In K. Porter, (Ed.) *Heal or die: Psychotherapists confront nuclear annihilation.* New York: The Psychohistory Press.

Normal Family Reactions to a Pathological World

In this section, Donna Hilleboe DeMuth, Priscilla Ellis, Sarah Greenberg, Bianca Cody-Murphy, Jonathan Reusser, and Jules Riskin have chosen to study some ways in which normal families handle the challenges of living in a world threatened by self-destructive behavior. Their common aim is to look at potential emotional responses experienced within these families as well as the resources that may exist within family systems for support and empowerment.

First, Donna presents a review of the relevant literature in Chapter 4, *Psychosocial Studies of Reactions to the Threat of Nuclear War*. In this chapter, she takes a look at how the studies conducted both by systemic thinkers and by those from other psychological disciplines inform us about the ways in which children, adults, and families deal with global survival issues.

Next, Priscilla, Sarah, Bianca, and Jon explore the effects on families of living in highly toxic environments. In Chapter 5, *Environmentally Contaminated Families: Therapeutic Considerations*, they offer some suggestions for understanding and healing the emotional wounds of these families. In addition, they focus on examining successful family mechanisms for coping with the stress.

In Chapter 6, *Family Interaction, Nuclear War, Earthquakes, and the Environment: An Empirical Pilot Research Study and Advocacy Implications*, Jules compares responses of volunteer families to the possibilities of nuclear war with their responses to an actual disaster, the earthquake in San Francisco in 1989. Using a standardized conjoint interview protocol, he suggests that already existing family structures may be more influential in determining the family's responses than the nature of the threat itself.

Donna then reports on a study of the effects of a structured, facilitated discussion of nuclear war on both volunteer families and the volunteer research team that conducted the studies. In Chapter 7, *The Family Interviewing Project: A Group of Clinicians Looks at Family Reactions to the Threat of Nuclear War,* Donna goes after nuclear war. She outlines ways in which the process of the team affected the research and, in turn, the ways in which conducting the study affected the team.

Chapter 4

Psychosocial Studies of Reactions to the Threat of Nuclear War

Donna Hilleboe DeMuth

No understanding of family therapists and their work in the global arena is complete without a brief review of the literature on the individual and family psychology of global issues.[1] Using the conceptualizations of Boyer (1985) as a base, I will also look at the relationship between the development of these studies and the historical and social context. Finally, I will address the question of the appropriateness of conducting studies of family reactions to global threats, given that these investigations have begun so recently.

STUDIES IN NUCLEAR PSYCHOLOGY[2]

Studies of Children

It is interesting that, given the small amount of available literature, so many researchers have investigated the potential impact of the nuclear threat on children and adolescents. There may have been an unspoken assumption that children would be more vulnerable to psychological trauma than adults. Perhaps investigators were motivated to alleviate what they viewed as the distress of children in the nuclear age. It is certainly possible that many adults find it easier to focus on children's pain rather than on their own (DeMuth, 1990a).

The earliest research on children was concerned with possible psychopathology. Escalona (1962) reported, in a study of 311 students, aged 10 to 17 years old, that 70% spontaneously revealed concern about future nuclear war. Schwebel (1965) reported, in a study conducted in 1962, that of 300 adolescents, 42% expected nuclear war to occur in their lifetime.

Later, Beardslee and Mack (1982), in a study of 1,100 adolescents, reported that this population experienced substantial nuclear anxiety and fears for the future. Beardslee and Mack postulated, as did Lifton (1987), that these fears could be associated with the current increases in substance abuse and with feelings of alienation experienced by many young people.

Other surveys of teenagers used more representative samples and embedded queries about nuclear war into more general questionnaires (Goldberg et al. 1985; Goldenring & Doctor, 1986; Lewis, Goldberg, & Parker, 1990). In these studies, correlations between nuclear concerns in young people and psychopathology were not found. Rather, Goldberg et al. found that teenagers who reported that they thought and worried about nuclear war more often reported greater feelings of efficacy about finding solutions to world tensions. Goldenring and Doctor also found that adolescents reporting high degree of nuclear worry were more apt to demonstrate higher social and academic functioning.

Both Goldberg et al. and Eisenbud, VanHoorn, and Berger Gould (1985) reported that children, in general, express less concern for the nuclear future as they become older. This finding was also noted by R. Snow (personal communication, 1982) in her work with schoolchildren in Massachusetts. Still, surveys from several countries reveal that the threat of nuclear war ranks among the first three worries reported by teenagers who responded to open-ended questions about their fears (Diamond & Bachman, 1986; Goldenring & Doctor, 1986; Oliver, 1990; Solantaus & Rimpela, 1986). Teenagers report that they almost never talk to adults about their thoughts and feelings about nuclear issues (Goldenring & Doctor, 1986; Oliver, 1990). The family is least often cited as their source of information about world events (Lewis, Goldberg, & Parker, 1990). One New Zealand study revealed that adolescents whose parents are social activists report a greater sense of efficacy about solving world problems than those who view their parents as unconcerned (Oliver, 1990). It must be noted, however, that Coles (1985), DeAngelis (1991) and DeMuth (Chapter 7) have raised concern that questionnaires may not adequately reflect the nuclear concerns of children.

Studies of Adults

The pioneering work of Alexander (1946); Frank (1964); Fromm (1974); Grosser, Wechsler, and Greenblatt (1964); Lifton (1967); and May (1950) set the tone for concepts derived from psychoanalytic practice (denial, repression, displacement, psychic numbing) to describe the ways in which adults deal with the stresses of living with the possibilities of nuclear destruction. These concepts characterized much of the subsequent study of adult reactions to the nuclear threat. Lifton assumed that even "survivors" who were distant from the bombings would be affected in ways similar to those immediately present.

Following Lifton's studies, there were no significant investigations for 15 years. Subsequently, Frank (1986), Lifton (1979, 1986), Macy (1981, 1983, 1991), Schell (1982), and Schwebel (1986) have postulated that it takes major psychological efforts for individuals *not* to keep global dangers in awareness. They speak of possible negative effects of the terror and despair that may underlie much public apathy. These notions, however, have not as yet been supported by research data.

French and VanHoorn (1986) studied individual reactions to viewing the television film *The Day After,* a fictional account of nuclear bombing of an American city. They found that exposure to the film created a strong immediate impact, which, however, did not lead to lasting changes in political attitudes.

Some interesting connections with the previously cited studies of adolescents have emerged. Adults who were more apt to take action on behalf of social causes also reported more consciousness of and worry about nuclear threats (Locatelli and Holt, 1986). Kanovsky (1989) also found that adults who were most concerned about nuclear war felt most positively about finding solutions.

It might be postulated then that expressed nuclear anxiety can be an indicator of personal strength in adults. The findings of Zweigenhaft (1985) suggest that adults' ability to tolerate dealing with nuclear issues correlated positively with the degree of general anxiety that they could bear. Fiske (1987), however, reports a positive correlation between general psychological vulnerability and the degree of expressed concern about nuclear war. The studies are just beginning.

Illumination of the issue of adult anxiety about nuclear war comes from Kanofsky (1989). He found that although nuclear war was not immediately salient for many of his respondents, when they did think about the subject, their degree of concern was apt to be substantial. In other words, frequency of reported concern was not necessarily equated with degree of concern, and expression of concern could be evoked relatively easily with stimulation from outside. Kanofsky's work, as yet unpublished, does offer a thorough analysis of the different factors possible within each adult's response to global threats. Using a theoretical model derived from Lazarus and Folkman (1984), he separates responses of his subjects to nuclear war into categories of appraisal strategies and coping strategies (emotional and problem solving). Thus, he reframes and clarifies the concept of *psychic numbing.*

Kanofsky addresses concerns also raised by Zur (1990). Both point out that many previous studies of both children and adults are not sufficiently rigorous in their design, their sampling, and their methodology.

Studies of Families

Studies of family interactions about the nuclear issue are sparse and did not begin until the 1980s (DeMuth, 1990a; Reusser and Murphy, 1990). Significantly, few family therapists have done empirical studies.

In the amazing synchronicity of the events of 1982, Greenwald and Zeitlin (1987) were interviewing families about nuclear war. Also, other projects had begun. Riskin, using a structured conjoint interview format, was observing families discussing nuclear war in front of a one-way mirror (Riskin, Chapter 6). Cody-Murphy, Ellis, and Greenburg (1987) in Boston were studying families of the survivors of the first atomic tests in Los Alamos. DeMuth (1990a) started a research collective in Maine, investigating the subsequent impact of family discussions about nuclear war on its members. Berger Gould in California was looking at adolescents discussing the topic with their families (Berger Gould, Moon, & VanHoorn, 1986).

Unwittingly, as these studies began, some investigations were following the pathology model of the earlier analytic thinkers. Berger Gould, Moon, and Van-Hoorn (1986); DeMuth (1985); and Zeitlin (1984) noted that many parents seemed ineffective in responding to their childrens' worries about nuclear war. We assumed that silence between generations might carry some of the same negative consequences as did the existence of other "family secrets," such as alcoholism and child or spouse abuse. Some family therapists also speculated that serious family pathology could result from the stresses of living under the nuclear Sword of Damocles (Bloch, 1984; Wetzel & Winawer, 1986).

Greenwald and Zeitlin published their findings in 1987. As Riskin and De-Muth continued their investigations, however, they noticed very few signs of overt psychopathology in the families they interviewed about reactions to the threat of nuclear war. Most of these families had not previously discussed the issue (see Chapters 6 and 7). The work of Cody-Murphy, Ellis, and Greenburg (1987) also suggested that the silence of families of atomic veterans, directly exposed to nuclear risks, may be a normal way of coping with such a severe stressor.

The most significant facts about the family studies are that there are few of them, that they are all qualitative, and that the samples are small. To date, no one has attempted to undertake a large-scale investigation of how families react to the situation of living with global dangers.

Disease Versus Health Models

Because of their passionate concern for survivors of the bomb as well as for their own future survival, it was probably inevitable that the earliest students of nuclear psychology were keenly aware of potential pathology in people's responses. The studies had an advocacy function and served as warning to professionals and lay people who were still reacting to the relatively recent terror of the bomb.

The degree to which the notion of psychological danger permeated the work of later investigators can be seen in their language. For example, an issue of *Psychology Today* (1984, 18, [4]) citing this work showed on its cover a vivid picture of an obviously frightened child, backed by a picture of the nuclear mushroom. The issue was entitled "Nuclear Fear: Growing Up Scared of Not Growing Up." On the title page of the same issue, an article by Yudkin (1984) was introduced with the statement "Nuclear war: Blowing up is making growing up hard to do" (p. 18). Videos of children from that era also featured their terror (Chivian & Snow, 1982; Verdun-Roe, Thierman, & Thierman, 1982). *Family Therapy Networker*

(1984, 8, 2) entitled its feature issue "The Nuclear Shadow." Articles by Bloch (1984) and Zeitlin (1984) were headed "Nuclear Secrets."

The exploration of nuclear concern in individuals and families has been enriched by incorporating some principles of learning theory, particularly the concepts of mastery outlined by Bandura (1977). Studies on resilience in children have also illuminated the issue of how individuals and families can carry on with little apparent distress in the face of such enormous dangers (Anthony & Cohler, 1987; Dugan & Coles, 1990; Rutter, 1988). It appears now that reactions to the stress of living under global threats may be understood more readily as normal coping devices than as defenses against preconscious terrors. Kanovsky (1989), Seligman (1990), and Staub (1990) all point out that a positive response to such stressful societal pressures depends on many factors, including the salience and meaning of the stress and the coping models to which the individual has been previously exposed.

Figley and McCubbin (1983) remind us that a family's reaction to a stressor is strongly influenced by its normal ethos: its appraisal both of the nature of the stressor itself and of its own resources. Using this model, effective students of family reactions to global danger will need to correlate their understanding of these family reactions to varying family structures and value systems. Finally, the humanistic model reminds us that successful psychological coping with planetary dangers may depend on a serious redefinition of the nature of the self in society, from an individualistic to a planetary consciousness (Conn, 1990; Mack, 1990; Macy, 1983, 1991).

Studies of the psychology of global survival reflecting humanistic and learning theory models were conducted at a time when international tensions seemed less threatening and when the reign of psychoanalysis was crumbling. There were also methodological differences in the studies. In the minds of these later researchers, therefore, it became easier to view silence within the family on matters of global concern as a learned response than as an entrenched psychological defense.

Coles (1990) makes an even stronger statement. He argues that the psychological concept of denial is an unacceptable substitute for the notion of the absence of *moral courage,* a quality which he believes to be the most significant coping mechanism available to both adults and children.

PSYCHOLOGICAL STUDIES OF GLOBAL THREAT AND SOCIAL HISTORY

There is another level on which psychological response to planetary survival can be understood. Boyer (1984, 1985) points out that the American public's response to nuclear proliferation has been correlated with the nature of political events and their manipulation by politicians and the media. In social history, he sees cycles of fear, reaction, activism, discouragement, and apathy, restimulated when global tensions break loose. In a similar way, Conn (1990), DeMuth (1990a) and Macy (1983) have maintained that individual response to planetary threats moves in repetitive cycles.

Thus, we might look at the development of a literature of global psychology between 1945 and 1980 in relationship to some significant historical events as well as to the societal reactions that Boyer (1985) has described.[3] (See Table 4-1.) In the

TABLE 4-1   A Time Line of Correlations Between Historical Events and the Development of a Psychology of Nuclear Awareness

Date	Historical Events	Social Cultural Context	Psychological Investigations
1945	Atomic explosions Hiroshima/ Nagasaki	Overwhelming national approval and relief from tensions of W.W. II	
1946	Publication of *Hiroshima* (John Hersey)	Realization/terror calls on moral imperatives and antinuclear activism	Am. Psychological Assoc. convenes conference on implications of nuclear age Franz Alexander
1947–54		Dawning of "atomic age" glamorizing scientific future, antinuclear activism recedes, media soothes public anxieties. Declining hopes for international control. Beginning fatalism about nuclear war recurring	GAP report does not mention nuclear war in list of social issues of concern to psychiatry Rollo May
1954–61	U.S./Soviet tests of thermonuclear bombs	Civil defense reliance increases after fallout scare. Only 4% of public concerned about nuclear war. Slowly, activism re-emerges. SANE and PSSR begin	
1962	Cuban missile crisis	Nuclear war fears are activated and then recede quickly	American Psychiatric Assoc. and Am. Acad. of Science Select Committee on Research on Threat of Impending Disaster Milton Schwebel Sybil Escalona

TABLE 4-1 *(continued)*

Date	Historical Events	Social Cultural Context	Psychological Investigations
1963–64	U.S./U.S.S.R. test ban treaty. J.F. Kennedy assassination	Tests go underground. "Deterrence" theory emerges. Nuclear prolification escalates again. Public apathy regarding nuclear war. Political focus on poverty war	Jerome Frank
1965–72	Vietnam war begins. Signing of ABM treaty. SALT I	Focus on immediate war efforts. Interest in nuclear issues disappears almost totally. Civil rights and anti-Vietnam issues occupy activists	R.J. Lifton Carl Rogers Erich Fromm
1973–78	Vietnam war ends	Beginning revival of awareness and activism against nuclear war	Isador Charny R.J. Lifton Karl Lorenz
1979	Three Mile Island nuclear accident. SALT II fails	Loss of illusions about "peaceful atom" and international controls of nuclear weapons	R.J. Lifton
1980	Ronald Reagan elected; strengthens military buildup against USSR	Rapidly increasing antinuclear activism	Beginning of the empirical works on nuclear psychology

Based on the work of Boyer (1985).

years between 1980 and 1990, which led ultimately to the breakup of the Soviet Union and the de-escalating of the cold war, work on the psychology of global survival was prolific.

The task of using psychological skills to understand the impact of global issues was taken up by professional organizations (American Family Therapists Academy [AFTA], American Orthopsychiatric Association,[4] American Psychiatric Association, American Psychological Association) and their publications. In 1983, leaders in the field of nuclear psychology, Richard Chasin and John Mack, formed the Center for Psychological Studies in the Nuclear Age[5] in Cambridge, Massachusetts. A Select Committee on Congress and Youth (1984) convened a symposium of experts addressing children's fears of war. International Physicians for Prevention of Nuclear War (later to receive the Nobel Peace Prize) convened an international conference on children and nuclear issues in 1985 and began to create links between psychotherapists from the Eastern and Western blocs. Research studies on children and adults were being published frequently, particularly in 1986 and 1987.

Yet as we have seen, relatively few family therapists have taken a major part in this intellectual excitement. Few conferences of family therapists include presentations relating to global survival.[6] The largest organization of marriage and family therapists (American Association of Marriage and Family Therapists [AAMFT]) has *not* appointed a task force on nuclear or environmental issues. The *Journal of the American Association of Marriage and Family Therapists* as well as *Family Process* have published no papers on the relationship of clinical practice to planetary dangers (DeMuth, 1990a).

In 1990, the newsletter of the *American Association of Marriage and Family Therapists* reported on a survey of the major social concerns of its members; global survival was not mentioned (Nichols, 1990). Even Minuchin (1991), often an eloquent spokesperson for issues of social context, remained silent. In a reminder to therapists that families' problems cannot be fully understood except as they are embedded in the culture, he did not include the possibilities of nuclear or environmental annihilation in his definition of contemporary culture.

In the waning days of the cold war, and even in the face of the 1991 military flareups in the Middle East, family therapists' interest in global issues may have diminished even further. At the same time, however, new energy for the support of using a global context has begun to emerge from the theoretical work of the constructionists and others. (See Chapter 1; Berger Gould, 1988; and DeMuth, 1990b.)

RELEVANCE OF FAMILY STUDIES IN GLOBAL PSYCHOLOGY

We have seen that family therapists have not as yet developed a major body of work in the psychology of global survival. The literature from sociology and social psychology, however, validates the importance of both family support in dealing with major external stress and family influence on the development of social consciousness in children. Both of these areas are well documented and extremely complex, and I shall touch on them only briefly.

Role of Family Support in Dealing with Stress

Many social psychologists have demonstrated that the role of family and community is crucial in the healing of the effects of stress resulting from either chronic or traumatic events (Cohen & Wills, 1985; Figley, 1986; Flannery, 1990; Kobassa and Pucetti, 1982; Perlman & Rook, 1987). Figley sums it up:

> There is little doubt that the family, plus the social support system in general, is the single most important resource in emotional recovery from disaster . . . before, during, and after other stressful times. (p. 40)

The studies of Erikson (1976) and Garula (1989) have shown the value of community support following man-made disasters. Similar findings have been reported in studies of individuals recovering from war trauma (Milgram, 1986) and of families reacting to stresses from the release of environmental contaminants (Ellis, Greenberg, Murphy, and Reusser, 1992; Chapter 5).

Even as early as 1942, Anna Freud described the psychological recovery of child survivors of the Holocaust in Nazi Germany as largely dependent on their banding together to form an artificially constructed family unit (cited in Garmezy, 1988). The maintenance of life itself may be enhanced by the availability of family support. Lynch (1977) reports that people without available family resources are much more vulnerable to physical illnesses, such as heart disease.

The family then is well documented to be a potential resource to aid in dealing with stress. We need to look further to understand why, in studies of reactions to more ambiguous global tensions, the family has not been a focus. We also need to understand why, in the few studies that do exist, it is found that most children do not discuss their concerns about the fate of the planet within their families.

Role of Family in Developing Social Responsibility

The family has a mandate from society to perpetuate the species. That mandate should therefore include the family's responsibility to raise children who will take some responsibility for maintaining future life on this planet. Coles (1986, 1990), Dunn (1987), Haan (1989), Gilligan and Wiggins (1988), and Kitwood (1990) have documented that the moral capacity of very young children is stronger than has previously been reported and that concern for others is a natural aspect of their development. Anthony and Cohler (1987), Rutter (1988), and other students of resilience in children point out that learning to take responsibility for others can be a protective factor in children subjected to stress. Staub (1975, 1990) sees the role of the family as primary in rearing what he describes as a "pro-social" child, stressing in particular its role in nurturance and in modeling socially responsible behavior.

Both Staub and Kitwood (1990) found that moral values in children are reinforced most effectively if the child has first taken some concrete altruistic action. Therefore, it would seem to be crucial that parents and teachers both model and support socially responsible behaviors in children while they are still young.

Resilience studies also indicate that the child who learns to deal with stressful events in supportive circumstances, such as within a well-nurturing family, is likely to develop not only greater resilience to additional stressors, but also a sense of mastery (Bandura, 1977), which he or she can use to deal constructively with stressors in adulthood (Anthony & Cohler, 1987; Dugan & Coles, 1990; Rutter, 1988). Kegan's (1982) developmental constructs support the role of a *holding environment*, such as the family, in making transitions from self-involvement to social involvement.

Family is the natural place for social responsibility to be cultivated. We have seen, however, that coping mechanisms that allow people to keep emotionally threatening issues in the background can make it difficult for them, as parents, to carry out their function effectively in relation to their family's responsibility to work towards preventing global annihilation (DeMuth, 1990a; Greenwald & Zeitlin, 1987).

SUMMARY

A brief review of the literature on psychological coping of individuals and families in response to threats to planetary destruction through nuclear war reveals the following:

1. Most commentators on the psychological impact of nuclear events have written from direct personal experience and from a theoretical perspective. Empirical studies reveal varying degrees of anxiety and concern about nuclear war in children and adults. These studies have been criticized for their methodological flaws.
2. Correlation between nuclear anxieties and psychopathology has not been investigated substantially. There is some indication that more well functioning teenagers and adults report more concern about the threat of nuclear war.
3. Children and teenagers report that they do not discuss worries about the future of the planet with adults.
4. Despite evidence of the potentially positive role of the family in supporting its members during stressful times and of its strong influence in helping children develop a sense of concern for others, there have been only a few small, qualitative studies of how families cope with living under the nuclear threat.
5. The degree of interest in the psychology of nuclear concerns seems to have a direct relationship to political/social events that tend to bring those events into public awareness.

NOTES

1. I am indebted to the work of Eisenbud, VanHoorn, & Gould (1985); Schwebel (1986); Kanofsky (1989); and Zur (1990) for both documentation and critique of research findings.
2. Much of the early research in the psychological effects of the nuclear dilemma was criticized for its methodological flaws (Kanofsky, 1989; Zur, 1990) and by lack of sufficient depth (Coles, 1985, 1986; deAngelis, 1991). In addition, most investigators have not differentiated sufficiently between the many possible components of affective responses to nuclear threat, according to Kanofsky and Zur.
3. It is interesting to note that at the same time as psychological investigations of nuclear issues were beginning, other large movements were having an impact on psychology,

i.e., the survivors movements, self-help and 12-step movements, feminism, and studies of resiliency in children.
4. It should be mentioned that the American Orthopsychiatric Association, although not specifically a family therapy organization, has taken a systems approach to global survival concerns and addressed them consistently in its conference program and its publications.
5. Now renamed "The Center for Psychological and Social Change."
6. The Ackerman Institute and AFTA have been notable exceptions.

BIBLIOGRAPHY

Alexander, F. (1946). Mental hygiene in the atomic age. *Mental Hygiene, 30*, 529–534.

Anthony, E. J., & Cohler, B. J. (Eds.) (1987). *The invulnerable child.* New York: Guilford.

Bandura, A. (1977). Self-efficacy: Toward a unifying theory of behavior change. *Psychological Review, 84*, 191–215.

Beardslee, W., & Mack, J. (1982). The impact of nuclear developments on children and adolescents. In *Psychological aspects of nuclear developments* (Task Force Report 20). Washington, DC: American Psychiatric Association.

Berger Gould, B. (1988). Bearing witness: Integrating political and professional work. *Newsletter of the American Family Therapy Association, #32*, 3–5.

Berger Gould, B., Moon, S., & VanHoorn, J. (Eds.) (1986). *Growing up scared: The psychological effect of the nuclear threat on children.* Berkeley: Open Books.

Bloch, D. (1984). Nuclear secrets: What do we tell the children? *The Family Therapy Networker, 8*, 30.

Boyer, P. (1984). From activism to apathy: America and the nuclear issue, 1963–198. *Bulletin of the Atomic Scientists 40* (7), 14–23.

Boyer, P. S. (1985). *By the bomb's early light; American thought and culture at the dawn of the atomic age.* New York: Pantheon.

Chivian, E., & Snow, R. (1982). *There's a nuclear war going on inside me: What children are saying about nuclear war.* [Videotape of classroom discussions] Boston, MA: International Physicians for Prevention of Nuclear War.

Cody-Murphy, B., Ellis, P., & Greenburg, S. (1987, March). *The atomic veterans' survivor project.* Paper presented at the meeting of the American Orthopsychiatric Association, Washington, DC.

Cohen, S., & Wills, T. A. (1985). Stress, social support, and the buffering process. *Psychological Bulletin, 98*, 310–357.

Coles, R. (1985, December 8). Children and the bomb. *New York Times Magazine.*

Coles, R. (1986). *The moral life of children.* Boston: Atlantic Monthly.

Coles, R. (1990, April). *The struggle for a spiritual life.* Lecture sponsored by Jackson Brook Institute and Bangor Theological Seminary, Portland, ME.

Conn, S. A. (1990). *Protest and thrive: The relationship between social responsibility and personal empowerment.* Cambridge, MA: Center for Psychological Studies in the Nuclear Age.

DeAngelis, T. (1991). Impact of war trauma hits children hardest. *The APA Monitor; 22*(8), 8–9.

DeMuth, D. H. (1985, June). *The state of the work on families and the nuclear threat.* Paper presented at the Interest Group on Nuclear Issues at the Annual Meeting of the American Family Therapy Association, Chicago.

DeMuth, D. H. (1990a). Some implications of the threat of nuclear war for families and family therapists. In M. Mirkin (Ed.), *The social and political contexts of family therapy.* Boston: Allyn & Bacon.

DeMuth, D. H. (1990b). The social consciousness of family therapy: A time of change. *Newsletter of the American Family Therapy Association, June,* 10–13.

Diamond, G., & Bachman, J. (1986). High school seniors and the nuclear threat, 1975–1984: Political and mental health implications of concern and despair. *International Journal of Mental Health, 15,* 210–241.

Dugan, T. F., & Coles, R. (Eds.), (1990). *The child in our times: Studies in the development of resiliency.* New York: Brunner/Mazel.

Dunn, J. (1987). The beginnings of moral understanding: Development in the second year. In J. Kajan & S. Lamb (Eds.), *The emergency of morality in young children.* Chicago: University of Chicago Press.

Eisenbud, M. M., VanHoorn, J. L., & Berger Gould, B. (1985). Children, adolescents and the threat of nuclear war: An international perspective. *Advances in International Maternal and Child Health, 6.*

Ellis, P., Greenberg, S., Murphy, B. C., & Reusser, J. (1992). Environmentally contaminated families: Therapeutic considerations. *American Journal Orthopsychiatry, 62*(1), 44–54.

Erikson, K. T. (1976). *Everything in its path.* New York: Simon & Schuster.

Escalona, S. (1962). *Children and the threat of nuclear war.* New York: Child Study Association of America.

Family Therapy Networker (1984), *8,* 2.

Figley, C. R. (1986). The role of the family and social support system. In C. R. Figley (Ed.). *Trauma and its wake. Vol II: Traumatic stress theory, research and intervention.* New York: Brunner/Mazel.

Figley, C. R., & McCubbin, H. I. (Eds.), 1983. *Stress and the family. Vol II: Coping with catastrophe.* New York: Brunner/Mazel.

Fiske, S. T. (1987). People's reactions to nuclear war: Implications for psychologists. *American Psychologist, 42,* 207–217.

Flannery, R. B. (1990). Social support and psychological trauma: A methodological review. *Journal of Traumatic Stress, 3*(4), 593–609.

Frank, J. D. (1964). *Sanity and survival.* New York: Random House.

Frank, J. D. (1986). Psychological responses to the threat of nuclear annihilation. *International Journal of Mental Health, 15,* 65–71.

French, P. L., & VanHoorn, J. (1986). Half a nation saw nuclear war and nobody blinked. A reassessment of the impact of *The Day After* in terms of a theoretical chain of causality. In M. Schwebel (Ed.), *Mental health implications of life in the nuclear age.* Armonk, NY: M.E. Sharpe.

Freud, S. (1930). *Civilization and its discontents* (Jean Riviere, Trans.). New York: J. Cape & H. Smith.

Fromm, E. (1974). *The anatomy of human destructiveness.* London: Jonathan Cape.

Garmezy, N. (1988). The stressors of childhood. In N. Garmezy & M. Rutter (Eds.), *Stress, coping and development in children.* Baltimore: Johns Hopkins University Press.

Garula, C. (1989, April). *Psychological effects of man-made disasters.* Paper presented at the American Orthopsychiatric Association, New York.

Gilligan, C., & Wiggins, G. (1988). *The origins of morality in early childhood relationships.* In C. Gilligan, J. V. Ward, & J. M. Taylor (Eds.), *Mapping the moral domain.* Cambridge, MA: Harvard University Press.

Goldberg, S., LaCombe, S., Levinson, D., Parker, K. R., Ross, C., & Sommers, F. (1985). Thinking about the threat of nuclear war: Relevance to mental health. *American Journal of Orthopsychiatry, 55,* 503–512.

Goldenring, J. M., & Doctor, R. (1986). Teenage worry about nuclear war: North American and European questionnaire studies. *International Journal of Mental Health, 15,* 72–92.

Greenwald, D. S., & Zeitlin, S. J. (1987). *No reason to talk about it: Families confront the nuclear taboo.* New York: WW Norton.

Grosser, G. H., Wechsler, H., & Greenblatt, M. (Eds.) (1964). *The threat of impending disaster: Contributions to the psychology of stress.* Cambridge, MA: M.I.T. Press.

Haan, N. (1989). Coping with moral conflict as resiliency. In T. F. Dugan & R. Coles (Eds.), *The child in our times: Studies in the development of resiliency.* New York: Brunner/Mazel.

Hersey, J. (1946). *Hiroshima.* New York: Bantam Books.

Kanofsky, S. (1989). *The possibility of nuclear war: Appraisal, coping and emotional response.* Unpublished doctoral dissertation, California School of Professional Psychology, Berkeley/Alameda.

Kegan, R. (1982). *The evolving self.* Cambridge: Harvard University Press.

Kitwood, J. M. (1990). *Concern for others: A new psychology of conscience and morality.* New York: Routledge, Chapman & Hall.

Kobassa, S. C., & Pucetti, M. C. (1983). Personality and social resources in stress resistance. *Journal of Personal and Social Psychology, 42,* 168–177.

Lazarus, R. S., & Folkman, S. (1984). *Stress, appraisal and coping.* New York: Springer.

Lewis, C., Goldberg, S., & Parker, K. R. (1989). Nuclear worries of Canadian youth: Replication and extension. *American Journal of Orthopsychiatry, 59*(4), 520–527.

Lifton, R. J. (1967). *Death in life: Survivors of Hiroshima.* New York: Simon & Schuster.

Lifton, R. J. (1979). *The broken connection.* New York: Simon & Schuster.

Lifton, R. J. (1986). *The Nazi doctors.* New York: Basic Books.

Lifton, R. J. (1987). *The future of immortality: And other essays for a nuclear age.* New York: Basic Books.

Locatelli, M. G., & Holt, R. R. (1986). Antinuclear activism, psychic numbing, and mental health. *International Journal of Mental Health, 15,* 143–161.

Lynch, J. J. (1977). *The broken heart: The medical consequences of loneliness.* New York: Basic Books.

Mack, J. (1990). *Changing models of psychotherapy, from psychological conflict to human empowerment.* Cambridge, MA: Center for Psychological Studies in the Nuclear Age.

Macy, J. (1981). Despair work. *Evolutionary Blues—An Interhelp Ouarterly, 1.*

Macy, J. (1983). *Despair and personal power in the nuclear age.* Philadelphia: New Society.

Macy, J. (1991). *World as lover, world as self.* Berkeley: Parallax Press.

May, R. (1950). *The meaning of anxiety.* New York: Ronald Press.

Milgram, N. (Ed.) (1986). *Stress and coping in time of war: Generalizations from the Israeli experience.* New York: Brunner/Mazel.

Minuchin, S. (1991). The seductions of constructionism. *Family Therapy Networker, 15,* 47–50.

Nichols, W. C. (1990). Therapists identify major issues affecting North American families in 1980's. *Family Therapy News, 21,* 1.

Oliver, P. (1990). Nuclear freedom and student's sense of efficacy about prevention of nuclear war. *American Journal of Orthopsychiatry, 60*(4), 611–621.

Perlman, D., & Rook, K. S. (1987). Social support, social deficit and the family: Toward the enhancement of well-being. In S. Oskamp (Ed.), *Family processes and problems: Social psychological aspects.* Newbury Park, CA: Sage.

Psychology Today (1984), *18*(4).

Reusser, J. W., & Murphy, B. C. (1990). Family therapy in the nuclear age: From clinical to global. In M. P. Mirkin (Ed.), *Political and social contexts of family therapy.* Boston: Allyn & Bacon.

Rutter, M. (1988). Stress, coping and development; Some issues and some questions. In N. Garmeczy & M. Rutter (Eds.), *Stress, coping, and development in children.* New York: McGraw-Hill.

Schell, J. (1982). *The fate of the earth.* New York: Avon.

Schwebel, M. (1965). Nuclear cold war: Student opinions and professional responsibility. *Behavior Science and Human Survival.* Palo Alto, CA: Science and Behavior Books.

Schwebel, M. (Ed.) (1986). Mental health implications of life in the nuclear age. *International Journal of Mental Health, 15.*

Schwebel, M. (1986). The study of stress and coping in the nuclear age: A new specialty. *International Journal of Mental Health, 15,* 5–15.

Select Committee on Children, Youth and Families (1984). *Children's fears of war.* [Hearing] Washington, DC: U.S. Government Printing Office.

Seligman, M. E. (1990). *Learned optimism.* New York: Alfred A. Knopf.

Solantaus, T., & Rimpala, M. (1986). Mental health and the threat of nuclear war—a suitable case for treatment? *International Journal of Mental Health, 15,* 261–275.

Staub, E. (1975). To rear a pro-social child: Reasoning, learning by doing, and learning by teaching others. In D. J. DePalma and J. M. Foley (Eds.) *Moral Development: Current theory and research.* New York: John Wiley.

Staub, E. (1990). *The roots of evil: The origins of genocide and other group violence.* Cambridge, MA: Cambridge University Press.

Verdon-Roe, U., Thierman, E., & Thierman, I. (1983). *In the nuclear shadow: What can the children tell us?* [Videotape of childrens' interview responses] Santa Cruz, CA: Educational film and video project.

Wetzel, N. A., & Winawer, H. (1986). The psychological consequences of the nuclear threat from a family systems perspective. *International Journal of Mental Health, 15,* 290–313.

Yudkin, M. (1984). When kids think the unthinkable. *Psychology Today, 18*(4), 18–25.

Zeitlin, S. J. (1984). Nuclear secrets: What do we tell mom and dad? *The Family Therapy Networker, 8*(31), 38–39, 62.

Zur, O. (1990). On nuclear attitudes and psychic numbing: Overview and critique. *Contemporary Social Psychology, 14*(2), 96–110.

Zweigenhaft, R. L. (1985). Race, sex, and nuclear war. *Genetic, Social and General Psychology Monographs, 111*(3), 283–301.

Chapter 5
Environmentally Contaminated Families: Therapeutic Considerations*

Priscilla Ellis
Sarah Greenberg
Bianca Cody Murphy
Jonathan W. Reusser[†]

Environmental contamination has become a global public health problem transcending geographic and generational boundaries. Most environmental contamination is man-made. Although there are instances of naturally occurring contaminants, such as radon gas, environmental pollution is largely a product of the industrial and technological developments of the last 50 years. Individuals, families, and communities throughout the world have been exposed to radioactive and chemical toxins from industrial and agricultural technology, nuclear weapons development and testing, and toxic waste disposal. The proliferation of environmental toxins makes the possibility of damaging exposure a concern for all families. Further, with increasing evidence and awareness of the varieties of environmental contamination, many are struggling with fears about living in a dangerously polluted world. These anticipatory fears increase levels of stress among those who may not yet have been actually contaminated (Brown & Mikkelsen, 1990; Edelstein, 1988; Vyner, 1988).

We became keenly aware of the effects of environmental contamination on families when we interviewed atomic veterans and their families as part of a research project (Murphy, Ellis, & Greenberg, 1990). Atomic veterans constitute the approximately 250,000 members of the U.S. armed forces who were routinely

*This paper originally appeared in *American Journal of Orthopsychiatry, 62*(1), p. 44–54.
†The authors would like to thank Marsha Pravder Mirkin for her valuable help with an early draft of this paper.

exposed to ionizing radiation during the above-ground nuclear testing program between 1945 and 1962 and the occupation and "cleanup" of Hiroshima and Nagasaki. As family therapists, we were interested in learning about the psychological impact of radiation exposure on the veteran and his family. The stories that emerged from our interviews parallel the experiences of others who have suffered from toxic exposure (Brown & Mikkelsen, 1990; Edelstein, 1988; Levine, 1982; Vyner, 1988; Wasserman & Solomon, 1982).

Most survivors[1] of environmental contamination never enter a mental health worker's office. Indeed, many do not define their experiences as psychologically injurious. None of the atomic veterans we met with reported seeking mental health counseling about their exposure. Nor did any resident of the Legler area of Jackson Township, New Jersey, a community where groundwater contamination led to serious health problems and community disruption (Edelstein, 1988). People cope with the impact of environmental contamination in a variety of ways ranging from denial to activism. Some people exposed to environmental contamination, however, may come to the attention of mental health workers through their own initiative, through outreach by professionals following a community disaster, or through referral from medical or other human service agencies. Therefore, in the face of this escalating health problem, mental health professionals need to educate themselves about the psychological impact of environmental contamination and the most effective ways of working with affected individuals, families, and communities.

STRESSES OF ENVIRONMENTAL CONTAMINATION

Stress is part of family life. How a family copes with stress depends on the nature of the stress, the family's and community's perception of the stress, and the family's characteristic patterns of functioning. Environmental contamination is a stress that is unique in terms of (1) its physical characteristics and resultant adaptational dilemmas, (2) the agent or cause of the injury, and (3) the institutional responses to contamination.

Characteristics of Contaminants

There are five primary characteristics of environmental contaminants that are central to an understanding of their psychological impact. The source of the contamination is usually invisible. The consequences are unpredictable and often delayed. The adverse health effects, if they do appear, usually become chronic and incurable. The effects may be transgenerational, owing to damage of the reproductive or genetic systems. Finally, these physical characteristics of environmental contaminants create particular adaptational dilemmas for those exposed.

Invisible. Many environmental contaminants are impossible to detect with the human senses. Some contaminants produce a sign of their toxicity, such as the heat from a radioactive blast or the smoke from poisonous coal fires. Even if the presence of a toxin has been detected or confirmed, however, it is difficult to determine the extent to which the toxin may have been absorbed by the body. There is thus uncertainty about the source and amount of toxicity to which one has been exposed. This uncertainty is one of the hallmarks of *invisible trauma* (Vyner, 1988).

The invisibility of a contaminant can make the environment feel pervasively unsafe, or it can contribute to the denial that many environmental survivors experience at some stage of their coping with contamination. If you can't see, hear, feel, smell, or taste it, maybe it wasn't there at all, or if it was there, maybe it wasn't that bad. When you can detect some aspect of it, however, like the residents of Centralia, Pennsylvania, who breathed in the fumes of underground coal fires, a remedy such as gas masks may either heighten anxiety or provide an illusion of control that later evidence (e.g., physical symptoms) challenges. This was the case for the atomic veterans who wore radiation badges, which were supposed to measure the amount of radiation to which they were exposed. They felt safe with the knowledge that their badges indicated they were not exposed to dangerous levels of radiation. Years later it became clear that the most damaging radiation (beta), absorbed in minute particles through the respiratory system, was not detectable by these external measurements (Saffer & Kelly, 1982; Uhl & Ensign, 1980; Wasserman & Solomon, 1982).

Unpredictable. Not only are most toxins impossible or difficult to detect and measure, but also their physical effects are varied and unpredictable and the cause of subsequent symptoms ambiguous (Vyner, 1988). Ionizing radiation, for example, has been linked to a variety of cancers, respiratory illnesses, and general systemic problems. The exposed person is thus faced with another set of uncertainties: No one can predict what may develop from exposure, nor can particular symptoms be conclusively linked with the exposure. One atomic veteran whom we interviewed had developed skin cancer within a year after his assignment observing bomb tests on board ship near the Bikini Islands. He was told that the cancer was probably due to exposure from the sun, not from the radioactive fallout. There was no way to prove what actually caused his cancer. Medical and scientific ambiguity about the effects of exposure compound the uncertainties about source and dose. This ambiguity, furthermore, fuels and complicates the political and legal controversies that surround the issue of environmental contamination.

Delayed. There is often a long delay between exposure and the appearance of symptoms. This delay can exacerbate feelings of uncertainty among those exposed. They are never certain whether they are really survivors or simply victims waiting for their diseases to appear. The wife of one atomic veteran, for example, told us that she checked her husband's back every morning for the appearance of cancerous lesions years after his exposure to radiation.

It is often the appearance of symptoms, sometimes many years after the exposure, that causes those exposed to begin to define their exposure as problematic. Moreover, the physical and psychological effects of contamination may assume an intermittent salience in the life of a family. Particular events or life stages, such as marriage or the birth of a child, may bring the issue of environmental contamination into prominence. Consideration of parenthood, for example, may raise fears about the transmission of genetic or health problems to children as a result of the parents' or grandparents' previous toxic exposure. Job changes and geographical moves may be linked with the fear or actuality of exposure. It may be such events or life stage issues that bring a family or family member into a medical or mental health office.

Chronic. The physical effects of toxic exposure are long-lasting and often recurrent throughout the life span. Health problems and illnesses associated with radioactive or chemical contamination include cancers, respiratory ailments, skin disorders, dental problems, circulatory problems, and immunological dysfunction (Bertell, 1985; Vyner, 1988). All of these have a chronic or recurring nature and confront families with the challenges of coping with chronic illness. Thus, those affected by toxic exposure, even if symptom-free for a while, must struggle with anxiety and fears about the eventual emergence of a chronic, possibly life-threatening illness. The uncertainties and anxieties themselves can become chronic. For example, residents of Woburn, Massachusetts, where drinking water had become contaminated by chemical toxins, feared that their immune systems had been permanently damaged (Brown & Mikkelsen, 1990).

Transgenerational. The health effects of many environmental contaminants transcend generational boundaries, sometimes appearing in the children of the exposed individuals. Ionizing radiation, for example, attacks the human body at the cellular level and is capable of causing genetic damage that can be passed on from generation to generation (Bertell, 1985). Some chemical toxins cause chromosomal damage, as in the contamination of the land around Love Canal, New York (Levine, 1982), or damage to the immune system, as in the contamination of drinking water in Woburn (Brown & Mikkelsen, 1990). Environmental toxins are more likely to cause greater damage to fetuses and young children than to adults. These characteristics cause those exposed to worry not only about the uncertainties of their own health, but also those of their children and grandchildren.

Adaptational Consequences. The multitude of uncertainties experienced by those exposed to environmental contaminants creates stress different from the stress of coping with a threat that can be perceived. Ambiguity and uncertainty heighten feelings of powerlessness and lack of control, which have been found to be associated with higher levels of stress in other situations (Vyner, 1988). As DeMuth (1990) noted with the nuclear threat, environmental contamination in its ongoing nature and lack of resolution creates a sense of ambiguity that has been seen as among the most debilitating aspects of stress for families. Higher levels of stress have been found in communities affected by toxic contamination than in comparable communities not directly affected (Edelstein, 1988). One investigator postulated that the loss of control caused by environmental stress can lead to depression and other psychopathologies (Gibbs, 1986).

Because there is so much ambiguity about the nature and consequences of toxic exposure, what becomes critical in the adaptation process is the family's *perception* of the threat. Given the lack of empirical data from which to understand the nature and effects of their exposure, people will construct their own interpretation. In the families of several atomic veterans we interviewed, some of the children had been born with, or subsequently developed, health problems, none of which had been linked by medical authorities to the father's radiation exposure. In almost every instance, however, the veteran and his wife believed that the problems were due to the exposure. One couple who had a daughter with a congenital back problem (scoliosis) and another with a hearing problem emphasized the robust health in their respective families of origin as evidence that their daughters' congenital problems were radiogenic rather than hereditary.

Toxic contamination challenges a family's framework for understanding the world, its "lifescape" (Edelstein, 1988). Beliefs about personal control, the value of technology, the safety of home and environment, and the trustworthiness of authorities are called into question and sometimes radically changed by the experiences associated with toxic exposure. In our interviews, the families of atomic veterans, especially the veterans themselves, struggled with the anger and sense of betrayal they felt toward the government and their own deep loyalty and patriotism (Murphy et al., 1990). In some instances, the veterans became disenchanted with the government; in others, their wives or children assumed that stance. Residents of Woburn, when asked why they did not move to another locale, responded that at least they knew where the Woburn water (by this time closely monitored by the Environmental Protection Agency) came from and they felt that there was "no safe place" to relocate (Brown & Mikkelsen, 1990).

Agent of Injury

There is considerable evidence of differences between peoples' responses to natural disasters and to man-made, technological disasters (Baum, Fleming and Singer, 1983). Human-caused disaster or pollution raises issues of human failure and responsibility. Because the contamination cannot be attributed to an act of God or nature, someone is to blame. Usually the cause or source of the contamination is a corporate or governmental entity, a fact that may raise issues of powerlessness and victimization among the families and communities affected by the contamination.

Paradoxically, in environmental contamination, the agent of injury is both human and impersonal. An environmental survivor, in contrast to a victim of a criminal assault, often cannot identify the assailant in a precise or personal way. The responsible agent may seem so impersonal or amorphous that it is difficult to focus and discharge anger toward it. As one Woburn resident put it, "At least if someone shoots you with a gun you know who did it" (Brown & Mikkelsen, 1990).

Others who have been exposed may be able to mobilize their anger toward governmental or corporate perpetrators. When residents of Legler, New Jersey, learned that a municipal landfill was being proposed for a site in their neighborhood, they organized their opposition and presented a petition to the township. The siting decision prevailed, however, and seven years later evidence of significant wellwater pollution was confirmed by the New Jersey Department of Environmental Protection. Anger and frustration among residents mounted and were directed primarily at the township (Edelstein, 1988). Similarly, as residents of Love Canal came to realize that their neighborhood was dangerously contaminated as a result of years of chemical waste dumping by the Hooker Chemical Company, they became increasingly suspicious and angry as they were met with denial and evasion by governmental authorities. Lois Gibbs (1982) helped to mobilize that anger into effective community action that eventually resulted in the relocation and compensation of residents of Love Canal.

Institutional Invalidation

When a family member or members are exposed to an environmental toxin, there is often invalidation of either the exposure itself or its effects by those in positions of power and responsibility. The invalidation can take several forms: outright denial that any contamination has occurred, disavowal of a relationship between the exposure and later health problems, or minimization of those problems. Atomic veterans were told before, during, and after their exposure to ionizing radiation that the radiation posed no danger to them. Residents of Centralia finally achieved their goal of relocation only through the government's acceptance of evidence of elevated stress levels, not medical problems, in the community (Garula, 1989). Evidence of chromosomal damage among Love Canal residents was disputed and eventually rejected by the Environmental Protection Agency (Vyner, 1988).

The stories of Fernald, Ohio; Hanford, Washington; and Rocky Flats, Colorado, to name a few, are remarkably similar. Communities come to realize, then mobilize around, evidence of unusual levels of illness and death, whereas governmental, corporate, and sometimes medical authorities deny, litigate, and occasionally settle—usually without ever validating—the claims of the contaminated. Economic motives; fear of legal liability; protection of reputation and image; and subordination of human and environmental welfare to economic, industrial, scientific, or military ends are the usual causes of institutional invalidation. Edelstein (1988) describes how individuals in contaminated communities are disabled by having to deal with "the complex institutional context made up of the various local, state, and federal agencies having jurisdiction over the contamination incident . . . (who surround) . . . their decisions with the aura of certainty" (pp. 118, 121).

Institutional invalidation compounds the tendency of some families to suppress their contamination experience. Worried and uncertain about the effects of their exposure, invalidated by external institutions, these families often experience feelings of alienation and isolation from the larger community. They may become stigmatized by others either within or beyond their immediate community. Children are teased, and activists are labeled troublemakers or oddballs. Stigmatization is common among contaminated populations (Brown & Mikkelsen, 1990). Residents of Woburn, Massachusetts; Centralia, Pennsylvania; Love Canal, New York; and Legler, New Jersey, all experienced stigmatization (Edelstein, 1988). As in other kinds of stigmatization, fear and anger are primary causes. In the case of environmental contamination, fear and anger about possible loss of jobs, property devaluation, and community notoriety lead to stigmatizing those who have been contaminated or who bring it to people's attention. The ultimate fear, for which stigmatization serves as a psychological defense, is of one's own vulnerability, of being contaminated oneself.

A vicious cycle may be set in motion wherein the physical or emotional symptoms of the survivors are used to invalidate their claims further. Labels such as paranoid, hysterical, or psychosomatic may be used to discredit their attempts to seek validation and compensation. In these ways, victims of environmental contamination can also become victims of contaminating social and political processes. As Vyner (1988) states:

> ... the mental states of people exposed to an invisible environmental contaminant should not be regarded as so many pawns in the political disputes that arise concerning the health effects of an exposure. Such a view is not empirically correct, and it damages the exposed individuals. ... Statements that blame exposees for their somatic illnesses are ... probably an attempt by the person or institution making the statement to claim that they themselves are not responsible for the illness/trauma in question." (pp. 172–173)

THERAPEUTIC CONSIDERATIONS

Disease of Society

Families affected by toxic contamination who show signs of stress and dysfunction should not be considered mentally ill. Environmental contamination is a disease of society, not of individuals and families. The ultimate and most appropriate cure for the disease would be its elimination or, at the least, adequate protection and compensation for the victims.

As family therapists, however, we may be asked to assist individual families or communities as they cope with the effects of environmental contamination. In addition to physical health problems, these effects can include depression in one or more family members, marital stress, despair, hypervigilance, post-traumatic stress syndrome, and even suicide (Brown & Mikkelsen, 1990; Edelsten, 1988; Vyner, 1988). The psychological effects of environmental contamination can be severe and disabling. Pathologizing these families, however, does them a serious injustice and disservice: It perpetuates the cycle of blaming the victim and interferes with the creation of a potentially helpful collaborative relationship. An understanding of the larger contexts in which the families that come to our attention live and function can make us more effective collaborators in their efforts to cope with the effects of contamination.

Environmental contamination upsets the basic assumptions underlying peoples' lives. We can view their efforts to cope with toxic exposure as in part a struggle to make meaning out of their experience, a process that may involve painful alteration of previously held beliefs. Although there may be commonalities in families' responses to environmental contamination, each family's response will be mediated by its ethnic, religious, and socioeconomic background and will interact with its characteristic coping styles and developmental life stage.

We need to learn more about the different coping patterns of those affected by environmental contamination. What enables some families to pull together and mobilize in active and creative ways in the face of toxic exposure, whereas some families are split apart or develop serious emotional symptoms in one or more members? More research is needed to answer these questions, some of which have begun to be addressed by family theoreticians in the context of stress and trauma in general (Figley, 1989; Olson, Russell, and Sprenkle, 1989).

Validation

Whatever the particular meanings a family and its members assign to the contamination experience, they have almost all experienced some kind of invalidation. Therefore, if the family believes that toxic exposure has occurred, the clinician should directly inquire about it. He or she must identify the contamination as an important occurrence in the life of the family to counteract the family's experience of invalidation. This affirmation signals to the family a willingness to hear their story and serves to invite more silent family members to talk.

Open Communication

In some families, the fact of toxic exposure may not be acknowledged openly and may even be kept a secret. Avoidance or secrecy may be due to a sense of shame and guilt about the exposure or a need to protect oneself and others from disturbing feelings associated with the exposure.

Victims of many kinds of trauma often blame themselves for both the injury itself and the physical and psychological consequences of the injury. Survivors of environmental trauma similarly may experience a sense of shame and embarrassment about their situation and symptoms. Parents particularly may feel ashamed and guilty about causing injury to, or not protecting, their children. As one atomic veteran we interviewed said, "I worry that her (daughter's) health problems are because of something I did." The family may not want others, friends or neighbors, to know of the exposure. Sometimes family members may even try to hide the exposure from each other. In our study, we found that some of the veterans did not tell their wives of their radiation exposure until years later.

In some instances, the secret is real. In others, it is a pseudo-secret. For example, in one family we interviewed, the parents thought that their children were unaware of the father's exposure but discovered in the family meeting that the daughter had known of it for years. Thus, the family therapist must be familiar with the impact of secrets on family functioning. He or she must recognize that family secrets "often serve complex family needs and maintain or (less often) disrupt established family patterns" (Roth & Murphy, 1986).

When the information about exposure is known, family members may still find it difficult to share their worries with each other. The families of the atomic veterans with whom we met had a tendency to protect themselves and one another from information or disturbing feelings about the radiation exposure. Parents protected children, and children protected parents by not talking about the exposure or by minimizing their concerns (Murphy et al., 1990). Studies of families of holocaust survivors have found a similar pattern of mutual protectiveness between parents and children: "The parents had to shield their children by not speaking about the horrors of the past while the children protect their parents by not asking questions, so as not to cause any more pain and suffering" (Obermeyer, 1988, p. 8). Similarly, families confronting the possibility of nuclear war have been observed to avoid the issue as a taboo topic (Greenwald & Zeitlin, 1987). Evidence from various studies of families coping with severe stress indicates that suppression, avoidance, and minimization are common if not normative coping devices (DeMuth, 1990).

Although there is disagreement in the family therapy and social psychology literature about the value of open communication for optimal family functioning, Edelstein's study of Legler residents suggests that families who were able to achieve a level of sharing and mutual trust around the contamination experience were more successful in coping with it and seemed to develop a stronger relationship (Edelstein, 1988). As DeMuth (1990) notes in her discussion of families and the nuclear threat:

> [T]here is potential for serious dysfunction when family members are not able to talk to one another about serious concerns . . . the ability to communicate painful feelings appropriately, according to the family's ethnic and typal style (Kantor & Lehr, 1975; McGoldrick et al., 1982) is crucial to the development of a sense of family cohesiveness and to the self-esteem of its individual members. (p. 306)

Respect for Differences

Family members may each respond differently to the contamination experience. It may be useful for the family therapist to normalize this aspect of family functioning, especially for families who have trouble accepting the differences and individuality of its members. Diverse responses to radiation exposure were expressed not only within atomic veteran families, but also by single members during the course of one interview. The continuum of response could be described as ranging from avoidance and denial (protection), through concern (for future generations), to outrage and anger (often about the invalidation experience). Responses could not be categorized simply for one family or even one family member. The responses were complex and could shift back and forth, even during a 2-hour interview (Murphy et al., 1990). Age, gender, family role, and the extent of exposure in the family may affect individual family members' responses. Women, for example, have often been more upset, angry, and outspoken about the toxic contamination of their families and communities than men (Pilisuk & Acredolo, 1988). After the accident at Three Mile Island, women residents of the area were found to be more distrustful than men of authorities (Brown & Mikkelsen, 1990). Indeed, many of the grassroots activists, some of whom come to assume national prominence like Lois Gibbs, are housewives whose concern for their children, their homes, and their communities becomes transformed into outrage and ultimately political action on behalf of others (Glendinning, 1987).

Men and women may differ in their economic or political investment in the source of the contamination. Men usually hold positions of greater power and make more money than women in industrial, scientific, or military employment (the usual sources of contamination). They may be less likely therefore to jeopardize their financial and professional power and security by blowing the whistle on the polluter. Even when men and women have comparable jobs, however, women may be more likely to subordinate economic or political considerations to their concern for the protection of human and environmental welfare. Theories about women's psychological development suggest that women tend to be more concerned with "relational" issues than men (Surrey, 1985) and are more likely to be motivated by an ethic of care and concern (Gilligan, 1982). Thus, women's psychological development may contribute to their joining together with others and taking an activist position in response to environmental contamination (Boston Women's Peace Research Group, 1992).

Age can differentially affect responses to contamination. In several communities near toxic exposure sites, the most concerned residents were the younger adults whose concern for their own or their children's health made them more fearful than elderly residents, whose children were grown and who were closer to the end of their own lives (Edelstein, 1988).

The needs of different family members are often not only different, but also conflicting; the atomic veteran, for example, may be most needful of silence and attention to matters other than his exposure just when his wife is becoming active, mobilizing her anger, or joining with others, or when his child, contemplating marriage, wishes to learn the facts about his or her vulnerability. At the same time that therapists validate the contamination experience of the family and encourage discussion about it, they must also affirm the different needs of individual family members for openness or protection around the issue of contamination.

Thus, the clinician needs to walk a fine line. The clinician needs to let family members know that he or she is aware of the experience of environmental contamination and is receptive to talking about it, while at the same time respecting the family's boundaries and their desire to protect each other. A family's difficulty in tolerating and accommodating the various needs and responses of different members is often greatest at a time of crisis or loss. It may be useful at some point to encourage family members to discuss their differing feelings and positions. It may sometimes be useful to interview members separately.

Not only will there be individual differences among family members at a given point, but also, as in any family process, there will be different stages of coping with the contamination experience for the family as a whole and its members. As in all family work, timing and pacing are crucial. Families have to be able to move in and out of awareness; their periodic need to protect themselves, to "live a normal life," as one atomic veteran put it, to focus on the positive, must be respected and supported (Murphy et al., 1990).

Empowerment

In our initial encounter with a family, we should heed the advice given by one environmental victim turned activist: The first question to ask is, what do you want? (Garula, 1989). It is sometimes easy to forget, in the urgency of the helper or the arrogance of the professional, to invite the client family to define its needs and goals. This is especially important with clients who have been victimized. Because victimization always involves the destruction of the victim's autonomy and control, their restoration is an essential part of the healing process. As in work with victims of sexual abuse, the first principle should be: "the locus of control is with the patient" (Herman, 1990).

Families who have been exposed to toxic contaminants, similar to families exposed to other traumas, often think their experiences are unique and find themselves isolated from others. Family therapists can initiate or encourage the development of support groups for exposed families. As Figley (1989) suggests from his work with traumatized families, one of the most important factors in successful treatment is the client's access to a social support system. Because family members may respond differently, some of these support groups may be specifically for the exposure victims themselves (if not all family members were exposed), parents, partners, or children. These groups help counteract the denial and isolation. In addition, they enable families to contribute to one another, enhancing their self-esteem and allowing them to use their experience in a helpful way.

Because of the multiple uncertainties about the health effects of toxic exposure and the stress associated with such uncertainty, families need access to information and education about the consequences of the toxic exposure. The clinician working with these families also needs to become informed to the best of his or her ability about the contamination and its potential consequences on both the exposed individuals and future generations. Families facing the aftermath of contamination will often be preoccupied with anticipating and identifying the effects the experience will have on their family. Because the family may have little idea of where to turn to find help in the wider community, the clinician should become aware of community resources. The clinician should also become an advocate for the creation of such resources where they do not already exist.

Transforming their own trauma into a vehicle for helping others is a well-recognized aspect of healing for those who have been victimized (Glendinning, 1987; Herman, 1990). The atomic veterans with whom we met wished to leave a legacy from their radiation experience for future generations. They hoped that others would benefit from their experience, and they encouraged us to use the interviews toward this end. Several action-oriented and self-help groups and organizations have been formed by survivors of environmental contamination: the National Association of Radiation Survivors (NARS), the National Association of Atomic Veterans (NAAV), the Relocation Action Network (RAIN), Citizen's Clearinghouse for Hazardous Waste, Inc., and Downwinders (for those living downwind of radioactive fallout from nuclear bomb tests). These groups have been variously involved in providing medical, legal, and technical assistance to fellow survivors and often give their members a sense of purpose and empowerment that help them cope with, if not transcend, the psychological injuries associated with their toxic exposure.

Therapist's Own Responses

Issues related to environmental contamination can evoke powerful reactions not only in clients, but also in therapists. Clinicians may feel outrage, despair, or helplessness as they listen to clients who are confronting environmental contamination. The clinician's feelings will also ebb and flow in a process similar to those of the clients. It is important that family therapists have supervision with supportive colleagues to monitor their feelings and to prevent their own responses from interfering with the clients' ability to come to terms with their experience of contamination.

If the therapist also has suffered the direct effects of toxic environmental contamination, he or she needs to pay particular attention to feelings and responses that might interfere with the therapeutic process. Overidentification with the victim, knowing what is "right" for the client, and a sense of helplessness and despair about the possibilities for change are some of the pitfalls for the therapist who has had similar experiences.

As family therapists, our primary responsibility is to work for the mental health of our clients. Toxic contamination is bad for our clients' physical and mental health. We should speak out against it. At the same time, we must recognize that our clients may not share our political beliefs. Some families are torn between economic interests and patriotic beliefs on the one hand and their reactions to their own contamination on the other. Clinicians need to be sensitive to and respectful of the dilemmas and conflicts with which their clients are struggling. We should also be aware that clients may undergo changes in their political views during therapy. Clients may want to take political action themselves at different times. The clinician, however, must avoid pushing the clients into action or condemning them for inaction even if the clinician believes in the importance of taking action herself or himself.

In our office, our first responsibility is to assist the family in its own process of coping with the effects of environmental contamination. Beyond the office, we can and should be free to take stands and actions on our own. We agree with Sholtz (1990): "Not taking political stands is impossible. If we do not speak out against public policy that we know to be bad for mental health, we are in fact supporting such policy" (p. 11). One of the most compelling public policy issues today is that of environmental contamination.

NOTE

1. The term *survivor* rather than victim emphasizes the strengths and coping abilities of those exposed to environmental contamination even though they have been victimized.

BIBLIOGRAPHY

Baum, A., Fleming, R., & Singer, J. E. (1983). Coping with victimization by technological disaster. *Journal of Social Issues, 39*(2), 117–138.

Bertell, R. (1985). *No immediate danger: Prognosis for a radioactive earth.* Summertown, TN: The Book Publishing Co.

Boston Women's Peace Research Group (S. Brooks, S. Conn, P. Ellis, S. Mack, B. C. Murphy, & J. Surrey) (1992). Women and peacemaking: The importance of relationships. In P. Green & S. Staub (Eds.). *Psychology and social responsibility: Facing global challenges* (pp. 271–289). New York: New York University Press.

Brown, P., & Mikkelsen, E. J. (1990). *No safe place: Toxic waste, leukemia, and community action.* Berkeley: University of California Press.

DeMuth, D. H. (1990). Some implications of the threat of nuclear war for families and family therapists. In M. Mirkin (Ed.), *The social and political contexts of family therapy* (pp. 355–381). Boston: Allyn & Bacon.

Edelstein, M. R. (1988). *Contaminated communities: The social and psychological impacts of residential toxic exposure.* Boulder: Westview.

Figley, C. R. (1989). *Helping traumatized families.* San Francisco: Jossey-Bass.

Garula, C. (1989, April). In B. C. Murphy (Moderator), *The psychological effects of "man made" environmental disasters on families and communities.* Panel discusssion conducted at the Annual Meeting of The American Orthopsychiatric Association, New York.

Gibbs, L. (1982). *Love Canal: My story.* Albany: State University of New York Press.

Gibbs, M. (1986). Psychological dysfunction as a consequence of exposure to toxics. In A. Leibovitz, A. Baum, & J. Singer (Eds.), *Health consequences of exposure to toxins* (pp. 47–70). Hillsdale, NJ: Lawrence Erlbaum Associates.

Gilligan, C. (1982). *In a different voice.* Cambridge, MA: Harvard University Press.

Glendinning, C. (1987). *Environmental hazards and human health: From victims to heroes.* Paper presented at Annual Meeting of the Association for Humanistic Psychology, Oakland, CA.

Greenwald, D., & Zeitlin, S. (1987). *No reason to talk about it: Families confront the nuclear taboo.* New York: WW Norton.

Herman, J. L. (1990, June). *The treatment of trauma: Incest as a paradigm.* Presented at Psychological Trauma Conference, sponsored by Harvard Medical School and Massachusetts Mental Health Center, Cambridge, MA.

Levine, A. (1982). *Love Canal: Science, politics and people.* Boston: Lexington Books.

Murphy, B. C., Ellis, P., & Greenberg, S. (1990). Atomic veterans and their families: Responses to radiation exposure. *American Journal of Orthopsychiatry, 60,* 418–427.

Obermeyer, V. (1988). Introduction. Special issue: Children of the Holocaust. *Journal of Family Therapy 15*(3), 1–10.

Olson, D. H., Russell, C. S., & Sprenkle, D. H. (Eds.). (1989). *Circumplex model: Systemic assessment and treatment of families.* New York: Haworth.

Pilisuk, M., & Acredolo, C. (1988). Fear of technological hazards: one concern or many? *Social Behavior 3,* 17–24.

Roth, S., & Murphy, B. C. (1986). Therapeutic work with lesbian clients: A systemic therapy view. In M. Ault-Riche (Ed.), *Women and family therapy* (pp. 78–89). Rockville, MD: Aspen Press.

Saffer, T. H., & Kelly, O. E. (1982). *Countdown zero.* New York: Putnam's.

Sholtz, D. (1990, August). *The politics of being apolitical.* Keynote address presented at The Association of Lesbian and Gay Psychologists, Boston.

Surrey, J. (1985). *The "self-in-relation": A theory of women's development.* Work in Progress #13. Wellesley, MA: Stone Center Working Paper Series.

Uhl, M., & Ensign, T. (1980). *G.I. guinea pigs.* New York: Wideview Books.

Vyner, H. (1988). *Invisible trauma: The psychosocial effects of the invisible contaminants.* Lexington, MA: D.C. Heath.

Wasserman, H., & Solomon, N. (1982). *Killing our own.* New York: Dell Publishing.

Chapter 6

Family Interaction, Nuclear War, Earthquakes, and the Environment: An Empirical Pilot Research Study and Advocacy Implications

Jules Riskin*

The original aim of the research to be described in this chapter was to study the effects of the threat of nuclear war on the psychological well-being of families and their members. When I began the project, I expected that families who discussed nuclear war openly would be better able to cope with the threat and would be psychologically healthier than families who did not discuss nuclear war. The research data have suggested, however, that the threat of nuclear war in itself does not have a significant effect on family and individual mental health status, nor is there a clear relationship between talking about nuclear war and psychological well-being. How families perceive, process, and respond to stresses of the threat of nuclear war and other environmental disasters appears to be strongly influenced by their own internal style, interactional patterns, and dynamics.

The idea for the first phase of the project came from my observing a videotape of a (focus) group of strangers discussing nuclear war. Two fortuitous occurrences, to be described subsequently, made it possible to conduct a second phase of the project, a *pre* and *post* study of the effects of the October 1989 (San Francisco

*I wish to thank Victoria Dickerson, Ph.D., Ben Hammett, Ph.D., Ferol Larsen, Ph.D., Joyce Emamjomeh, Shirley Riskin, and many other members of the MRI staff for their generous help on this project. I also thank those colleagues and friends whose financial generosity helped make this work possible. Most importantly, I thank the ten research families without whom there would not have been a project.

Bay Area) Loma Prieta earthquake on the same group of families who were subjects for the nuclear war project.

In conducting this project, I have not been a neutral researcher/observer. Much of my career has been spent conducting research on families, and I am a firm believer in taking a rigorous, objective approach to professional studies. The subject of family interactions and nuclear war, however, has had impact on me personally in a much more powerful way than has any previous focus of investigation. For that reason, I shall now summarize some of my assumptions, premises, biases, and relevant values. I shall therefore be in a stronger position to control for unintended ways in which those subjective factors might intrude into the execution and reporting of the research. Some, but not all, of these assumptions are supported by research findings. They are as follows:

- Time is running out. People ought to get more involved in nuclear and environmental issues before it becomes too late to reverse destructive changes.
- Researchers need to keep a clear distinction between what we believe people *ought* to think, feel, and do about nuclear and other environmental threats and the inferences we draw from what we actually *do* observe.
- It is inappropriate for therapists to introduce nuclear or environmental topics into the therapy arena, unless families or individuals make it reasonably clear that they believe these issues might be affecting them.
- It is a good idea for parents and children to talk together about environmental matters. Parental modeling can have a positive influence in this area, as in others, on children; children who grow up in families in which these topics are discussed will become more interested and more likely to become socially responsible adults than children of families who do not discuss these topics.
- It is important to observe family interaction as parents and children together discuss nuclear war and other environmental dangers. From family research and family therapy, we know that the whole is different from the sum of the parts.
- Directly observing parents and children discussing nuclear war and the environment may provide insights about the processes families use to avoid the discussion of potential environmental catastrophes.
- Family and individual mental health status, psychopathology, and family dysfunction may not be of primary relevance to the following question: What knowledge about families would be useful for family therapists and researchers so that they could influence people to overcome their inertia and indifference, to modify their thinking and feeling about, and eventually their behavior toward, their environment? That is, what will influence the members of families—the parents today and their children when they attain adulthood—to become more responsible, actively involved, engaged citizens in the effort to prevent the continuing degradation and destruction of our environment?

For reasons related to these biases, my focus has shifted away from the effects of external catastrophes on family and individual mental health to the question of how family therapists and researchers can use their skills, *outside* the consultation room, to influence families toward becoming more involved with environmental issues. Family therapy is an arena for change, and family therapists are experts in influencing families to change. I am interested in ways that family therapists/researchers can use their knowledge to become advocates for the environment, including the prevention of nuclear war.

This chapter therefore has two sections. In the first part, as a researcher I shall report on this project. In the latter part of the Discussion, I shall switch roles and become an advocate.

REVIEW OF THE LITERATURE

The empirical study of the effects of the threat of nuclear war on family life has become a focus of interest only in the last few years. To my knowledge, there are only three groups of investigators who have actually been observing families and collecting data on family interaction and the threat of nuclear war (DeMuth, 1990; Greenwald & Zeitlin, 1987; Riskin, 1988). A few writers have theorized but have not presented empirical data about families and nuclear war (Hesse, 1986; Marciano & Sussman, 1986). A few collections of articles describing empirical studies have been published, but these have almost entirely focused on *individuals'* responses to survey or questionnaire items relating to nuclear war (Schwebel, 1986; Solantaus, Chivian, Vartanyan, & Chivian, 1985). Several of these articles have suggested a relationship between the nuclear threat and mental health (e.g., Escalona, 1982; Mack, 1986). A few have expressed various degrees of doubt about the strength of such a relationship (Coles, 1985; Fiske, 1987; Frank, 1986; Locatelli & Holt, 1986; Zur, 1990).

I am not aware of any studies that include both *pre* and *post* components on how families cope with the effects of natural disasters. The study of the relationship between the threat of nuclear war or other environmental disasters and family interaction is thus essentially a young field of investigation.

METHOD[1]

Recruitment and Aims

At the outset I must emphasize that any inferences and conclusions that can be drawn from the work to be described are extremely tentative and severely limited by the small sample and its homogeneous composition. This project was a pilot study, and there were no specific hypotheses. My research associate, Dr.

Victoria Dickerson, and I did have a general aim: to explore whether the threat of nuclear war is a significant stressor of families and, if so, how they cope with it as compared with other stressors. There were several guiding questions, such as (1) do families talk easily about nuclear war or not, and how; (2) how do they *avoid* discussing it, and is "avoidance" a correct characterization; (3) how do they cope with the nuclear threat as compared with how they cope with other external stressors; (4) how does their communication style about ordinary day-to-day topics compare or contrast with their communication style when discussing nuclear war; and (5) is talking or not talking about nuclear war related to talking or not talking about other family topics, and is it related to the level of community involvement of the parents or to whether they are pro nuclear defense or pro arms reduction?

Ten families were referred to the project, by colleagues who knew them socially, by other families, and by self-referral. The families were recruited and interviewed from May, 1987, through June, 1988, and for the postearthquake phase of the project from November, 1989, through January, 1990. Criteria for participating in the study included an intact family with at least two children, none younger than age six years, and a willingness to be interviewed about external stresses, including the possibility of nuclear war. Mental health and therapy status were not relevant criteria.

I telephoned the ten families and all agreed to a home orientation visit. At that meeting, with the parents and children present, I outlined the project and offered them a $50.00 honorarium for participating. I asked each family to discuss, after I had left, whether they would participate and then to call me in a few days about their decision. Nine families agreed to participate in an interview at the Mental Research Institute (MRI), and one family agreed to a home interview. Thus, there were no outright refusals.

The sample represented an extremely narrow socioeconomic range. All families were from the Silicon Valley area of California. All parents were upper middle-class professionals or homemakers and community volunteers, and all but one had college or graduate degrees. There was considerable diversity, however, within the homogeneity, and the group was fairly representative of the well-educated professional class in the community. The families included nine with two parents and two children and one with two parents and three children. There were thus 20 adults ranging from 35 to 60 years old at the time of the first interview and 21 children ranging from six to 19 years old. Eight families were white, one was Afro-American, and one had white parents and adopted Afro-American children. There was a wide spectrum of political views from conservative to liberal, from advocates of strong pro nuclear defense to supporters of a bilateral nuclear freeze and arms reduction; a range of community involvement from little to much; a range of environmental and (anti) nuclear involvement from none to full-time occupation; a range of religious beliefs from atheist through agnostic to very devout; and considerable variation in the amount of talking about nuclear war and other world issues, ranging from no discussion to a great deal of discussion.

First Interview (at MRI) and Related Data (5/87–6/88)

The MRI interview was standardized and semistructured and lasted about $1\frac{1}{2}$ hours. A group of experienced family researchers and therapists representing a wide diversity of political views participated in creating the interview questions and in observing families behind a one-way screen. This diversity helped us to minimize the degree to which our own biases might intrude into the interview. Interviews were audiotaped and videotaped. They proceeded from exploring ordinary day-to-day topics to progressively more stressful scenarios. Some questions were designed to serve as controls for other topics. Discussion time for each question ranged from 3 to 8 minutes, with an average of about 5 minutes. Half the interviews were conducted by Dr. Dickerson and half by me. All questions were read from cards to insure standardization and to reduce subtle clues the interviewer might give about desired responses (*interviewer bias*). During the family discussion of the topics, the interviewer left the interview room, as indicated. The whole family was present for every question except one, as noted.

An outline of the interview is as follows:

- Plan something the family could do all together. (Interviewer leaves.)
- What advice would you give to a neighbor family whose child was being teased by a bully? (Interviewer leaves.)
- Each person write on an index card three items, on any topic from personal to global, that worry you. (Interviewer present.)
- Discuss an external stress that you have experienced, for example, sudden job change, death of a relative or friend, or being in a hurricane. (Interviewer leaves.)
- Here is an imaginary scenario: Discuss what you would do if seismologists were to predict with a high level of confidence that there would be a major earthquake in the next three months on a fault quite near your home. (Interviewer leaves.)[2]
- What does the idea of nuclear war bring to mind? (Interviewer present.)
- Is it a good idea or not for families to discuss nuclear war? The children please discuss without their parents present; then the parents without the children; then the whole family discuss the topic together. (Interviewer present.)
- Some people are pro strong nuclear defense, and some are pro bilateral nuclear freeze and nuclear arms reduction. What are your views? (Interviewer present.)
- How could people get you more involved in working for groups supporting your point of view? (Interviewer present.)
- What effects, if any, does the possibility of nuclear war have on your lives, today or in the future? (Interviewer present.)
- Scenario: Tension is escalating in the Persian Gulf, and a U.S. ship has suffered hundreds of casualties. Please discuss what the United States should do. (Interviewer leaves.)
- Scenario: Tension between two Middle East countries, A and B, has significantly escalated. Country A threatens to launch a nuclear warhead against

Washington, D.C., if the United States comes to the aid of country B, with whom we are friendly. Please discuss what the United States should do. (Interviewer leaves.)
- Scenario: You hear on an emergency broadcast that full-scale nuclear war has broken out and that in 25 minutes many nuclear bombs will reach Silicon Valley. What would you do? (Interviewer present.)
- What can citizens do to help prevent nuclear war? (Interviewer present.)
- What do you think of these questions? Did the interviewer's own biases intrude? (Interviewer present.)

Dr. Dickerson and I spent about 2 hours at their home with the family who refused the MRI interview, discussing their reasons for refusing to be interviewed at the MRI and reviewing how they might have answered the interview questions. (Only the parents participated in this interview. Their reasons for refusing to come to the MRI to be interviewed will be discussed later.)

In addition to the interview, other data were collected:

- Demographic information on each family, including questions on education, occupation, income, religious preference, race, and history of therapy.
- California Personality Inventory (CPI) (Gough, 1987), completed by everyone over 12 years old. (This is similar to the Minnesota Multiphasic Personality Inventory [MMPI], but is less pathology oriented.)
- Activity sheets for each person, covering activities in the local community, non-nuclear political activities, and nuclear-environmental activities.
- FACES III (Olson, Portner, & Lavee, 1985), which assesses family adaptability and cohesion, and F-COPES (McCubbin, Larsen, & Olson, 1982), which assesses family coping styles. Both tests were administered to all family members.
- Ratings by the interview observers of the Family Interaction Scales (FIS) (Riskin, 1983) immediately after the interview.
- A "clinical" discussion of the interview by the observers, immediately after they rated the FIS.

Second Interview (at home): Postearthquake Interview (10/89–1/90)

In the midst of our doing the data analysis, the Loma Prieta earthquake of October 17, 1989, struck. Although a disaster for the community, for us it was the second fortuitous event (see note 2). Within a few days, I began contacting the original ten subject families, and all ten agreed to be interviewed about their experiences with the earthquake. Families were interviewed at their homes, from late October, 1989, through January 1990. Because time was critical, it was not possible to standardize the conditions of this round of interviews. Seven were videotaped with the aid of a colleague. I conducted the three other interviews by myself and made only audiotapes. Two of these families had moved before the earthquake to other states; they were interviewed by telephone; one family was videotaped and the other audiotaped. Except for two children who were now out of the country, all members who participated in the first interview participated in the second one.

The purpose of the interview was twofold: (1) to compare how families coped with an actual environmental disaster, the earthquake, with how they coped with the hypothetical earthquake in the interview two years earlier; (2) to explore what families believed would need to change for them to become more involved in environmental issues than they were now. (This second purpose reflected a shift in my own interests from the original project's emphasis on the [psychopathological] effects of the threat of nuclear war on families and also an expansion of my focus to broader environmental concerns.)

The interviews took an average of 45 minutes. The questions were as follows:

- Describe what each of you felt, thought, and did when the earthquake struck.
- How have you been affected by the earthquake? Any residual feelings?
- In hindsight, is there anything you would have done differently to protect yourselves against the consequences of the earthquake?
- There are predictions that a bigger earthquake will soon come. Are you worried that "the other shoe will drop?"
- What sense of control do you feel you have over the consequences of the next earthquake? What can you do to minimize damage?
- May we look at the videotape of your discussion of two years ago about a hypothetical earthquake? (All families were eager to watch the tape.) What are your reactions?
- There are other major environmental problems, for example, ozone damage, hothouse effect, pollution. Whatever your current level of involvement in these issues, what would have to happen for you to become more involved than you are now?

The design of this two-step project was thus both cross-sectional and longitudinal. The cross-sectional components were the data from the first interview. The longitudinal part was the preearthquake and postearthquake data and the data about involvement in nuclear and environmental issues.

DATA ANALYSIS

Summary of Data

1. MRI interview on coping with the threat of nuclear war and including a question on a hypothetical earthquake scenario.
   - Clinical judgments made by observers of the MRI interview.
   - FIS ratings made by the same observers.
   - 75-item questionnaire, quantitatively rating families' responses to the interview topics.[3]

- Paper and pencil data.
  FACES
  F-COPES
  CPI
  Three worries (done during the interview)
  Demographic data
  Activities sheets, including community, political (non-nuclear), and nuclear/environmental categories.
2. Postearthquake interview.
   - Clinical-impressionistic judgments about the process and content of the interviews.
   - FIS ratings.
   - 14-item questionnaire quantitatively rated; this questionnaire incorporated the same items that were used to rate the hypothetical earthquake ("prequake") scenario in the first, that is, MRI, interview.
   - Qualitative analysis of families' responses to how to become more involved with environmental issues.

Organizing the Data: Major Categories

It is evident that although only ten families were processed, a tremendous amount of data was collected. We constructed several major categories, derived in part from family interaction research literature and from the literature on individuals and the threat of nuclear war. There is some overlap among them.

The major categories are as follows:

- Demographics
- Mental health status
- Activity level
- Communication-interactional style
- Control/efficacy
- Feelings
- Expressed interest
- Opinions, attitudes, and beliefs
- Developmental factors
- Parental expectations and observer bias
- Involvement
- Family adaptability, cohesion, and coping style

Results

Although the N of only 10 families precludes meaningful statistical tests of significance, suggestive trends can be identified and will be discussed later. (The quantitative results will not be formally discussed in this chapter but will be presented at a later date.) These trends have been suggested in part by scattergrams based on the major variables. Short vignettes from the interviews (with families' identifications altered to protect confidentiality) will be used to illustrate these trends.[4]

Demographics. The ten families were quite homogeneous with respect to demographic variables, but within this homogeneity, there was a wide range in most other categories.

Mental Health Status of Families and Members. This was assessed by (1) clinical judgments made by observers of the MRI interview and viewers of tapes of both interviews, (2) the average of the two parents' scores of Vector ("Level") III of the CPI (Gough, 1987; personal communication, 1988), and (3) a global rating of each family's level of functioning. These ratings were an average of ratings made independently by myself and several colleagues who were quite familiar with all the families but who had not discussed them with one another for almost two years. In general, this population was a highly functioning group of families and individuals (Riskin, 1982). On the family global rating scale (1 = totally dysfunctional and 10 = highly functional), they ranged from 6 (moderately well functioning) to 9.5 (very high level of functioning), with an average of 7.9. On the combined parental CPIs, the adults were functioning at a moderately superior to very superior level. (Several of the children's scores were of questionable validity.) Clinical judgments were consistent with the global ratings. Mental health status was not related to level of interest or opinions about nuclear defense or environmental issues, to sense of efficacy, to expression of feelings about nuclear war or earthquakes, or to level of activity.

Activities Level. This was assessed by scoring the "activities sheet," which all family members had completed. Subjects rated their own activities. The researchers then grouped the activities into (1) local community activities (e.g., church, school extracurricular programs); (2) political activities (e.g., attend city council meetings, vote); (3) environmental and pronuclear/antinuclear activities (e.g., member of Physicians for Social Responsibility [PSR]). *Community* activities ranged from minimal to very much. These were not related to the other areas of activities. *Political* activities also ranged from minimal to much. In all families, the parents at the very least voted fairly regularly, and many wrote letters to their congressional representatives.

There was also a wide range of *nuclear* activities. Two sets of parents were highly involved in an antinuclear organization, volunteering 10 to 20 hours per week at the local office. One set of parents devoted several hours per month attending meetings to oppose schools' teaching courses relating to nuclear matters. One of the antinuclear families functioned at a very high level; in the other, there was a moderate level of parent-child tension. There was also moderate tension in the family of the parents opposed to nuclear studies. One teenager out of a total of nine was actively involved, independently of her family, in a world-affairs discussion group. Her parents were passively pro arms reduction: Mother was "only" a dues-paying member of one organization, and Father wore another organization's emblem "which at least gets other people at work to ask what it means."

The general level of *environmental* activities was rather low and passive; most families participated in local community recycling programs, and several mentioned not using styrofoam cups, but not much more. One father was professionally active in the environmental area, and one family said they were shifting their investments to an environmentally oriented mutual fund. Overall, the activity levels were not related to the level of family functioning (mental health status) or communication style.

Family Style, Communication, and Interactional Patterns. This category was assessed by (1) clinical judgments; (2) quantitative ratings using the FIS, for example, the ratio of "friendliness" to "unfriendliness" and the ratio of "agreements" to "disagreements" (Riskin, 1982); (3) some of the "process" items on the MRI interview questionnaire, for example, the family discusses the "bully" topic in an aggressive or in a conciliatory way.

The data strongly suggest that family style is consistent across all topics, from mundane issues to nuclear war and environmental issues, to pre and post discussions of earthquakes, and that at least some families do not discuss nuclear war for reasons more related to their specific style than to the specific topic of nuclear war. Further, the data indicate that the MRI (nuclear and hypothetical earthquake) interview was representative of family style. The style at MRI was quite similar to the patterns at the earlier, home orientation interview and to the family style at the postearthquake interviews at home two years later.

There was a positive association of some of the interactional variables with the level of family functioning; for example, several families had a high ratio of "agree" to "disagree" and of "support" to "attack" and also scored 9 to 9.5 on the global ratings, and several had low ratios and scored 6 to 7.5. Families whose style was quite assertive/aggressive in discussing the "neighborhood bully" topic were also assertive/aggressive in discussing the "countries A and B" scenario. Also, their substantive positions tended to parallel their interactional styles.

Some brief illustrative vignettes follow:

Family A

Family A has a daughter age 13 and a son age 10. This family chose not to be interviewed at MRI. The stated reasons were the parents' concern that discussing nuclear war might be stressful for the children and that the children would feel uneasy when left in the interview room by themselves. This family viewed the external world, ranging from experiences of daily living to global issues, as inhospitable. Mother said that during some nearby helicopter maneuvers a few years ago she had been concerned that a helicopter might crash into their house, which was on a steep cliff. The younger child had once been hit by a bar of soap while taking a shower when a moderate-sized earthquake had struck and was uneasy about taking a shower alone for the following year. The family also had made detailed preparations on how the children should protect themselves against rattlesnakes, which were not rare around their new home.

Family B

Family B was strongly assertive in style.

Son (age 19): Say country A is irrational and calls our bluff, and say they don't think we'd do it [retaliate with a nuclear bomb if they fired a bomb on Washington, D.C.].

Mother (overlaps): Then we *have to do* it.

Son: Then you'd nuke them?

Mother: You bet your life we do!

Father: You have to do it!

Mother: You have to do it!

Father: . . . That's the whole point of deterrence—the aim of deterrence is to deter . . . the one way you prevent nuclear war is threatening it.

Daughter (age 15): (Talks into microphone) O.K., next scenario. (She had made a similar comment after the family discussed "plan something together" for a few minutes.)

In the same family, the father emphasized to the interviewer that it is conceptually wrong to isolate nuclear war from "geopolitics," and Mother whispered to him, "you're pontificating." The family discusses geopolitical matters frequently at home; Son participates, Daughter does not. Later in the interview, Father emphasizes that Daughter needed to understand more about history, that " . . . she needs some books, I can give her some books to read." At the end of the interview, the family was asked if they felt stressed. Mother laughingly said, "This is the tone of our dinner conversation." Their style is quite consistent across contents.

Family C

Family C talks quite openly at home about the horrors of nuclear war. The children were asked whether their friends talk about nuclear war with their parents:

Daughter (age 15): We talk openly about it, me and my friends, but a lot of them, I'm sure, don't talk about it to their families . . . just because a lot of my friends don't have that great a relationship with their families. Like, they're divorced, or they don't discuss anything with their families.

Family D

Family D parents have many strong differences of opinions on a variety of topics, including that Mother is pro–Strategic Defense Initiative (SDI) and Father is skeptical. Because they differ so strongly, they do not discuss nuclear war or SDI, even though Father is a scientist in a related field. The children rejoined the parents so they could all talk together about whether to discuss nuclear war:

Daughter (age 13): What did you guys say?

Mother: Well, we disagreed (laughs). That won't surprise you.

Daughter: No.

Mother: Dad said we should talk and I said I didn't see much point to it.

In the same family, three older children had been away at college during the MRI interview. A few months later, the "big kids" came home for vacation. Mother invited me to their home to show the whole family the videotape of the interview. After viewing the tape:

Son (age 22) (in a friendly tone): For me it was interesting psychologically. I think they all responded so typically of themselves.

Interviewer: This [the MRI interview] is a typical cross section of the family?

Daughter (age 20): Right.

Son: Right.

In the scoring of the interview questionnaire, there were 35 instances in which the ten sets of parents sharply disagreed with each other on a variety of topics, including "plan something together," the hypothetical earthquake scenario, and stance toward nuclear arms. Three sets of parents, including families who are the most assertive/aggressive by other measures, had 60% of all these disagreements. Clearly intensely disagreeing, even arguing, is a general characteristic of these families and not restricted to global issues.

Most of the families, on viewing the tape of the hypothetical earthquake scenario from two years earlier, which was shown during the postearthquake interview, commented that there were no surprises. "We still are just like we were two years ago."

Control: Sense of Efficacy. This category was assessed by clinical judgments and questionnaire ratings on the extent to which family members feel or believe they have, or could have, control versus powerlessness in helping to prevent nuclear war and in minimizing the consequences of an earthquake or other potential environmental disasters.

Families varied widely in their sense of control. For given families, control tended to be consistent across topics (although it does not clearly correlate with [self-defined] "activities"). In particular, control over the consequences of an earthquake (both hypothetical and actual) was moderately associated with a sense of control over preventing nuclear war. Also, the more remote the topic from the personal lives of the families, the less the sense of control; the more personal and immediate the topic, the greater the sense of control. Some illustrations follow.

Family A

Father expressed a low sense of control over nuclear issues and that "it's very difficult to measure the individual impact of any one individual at any time." The parents, however, described how, in preparation for moving to a new house in an area known to have rattlesnakes, they devoted much time and effort to teaching their young children to be alert for and appropriately fearful of rattlesnakes, and the "do's" and "don'ts" of behavior if they were ever close to one. They perceive rattlesnakes to be a clear and immediate danger, about which direct and immediate action can be taken. Father contrasts rattlesnakes with lightning: "You really can't do anything about lightning."

Family B

Son (age 19) said he couldn't do anything about nuclear war, but that "[I] certainly have control over coping with AIDS."

Family D

Son (one of the "big kids," age 22 [see p. 12]), who has well-defined future goals and plans says: I'm kind of apathetic [about preventing nuclear war] . . . and . . . there's things that are more pressing which I do have an effect on and which I can resolve. . . .

Family E

Family explicitly uses the "countries A and B" scenario to teach their children (ages 11 and 7):

Mother: [This scenario is] real, and [that's] why we have to work now, because this is, this is proliferation.

Daughter (age 11): [It's good to talk about nuclear war because] . . . people will know more how to prevent it . . . [and then] maybe they can write to somebody, like the President.

Family F

Father: Seeing that film ["The Last Epidemic"] was a devastating experience for me . . . and, uh, it really changed my priorities . . . and I started working with other people on it.

Mother: Even to the point of doing it full time.

Father: And as a result, I, I have found that, uh, instead of being devastated I feel more hopeful and I'm not discouraged.

Feelings. This category was based on the three written "worries" from the MRI interview, the interview questionnaire ratings, and clinical judgments on whether the nuclear threat and the hypothetical and actual earthquakes were topics about which the subjects seemed frightened or worried.

In general, those people who were more active in nuclear matters tended to express their feelings about nuclear war spontaneously. Most others, when explicitly asked, also expressed their feelings, but they appeared quite deliberately not to dwell on painful feelings; they actively suppressed, or *selectively inattended* to them.

Family G

Daughter #2 (age 15): [When asked her view of talking about nuclear war] I'm not a world leader, I don't vote, so . . .

Father (interrupts): You will be in three years.

Daughter: Right, but I don't now so I haven't thought about it . . .

Mother (interrupts): Hmpph. Do you discuss these issues with your friends?

Daughter #1 (age 18) (overlaps): No. Why do you want us to ruin our day by talking about nuclear war? We don't just come up and say, "Well, let's talk about nuclear war now." That's stupid.

Daughter #1 (a few minutes later, describing a videotape about Hiroshima): People, you just see their skins falling off (pulls hand down over face). . . . You can see their skin, they have, like, no jaws, ugh! Their eyes fall out, ugh!

Daughter #2: I don't like talking about it . . . why ruin your day?

Father: Girls, where have you been, anyway! What if there was a way for you to prevent World War III?

Father (when parents are alone): The kids aren't interested in talking about nuclear war [like we are]. We've failed, just as we failed to get them interested in back-packing.

Family B

Son (age 19): [Talking about nuclear war] isn't stressful. The only thing *I'm* worried about is my parents want me to get a job, that's stress, my parents, you know, want me to go to school and how my grades are. . . .

Family C

Son (age 13, in response to "what does nuclear war bring to mind?"): Well, really, I mean, I'm sort of used to living with it. I realize the fact that any time I could be completely obliterated, with only having a half-hour's warning. I mean, there's not really much that I can do about it yet. So it just doesn't bother me that much (neutral tone of voice).

Family H

Son (age 13): I don't like talking about [nuclear war] 'cause it makes, it makes me think, you know, more about well, what if, and then starting getting all these— crazy, and then you go around being paranoid. [But] the other day my friend and I talked about it, and, you know, it wasn't anything big. I—, it just depends on how you talk about it.

Mother (later): I think [talking about nuclear war here] brings it home. [Other-wise] it's in the distance, you don't really have to deal with it that much . . .

Son (interrupts): It's a little like playing volleyball, keep it out there (he shoves his arms as if pushing a volleyball away).

Those people who were more upset in discussing nuclear war (as judged by both their verbal and nonverbal behavior) also tended to be more upset about earthquakes, both real and imaginary, and a variety of other subjects.

Family A

Mother felt that her enjoyment of her lovely view of Silicon Valley had been destroyed ever since, several years ago, she had seen in her local newspaper a drawing depicting the destruction if a nuclear bomb were to be detonated in the heart of the valley. This woman also reported a variety of mild fears in herself and in other family members.

Family G

Mother was quite dramatic in expressing her fear of both nuclear war and earthquakes.

Expressed feelings were, as expected, related to family and individual interactional style.

Family C

Mother is an office administrator and values rationality highly. Following the earthquake, she was quite "devastated." Not, however, about the earthquake itself, but because her staff had criticized her for being "insensitive to *their* fears." Earlier she had said that in her view the likelihood of nuclear war has "gotta be low, otherwise I couldn't continue to live the life I'm living." She is a dues-paying, but otherwise passive, member of an antinuclear organization.

Methodologically "feelings" are complex to assess and define operationally, and there are pitfalls in making inferences from observed behavior and in interpreting that behavior. Some examples may illustrate this.

Family D

Mother (to her children, ages 13 and 8): [The possibility of nuclear war] doesn't scare me. I've told you kids, you don't harbor fear. When you're afraid, you find a way to do what you can, and then you put the rest in the hands of God and you don't anguish or worry about it. And so I think that it's cowardice that makes people so afraid of all this most of the time, and I'm not a coward. I'm not afraid. No, that doesn't make me afraid. (She then quotes Shakespeare that) " . . . it seems to me most strange that men should fear; seeing that death, a necessary end, will come when it will come" (forcefully stated). I believe very strongly that my family will be reunited after this life is over.

One might infer that she is denying her fear; however, she is devoutly religious and may have felt that the interviewer was discounting her view that the soul is eternal. It is not self-evident which interpretation (if either) is correct.

Family I

In Family I, with two children, ages 8 and 6, who at this time were out of the interview room, Father and Mother both said they weren't afraid of nuclear war:

Mother: I think that probably the only fear that I have, because I believe that our soul is eternal, you know . . . we would go to heaven . . . and be with the Lord . . . if there were a nuclear holocaust and there were some of us left (the last phrase spoken with much feeling).

In response to a question about stressful experiences, the same family told of moving from the Midwest to Silicon Valley. They used two cars, and during the trip encountered heavy fog. One car broke down:

Mother: That was pretty scary.

Son (age 6): A truck almost hit the other car.

Interviewer: How did you folks cope with that?

Father: We prayed a lot.

Mother: Yeah, we prayed.

Father: We believe in prayer.

Family J

During Family J's wrap-up question, Son #1 (age 19) says: There's no way you could get any stress out of us on any topic.

(Many overlapping yeahs.)

Daughter (age 17): We know who we are and we go home with our lives and you [interviewer] go home with your self.

(Son #2, age 14 and mentally retarded, is present.)

Son #1: You could [push] about mental retardation and make it bothersome to me and that's about it. I'd say, "Oh well, that's it. Life goes on."

(Entire discussion is spoken in a relaxed, neutral tone.)

The children's comments could be interpreted as masking a deep fear. Alternatively, their statements could be viewed as reflecting very high self-esteem and confidence. The observers favored the latter view.

Family H

Family H discussed the consequences of nuclear war: annihilation, the end of the world. Affect during the discussion was neutral. Again, it was not self-evident whether this was a manifestation of defense or whether the topic was so remote that a neutral affect was appropriate.

In contrast, the "25 minutes to go" question was asked of the last three of the ten families at the MRI interview and elicited much more affect. There was considerable joking in two families, and one set of parents (from an activist family) had tears in their eyes.

Expressed Interest Level. Expressed interest in nuclear war and other environmental issues was assessed by clinical judgments and on relevant items from the MRI and postearthquake interview questionnaires.[5]

Levels ranged from highly interested to quite bored. In general, the more remote or abstract the topic, the less interest families expressed. As with feelings, there was much more interest in earthquake preparedness immediately after the Loma Prieta earthquake than several months later (see p. 109).

For most families (except for three mothers, who candidly stated their fears), the hypothetical earthquake was a neutral exercise. Most families also discussed the abstract topic of nuclear war neutrally. As the scenarios became more concrete and vivid (progressing from: "Should families talk about nuclear war," to the "Countries A and B" scenario, to "25 minutes until the bomb drops"), expression of both interest and feelings became stronger.

A possible relationship between interest in nuclear war and family interactional style is suggested by the following.

Families E and F

Families E and F are quite similar along many dimensions. Both sets of parents are the same ages and are highly involved in the same antinuclear organization. Both families have two children, ages 11 and 7 and 11 and 8. But their interactional styles differ. The first family has a slightly tense emotional climate, and the mother tends to monitor the older child's behavior closely. The second set of parents are more relaxed with their children. The older child of the first family is not interested in discussing nuclear war; the older child of the second family is *quite* interested.

The actual occurrence of the October, 1989, earthquake created much more interest in earthquake preparedness than did the hypothetical scenario, even though none of the ten families experienced any significant personal damage or disruption of their lives. Earthquakes are more immediate, palpable and personal than the possibility of nuclear war.

Family I

Family I, when presented with the hypothetical, pre-earthquake scenario:

Father: (laughs)

Mother: I have a very quick answer to that: we'd move!

Overall interest in the destruction of the environment was not high. In six of the ten families, the environment was clearly of low priority. Some typical comments follow.

Family A, Father: I guess it's all theoretical right now because I don't, there's nothing that I'm so concerned about that it over—that is stronger, takes precedent, to normal family life.

Family B, Father: Every few years there's another problem that is threatening us with catastrophe. But this hysteria is very short-lived.

Family C, Mother: At least one can always give money . . . I think if I felt it was sufficiently severe [that I'd do more].

Family C, Father: I would have to be convinced that the threat was more serious than it now seems to be.

Family G, Father: [I need to see] . . . destruction in the San Francisco Bay, or the Pacific flyway having no birds left in it because the chain was broken somewhere along the flyway.

Family J, Mother: What I have *had* to do is set priorities . . . [and other issues have higher priority].

The other four families, including the two active members of an antinuclear group, were much more actively interested.

Opinions, Beliefs, and Attitudes. This category was assessed by ratings of the interview questionnaires and clinical judgments. Families were asked whether they favored strong nuclear arms defense (SNAD) or bilateral freeze and nuclear arms reduction (BNAR). Two of the SNAD families were highly assertive/aggressive in style. Another SNAD family (Father is a career military officer) was extremely gentle and mild-mannered. Two of the BNAR families were also quite aggressive in style. Thus, there was no clear relationship between attitude toward nuclear arms and family style. There was also no relationship between these attitudes and family or parental mental health status.

In response to the hypothetical (pre) earthquake question, the dominant theme expressed by both parents and children was: There are disasters everywhere, and you can't run from them. In the postearthquake interview, the three mothers who had said during the pre-earthquake interview that they want to leave this area still wanted to move away.

The question about the environment in the postearthquake interview elicited attitudes similar to families' "interests." Most families thought it was important to do some recycling, and several children said that it was a good idea not to use styrofoam cups or hair sprays with chlorofluorocarbons. Many individuals, both adults and children, did not believe there was yet sufficient evidence about ozone destruction, acid rain, and so forth to make a sound judgment. A typical comment was as follows.

Family C

Father (scientist): The problem is [that] for every expert who says—I mean I'm technically acute enough that I could find out a lot about this stuff. People have been studying the ozone while I'm right in the next office, but for every scientist or expert who says one thing, there is a scientist or expert who says something else. Unfortunately it seems to me the evidence is still ambiguous. Hopefully, if it ever becomes unambiguous, it won't be too late, but maybe it will be. (This father wears a lapel button of a peace organization.)

Developmental Factors. Some of the attitudes, levels of interest, and feelings expressed may be related to the age and sex of the family members as well as to family style. Three male children were quite aggressive in discussing the "bully" question and the "Countries A and B" scenario.

Family F, Son (age 11): Call the bully's parents, and then, if the bully's parents don't solve it then they (gestures as if stabbing himself).

Family E, Son (age 6): (He is describing what a bully once actually did.) He was punch, and punching, so the, the [other] kid started *ble-e-e-ding* in a while (he punches the air with his fists).

Family H, Son (age 11): (In discussing Countries A and B) I think if Country A did that [nuclear attack on Washington, D.C.], we might nuke one of their cities.

Eight of the nine adolescents in the entire sample said they were not interested or worried about nuclear war because of concerns such as school, social life, soccer practice, and a feeling there was nothing they could do anyway. Their responses might be typical of many in that age group.

Family J

Daughter (age 17): [I wouldn't do] much more than writing checks or letters, because I've got too much going in my own life (scholarship society, minority group activities in school) to be worried about something I can do nothing to [control].

Parents varied considerably about the appropriateness of discussing nuclear war with or in front of their children.

Family A, who decided against the MRI interview, said they were concerned that their 13- and 10-year-old children would become upset over a discussion of nuclear war.

Family E, Father: My boy (age 7) has more pressing concerns than nuclear war: Is Susie still chasing him around the playground trying to kiss him. However, we've been active [in an antinuclear organization] since they were born, [and] . . . I don't think we have the opinion that you need to hide it from them.

Parental Expectations. Not only interviewer bias, but also parental expectations of course influence the children's attitudes about nuclear war. Both sets of parents in two families are heavily involved in a peace organization. The fathers and mothers are about the same ages, and both families have two children, ages 11 and 7. In response to the question "is it a good idea or not for families to talk about nuclear war," the following interchanges occurred.

First Family

Mother: But otherwise you would rather not talk about it?

Child #1: Right.

Mother: And why is that?

Child #1: I don't know.

Father: Just because it's so bad? (very gently)

Child #1: Yeah.

Child #2: Uh huh.

Father: So scary?

Child #1: Um hum . . .

(One minute later):

Mother (to Child #2): Is it something to talk about or not? Hmm? (neutral tone)

Child #2: I don't want to.

Mother: Why?

Child #1: (Whispers) . . . basketball.

Mother (to Child #1): Don't be silly.

Child #2: (Interrupts): . . . cause I get, get maybe get worried.

Father: Maybe have bad dreams or something? (tone very solicitous)

Child #2: Um hum.

Second Family

Father: Should we talk about nuclear war?

Child #1: Uh huh.

Child #2: No.

Father: Why don't you think so?

Child #2: Because.

Father: Can you say more than "just because"?

Child #2: Uh uh. ("no")

(Father gently restrains Child #2 from standing up.)

Mother: Is it scary for you to talk about, or is it boring for you to talk about? (matter of fact, neutral tone)

Child #2: Boring.

Father: It's boring?

Child #2: Uh huh.

Father in the first family had expectations, conveyed by words and tone of voice, that may have limited or cued his children's choice of responses. Both parents in the second family by their words and tones gave child #2 more options.

Involvement. This category overlaps many of the others, including control. I am using it to refer to some of the common themes expressed to account for people's level of participation in nuclear, earthquake, or environmental activities.

In response to "what can people do to help prevent *nuclear war,*" several people said: One person can't do anything, so I do nothing. Other typical responses were as follows.

Family G, Mother: (pays dues to an antinuclear organization): I don't know [what else I can do]. And I have the guilts about it. I'm—give me more hours.

Family D, Son ("older kid," age 22, interviewed later, after he had seen a videotape of his family's MRI interview, at which he was not present): What makes me kind of apathetic about the whole thing is that it really doesn't affect me right now and that makes it hard for me to relate to it as a real crisis.

Same family, Daughter (age 19): There's a group at school for peace, and they stand around on Thursdays, and, in groups, with their signs up, and I, they discuss, uh, things like Nicaragua and Honduras, nuclear war . . . and when I walk by I think, "why aren't they studying?" (Laughs)

Son (very active in campus affairs): Well, getting an education . . . [is more important].

The *hypothetical earthquake* scenario elicited the same theme that although most families believed that there were many actions that "probably should" be taken, in fact most families had made minimal preparations. Several wives reminded their husbands that they had asked for the water heaters to be fastened and so forth but that nothing yet had been done.

Family G

Mother: We would have enough water, we would, we would stake the water heater and our new furnace to the wall—I think that's been requested in the past (looks at father)—we would make sure we had enough water and enough food.

At the *postearthquake* interview, several families joked that the "Big One" was still to come. Only one family had made serious preparations before the earthquake. The mother was also quite active in neighborhood earthquake preparedness programs. Several people, adults and children, said, "why worry, there are dangers everywhere."

The *environmental* question at the end of the postearthquake interview focused on becoming more involved in environmental issues. Most families are minimally involved (local recycling, not using styrofoam cups) and have no plans to become more involved in the near future. The major themes present included the following: there's not enough evidence, the experts disagree, I'm too busy, one person wouldn't make a difference, it's not personal enough.

Family H, Son #1 (student, age 17): Well, I'd have to see [damage] go past, you know . . . where there's no rain forest left or suddenly all summers are 110 degrees.

Family A, Father (business executive): . . . *If* there was something I could really do to make a difference and it was more impending, [then] I think I would get involved . . .

Family B, Father (writer): I'd have to be convinced there's a danger. There is really no good scientific evidence. . . . This catastrophic prediction is pretty . . . hysterical.

Family C, Mother (office administrator): . . . this year is going to be a terribly, terrible, stressful and busy one at work . . . I think if I thought it [environmental threat] was sufficiently severe, that I would try to do something even so.

Family I, Mother (homemaker, school and church volunteer): I do not see . . . concrete things for us to do [other than not buy tuna fish]. I think everyone would need to get together and say "we will change and you will change" and then we'll all make a difference.

Family D, Father (scientist): If one were presented with compelling evidence that one of these problems was really severe, then I would be inclined to talk to people about it.

Family D, Mother (who is quite involved in a community earthquake preparedness program): Talking about [the environment] right now makes me think I will go ahead and . . . *do* write to the President [about acid rain].

Family G, Father (electrical engineer): My answer is almost the same as my daughter's (age 20). I would have to see or feel, um, change, damage to the environment I live in. (Mother makes contributions to environmental organizations.)

Family J, Mother (director of a community agency): I'd need a profile of statements from someone who, from a scientist who really understands [environmental issues], like the Surgeon General [on cigarettes and cancer].[6]

The two families who were deeply involved in an antinuclear organization were also quite involved in environmental activities.

Family Adaptability, Cohesion, and Coping Style. These data are being analyzed and will be reported in future papers.

DISCUSSION

I wish to re-emphasize that generalizations from this research are extremely limited by the very small size and homogeneity of the sample. Statements of a general nature should therefore be regarded only as suggestive trends and as hypotheses to be tested on larger samples.

Direction of Causality

Although causal direction cannot be deduced from cross-sectional studies, the data support the impression that a family's unique internal relationships and interactional style influence its perception, processing of, and responses to the external environment, including the threat of nuclear war. Indeed, the interactional style may be at least as significant as the nuclear war threat per se in determining the impact of that threat. People's prior status may be irrelevant if a general nuclear war were actually to occur, but their way of coping with the *threat* is not independent of prior experience.[7]

The family and its members are not blank screens. This would seem to be a trivial observation, and it is certainly not news to many schools of psychotherapy or social scientists (Hill, 1949). I believe, however, that some of the research in this field has tended to minimize or even ignore the family's active role in mediating external stimuli. Therefore, this simple premise does need restating. Clinical examples from the subject families (several cited in the Results section) support this view. For example, parents and children who tend to avoid discussing emotionally charged topics, for whatever reason, will tend to avoid discussing such potentially terrifying subjects as nuclear war.

I am not suggesting that the threat of nuclear war has no impact on families. In this present sample, however, I find significantly less impact than some of the literature has reported.

Mental Health Effects

We did not see evidence that the threat of nuclear war affected individual mental health or family functioning, in the sense that *mental health* implies a framework of pathology or well-being. In fact, the family that said its members *were* affected was the one in which the physical environment generally was perceived as unfriendly; this family was mildly phobic about several potential threats, local to global. (It is of course possible that we were not looking at the relevant issues or did not examine our data in sufficient depth.) I am not arguing that the external threats studied here had no psychological consequences; I am stating that this project provided no evidence that these stressors in themselves significantly contributed to psychopathology. Although it is difficult to believe that ongoing exposure to the threat of nuclear war does not influence people psychologically, it may be in ways that cannot be measured by traditional mental health assessment techniques.[8] The observation that an 18-year-old girl was repulsed by the thought of nuclear war and said, "ugh, why ruin my day, why talk about it," does not necessarily lead to the conclusion that she is chronically burdened by visions of her skin peeling or of the destruction of the earth and her own futurelessness. Similarly, one might expect children, if asked, to say that it would be scary if their parents were to die, but that fear does not ordinarily obsess or paralyze them. Or one would expect children who live in tornado country to be afraid of tornados, but not that they would necessarily be emotionally constricted by that fear in itself. The whether and how of the *emotional* impact of these possible disasters depend also on other factors, including the family emotional climate and how the family interacts or communicates about them.

There was no evidence from the study families that the threat of nuclear war contributed to a "sense of futurelessness." On the contrary, all the teenagers were quite concerned with future plans, including college and careers after college. It may, however, contribute, as one of the many complex factors, to today's young people's increasing indifference to public affairs and issues of the larger world (Oreskes, 1990).

It might be argued that because of likely total annihilation, nuclear war is qualitatively different from other disasters; this, however, seemed too abstract to have an impact on the mental health of subject families. The whole world may be on a course of self-destruction from nuclear or environmental devastation. In my view, however, this is not a *mental health* issue (unless that term be synonymous with *psychological*). I do believe that nuclear war and environmental degradation threaten our existence, and I will address family therapists/researchers' potential contributions to survival in the final section of this chapter on "Advocacy."

Interest: Salience

Nuclear war had low salience for most subject families. They were more concerned with jobs, school, family, and social life. Interest in earthquakes peaked immediately following the Loma Prieta earthquake, and that passed within a few months. Although most people acknowledged, when asked, that the consequences of nuclear war, earthquakes, and environmental degradation would be devastating, the concepts seem so remote from daily lives that they are of low salience. People are concerned with matters that personally interest them, that directly influence them, and over which they feel they have some sense of control (sense of efficacy).

Our findings support Fiske's observation that, " . . . although people certainly report concern when asked, the issue (of nuclear war) simply is not emotionally central for most people most of the time" (Fiske, 1987).

Ornstein, prominent child psychoanalyst, has stated, " . . . most families and children I see in my practice are thoroughly preoccupied with their problems relating to daily living: school performance, financial and marital problems, drug abuse, social relationships, peer acceptance, etc. . . . To be politically alert, to care about water and air pollution, the arms race and the size of the national budget deficit is a luxury—available to those whose daily lives are in relatively good order" (A. Ornstein, personal communication, 1988). This last observation, however, has been questioned by researchers (Ardila, 1986).

There are important reasons why many families (not just clinical families) do not discuss nuclear war, but the reasons may lie more with the nature of the particular family than with the horrors of the subject. Similarly, families see the potential destruction of the environment as abstractly important, but, as with nuclear war and earthquakes, it has low priority in their daily lives.

The two families for whom nuclear war and environmental issues had high salience were not distinguished from the low-salience families in terms of overall family functioning or communication style. This would suggest that other factors, for example, their internal family dynamics, might be more relevant in accounting for the difference.

Common Denominators

Although there are magnitudes of differences in the consequences of a general nuclear war, a large earthquake, and environmental deterioration, there are also parallels in how the subject families perceived and responded to the threats of their occurrences. The Loma Prieta earthquake frightened millions of people, including most members of the research families. Initially it was personal, immediate, and concrete, and some families took immediate preventive action for the next one. But there was little reinforcement, and memories of the earthquake faded.[9]

Most families and their members have taken very little action about nuclear war, earthquakes, or the environment. They seemed as unconcerned (with a few exceptions) about the *inevitability* of another 7.0 or larger earthquake in the San Francisco Bay area as they are about the possibility of nuclear war or environmental destruction.

Feelings: Denial

In discussing the threat of nuclear war or damage to the environment, I have not used the term *denial* or the related concept, *psychic numbing*. These concepts are complex, are often highly inferential, and may be pejorative; reliability is, therefore, difficult to establish. They are often used with a connotation of pathology (not necessarily intended by the originator of the term psychic numbing [Lifton, 1990]), which I have tried to avoid.

Family members, when asked, often expressed their feelings about nuclear war. Sometimes comments were blandly stated, and the meaning of this blandness is subject to differing interpretations. I view it as more related to the remoteness of the topic rather than to (pathological) denial. The insidious effects of environmental degradation may also be regarded as too remote by most people. The concept of denial, however, may be more relevant to describe family and individual reactions to earthquakes. Most of the study families did not appear bothered by seismologists' predictions that a major earthquake in the next 30 years is a virtual certainty. In this case, people are clearly excluding a part of their own immediate reality—no less than a denying alcoholic—and this could have dangerous consequences.[10]

Whatever the appropriate label, however, there is a middle ground. Constant focus on the horrors of nuclear war or on the effects of a major earthquake could paralyze people in their day-to-day living. Paying no attention whatsoever to earthquake preparedness (leaving aside nuclear war) could be damaging to people's health.

Involvement

There were common themes among the nonactivist families: lack of concern, low interest, lower sense of efficacy than in activist families. Also, families were not consistent in their activity levels across the three topics of nuclear war, earthquakes, and the environment. The reasons given, however, for noninvolvement in the first (pre-earthquake, MRI) interview and in the second (postearthquake) interview were fairly consistent. That is, they were similar over a two-year time interval.

Paul and Anne Ehrlich asked: "Why isn't everyone as scared as we are [about the population explosion]?" (Ehrlich & Ehrlich, 1990, p. 22). They suggest an answer: "People are not scared because they evolved biologically and culturally to respond to short-term 'fires' and to tune out long term 'trends' over which they had no control." This speculation is quite consistent with our findings.

CONCLUSIONS FROM RESEARCH

The findings from this project suggest that the level of psychological functioning of the study families and their members is not significantly affected by the threat of nuclear war or by predictions of major earthquakes or of irreversible, catastrophic environmental destruction. These threats have low salience, and their remoteness for most families is more relevant in explaining families' lack of interest than is a framework of psychopathology. The data suggest that how families cope with these external stressors appears to be more influenced by their internal family interactional and personal style and emotional climate than by the nature of the stressors in themselves. This is the case regardless of the enormity of the consequences of nuclear war and other forms of environmental destruction and even though our theories about psychopathology might suggest that families *ought* to be more distressed.

*   *   *

ADVOCACY IMPLICATIONS FOR FAMILY THERAPISTS AND RESEARCHERS

These impressions lead me, as a concerned citizen, to speculate on how to identify those family characteristics that allow families to be accessible to influence. The aim of such knowledge is to be effective in persuading more families and their members to become involved in efforts to prevent the continuing deterioration of our environment.

I shall therefore shift roles from that of researcher to that of advocate. In the real world, there is of course overlap. Clinicians and researchers are never completely neutral observers: Their attitudes and values do influence their clients and their own interpretations of data. And advocates have explicit or implicit frameworks for explaining the phenomena they want to influence. I believe, however, that it is useful and ethical, at least conceptually, to maintain this distinction.

Therapists' special area of competence is in bringing about change in people's thinking, feeling, and behavior—at a personal level. The mental health status of families and individuals, the framework of psychopathology, and the functional/dysfunctional level of families may not be relevant, however, in explaining their interest or lack of interest in nuclear war, earthquakes, and the environment. But their feelings and attitudes *are* relevant. Therapists, because of their particular qualifications, are potentially in a unique and strong position to influence people to become motivated to change their attitudes and behavior about the broader environment and to become more involved. Such changes are independent of mental health issues. As previously stated, I believe that the arena to achieve such changes belongs outside the therapy room.

The results of this study indicated that families, for the most part, are relatively unconcerned with the stressors we investigated: the threats of nuclear war, of destructive earthquakes, and of environmental degradation. These are simply low-priority items. Understanding the processes that families use to ignore or "inattend" to these threats may, however, be useful for us as advocates, to develop methods of helping families overcome the resulting inertia and indifference and of motivating them to change. Families are telling us what *won't* work; by appropriate investigation, we can learn from them what *will* work.

Earthquakes are not as abstract or remote as nuclear war, and they are not as obscure or as insidious as environmental change; but, despite this group's generally high level of functioning, most people were not taking appropriate measures to press local and state governments to secure dangerous areas, such as toxic chemical sites, or to strengthen vulnerable overpasses, schools, and hospitals; nor were they doing much of what should be done at home for earthquake preparedness. Some of the principal reasons given were: It's inconvenient; it won't happen to me; the odds are against it; there are dangers everywhere; it's too expensive; it would require major changes in social, economic, and political priorities.

Likewise, most families interviewed in this project do not have a sense of urgency about the accelerating pace of destruction of the environment and are quite comfortable with their own personal lives. Many people stated that they needed more evidence before they would consider becoming involved. The typical responses given to "how to get you more involved in environmental issues" are disheartening.

One mother said: I may be the ostrich of my town, but I really don't think much about these matters.

A 19-year-old girl, quite active in her community: We are [too] busy with our lives, we live full lives.

The members of these families are quite intelligent, highly educated, and highly achievement oriented and live in an affluent, politically sophisticated community. Many are active in local community affairs, and they vote and write occasional political letters. If *this* group is not, in the Ehrlichs' words, as "scared as we are," what about all the others? Yet their comments paradoxically contain *encouraging* information. By articulating their reasons for noninvolvement, these families are thereby implicitly and sometimes explicitly suggesting ways they *could* be motivated to change and how they *could* become more involved.

As agents of change, therapists can influence families and individuals to become more involved in environmental issues, but to do so we must be willing to explore approaches that for most of us are nontraditional. This requires a shift from our roles as professionals helping patients and clients who come to us with personal "illness" or family "problems." With the shift from a psychotherapy framework, we would be attempting to bring about change by using our skills in the social and political arenas. As concerned citizens, we would become "applied" family therapists.

Some therapists, as concerned citizens, have transferred skills used in the consultation room into the community by, for example, participating in organizations such as Physicians for Social Responsibility and Psychologists for Social Responsibility and in using educational approaches. Others have been meeting with groups of families and parents in schools, churches, and community centers, encouraging them to express their concerns about nuclear war (DeMuth, 1990; Reusser & Murphy, 1990). I shall suggest some additional areas in which researchers and therapists might focus their efforts.

We need to study a larger, more heterogeneous group of uninvolved families than only white upper-middle-class Americans. We do not know whether research findings based on one socioeconomic group can be generalized to others.

Additional families who already *are* active should be studied. What has contributed to their placing environmental issues at high priority? (This would be parallel to studying "healthy" families, rather than focusing exclusively on psychopathology [Riskin, 1982]). Members of established antinuclear and environmental organizations could profitably be interviewed with their families: What contributes to their feeling efficacious, being concerned and active? I think it is clearer why families are *not* scared than why the Ehrlichs *are*. People like the Ehrlichs should be interviewed to find out what makes it possible for them to allow themselves to "feel scared." Further, we must consider how knowledge about activists can be translated into useful information for motivating nonactive families.

Therapist/researcher-advocates might meet with nonactivist therapists, to learn why so many are indifferent or unwilling to become more involved. It may be for reasons similar to those given by the uninvolved families of this study or for other reasons, for example, financial ones or discomfort and uncertainty about community reactions. Perhaps some uninvolved therapists can be influenced to become more active, and a wider professional audience than those of you who read this book can be motivated toward increased involvement. Otherwise, we continue to do more of the same, "preaching to the choir."

The following comments recently appeared in the *New York Times:* "The Republican National Committee regularly assembles demographically balanced groups of voters to probe their feelings about politics. Mr. Atwater [Chairman, R.N.C.] sits watching behind a one-way glass" (Toner, 1990). If politicians can use psychological insights about change to mold public opinion, why shouldn't we? Therapist advocates might do well to learn what techniques market researchers use to study how to influence people to change, especially their use of ad hoc groups assembled to discuss their thinking and feelings about a specific topic (focus groups). Market research provides information to the mass communications networks, which then becomes translated into advertising and even the content of major television programs, powerfully affecting peoples' feelings, beliefs, and actions. As therapists, we might not find their methods of influence desirable, especially as they use their techniques intentionally to "manipulate" their customers. Therapists traditionally prefer techniques that encourage people to take control of their own lives in ways that would be growth producing. How much more important, then, that we learn how to apply persuasive techniques to assist others in ways that could not only further peoples' personal lives, but also further their continued growth and development within this healthy planet. If a goal of therapist/researcher-advocates is to change people's attitudes and behavior through reaching wider audiences and successfully influencing them to become more involved in environmental matters, collaboration with market researchers may be worth exploring.

Therapist/researcher-advocates could also use their clinical skills in overcoming resistance to change by working as consultants to environmental organizations, offering suggestions to their publicity departments on effective means of educating and influencing families, perhaps through articles in their periodicals or in their public service advertisements. In the present research, for example, families often used vivid imagery in describing their feelings and attitudes toward the environment, and the language they used might well suggest how a larger audience could be influenced through appropriately targeted advertisements.

I believe that family therapist/researcher-advocates should use their special skills to learn how to overcome families' lack of interest and passivity and to understand more about those factors that enable some families and their members to be active. Such investigation, based on psychological principles, need not, however, depend on a framework of *mental health* or *psychopathology*. With increased knowledge, as *applied family therapists* working in the community, we shall be in a stronger position to stimulate families' interest and influence them to become active participants in the effort to preserve our environment.

I should like to close with comments from two of the research families that offer both advice and encouragement for "applied" therapists:

Interviewer: What could an activist organization that advocates your points of view about nuclear weapons do to try to get you more involved?

Father: They'd want to raise our level of concern.

Daughter (age 13): (Overlaps) . . . Telling us, telling us what it does.

Mother: What? What does?

Daughter: What damage.

Son (age 8): Telling us how terrible it is.

Daughter: Yeah.

Father: Well, that would . . .

Daughter: (overlaps) Raise our level of anxiety.

Father: (continues) . . . raise our level of interest. However, if they really want to get us hooked, they would have to indicate how, uh, participating could be effective.

Mother: Yeah, I agree with that.

Another Father: (talking with his family [wife, son age 17, and son age 15] about becoming more involved in environmental issues) When I was my boys' age I used to be able to go up in the mountains and drink out of any stream and have wonderful fresh water that I could just dip with a cup, and now, of course . . . we have to carry a little pump. So we've adapted, but that to me is a real loss. I miss that freedom of being able to just drink out of the waters . . .

Interviewer: For you that was tangible.

Father: Very tangible. Seeing my boys not have a freedom that I had . . . moves me at a deep inner level, and I wanna do, do that much, anyway.

NOTES

1. I am including a detailed account of the research method. I believe strongly that it is important to document the empirical base on which the Results and Discussion are based, particularly in a research arena so emotionally charged as this one is.
2. The inclusion of this question was the first fortuitous event. It was included as a control for later questions on nuclear war. After the Loma Prieta earthquake, it became the *pre-earthquake* baseline question.
3. The ratings on this questionnaire were done independently by me and a researcher who was previously totally unfamiliar with the project. Interrater reliability was satisfactory; differences were resolved by discussion.
4. There is a methodological pitfall in that I could be selectively choosing those examples that support my own biases and ignoring the ones that are contrary to them. I have attempted to guard against this.
5. I use the term *interest* as a general heading because it is a more neutral term than *acknowledgment* and the related term *denial*, which might imply pathology.
6. These views were epitomized by a scientist and colleague of mine: "I'd need to be convinced that my grandchildren would be wearing gas masks."
7. I believe this observation holds for the short-term. Over the long-term of several decades, the reciprocal interactive effects may or may not be more nearly equal. Such determination would require a long-term longitudinal study.
8. Many people who grew up in the Great Depression of the 1930s were profoundly affected in their psychological development and in their view of the world. This does not necessarily imply, however, that the Depression had a psychopathological effect

(although for some vulnerable individuals it may well have contributed to such effects).

9. Quite similar to the findings on the research families, comments and references in the wider community to the Loma Prieta earthquake faded within a few months. On December 31, 1989, 2 ½ months after the earthquake, the Sunday *San Jose Mercury News* (cir. 320,000) published a 16-page supplement on the Hayward fault, a major earthquake fault that runs through many communities on the east side of the San Francisco Bay, with a total population of over 2 million people (*San Jose Mercury News*, 1989). The supplement stated that seismologists are predicting that there is a 50% chance of 7.0 (Richter scale) or larger earthquake happening at *any* time in the next 30 years along the Hayward fault. It was estimated that thousands of people would die immediately, that hundreds of thousands would be seriously injured, and that devastation would be widespread. The tremendous risk to vulnerable office buildings, hospitals, schools, freeways, and overpasses was explicitly and graphically portrayed. Details were presented about preventive measures that could and should be done as soon as possible. Since that supplement appeared, I have not heard *any* unsolicited comments from clients, friends, or relatives who live along the Hayward fault about the fault's enormous, potentially devastating power or even any mention of the existence of the fault itself. In the spring of 1990, there was a series of minor earthquakes near, but not on, the Hayward fault. For a few weeks, the media gave some attention to earthquake preparedness, but once again, interest quickly dissipated. As is generally the case when people are faced with unpleasant or painful experiences that are not reinforced, earthquakes had lost much salience by the time the article appeared. This observation closely parallels the findings on the effects of the television movie about nuclear war, *The Day After* (French & Van Hoorn, 1986).

10. This opinion, of course, could simply be viewed as pejorative because of a "bias" of mine, since I am quite fearful of the possibility of earthquakes.

BIBLIOGRAPHY

Ardilla, R. (1986). The psychological impact of the nuclear threat on the Third World: The case of Colombia. *International Journal of Mental Health, 15* (1–3), 162–171.

Coles, R. (1985, Dec. 8). Children and the bomb. *New York Times Magazine*, p. 36.

DeMuth, D. H. (1990). Some implications of the threat of nuclear war for families and family therapists. In M. P. Mirkin (Ed.), *The social and political contexts of family therapy* (pp. 355–382). Boston: Allyn & Bacon.

Ehrlich, P., & Ehrlich, A. (1990). The population explosion: Why isn't everyone as scared as we are? *Americus Journal*, Winter, 1990, pp. 22–29.

Escalona, S. (1982). Growing up with the threat of nuclear war: Some indirect effects on personality development. *American Journal of Orthopsychiatry, 52,* 600–608.

Fiske, S. T. (1987). People's reactions to nuclear war: Implications for psychologists. *American Psychologist, 42,* 207–217.

Forrest, K., & Warrick, R. (1989, March). *Market research*. Panel discussion at Annual Meeting of Physicians for Social Responsibility, Palo Alto, CA.

Frank, J. D. (1986). Psychological responses to the threat of nuclear annihilation. *International Journal of Mental Health, 15* (1–3), 65–71.

French, P., & Van Hoorn, J. (1986). Half a nation saw nuclear war and nobody blinked? A reassessment of the impact of *The Day After* in terms of a theoretical chain of causality. *International Journal of Mental Health, 15* (1–3), 276–297.

Gough, H. G. (1987). *CPI: California Psychological Inventory, Administrator's Guide.* Palo Alto: Consulting Psychologists Press.

Gough, H. G. (1988). Personal communication.

Greenwald, D. S., & Zeitlin, S. J. (1987). *No reason to talk about it: Families confront the nuclear taboo.* New York: Norton.

Hesse, P. (1986). Children's and adolescents' fears of nuclear war: Is our sense of the future disappearing? *International Journal of Mental Health, 15*(1–3), 93–113.

Hill, R. (1949). *Families under stress.* New York: Harper & Row.

Lifton, R. (1990). The genocidal mentality. *Tikkun, 5*(3), 29–32.

Locatelli, M. G., & Holt, R. R. (1986). Anti-nuclear activism, psychic numbing, and mental health. *International Journal of Mental Health, 15* (1–3), 143–161.

Mack, J. E. (1986). Approaching the nuclear threat in clinical work with children and their families. In B. B. Gould, S. Moon, & J. Van Hoorn (Eds.), *Growing up scared? The psychological effect of the nuclear threat on children* (pp. 25–38). Berkeley, CA: Open Books.

Marciano, T. D., & Sussman, M. B. (Eds.) (1986). Families and the prospect of nuclear attack/holocaust [Special Issue]. *Marriage and Family Review, 10*(2).

McCubbin, H., Larsen, A., & Olson, D. (1982). *F-COPES.* St. Paul: Family Social Science, University of Minnesota.

Olson, D., Portner, J., & Lavee, Y. (1985). *FACES III.* St. Paul: Family Social Science, University of Minnesota.

Ornstein, A. (1988). Personal communication.

Oreskes, M. (1990, June 28). Profiles of today's youths: Many just don't seem to care. *The New York Times,* A1.

Reusser, W., & Murphy, B. C. (1990). Family therapy in the nuclear age: From clinical to global. In M. P. Mirkin (Ed.), *The social and political contexts of family therapy* (pp. 395–407). Boston: Allyn & Bacon.

Riskin, J. (1982). Research on "non-labeled" families: A longitudinal study. In F. Walsh (Ed.), *Normal family Processes* (pp. 67–93). New York: Guilford.

Riskin, J. (1983). *Family interaction scales.* Unpublished manuscript.

Riskin, J. (1988, April). *Family interaction, stress and nuclear war.* Paper presented at Symposium: Growing Up in the Nuclear Age, Palo Alto, CA.

San Jose Mercury News (Dec. 31, 1989). We are not prepared: Special Section.

Schwebel, M. (Ed.) (1986). Mental health implications of life in the nuclear age. *International Journal of Mental Health, 15* (1–3).

Solantaus, T., Chivian, E., Vartanyan, M., & Chivian, S. (Eds.) (1985). Impact of the threat of nuclear war on children and adolescents. *Proceedings of an International Research Symposium.* Helsinki-Espoo, Finland. Boston: IPPNW.

Toner, R. (1990, March 19). The trouble with politics: Running vs. governing. *The New York Times,* 1.

Zur, O. (1990). On nuclear attitudes and psychic numbing: Overview and critique. *Contemporary Social Psychology, 14*(2), 96–119.

Chapter 7

The Family Interviewing Project: A Group of Clinicians Looks at Family Reactions to the Threat of Nuclear War

Donna Hilleboe DeMuth

Wherever one decides to draw the line between the subjective and the objective, it is clear that we don't stand outside creation like gods, with the power to describe the world with perfect objectivity. It is not just that we affect what we observe by the very act of observation; the world is filtered through our senses, and the information is processed and sorted into patterns by our brains. We only see light in a tiny band of the electromagnetic system.
——*George Johnson* In the Palaces of Memory
(quoted in Noted With Pleasure (1991). The New York Times Book Review, p. 39)

The point of becoming an amateur scientist is not to compete with professionals on their own turf, but to use a symbolic discipline to extend mental skills and to create order in consciousness. On that level, amateur scholarship can hold its own and can be even more effective than its professional counterpart.
—*Mihalyi Csikszentmihalyi (1990).* Flow: The Psychology of Optimal Experience, *p. 141*

This is the story of my work with a group of overly busy therapists who cared about the state of the world, who felt powerless in the political process, and who decided to band together to use their professional skills to understand more about how "normal" families coped with the same dilemma. It is also the story of 30 families who honored our group by letting us observe what happened when they talked together about nuclear war and by letting us study the impact of that discussion on them.

I will tell both stories in the same chapter, reflecting our group's commitment to integrating the research task with its own process. I will also write in a personal style. I am uncomfortable taking a purely academic stance in regard to issues that

I know may make it impossible for my grandchildren to live out their lives on this earth. I cannot simply observe from a distance the possibility that our planet may not survive its technological assaults. The so-called clear logic of "masculine thought," in Ruddick's terms (1989), does not seem complex enough for me to approach a subject of such impact. I will therefore link the professional focus with the personal and infuse it with my own anecdotal, more traditionally "feminine" style.

Furthermore, the work of Maturana (1991), Steier (1991), Jorgenson (1991), and other constructivists convinces me that, similar to psychotherapy, research is a circular, reflective procedure in which researchers themselves must always be seen as part of the field being studied. We cannot ignore our own impact as we attempt to make sense of the facts we collect.

It is my hope that our work will inspire other clinicians to use their skills to help understand how families deal with threats of planetary annihilation. I hope that the ups and downs of our group can serve others both as encouragement and as warning.

I want to emphasize that as research team members we were facing the same issues as were the families we studied. In some important ways, our processes replicated those of the families. The systems were different, of course, and the parallels are not exact. The team, however, became somewhat like a family as we worked together with a common purpose and grew close to one another. We developed our own myths and rituals and our own rules for inclusion. We have a history and anniversaries and losses.

In the first part of this Chapter, I will describe the group, review our history, and use a developmental framework to understand our process.

In the second part, I will describe briefly the methodology of the final research design, report on its findings, and suggest some areas for further study.

In the third part, I will comment on some of the similarities and differences in how both the group and the families managed the task of focusing on issues of global survival.

THE STORY OF THE RESEARCH GROUP[1]

Beginnings

The Family Interviewing Project officially began in the spring of 1985, through my separate conversations with two friends, Joe Melnick and Kathleen Sullivan. We were enraged and terrified about the mounting nuclear tension between the United States and the U.S.S.R. We were also cynical about traditional ways of effecting social and political change.

All three of us were dedicated and experienced therapists and were trying to manage very busy practices. We were political liberals and had had a history of activism, much of which had been latent since our post-Vietnam burnout. No one was comfortable with political inactivity; we felt guilty a great deal of the time but did not know what to do about that guilt. We were attracted to a research project because it gave us a way to integrate our professional lives with our serious concerns for the survival of the planet.

At first, I was the only one knowledgeable in the psychology of nuclear concerns. I had done a great deal of reading and, through the American Family Therapy Academy, had made contact with other therapists who were interested in how families dealt with threats to global survival. I had begun to offer educational programs to parents and professionals concerned about *children's* fear of nuclear war.

At that time, there were no published studies of the ways in which families were coping with the challenge of living under a nuclear Sword of Damocles. We became interested in the work of David Greenwald, Wendy Foreman, Jon Reusser, and Steve Zeitlin, who were beginning to interview volunteer families, looking at the barriers to communication that they believed might exist between parents and children as they talked together about nuclear war.

On the first sunny day in May, Steve came to Portland, Maine, to present his work to a group of 25 of our colleagues. There was silence in the audience as we viewed his videotapes of families discussing nuclear war together. Some of us had tears in our eyes. Joe Melnick spoke for the group: "I don't want to face the feelings I have right now."

Immediately a central issue emerged for us. It was a dilemma that each of us had been facing alone and that, ultimately, we would ask our families to face. How could we deal with such intensely evocative material? We wanted to learn. Given these feelings, however, how could we possibly consider ourselves capable of doing credible research? How could we work without becoming overwhelmed or, at the least, biased by these feelings?

Our first task then was to form a group and to learn to manage the feelings effectively. We began by developing a trusting climate and continued to consider the supportive aspects of the group to be as important as the work to be done.

Twelve of us decided to continue looking at the issues that Steve had raised. We were excited and energized at the prospect of interviewing families in Maine. We hoped in that way to develop a research question that we could later explore in a more systematic fashion.

We also experienced anxiety, which emerged immediately in our concerns for the practical aspects of the work. In addition to constraints of time, there were also major organizational problems ahead of us. Grant writing and data collecting were foreign to most of us. We had no funds. Only four of us had done any recent research, and only four were experienced family interviewers. Many of us felt inadequate to the task and would continue to feel this way from time to time through the life of the project.

We also felt exposed to the community. We lived and practiced our profession in the small world of southern Maine. Our work would be critiqued, both politically and professionally, in an open system. We would also, as it turned out, find that we had invaluable support from this same community, support that often emerged at the times when it was truly needed.

Our First Pitfalls and Recovery

Perhaps our decision to begin the work by listening to family discussions rather than by collecting "objective" data came because, as clinicians, we felt most comfortable with person-to-person contact. By starting this way, however, we immediately faced a challenge that affected the entire life of the project. To our surprise, we had difficulty making arrangements with friends and colleagues to interview them with their families. They expressed fear that their children would become too upset. Some were less direct and simply didn't call back. One parent asked if we would have psychiatric backup available should it be needed. One member of a professional group we approached feared that our discussions might stimulate suicidal wishes in adolescents.

Our own anxieties multiplied. We fantasized about malpractice suits and the loss of professional credibility. We had become consumed by the realities of the very question we were interested in: Why is it that families avoid discussions about nuclear issues?

After several meetings in which scheduled families did not show up for interviews, we felt stuck. We were more conscious of our fatigue. Some members dropped out. We could not focus on the next task.

There was a breakthrough, of course, the first of many such cycles of paralysis and renewal that ensued.

Denis Noonan was the catalyzer. He led us to a deeper level of personal exploration before we shifted back to task. He asked us to say out loud to one another the questions that we had been afraid to ask the families we would be seeing: Would I be burned up? Would I be with my children when it happened? Would there be anything but scorched earth for them to live in?

Even as I write, six years later, I can feel the immediacy of the terror we had been skirting. As Macy (1981, 1983) had suggested, facing it together made it less terrifying. This simple and profound concept never left us; as we developed our work, we bonded in a unique way. For many of us, it was the first time that we had talked to anyone else in depth about the personal reality of living in the face of nuclear threats. For all of us, the sharing not only reduced the terror, but also gave us a stronger sense of purpose and some clues about ways to proceed.

The next step was both to solidify our own sense of competence as interviewers and to look further into our own resistance. We agreed to interview each others' families, using co-facilitators for support, with other group members observing behind the one-way mirror. Not surprisingly, even we, who were highly motivated, found it difficult to get to the interviews. We forgot our own appointments. Our children came reluctantly and either did not open their mouths or else made nasty comments. We argued with our spouses before, after, and during interviews.

Thus, our own experience was validating what we had known as clinicians and what we were beginning to learn as researchers. One way that individuals and families cope with the ongoing, intractable presence of the threat of major future disaster is by focusing their lives on the immediate and manageable

(DeMuth, 1990; Kanofsky, 1989). Any disturbance to that coping mechanism is experienced as disruptive and may be resisted even when a conscious attempt to face the difficult reality is present.

We had other challenges ahead. As interviewers, we had to learn how to subdue our clinical impulses to intervene when distress surfaced within the family. We had to learn not to interrupt the flow of the family's interactions to let members help each other to express their feelings. We had to learn not to cry when children talked poignantly about their fears of the bomb's destructiveness.[2] We had to learn, as we went along, to think more clearly and critically about what we observed. We practiced using factual data to back up our observations.

Despite these challenges, or perhaps because of them, the experiences of working together, alternating as subjects, as interviewers, and as observers, soon made it clear that we were indeed a working team as well as a support group.

Our group's beginning mirrored the stages of the despair/empowerment cycle (DeMuth, 1990) (Fig. 7-1). The cycle continued to repeat itself in varying forms through the life of the project. Understanding this was extremely helpful to us as we persisted in the work.

As individuals, we had moved out of our own sense of helplessness by surfacing our concerns for the world and joining together as a working group. We quickly moved back to paralysis when our anxieties mounted and with the first discouragements. Denis' group intervention moved us deeply into the feelings/connection phase of cycle, and the release of our energy was profound, lasting for well over a year.

Figure 7-1   The Despair/Empowerment Cycle

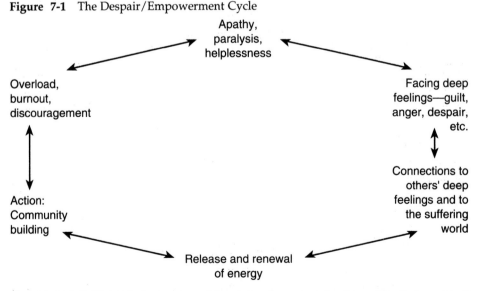

From DeMuth, D. H. (1990). Some aspects of threat of nuclear war on families and family therapists. In M. P. Mirkin (Ed.), *The political and social contexts of family therapy*, p. 377. Boston: Allyn & Bacon.

Developing a Research Design[3]

During the year 1986–1987, we continued to build community, work on tasks, and develop skills. It was a time of high energy and cohesion for the group. This was also a year in which we had considerable reinforcement from our supporters and were asked to speak frequently about our project to the community.

During this lengthy "high" phase, we also mastered the literature of nuclear psychology, developed our research questions, and created an interview format, which we tried out on eight families of friends and colleagues.

As our thinking progressed, we became more curious about the major resistances to family nuclear discussions that we had encountered. Was there any basis for the fears expressed by parents and by other professions? Was talking about nuclear war within the family really so unsafe? We were intrigued with the findings of Goldenring and Doctor (1986), Schwebel (1986), and others that most children and adolescents had serious concerns about the possibility of nuclear war but did not discuss those with their parents. We wondered why.

Our resources did not allow us to develop a research design that could focus on *why.* We decided instead to focus on the possible consequences of family discussions about nuclear war. We hoped to see if parental resistance to talking about nuclear war with their children was indeed based on a realistic appraisal of the potential impact of such discussions.

Thus, we designed a study that attempted to measure some reactions of individual family members to a structured, facilitated family discussion about nuclear war. Our hope was to interview 30 families and to use a control group of 30 families who would be given the same pre and post questionnaires but not be interviewed. We believed that, following a structured, facilitated family interview, family members would feel more connected to one another, more positive about the world situation, more apt to discuss nuclear topics, and more inclined to political/social action. We also believed that children would not experience emotional or behavioral difficulties following the interview. (See Appendix I.)

Working with—and Against—Our Biases

No discussion of the development of our thinking would be complete without mentioning some of the biases we brought from our work as clinicians, from our wish to make a social impact, and from our own group experience. I believe that the strength of our work, in fact, was in our ability to identify these biases and to challenge our own assumptions.

Family Members Would, After Talking Together, Be Motivated to Take Political Action. The first bias came from our assumption that families would experience a similar sense of relief from despair as we had after sharing together our deep concerns for the world and that this would also release their energy for social activism. Our own experience had been so profound that we literally ignored information from our reading that could have corrected this bias. For example,

Lieberman, Yalom, and Miles (1973) had already studied participants' reactions after attending encounter groups and learned that immediate *peak experiences* did not last nor necessarily result in the absence of follow-up in sustained behavior change. French and Van Hoorn (1986) had demonstrated that very few subjects changed their political or social views subsequent to viewing the TV production of *The Day After*, which had graphically depicted the horrors resulting from atomic war.[4]

We were supported in our belief system by Macy's (1981, 1983) work and that of McVeigh (1982), who postulated that nuclear despair could be relieved by the powerful connections occurring when people talked together about their concerns. We were also influenced by the fact that almost all of the families we interviewed told us immediately afterward of their positive responses to the experience. As therapists, we may have overvalued the impact of our own interactions with clients and thus assumed that research subjects would also have a powerful reaction to our intervention. This grandiosity, unfortunately, created many problems as we attempted to implement our research design.

Intergenerational Silence About Nuclear War Results in Family Dysfunction.
Another bias came naturally to us as clinicians and also reflected the current state of available knowledge in the psychology of nuclear peril (see Chapter 4). We were making assumptions from a disease model. We projected negative consequences when children experienced concern for the world and did not discuss these concerns with their parents, using the model of the dysfunctional "family secret." We were reinforced by Zeitlin's conclusions (1984) that many of the parents he observed were not able to offer children sufficient support in their concerns about nuclear war.

We conceptualized that personal and family dysfunction would result from nuclear angst, and, as clinicians, we were motivated to intervene. We saw our research, ultimately, as a way to help relieve the personal pain of families living under global tensions. Thus, we tended to overfocus, in our first family interviews, on signals of personal distress.

Fortunately, we were aided in correcting our bias by our years of experience as observing clinicians. We soon realized that our families did not appear to be dysfunctional, even when discussing such a distressing topic. We noticed that family members, as a whole, used appropriate affect, kept eye contact, and offered gestures of support to one another as they talked. We became accustomed, as we went on, to watching children talk expressively about their fears around nuclear war and then to reconstitute quickly to age-appropriate normal behavior.[5]

As we developed the operational format for the study, our basic notions began to change. Armed with newly published studies on resilience (Anthony & Cohler, 1987; Rutter, 1987), we began to have more faith that children could, with sufficient support, face extremely difficult challenges without becoming impaired. We also began to conceptualize the silence between generations more as a normal way of coping with global survival issues, which were always present in some way but easily placed in the background. The work of social psychologists, particularly Figley and McCubbin (1983) and McCubbin and Patterson (1983), came to our attention, and we realized that normal families in other circumstances of long-term stress used suppression as a survival tool. Our experience was that silence as a coping device could be relatively easily changed *when a family was ready to talk and assisted to do so.* This discovery had, I believe, a positive effect on our subsequent interviews, allowed us to relax and to enjoy the families we encountered.

The Research Interview Should Impose No Harm on the Families. Finally, our bias as clinicians and as members of a support group influenced us to design a study that, we hoped, would guarantee that there would be no subsequent harm to our subject families. Our interviewing style came to reflect a sense of the common concerns that we and our families shared. We were *all* living in an extremely difficult era and all finding it difficult, at times, to cope. Thus, as researchers, we intended not only to be benign in our interventions, but also to be quietly emphatic. In whatever way the family showed its coping style, even when at times its members violated our own personal or political code, we were learning to understand and accept differing mechanisms for psychological survival.

This clinical/ethical stance informed the interview schedule that we developed. We would move gradually with families into the experience of being exposed to questions that might elicit strong feelings. Based on the work of Schwebel (1986), the schedule used a "funnel" design. (See Appendix II.) We started with questions about the family itself, went to questions about their knowledge of current events and of nuclear issues, and led up to a provocative question about how family members would react if they learned the bomb would drop in just a few hours.

Using Macy's (1983) experiences and suggestions from the educational programs of the Brookline schools (R. Snow, personal communication, 1982), we decided to end our interviews with an emphasis on problem solving and capitalize on each family's ability to reconstitute after facing traumatic material.

It is, of course, true that by conducting this kind of interview, we were limiting the rigor of our research approach. We were weighting the possibility that we would not impose emotional damage upon family members. Our bias, not only as ethical clinicians but also as social activists, prevailed. We truly did not want to provoke powerful negative reactions. We had come to believe, from our readings and our own experience, that the family discussions would not be harmful. It is thus not surprising that the absence of any subsequent behavioral indications of harm to children was one of the most consistent findings in our small and selective sample of families.

Surviving Difficulties with Recruitment

By the fall of 1987, our research design was sound, even though too complex. We had an excellent format for interviewing, which has stood the test of time. We had honed our interviewing skills and were ready to go. It was another peak time for our energies.

The slowdown came when the subject families who had been promised by our community supporters did not materialize. We put hours of effort into recruitment and asked for help wherever we could. By the spring of 1988, however, we had interviewed only ten families. We laughed and cried at our earlier innocence.

Paradoxically the very question we were exploring—what *is* the impact of family discussion about nuclear war?—was being answered by our community as if they knew that the impact would be negative. Should we have worked on a grant application or raised funds so we could have paid families for their time and hired an assistant for recruitment calls? Did we infect the community before our own anxieties were relieved? Or, more likely, were we running counter to other norms, for example, that family members rarely came together to talk about any emotionally tinged subjects, or that Maine culture reinforces family privacy? We never were able to answer these questions but often wished that the research design had allowed us to explore them.

Nonetheless, we had recruited ten families and conducted what we believed to be ten highly interactive family interviews. Our volunteer families, most of whom had never before discussed nuclear war together, seemed able to speak freely to one another about the world's problems.

Reviewing, Revising, and Renewing

In the summer of 1988, we moved into another phase of the cycle, which again strongly tested our ability to change and grow. When we reviewed the tabulations from our first set of postquestionnaires,[6] we had to face the fact that a number of our original hypotheses were not substantiated. Three weeks after the interview, our postquestionnaires revealed that family members had not held further discussions about nuclear war, nor had they contemplated taking political action, nor did parents report feeling more competent about talking with their children about nuclear concerns.

On reviewing the data, our first impulse was to assume that our measures were inadequate. Therefore, we revised our questionnaires to be more specific and added an exercise using individual and family mandala drawings to the interview procedure.

Of greater concern to us was that our organization for collecting data had broken down and many returns were incomplete. The group itself seemed to be falling apart as well. Our spirits were low. We lost some members; we had unresolved arguments among ourselves. Several proposals to present our work at national conferences were rejected. We were no longer getting requests from the community to talk to groups nor money from our network to help with postage and supplies.

In moving out of the down cycle, new energy came from several people outside the group who joined us in significant ways. One was Robert Jay Green,[7] who affirmed that our proposal was valid. A skilled research veteran, he helped us to simplify our design. Another source of energy came from Bruce St. Thomas, a gifted art therapist, who inspired the use of individual and family drawings. In addition, Burtt and Gladys Richardson[8] volunteered to find us the families we needed for the second stage of our study.

We had been given the nudge we needed to move on.

Developmental Process

The story of the group now begins to cycle more slowly, with increasing periods of stasis, more times of discouragement, and more infrequent episodes of high energy. Our experiences of interviewing the 11 families who would become the focus for the major findings of the study (discussed later) were rich and wonderful. We were confident of our skills. The interviewed families thanked us warmly for the experience. Even children who had come reluctantly told us it had been "fun." These were our highs.

In 1988–1989, however, our group began to lose more members, and the gap was enormous. By the summer, we had to face the reality that we had no more energy for recruiting families. Therefore, our study would not be as complete as we had hoped. Even worse, our organizational skills had again broken down. We were missing major parts of our data.

What had happened? In retrospect, it is easier to piece it together; at the time, it seemed like failure. There are some simple explanations. For example, after four years, it is natural for people to run out of energy. Some of our members simply burned out, and some were ready to move on; their interests and ideas had changed. For some, the group no longer provided a necessary supportive function. In addition, cold war tensions had begun to relax, and the pressure of concern about nuclear issues had lessened for many. The fire had run down.

As I have been writing, however, I have gained new understanding of the loss of our members. I now see that a group such as ours was necessarily a temporary system. It served an extremely important function in giving us a safe place in which to make a transition to a new phase of development (Kegan, 1982). Kegan sees development of self as a circular process of moving from phases that primarily deal with individual concerns to phases that deal with concern for others. He names, as an important life-cycle stage, the move from the institutional self, concerned with competence and individuation, to an interindividual self, concerned with developing a mature sense of intimacy with the outer world.

It now strikes me that most members of our group had clearly won their stripes in the institutional phase as competent and recognized professionals and were ready to move into a new relationship with the world. Unknowingly, we aided in the transition by creating, in Kegan's terms, a holding environment: a group whose function was, in part, to prepare its members to move into a new form of development. Some members left, I believe, because they truly were not ready for that transition; others left because they no longer needed the holding environment. Not surprisingly, several went on to develop social action projects of their own.

A clue that validates this way of understanding the group's process came from Kathleen, who had been one of our core members. After leaving the team, she developed a creative program for empowering children to work together on environmental issues. "I don't feel lonely any more," she said. She had found community and no longer saw herself as alone in a dangerous world. I believe this was true for many of us, whether we stayed with the group or moved on.

Coming to the End

As we faced the task of pulling together the data from questionnaires, drawings, and interview notes from our second set of families, I reluctantly agreed to take leadership. I find handling details difficult and was fearful that I could not learn how to keep track of the masses of data we had accumulated. It seemed crucial to me, however, that if our task was to move to completion, someone had to take charge.[9]

Since that time, the work has been tedious. Still there have been times of great satisfaction as we have come together, seen some connections, and realized how much we have learned. It may be that despite our inexperience, our slowness, our focus on our own process, our inefficiency, and our grandiosity; despite our small sample; despite all the questions we wished we had asked and the ones that we did ask that turned out to be unproductive; and despite the paper we wasted on revising and the time wasted on telephone calls that got us nowhere, it may be that we have come through. We have used our gifts as clinicians and as explorers to illuminate in a small way the issues that families face in this terrible and perilous age. We have some ideas from our work that we can offer to other researchers who will have more logistical resources and can build on our pioneering efforts. We have a sounder base for the ideas we will offer to our community.

Most of all, we have learned a great deal about how to live in the constant uncertainty of our global future. We have extended our practices beyond the walls of our clinical offices and in doing so, I believe, have bridged a little of the gap between studying and healing that we had artificially imposed on ourselves.

METHODOLOGY AND FINDINGS

This section will focus on what we learned from the second subset of our research sample. As mentioned earlier, our data are more complete for these 11 families and, we believe, more relevant to our research questions.

Methodology (See Appendix I)

How Were the Families Recruited? Burtt and Gladys Richardson, a pediatrician and pediatric educator in a small town near Augusta, Maine, sent a letter to 50 parents of their 10- to 13-year-old-patients, describing the research project and asking for volunteers. When the letter elicited no response, both Burtt and Gladys made standardized phone calls to parents urging them to volunteer. When asked, almost all of the parents in the study indicated that they had come because of the influence of Burtt and Gladys.

What Procedures Did We Use? The interviews were conducted in the Richardsons' comfortable offices, which were familiar to the families. To begin, family members were greeted by the interviewer and given a written questionnaire to fill out.[10] The interviews followed, taking approximately $1\frac{1}{2}$ hours. During the session, each interviewer filled out a standardized form to record content of family discussion and also rated, on a standardized form, the family's interaction while drawing together.

Three weeks later, postquestionnaires similar to the prequestionnaires were sent to the parents of these families.[11] Seven responses were received. One year later, two of us telephoned the parents of all the families for a brief follow-up. We also talked with Burtt and Gladys to learn their impressions of the families' reactions subsequent to our interviews.

What Were the Families Like? Given the fact that we had made many contacts with families who had expressed some interest in our work but had declined to be interviewed, we were interested in the kinds of families who were actually willing to volunteer to discuss issues about nuclear war with one another.

The parents, mostly in their late thirties and early forties, described themselves as primarily middle-class and middle-of-the-road politically. They were all white and about equally Protestant and Catholic. Most had completed high school; only a few had post high school degrees. The parents reported seeing themselves as competent in their roles; they saw very few behavioral problems in their children.

From interviewer ratings of family drawings, we observed that the great majority of these families worked well together, were communicative and supportive of one another, and were also able to work independently of each other. From interview notes and from analysis of the family drawings, we noticed that most family members seemed to have a positive, optimistic outlook about life in general.

From subsections of the McMaster Family Assessment Device (Epstein, Baldwin, & Bishop, 1983), we found remarkable consistency for both parents and children. Most family members reported that they believed their families to be close and very communicative with one another.

Findings

How Did the Families Deal with the Threat of Nuclear War?

Attitudes Before the Interview. Few parents reported having been involved in the peace movement, nor had the families discussed nuclear war with one another before the interview. Many individuals believed that other family members did not know how they felt about nuclear war.

From our preinterview questionnaires, we learned that many more parents than children believed it might be too upsetting to other family members to discuss nuclear war together. Most parents, however, rated their competence to handle such discussions as "high."

Children were much more apt than their parents to report that they believed it to be "very likely" that there would be a nuclear war in their lifetime. Few people indicated that they were "very worried" about nuclear war or, indeed, about any other issue. Yet as we looked at their total scores, nuclear war rated second to a family member dying among all the concerns they faced.[12]

Attitudes During the Discussions. We did not have a standardized procedure for recording family process, but our detailed interviewing notes revealed that we thought most families seemed to be able to discuss the subject of nuclear war freely. We did not notice many of the signs of family dysfunction that Greenwald and Zeitlin (1987) had reported (e.g., parental overprotectiveness, lack of support for children's concerns, deflections, or intellectualizations). As previously mentioned, we had designed the structure of the interview in a way that we hoped would encourage healthy responses from the family.[13]

The experiences of family members drawing together also reinforced our sense of family competence. Many parents expressed surprise at the strong images drawn by their children and also reported feeling awkward in making their own drawings. Parents and children, however, seemed able to engage with an appropriate lessening of generational boundaries and showed relatively little discomfort about sharing deep feelings with each other. By opening the questions about nuclear issues privately (both in questionnaires and drawings), we had given both parents and children a chance to mobilize their own internal process before moving into intergenerational dialogue.[14]

Family Members' Reactions to Affective Material. Many family members talked movingly in response to the questions "Talk together about what you have heard about world events recently" and "What do you know about nuclear war?" We had expected only informational responses to these questions early in the interview. It was clear that most parents and children were knowledgeable about and very aware of the dangers. Typical answers here were "we could all blow up," "the politicians don't know how to solve the problems," and very frequently "I don't want to think about it," followed by a statement of great worry or concern about the future of the world.

We gathered another interesting impression in looking at our families' responses to question #7 ("Talk to one another about what you think it would be like for you if you learned that a nuclear bomb was going to be dropped in our state in a very short time."). Our notes indicated that most families were complete in their responses, many of which seemed very affect laden. Family members talked about their wishes to be together if the bomb should drop. Many had thoughts of flight, including suicidal wishes. Both adults and children produced fantasy solutions, for example, leaving on spaceships or calling together a summit of world leaders, which implied a kind of power only superheroes are capable of achieving. Some solutions were naive: such as "driving to Florida." Some members became tearful while talking or reached out to touch another family member. There was a minimal amount of joking.

Significantly, however, despite the intensity of reactions to question #7, in all cases the families were able to move on to the next question: "What ideas do you all have about how to keep a nuclear war from happening?" Their ideas focused mainly on both moral/spiritual solutions, such as increasing respect and love between different peoples, and educational ones, for example, learning more about other cultures and about alternative methods of conflict resolution. There seemed to be less hope about political solutions, although some hopes for better communication between world leaders were expressed. One child said, "Let's throw all the bombs in the ocean"; another wanted to shoot them to the moon. A few slightly more sophisticated plans for world disarmament were proposed, mostly by adults.

Family members' statements, according to our notes, on the whole were positive. Only two families continued to express despair. All were able to work together effectively to produce a family drawing about their hopes for the world.

Differences Between Verbal and Nonverbal Responses. One of our most important incidental findings, we believe, is that when we analyzed responses from *all three* instruments measuring nuclear concerns we found that each one of our twenty-nine subjects showed a significant degree of concern about global survival.[15] Any single measure of nuclear concern would not have revealed this information.

Some family members who had expressed a low degree of concern in questionnaires or on the Goldenring and Doctor (1986) scale had created individual mandala drawings that rated very high on the anxiety scale. Other drawings, which scored relatively low on the anxiety measures, were done by family members who had expressed a high degree of concern on either the prequestionnaires or the Goldenring-Doctor scale. A dramatic example came from one family in which the preadolescent child refused to fill out any questionnaires or to talk during the interview. Her only comment was that she was not at all concerned about nuclear war. Her drawing, however, was heavily loaded with anxiety figures (Fig. 7-2). Her younger sibling, in contrast, spoke frequently and with considerable affect of his concerns and reported on the questionnaire that he felt nuclear war was highly likely to occur. He thought about it often and put nuclear war in the highest category of worry on the Goldenring-Doctor scale. His drawing, nevertheless, was rated extremely low on anxiety levels (Fig. 7-3).

It seems clear that the discrepancies between verbal and nonverbal measures of nuclear worries in our subjects support Coles' (1985, 1986) concern that investigations about global survival issues must be conducted in considerable depth to be valid. We also believe that our findings are consistent with those of Goldenring and Doctor (1986), who reported that adolescents showing the highest verbalized levels of concern about nuclear war tended to be those who functioned best, both

Figure 7-2   Individual Drawing, Family Member *N* (Age 11 Years)

socially and academically. It is possible that our young subject who talked so readily and identified his fears so clearly in words may not, in fact, have had a deep and pervasive terror of nuclear war. Because of his expressiveness, he may have received from parents enough support and reassurance to help him feel secure. Further research using nonverbal or expressive approaches would be extremely important in expanding our understanding of both individual and family ways of coping with threats of global destruction.

Homeostatic Mechanisms Mediating Nuclear Discussions. Somewhat to our surprise, we found little support for the existence of a family worry bearer, whose degree of anxiety was markedly greater than those of other family members. On the contrary, our interview notes seemed to indicate that families had a natural kind of rhythm in which members moved from statements of despair to those of hope.

We are extremely curious about this patterning and hope that other researchers may be able to understand how families make shifts that allow them to stay centered when topics of potential toxicity are brought up.

Such a balancing act may keep intense feelings in control but may also diminish the edge of anxiety that we know is necessary for action to take place (Lazarus, 1964). If the family is to be the matrix for developing social conscious-

Figure 7-3   Individual Drawing, Family Member *N* (Age 8 Years)

ness in its members, somehow its members must learn ways to unbalance safely to allow enough anxiety to emerge as a goad to action.

In one family, I observed a mother and her daughter creating a remarkable dance. Each time the mother stated her deep concern for the fate of the planet, her 13-year-old daughter countered by stating her belief in the power of the army to keep the Russians from annihilating us. When the mother finally shifted her position and revealed her belief that we were beginning to negotiate more positively with the Soviets, her daughter poured out, in a powerfully emotional statement, the degree to which she worried about the possible destruction of the world through nuclear war. It seemed that taking different steps in the dance had allowed each of them to explore ambivalence and finally to connect supportively about their concerns.

What Did the Families Report Subsequent to the Interviews?

There Were No Reported Negative Consequences.   The original question for our study had been to look at the consequences of a structured, facilitated family discussion of nuclear issues on family cohesiveness and communication and on the reported behavioral expressions of despair or anxiety among its members. From our interview notes, we saw that most family members reported positive feelings immediately after the interview. The most commonly used word to describe feelings about the experience was "good." A number of parents said "interesting." In every family, members responded that it would be a good idea for other families to talk together about nuclear war. This was true even for the families in which one or more members had expressed feelings of anxiety before or during the discussion.

Three weeks later, all seven sets of parents who returned postquestionnaires still reported that they felt positively about their experiences. There was no negative reaction. No children had any behavioral problems after the interview, and none of the parents felt that the interview had been too upsetting to any family member. Many parents felt, after the discussion, that other family members better understood their views about nuclear war.

We thought it important that, three weeks later, a significant number of parents had shifted their predictions about the likelihood of nuclear war occurring in their lifetimes from "not likely" to "very likely." We might suspect that for these subjects nuclear awareness and concern had been heightened. Their children, nevertheless, were not reported to have shown any negative behaviors.

One year later, we talked to one of the parents of all 11 families on the phone. They still had specific memories about the interview and felt positive about the experience, particularly in terms of understanding their children better.

We believe that our finding that there was no reported negative impact subsequent to our families' discussing nuclear war together, despite the high level of affect in some of their interaction, is extremely important, despite the small sample, the bias of the interview questions toward "doing no harm," and the selectivity of the subjects. This finding may be reassuring to parents as they respond to their children's concerns about global survival. Educators may also look to this finding when parents turn to them for advice about encouraging the topic of global survival to be discussed within the family.

Other researchers may want to suggest to prospective subjects that, in our study, a structured interview about nuclear war did not prove to be upsetting for 11 volunteer, self-described functional families.[16]

We believe that the structured and sequential nature of our interview format as well as the positive self-concept of our subject families and our own positive point of view were all factors that were significant in this finding. Obviously the finding needs further testing to be valid. We would like very much to have our interview schedule repeated with a larger and more representative number of families.

There Were Few Reported Positive Changes.   Three weeks subsequent to the interviews, there was no reported change in parents' feelings of family cohesion. None of the families had discussed nuclear war again, nor did any parents contemplate taking social action. Some parents did, however, feel that they better understood other family member's feelings about nuclear war.

As I mentioned earlier, it is clear that one family discussion on nuclear war in itself was not powerful enough to have a major impact on family members' attitudes or behavior.

We would like to see further studies, with more sophisticated design and measures, look at the effects on families of repeated discussions. It would also be interesting to test other ways of strengthening the discussion's impact, such as ending the discussion with support for the family to take action.

Our findings, of course, lead us to examine whether there is any value at all for families in discussing global issues together, beyond the feeling of well-being that the discussions seemed to inspire. At first glance, our study and that of Riskin (see Chapter 6) seem to suggest that there is no apparent pathological consequence for families if they do not discuss their concerns. We also suspect from the investigation of Blair (1988) that the personality traits of children may be more influential in determining their attitudes toward nuclear war than the existence of discussions with parents. We also know that many other factors beyond conversation guide families into taking political or social action. For example, many social psychologists find that children learn concepts of morality primarily by taking moral actions (Mirowsky & Ross, 1989; Oliver, 1990; Staub, 1975, 1989). Parents who model altruistic acts and encourage their children to try altruistic behavior are likely to see children develop a positive stance toward social action. Staub (1975) has found that parental warmth, modeling, and assignment of responsibility to children are more important than verbal interaction in developing an altruistic viewpoint.

I believe, however, that the not talking about global dangers may have more subtle and long-range consequences for family members. Again, Staub reminds us that the absence of speaking out against assaults to the planet is in effect a statement of support for the assaults. Oliver's (1990) study of teenagers in New Zealand indicates that their own lack of faith in activism is supported by the silence of their parents and other adults. Stevens (1982), who studied development of political attitudes in school-aged children, noted the importance of parents' offering children the cognitive tools for dealing with the complexities of the larger world, primarily through language.

I also believe that there may be another long-lasting effect from family silence on matters of global importance. In our structured family discussions, we observed family members demonstrating excellent problem-solving skills as they faced together some of the terror of nuclear war. We know from studies of resiliency in children (Anthony & Cohler, 1987; Dugan & Coles, 1990; Rutter, 1987) and from Bandura's (1977) work on efficacy that successful mastery of emotional challenges in childhood, with adult support, leads to increased competence in meeting the demands of adult life. We saw in our small study that families could both support each other and be competent in discussing how to deal with nuclear issues. I believe that children deprived of an opportunity to wrestle with world survival issues within their supportive families may lose a major opportunity to develop a positive stance toward solving the problems of survival.

Our study suggests that one discussion alone is not enough to offer either children or their parents adequate support to maintain such a positive stance, which I believe necessary to encourage activism. We need to find ways to enhance, within families and other institutions, children's sense of empowerment in relation to solving world problems.

SIMILAR PROCESSES IN TWO INTIMATE SYSTEMS

There are ways in which the findings from the families in our study parallel some of the process of our research group. It seems as if bringing global survival issues more directly into awareness may have stimulated similar coping devices in most of us.

It Was Safe to Discuss Difficult Topics

Both our research group and our families seemed able to use the connections to one another to be able to discuss the most terrifying of all topics, nuclear holocaust, without negative consequences. In addition, for the research group, there have been many positive consequences. Six years later, most of us now feel more optimistic and energetic about the possibilities of working toward a global future than we did before we started.

Similar to many of the parents in our families, talking together about nuclear war did raise our awareness and, temporarily, our anxiety. Talking also helped us to break through impasses, to face our own self-deceptions from time to time, and to free up energy for the work.

We believe that it is normal for individuals, families, and groups to have nuclear anxiety, manifested in many different ways, and also normal for them to put the anxiety aside to carry on with their lives. We found, both in ourselves and in our competent families, that this process took a natural course and could be counted on. It was another manifestation of the despair/empowerment cycle. It is again important to note that both we and our families openly knew that we had a choice about when to face the anxiety or express it and when to put it aside.

Connection in Itself Did Not Necessarily Lead to Activism

Intimacy and support were not the only ingredients in our group's developed sense of empowerment. We also had to do our work and feel reinforced in that work both from the community and from the joy of the work itself. In contrast, without a specific project to work on, the "good feelings" expressed by family members subsequent to interviews were not in themselves enough to stimulate action.

Other factors, in addition to intimacy, which we found were needed for our group to do its work included the following:

1. Clear leadership, a sense of structure, and a plan of action that was appropriate to our resources and abilities.
2. Ways to develop necessary skills, including getting outside help when necessary.
3. Stimulation and support from outside ourselves during the inevitable doldrums.
4. Developing a philosophy in which cycles of energy and withdrawal were seen as natural and low points were not viewed as indicators of failure.

I propose that some of the same factors might also be applicable for families who want to move beyond feeling overwhelmed into taking a more active position in regard to world problems.

Everyone Needed a "Parent"

This "parent" may be defined as an individual or institution seen as strong enough to offer both leadership and support as people make a choice to bring global survival issues into their consciousness. It was clear, both for our group and for our families, that impetus from a mentor outside the system had been necessary to stimulate us to deal with issues of nuclear war. For our group, the leadership had come first from pioneers in the field of nuclear psychology and then from Joe, Kathleen, and me. For the families, leadership to begin facing nuclear issues, had come from trusted medical caretakers.

Without someone to initiate and to offer support, our families had simply not talked about nuclear war before the interview. Yet in prequestionnaires, most of the parents stated that they had felt competent to do so. They demonstrated their competence once the interviews started. They had needed help to begin. Without ongoing support, they did not continue their discussions and were apparently unable to maintain their sense of empowerment.

For the research group as well, continued focus on the task required frequent reinforcement from "parental" outsiders, for technical assistance and validation of our worth. Finally, we could not complete our task until I took on a parental role in managing our business affairs, and the group became slightly more hierarchical in its structure.

Focusing on Global Issues Demands Competence

Our families defined themselves as well functioning and were viewed that way by us; our most involved group members were highly competent clinicians. We have, of course, no way of assessing whether families (or professionals) who do not see themselves as functional are less likely to engage in focusing on world problems. Exploring this question, however, would make an interesting research project.

I have already mentioned that our group process reflected the fact that many members were moving from a phase of development in which they were focused on self to one in which they were able to focus on concern for others. For our parents as well, we might speculate that their willingness to be interviewed came from a developmental shift in their willingness to look at their concerns for the world more deeply.

Like the other researchers I have mentioned, we focused on well-functioning families. Other investigations will be needed to learn how are less well developed families deal with global tensions.

A Shared World Vision Helps

Another reflection of the competence of our families to focus on world concerns came as we observed the richness and complexity of their drawings of hope

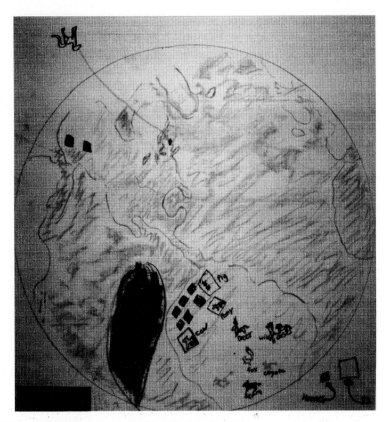

Figure 7-4   Family Drawing of Hope for the World

for the world as well as their responses to this question at the end of the family interview (Fig. 7-4). The drawings revealed beautiful themes of human connectedness, often showing physical contact between people of differing races and nations. Many families felt that people all over the world had much in common. They spoke of their belief that communication could help to straighten out misunderstandings without the use of war. Their respect for the natural beauty of the world and for the rhythms of the forces of nature was impressive. Even though not all of them were practicing a formal religious discipline, almost all displayed a belief in a benign purpose in the universe and an optimism that the world was designed in such a way that healing could take place.

As therapists, we too were joined in a common belief that human connections, communication, and understanding were powerful forces for healing, despite our superficial stance of cynicism toward our "trade." We did not all use spiritual symbols for our belief systems, but I think most of us had a deep trust in the natural world and in the essential goodness of human nature. We also believed in our group and had a shared vision of its importance. I believe that without these shared values, we would not have been able to sustain our work to the point of conclusion.

Family therapists can be discouraged about the complexities which arise when they enlarge the context of their work to a global perspective. My experience in the research group has led me to believe that we have nothing to fear if we stretch context absolutely as far as possible, to the extent of the universe, so that its goodness can be in our awareness as well as its pain.

By allowing ourselves to feel the unimaginable horror of the possibilities of our own annihilation, our group gained much more than we suffered. And much of the gain was in the restoration of hope that we experienced when we came together or when we observed our families as they came together, no matter how brief the time may have seemed.

> People have to learn to talk together so they won't want to set off missiles. The more people share a universal fear, the more hope we have.
>
> Mother of two, responding to a
> question about how nuclear war
> could be avoided.

> Knowing is terrifying
> And not knowing is terrifying
> But not knowing can kill us
> And knowing can save us.
>
> Anonymous third-grade student,
> Brookline (MA) Schools

Appendix I
Purpose and Measures

PURPOSE

The purpose of this study is to explore the impact of a structured conjoint family interview about nuclear issues, led by a trained facilitator, on

1. Individual family members' awareness and concern about nuclear issues.
2. Individual perceptions of how well other family members understand their thoughts and feelings about nuclear war.
3. Children's behavior, relative to anxiety and depression.
4. Family attitudes toward discussing this issue together.
5. Parents' perception of their own adequacy in discussing this issue with their children.
6. Parents' interest in social activism.

It is predicted that three weeks after the interview family members who have participated will report:

1. Greater awareness and concern about nuclear issues than before the interview.
2. Increased feelings of being understood by other family members relative to issues of nuclear war.

continued

Appendix I
Purpose and Measures, continued

3. Little or no change in children's behavior that might indicate anxiety or depression.
4. Having more frequent discussions about nuclear war.
5. Greater feelings of adequacy in dealing with family discussions of nuclear issues.
6. An intention to participate in a social action program promoting peace concerns.

DESCRIPTION OF INTERVIEW PROCEDURES AND MEASURES

Before being interviewed, each family member will fill out confidential questionnaires with basic demographic information. Children aged 11 years and older and parents will be given the Affective Responsiveness and General Functioning subtests of the McMaster Family Assessment Device (Epstein et al., 1985), which gives an overall assessment of the general level of family functioning. All family members aged 11 years and older will fill out selected questions from the Goldenring-Doctor Measures of Concern Scale (Goldenring & Doctor, 1986) and a series of questions about their reactions when they think about nuclear war. They will also answer questions about the frequency of family discussions about current events and about nuclear war. They will rate themselves on their level of social activism and on how well they believe other family members understand their thoughts and feelings about nuclear war. Parents will fill out a checklist of behavioral symptoms relating to anxiety or depression that any of their children may be demonstrating. They will also rate themselves in terms of their feelings of adequacy in discussing nuclear war with their children and in regard to concerns that such discussions might be too upsetting to the children.

After introductions and explanations, interviewers will conduct a standardized conjoint family interview in a familiar office setting, with all family members present (see Appendix II). The interview will include individual drawings about concern for the world and a family drawing of hope for the world. In closing, the interviewer will ask for comments about the interview, thank the family members for participation, and ask them to return a questionnaire to be mailed out in three weeks.

Three weeks later, participating family members will be asked to fill out a questionnaire reporting on their reactions subsequent to the interviews. The questionnaire will include some questions from the Horowitz Measure of Impact Scale (Horowitz, 1979).

One year later, parents will be telephoned to report on their recollections of the interview.

Appendix II
Interview Schedule

INTRODUCTION AND JOINING

1. Please make yourselves comfortable. (Rearrange seating if necessary.)
2. To parents: Please feel free to deal with the children the way you normally do and to interrupt the discussion if you have any concerns.
3. Now I would like to get to know a little about each one of you.
   To each member:
   Your name is _____ ?
   Where do you go to school? *or* Where do you work?
   How old are you? When is your birthday?
   Could you tell me one thing about yourself that you think might be interesting? (a hobby, a special interest, something you have done recently that you enjoyed)
4. In our study, we are interested in learning how families react when they talk with each other about living in the nuclear age.
5. Now I would like to ask you to begin talking together as a family about some important things. I will ask a few questions, but mostly I will be sitting back and letting you talk to one another about your thoughts and feelings. I will also be asking you to use the art material (point it out) as another way of expressing yourselves.
6. First, could you talk to each other about how you decided to join our project and come to this discussion today?
   Who first brought it up? Could you tell your family why you brought it up?
   How did the rest of you react?
   What did you think the discussion today would be like?
   Did you do anything to prepare for coming in today?

STRUCTURED QUESTIONS

1. Use your imagination to describe the earth today. Think about some of the worldwide problems and threats to human life and to nature. Select the art materials of your choice, and feel free to explore your thoughts and feelings about your concerns for the world. Anything you put down on the paper will be just fine: You will not be graded! Using the circle, draw whatever comes to your mind. After you have completed your drawing, add a title or any words that come to mind as a description of this image.
2. Now, will each of you talk to your family about your drawing? (After 5 minutes, give a time limit.)

continued

Appendix II
Interview Schedule, continued

3. Next, can you talk together some more about what you have heard about how things are going in the world today. For example, what have you seen or heard on the news that you have on your mind?
    Probes. To parents: You might ask your children what they have heard recently/what they think about what they have heard. Is there anything else that anyone has had on their minds from the news?
4. Have any of you heard about nuclear weapons? If so, what have you heard?
5. Have you ever talked to each other about nuclear war? If so, who has talked? If not, why do you think you have not?
6. Now I am going to ask you to talk together, as a family, telling your thoughts and feelings about the possibility of nuclear war happening.
    Probes. To parents: Would you like to ask the children again how they feel? Is there some reason you find it difficult to talk about this subject? Is there anyone else you think it might be easier to talk with? Is there anything else anyone would like to say to one another?
    (Be sure to continue focus on family interaction here: Do not begin to interview individual members to draw them out. If family members choose not to talk, do not press them.)
7. Next, I would like to ask you to talk to one another about what you think it would be like for you if you learned that a nuclear bomb was going to be dropped in our state in a very short time.
8. You have talked together about what it would be like if a nuclear bomb was actually dropped. Now I would like to ask you what ideas you all have about how to keep a nuclear war from happening? Please share your ideas with one another.
9. Next, will you turn to your imaginations again? Would you let yourselves imagine a world without the possibility of nuclear war? Let yourselves concentrate on whatever feelings you might have of hope for the world. Now, you may choose art materials again, and this time I will ask you to create a drawing *together*, using this sheet of paper. Any images, symbols, or colors that come to mind are just fine; use anything that will help you express your thoughts and feelings.
10. Please feel free to talk to one another as you draw. (After 10 minutes, give a reminder of remaining time.)
11. Now that you have finished, please add a title or any words that come to mind.
12. Could you now talk to each other about the drawing and what hope for the world means to you?

CLOSING

1. We are beginning to come to the end of our discussion. I'd like to ask you all how you have felt about talking to each other today about nuclear war.
2. Do you believe that it would be good for other families to talk to each other about nuclear war? Why, or why not?
3. Do you have any ideas about other questions we might have asked families in our study?
4. Would you like to hear about the results of our study? I would also be happy to meet with you again if anything else comes up that you would like to discuss.
5. In a few weeks, we will be mailing you some more questionnaires to fill out. It is really important for our study that these questionnaires be completed on time, so I hope you will be able to help us out by filling them out as soon as possible after you receive them. Please feel free to call me if you have any questions about this.
6. Before you leave, I want to thank you all very sincerely for being a part of our study. I have really learned a great deal from being with you all and enjoyed getting to know you. As a family, you have helped so much in increasing our understanding about some very important issues. Thank you again.

NOTES

1. Our group is a collective, and I, designated for the moment as the spokesperson, cannot begin without noting the presence of the others. There are those who have stayed with the project to the end. They are Joe Melnick, clinical psychologist and former college professor, our most experienced and therefore sometimes arrogant researcher, guiding light, process leader, healer and supporter; Bruce St. Thomas, art therapist, brilliantly gifted in understanding children, who showed us how to deepen our work through drawings; and Denis Noonan, pastoral counselor, a mover from the heart, who helped us break through impasses when we faced our terrors, both of nuclear war and of the computer printouts. Some members of the group became peripheral but stayed on to help from time to time: Bonnie Lazar, Kathleen Sullivan, and Mary McCann. Others joined us for a while, contributed substantially, and then moved on: Carol Lohman, Cheryl Eberhardt, Ben Chandler, Macy Whitehead, Cindy Lambert, Paulette Gosselin, Mary Jean Mork. These people are all still a part of the group's history and spirit.
2. I was the only interviewer who never learned not to cry. I did, however, learn to cry noiselessly so my tears did not disrupt family conversations.
3. Dr. Richard Steinman of the Department of Social Work, University of Southern Maine, was our guide and mentor through the first part of our research design.

4. Later the studies of Fiske (1987) would reinforce the notion that a sense of concern or fear about nuclear war was insufficient impetus to encourage development of social activism in her subjects.

5. J. Riskin (see Chapter 6) was interviewing families in California and coming to similar conclusions.

6. The data were collated thanks to the hard work of Alissia Melnick.

7. California School of Professional Psychology; Editorial Board of *Family Process*.

8. The Richardsons maintain a pediatric practice in a small town 50 miles north of Portland, ME.

9. Another breakthrough came when Tom McDonald, an able statistician, volunteered his time to help pull our results together.

10. Joe, Bruce, Kathleen, and I were the interviewers.

11. There was considerable confusion regarding which parts of the postquestionnaires were actually sent out; some data were lost.

12. This replicates a finding by Goldenring and Doctor (1986), who had administered the questionnaire to a large sample of American adolescents.

13. It is interesting to reflect on the differences between the two research projects. Greenwald and Zeitlin were able to use videotapes, so their analysis could be much more complete than ours. All of our questions were designed so family members would respond to each other rather than to the interviewer. We deliberately were intensifying the focus on family interaction. In addition, our interview format was highly structured. Perhaps the most important factor in our differences from Greenwald and Zeitlin is that we were interviewing three years later, when the tensions of the cold war were beginning to ease. Furthermore, we were studying semirural Mainers living in a different culture than that of Boston or Philadelphia.

14. This replicates the experience of Berger Gould (1983). In working with multifamily groups discussing nuclear topics, she found that more interactive intergenerational discussions occurred after parents and children had had an opportunity to talk separately in peer groups.

15. Prequestionnaire self-report, Goldenring-Doctor scale, (1986), and analysis of individuals' drawings, rated independently on eight objective variables of anxiety. (Contact author for more detailed information.)

16. The ten families in the first (pilot) phase of our study also reported no behavioral distress in family members subsequent to the interviews, based on parental report, and little negative impact based on the Horowitz Measure of Impact Scale (1979).

BIBLIOGRAPHY

Anthony, E. J., & Cohler, B. J. (Eds.) (1987). *The invulnerable child.* New York: Guilford.

Bandura, A. (1977). Self-efficacy: Toward a unifying theory of behavior change. *Psychological Review, 84*, 191–215.

Berger Gould, B. (1983, June). Presentation to the Interest Group on Nuclear Issues, Annual Meeting of the American Family Therapy Association, San Francisco. *Young people's attitudes to threat of nuclear war after an international crisis.*

Blair, P. H. (1988). *Children's anxiety about nuclear war.* Unpublished raw data.

Coles, R. (1985, December 8). Children and the bomb. *New York Times Magazine.*

Coles, R. (1986). *The moral life of children.* Boston: Atlantic Monthly.

Csikszentmihalyi, M. (1990). *Flow: The psychology of optimal experience.* New York: Harper Perennial.

DeMuth, D. H. (1990). Some implications of the threat of nuclear war for families and family therapists. In M. P. Merkin (Ed.), *The social and political contexts of family therapy.* Boston: Allyn & Bacon.

Dugan, T. F., & Coles, R. (Eds.) (1990). *The child in our times: Studies in the development of resiliency.* New York: Brunner/Mazel.

Epstein, N. B., Baldwin, L. M., & Bishop, D. S. (1983). The McMaster family assessment device. *Journal of Marital and Family Therapy, 9,* 171–182.

Figley, C. R., & McCubbin, H. I. (Eds.) (1983). *Stress and the family. Vol II. Coping with catastrophe.* New York: Brunner/Mazel.

Fiske, S. (1987). People's reaction to nuclear war. *American Psychologist, 42,* 207–217.

French, P. L., & Van Hoorn, J. (1986). Half a nation saw nuclear war and nobody blinked: A reassessment of the impact of *The Day After* in terms of a theoretical chain of causality. In M. Schwebel (Ed.), *Mental Health Implications of Life in the Nuclear Age.* Armonk, NY: M. E. Sharpe.

Goldenring, J. M., & Doctor, R. (1986). Teenage worry about nuclear war: North American and European questionnaire studies. *International Journal of Mental Health, 15,* 72–92.

Greenwald, D. S., & Zeitlin, S. J. (1987). *No reason to talk about it: Families confront the nuclear taboo.* New York: Norton.

Horowitz, M. F. (1979). Psychological responses to serious life events. In V. Hamilton & D. M. Warberton (Eds.), *Human Stress and Cognition.* New York: Wiley.

Jorgenson, J. (1991). Co-constructing the interviewer/co-constructing the family. In K. Steir (Ed.), *Research and Reflexivity.* Newbury Park, CA: Sage.

Kanofsky, S. (1989). The possibility of nuclear war: Appraisal, coping and emotional response. Unpublished doctoral dissertation, California School of Professional Psychology, Berkeley/Alameda, CA.

Kegan, R. (1982). *The evolving self.* Cambridge, MA: Harvard University Press.

Lazarus, R. S. (1964). A laboratory approach to psychological stress. In G. H. Grosser, H. Wechsler, & M. Greenblatt (Eds.), *The threat of impending disaster: Contributions to the psychology of stress.* Cambridge, MA: M.I.T. Press.

Lieberman, M. A., Yalom, I. D., & Miles, M. B. (1973). *Encounter groups: First facts.* New York: Basic Books.

Macy, J. R. (1981). Despair work. *Evolutionary Blues—An Interhelp Quarterly, 1,* 36–47.

Macy, J. R. (1983). *Despair and personal power in the nuclear age.* Philadelphia: New Society.

Maturana, H. R. (1991). Science and daily life: The ontology of scientific explanations. In F. Stier (Ed.), *Research and Reflexivity.* Newbury Park, CA: Sage.

McCubbin, H. I., & Patterson, J. M. (1983). The family stress process: The double ABCX model of adjustment and adaptation. *Marriage and Family Review, 6,* 7–37.

McVeigh, K. (1982). The hunger to be heard: Children and nuclear war. *Humpty Dumpty Reports: An Interhelp Journal,* 8–9.

Mirowsky, J., & Ross, C. (1989). *Social causes of psychological distress.* New York: Aldine de Gruyler.

Oliver, P. (1990). Nuclear freedom and students' sense of efficacy about prevention of nuclear war. *American Journal of Orthopsychiatry, 60*(4), 611–621.

Ruddick, S. (1989). *Maternal thinking: Toward a politics of peace.* New York: Ballantine.

Rutter, M. (1987). Psychosocial resilience and protective mechanisms. *American Journal of Orthopsychiatry, 57,* 316–331.

Schwebel, M. (1986). The study of stress and coping in the nuclear age: A new specialty. *International Journal of Mental Health, 15,* 5–15.

Staub, E. (1975). To rear a pro-social child: Reasoning, learning by doing and learning by teaching others. In D. J. DePalma & J. M. Foley (Eds.), *Moral development: Current theory and research.* New York: Wiley.

Staub, E. (1989). *The roots of evil: The origins of genocide and other group violence.* Cambridge, MA: Cambridge University Press.

Stier, F. (1991). *Research and reflexivity.* Newbury Park, CA: Sage.

Stevens, O. (1982). *Children talking politics: Political learning in childhood*. Oxford: Martin Robertson.

Zeitlin, S. (1984). Nuclear secrets: What do we tell mom and dad? *Family Therapy Networker, 8*, 31, 38–39, 62.

Zur, O. (1989). On nuclear attitudes and psychic numbing: Overview and critique. *Contemporary Social Psychology, 14*(2), 96–110.

Intervening on the Global Level

The work now moves to an international focus. It concerns itself with interventions, based on family systems thinking, made by Richard Chasin, Margaret Herzig, Katharine Baker, Benina Berger Gould, and Hinda Winawer. Each intervention took a strikingly different form.

Richard and Margaret, in Chapter 8, *Creating Systemic Interventions for the Sociopolitical Arena*, describe several workshops, retreats, and dialogue sessions that they have conducted. They use principles and techniques familiar to family therapists to promote understanding and collaboration between groups with divisive boundaries, be they political, personal, ideological, or professional.

Katharine writes, in Chapter 9, on *Teaching Family Theory and Therapy in the Soviet Union: A Continuing Experiment in Citizen Diplomacy*. Using principles of Bowen family therapy theory with Soviet psychotherapists, she facilitates conversations about cutoffs and losses sustained by the generations owing to collectivization, political purges, the ravages of World War II, and the more recent Chernobyl catastrophe. She deals with common feelings of depression and hopelessness, going as a teacher and coming back as a learner.

Benina, in Chapter 10, *From the Outside In: The Human Side of Crisis Management*, enters the culture of academic defense analysts as one visits a new and odd country. She allows herself to be inducted into the "nuclear club." She chronicles her experiences and reworks them, using family systems thinking. An oral history of the cold war era emerges, which leads to increased respect for and knowledge about a group of people we all have little access to or knowledge of, those who build nuclear weapons and make suggestions for policy.

Hinda also gives an account of entering a new system, this time the war-torn country of Nicaragua, in Chapter 11, *Scenes from a Revolution: Reflections of a North American Family Therapist*. In the process of teaching Central American women, she realizes how much we at home can learn from revolutionaries. She makes explicit the personal dimensions of being a woman, mother, North American, Jew, and family therapist in the political context.

Ultimately each author in this section has gone to another country, found a form for working that fit the context on a global level, and then brought home knowledge about how to work in "our own backyard." The process is reciprocal.

Chapter 8

Creating Systemic Interventions for the Sociopolitical Arena

Richard Chasin
Margaret Herzig*

Sociopolitical systems, like families, experience times of struggle. Some of these struggles are akin to developmental crises. For example, as a nation modernizes, it strives to enter the future with a new identity, while retaining roots and rituals from the past. Other sociopolitical struggles, such as war, are like acute trauma. A nation ravaged by war must grieve its losses before it can move beyond suspicion and hatred and toward productive interaction within and across its borders, just as a family must mourn lost members before its survivors can restructure their relationships and fully rejoin the larger community (Montville, 1989).

In our work, we have concerned ourselves principally with a third type of sociopolitical struggle, one that resembles families stuck in chronic conflict. In political stalemates such as the Arab-Israeli conflict, the 40-year cold war, and the

*We take full responsibility for the authorship of this chapter but gratefully share credit for the work reported with *Laura Chasin,* who has been involved in virtually all of it, in roles ranging from supportive presence to guiding light, and *Paula Gutlove,* whose commitment to peacemaking is inspirational. We also gratefully acknowledge *Sallyann Roth* and *Carol Becker* for the creative and thoughtful ways in which they have brought their manifold skills to bear on one of the major projects described herein.

The authors wish to acknowledge the generous support of the United States Institute of Peace; the Fund for Peace; the Carnegie Corporation of New York; the Ploughshares Fund; the Joint Foundation of New York; the NARA Fund; and several individual donors, including Dr. Loring Conant and Reverend Louise Conant, Dr. and Mrs. John Constable, and others who wish to remain anonymous.

abortion controversy in the United States, the adversaries commonly behave like family members stuck in "games without end" (Watzlawick, Beavin, & Jackson, 1967). Such adversaries come to view each other as dangerous enough to justify wars—hot wars, cold wars, or denigrating wars of rhetoric. Those on each side believe they hold the high moral ground and are prey to unprovoked attacks from the other side, which they see as power hungry, self-centered, destructive, and perhaps even deranged. Each side enlists bands of allies to support its own interpretation of history. The opponents' interactions are almost ritualized, and their strife, although costly, resists resolution. Such patterns of interaction often resemble couples engaged in acrimonious divorce litigation. As embattled spouses review their shared history of accusation and defense, they each find "proof" of their own innocent victimhood and of the other's unwarranted attacks and wrongdoing. Friends and family members are induced to take sides. Over time, the stakes in their marital battle become higher and higher (as do their legal bills).

Given that some of the most damaging and dangerous political conflicts in recent decades so closely resemble the problems that therapists are called on to help resolve in "stuck" families, it is surprising that the field of political psychology has heard little from family systems thinkers and that so few family therapists have brought their approaches into the realm of political intervention.[1] By contrast, the annals of political psychology are replete with concepts extrapolated from individual psychodynamic therapy.[2]

In our interventions with groups in chronic conflict, our general objective is to lead participants away from deadlock and toward authentic dialogue. We describe these interventions as *systemic* in a broad sense because they involve methods drawn from different schools of family therapy. Some of the methods we use are similar to those found in structural family therapy. These include instructions designed to obstruct apparently unproductive interactive cycles and to promote the development of interactive patterns that allow growth and problem solving. Other methods are akin to Milan school and Milan-derived systemic ideas and practices. These include careful attention to each person's views and a particular form of questioning that increases the number and variety of connections and distinctions that participants make. The enhancement of the field of relationships and ideas stimulates the participants to think and act in new ways, similar to what one hopes for in *therapeutic conversation* (Penn, 1982, 1985; Roth, 1992; Tomm, 1987, 1988).

Although our primary focus has been on chronic sociopolitical conflict, we have a secondary interest in people who share some important political objectives but do not collaborate with each other. We refer to these groups as *strange bedfellows*. Groups of strange bedfellows are analogous to mildly disengaged families, in which there is little or no overt strife, but the full potential of coordinated action is not realized because of their distance and isolation from one another. In the public arena, people who might collaborate productively are isolated for many reasons: cultural differences, geographic distance, narrow professional identifications, sharply different cognitive styles, and so on. As in families, there are hybrid forms; that is, there are sociopolitical groups that are partly conflicted and partly disengaged.

The approach used with strange bedfellows is drawn only partially from family systems practice. Although we use some structural therapy methods to prevent these individuals from remaining isolated and apply some systemic methods to enrich their conversations, we rely heavily on brainstorming methods, especially exercises in which participants are asked to suspend judgment and criticism, while supporting one another in the rapid generation of many varied ideas. Even though brainstorming sessions with strange bedfellows are quite different from interventions in situations involving chronic conflict, we include a discussion of them because they often bear interesting similarities to interventions in conflict and because there are situations that call for some blend of systemic and brainstorming methods.

Some of our systemic interventions have been carried out under the auspices of the Project on Promoting Effective Dialogue at the Center for Psychological Studies in the Nuclear Age and some under the auspices of the Public Conversations Project of the Family Institute of Cambridge, both of which are described here.[3] Most of the brainstorming interventions were ad hoc events, concerned with neither of these projects.[4] As we are the only people who have worked intensively on the full range of these efforts, we report on them here, on behalf of ourselves and our many collaborators.

PROJECT ON PROMOTING EFFECTIVE DIALOGUE

The Project on Promoting Effective Dialogue was founded in 1986 by Richard Chasin, a psychiatrist and family therapist, primarily to explore ways in which family systems theory and techniques might inform an analysis of the arms race and help shape systemic methods for political intervention. In 1987, he was joined by Margaret Herzig and in 1989 by Paula Gutlove.[5] Over the course of our work, we have become involved in, or initiated, meetings that brought together people who had chronically opposing political views or who at least held damaging assumptions about each other. We looked for opportunities to use systemic interventions to help participants bypass their usual, ritualized, hostile interactions and to promote authentic dialogue.

Four of the seven meetings designed and implemented by this project were systemic interventions in chronic conflict, conducted in the context of international workshops on stereotyping. Richard Chasin designed the first workshop on stereotyping for the 1987 World Congress of the International Physicians for the Prevention of Nuclear War (IPPNW) in Moscow. We have adapted that workshop for three subsequent IPPNW World Congresses in Montreal, Hiroshima, and Stockholm. Each workshop presented its own particular challenges; thus each required a different approach.

Back home in Boston, in the spring of 1988, our project sponsored a systemic intervention into a stuck conversation between two American groups whose attempts to collaborate had been less than satisfying and productive: defense analysts and peace activists. We asked Australian family therapist Michael White to facilitate a conversation among members of these two groups.

In addition, the project created and designed two weekend-long brainstorming meetings. The Entertainment Summit Retreat, held in March 1987, provided a private and peaceful retreat for leading American and Soviet filmmakers, after they had spent a hectic week in public and private meetings in Hollywood as part of a Soviet-American filmmakers' exchange. Three years later, we convened a Dialogue Workshop, to promote collaboration and networking among disparate scholars and practitioners in the emerging field of interactive conflict resolution. It was, in effect, a facilitated retreat for professional facilitators.

PUBLIC CONVERSATIONS PROJECT

The Public Conversations Project was initiated in December 1989 by Laura Chasin, a clinical social worker, who had collaborated with her husband Richard in the design and implementation of several brainstorming meetings in the mid-1980s. She has also participated in many of the systemic interventions sponsored by the Project on Promoting Effective Dialogue. She convened two brainstorming weekends on the abortion controversy in 1989 and 1990. She initiated the Public Conversations Project after viewing a televised debate about abortion in which the participants squabbled, while the moderator either made ineffective moves to interrupt the accusations or sat helplessly, apparently unable to slow the verbal escalation or promote genuine dialogue.

At the time of this writing, the Public Conversations Project has designed and implemented a series of 18 systemic interventions we refer to as *dialogue sessions*. Throughout the Project, our team has included the authors of this chapter, Laura Chasin, Carol Becker, and Sallyann Roth.[6] We have used systemic approaches to other "hot" sociopolitical topics, but most of the sessions conducted to date have been on the abortion issue.

A complete list of interventions and meetings organized by the Project on Promoting Effective Dialogue and the Public Conversations Project is presented in Tables 8-1 through 8-3.

GENERAL OBSERVATIONS

Much of our work has been guided by observations that we have made about patterns of behavior in chronic sociopolitical conflict and the role of the media in defining and sustaining those patterns.

Behavior Patterns in Chronic Conflict

Families in chronic conflict tend to interact in rigidly choreographed patterns and have conversations that are predictable and unproductive, particularly when

TABLE 8-1 Experiential Workshops on Stereotyping at World Congresses of International Physicians for the Prevention of Nuclear War (IPPNW)

Year and Place	Name of Meeting	Sponsor	Participants	Core Colleagues Involved	Key Outside Collaborator(s)
1987, Moscow	IPPNW Workshop on Stereotyping	PPED	42 delegates from 15 countries	L. Chasin, R. Chasin, Gutlove, M. Herzig	Marat Vartanyan
1988, Montreal	IPPNW Workshop on Stereotyping	PPED	80 delegates from 10 countries	L. Chasin, R. Chasin, M. Herzig	Marat Vartanyan
1989, Hiroshima	IPPNW Workshop on Stereotyping	PPED	71 delegates from 16 countries	R. Chasin, Gutlove, M. Herzig	Cathy Colman, Shoichi Takizawa, Merry White
1991, Stockholm	IPPNW Workshop on Stereotyping	PPED	40 delegates from 15 countries	R. Chasin, Gutlove, M. Herzig	

TABLE 8-2 Facilitated Conversations: Interrupting Stuck Debate, Fostering Dialogue

Year and Place	Name of Meeting	Sponsor	Participants	Core Colleagues Involved	Key Outside Collaborator(s)
1988, Boston	Defense Analysts and Peace Activists in Dialogue	FIC and PPED	Two defense analysts and two peace activists, interviewed by Michael White	L. Chasin, R. Chasin, Gutlove, M. Herzig, Roth	Terry Real, Kathy Weingarten, Cheryl White, Michael White
1990–present, Boston	Pro-Choice–Pro-Life Dialogues	Public Conversations Project at FIC	15 sessions with more than 70 individuals who self-describe as "pro-choice" or "pro-life"	Becker, L. Chasin, R. Chasin, M. Herzig, Roth	Peter Cook, Terry Real, Kathy Weingarten

TABLE 8-3 Brainstorming Retreats with Strange Bedfellows (Brainstorming Interventions)

Year and Place	Name of Meeting	Sponsor	Participants	Core Colleagues Involved	Key Outside Collaborator(s)
1983, Tarrytown, NY	Exploratory Meeting on the Nuclear Deadlock	private	40 diverse American experts on the arms race (not really a brainstorming session; see text)	R. Chasin	John Mack
1985, Martha's Vineyard, MA	Popularizing Peace	Microsecond	40 Hollywood video/film professionals and East Coast intellectuals and peace activists	L. Chasin, R. Chasin	Norman Fleishman
1986, Martha's Vineyard, MA	Revisioning the American Dream	private	30 activists, video/film professionals, political consultants, and elected officials	L. Chasin, R. Chasin	
1987, Tarrytown, NY	Entertainment Summit Retreat	Mediators, Inc., and PPED	30 leading American and Soviet filmmakers and other American "influentials"	L. Chasin, R. Chasin, M. Herzig	Mark Gerzon
1988, Martha's Vineyard, MA	Strategies for Meeting Needs of Children	Children's Defense Fund	40 activists, media professionals, political consultants, and religious leaders	L. Chasin, R. Chasin, M. Herzig	Hillary Clinton, Marian Wright Edelman
1989, Martha's Vineyard, MA	Communicating about Abortion	private	40 activists, health care professionals, political consultants, and elected officials	L. Chasin, R. Chasin, M. Herzig	Betty Carter, Ira Hirschfield, Evan Imber-Black, Caroline Marvin
1990, Martha's Vineyard, MA	Abortion: Moving Beyond the Single Issue	private	40 activists, health care professionals, political consultants, and elected officials	L. Chasin, R. Chasin, M. Herzig, Roth	Ira Hirschfield, Caroline Marvin
1990, Tarrytown, NY	Dialogue Workshop: Facilitating Facilitators	PPED	25 experts in international conflict resolution	L. Chasin, R. Chasin, Gutlove, Herzig	Ira Hirschfield, Caroline Marvin

---

Key to Tables 8-1, 8-2, and 8-3

Organizations

Children's Defense Fund, Washington, D.C.–based advocacy group.
CPSNA, Center for Psychological Studies in the Nuclear Age, Harvard Medical School (renamed in spring 1992: Center for Psychology and Social Change).
FIC, Family Institute of Cambridge (Watertown, MA).
Mediators, Inc., socially conscious film production company in Los Angeles.
Microsecond, L.A. group promoting peace in film/video. Funded by Tides Foundation (San Francisco).
PPED, Project on Promoting Effective Dialogue, sponsored by CPSNA.
USIP, United States Institute of Peace, Washington, D.C.

Collaborators

Betty Carter, Director, Family Institute of Westchester.
Hillary Clinton, Chair, Children's Defense Fund, Washington, D.C.
Cathy Colman, Dept. of Psychiatry, Harvard Medical School.
Peter Cook, writer and producer, WGBH-TV, Boston.
Marian Wright Edelman, President, Children's Defense Fund, Washington, D.C.
Norman Fleishman, Director, Microsecond.
Mark Gerzon, President, Mediators, Inc.
Ira Hirschfield, President, The Evelyn and Walter Haas, Jr., Fund, San Francisco (formerly Head, Philanthropy Office, Rockefeller Family and Associates).
Evan Imber-Black, Professor, Albert Einstein College of Medicine.
John Mack, Founder of CPSNA. Former Chair, Dept. of Psychiatry, Cambridge Hospital, Harvard Medical School.
Caroline Marvin, Co-director, Family Institute of Cambridge.
Terry Real, Faculty, Family Institute of Cambridge.
Sallyann Roth, Co-director, Family Institute of Cambridge.
Shoichi Takizawa, Vice-president, Kamo National Hospital, Hiroshima, Japan.
Marat Vartanyan, Director, All Union Research Center in Psychiatry, Moscow.
Kathy Weingarten, Co-director, Program on Narrative Therapies, Family Institute of Cambridge.
Cheryl White, Editor and publisher, Dulwich Centre Newsletter, Adelaide, Australia.
Michael White, Director, Dulwich Center, Adelaide, Australia.
Merry White, Dept. of Sociology, Boston University.

---

they are dealing with the chronic problem area. The repertoire of each participant and of the family as a whole is narrow and unvarying. Long-standing political adversaries also show limited, ritualized patterns when conversing with each other about their dispute. Other similarities between conflicted families and political opponents that we have observed include:

1. People on one side do not listen to those on the other side.
2. Questions posed by one side to the other side tend to be rhetorical and often are designed to reveal suspected inconsistencies or ulterior motives on the part of the side being questioned.

3. Members of an opposing alliance are seen as being all alike; the most extreme leaders of the opposition are assumed to be representative of the entire group.
4. Within each alliance, members de-emphasize differences among themselves, especially in the presence of an adversary. This behavior tends to reinforce the other side's perception that their opponents are all alike.
5. Those who join neither side are viewed as suspect by both sides.
6. Blaming the adversary is common. Taking responsibility for problems is uncommon.
7. Mind reading of the other side is common; genuine curiosity about what they really believe is rare.
8. Fixed opinions about the other side are common. Open-mindedness is uncommon.
9. Statements made by the other side that indicate openness to conciliation are seen as propaganda ploys or as revealing logical inconsistency.
10. Fixed and simple convictions are openly displayed. Complexity, ambivalence, confusion, and inner conflict are concealed.
11. Adversarial parties to a stalemated controversy tend to think that it is valuable to persist in the struggle, even though people who are outside the controversy may tell them that the persistence of the deadlock may well be more destructive than almost any alternative outcome.

Influence of the Media on Sociopolitical Conflict

Media presentations often accentuate polarization in entrenched sociopolitical conflicts. In the name of fairness, both sides need to be represented. To sell newspapers and television shows, the sides are often dramatically pitted against each other. Because combat is more exciting than conciliation, television moderators tend to foster debate rather than facilitate dialogue. They often devise and then lightly referee arguments rather than aid mutual understanding.

Some media presentations foster extreme stereotypic images of each side. They commonly offer a fixed definition of the controversy, suggesting only two options for resolution: a victory for one side or the other. Members of the viewing public tend to line up on one side or the other (often, we believe, with unconscious ambivalence). Those who are offended by both sides and by the "uncivilized" nature of the debate may become "turned off" to the issue. These people imagine that their own views or their preferred method of discussion have no place in the controversy. They become silent and, through their silence, disempowered.

Although there is no strong analogue to the media in family conflicts, the effects of extended families and social networks on couples in conflict sometimes resemble the media's influence on sociopolitical conflict. These "noncombatants" forces create definitions of the couple's conflict that become part of the couple's reality and may serve to close rather than open options for resolution of the conflict.

With these observations in mind, we have planned our interventions carefully to lead participants away from deadlock or disengagement and toward authentic dialogue and collaboration. A summary of most of our interventions follows.

SYSTEMIC INTERVENTIONS BY THE PROJECT ON PROMOTING EFFECTIVE DIALOGUE

IPPNW Workshops on Stereotyping

IPPNW Background. The first four systemic interventions were conducted as workshops on stereotyping at four annual World Congresses of the IPPNW. IPPNW was founded in 1980 by a small group of Soviet and American physicians, scientists, and influential citizens committed to using their prestige, credibility, experience, and skills to avert nuclear catastrophe. Five years later, IPPNW was awarded the Nobel Peace Prize. By the end of its first decade, IPPNW had affiliates in 69 countries, representing more than 250,000 members. Participation in IPPNW World Congresses has increased over the years from a small group of founders to several thousand. The early Congresses drew mostly representatives of NATO and the Warsaw Pact countries. The past three Congresses have drawn greater numbers of delegates from South America, Africa, and Asia.

Delegates to IPPNW World Congresses come from many cultures and ideologies, but they are strongly bonded by their realization that if a nuclear war were to be fought, physicians and medical institutions could offer nothing of significance to repair the damage. They share the belief that if physicians are to fulfill their mandate to promote health and save lives, they must adopt a preventive approach to the nuclear threat. Although IPPNW activists have often had strong disagreements (particularly before 1988), these have been somewhat tempered by shared goals and sometimes obscured by pseudomutuality; rarely have these activists publicly explored their serious differences.

General Design of the IPPNW Workshops. When Richard Chasin, a long-time member of IPPNW, was asked to contribute something to the 1987 Congress in Moscow, he thought: Why not encourage this group to uncover and dismantle some of the negative stereotypes that are fueling mutual suspicion and antagonism between Americans and Soviets and accelerating the arms race? The initial challenge was to bring potentially insulting stereotypic images to the surface, without engendering the escalating cycle of attack and counterattack that had made so many other Soviet-American exchanges risky and futile. It occurred to Chasin that this goal might be achieved by asking the Soviet and American groups *not* what stereotypes each held of the other—which would activate hostility and defensiveness—but what stereotypes each thought the other held of them. The circularity of this question would allow for damaging and injurious stereotypes to accumulate in the room without anyone making an accusation or negative attribution about an adversary group.[7] Then after each group had listed the stereotypes they felt others held of them, they could disavow some of these stereotypes as inaccurate, insulting, or both. Chasin developed this workshop design in consultation with Soviet colleagues a few days before the 1987 Congress, and they decided to try it out. The workshop was so well received that it has been adapted for implementation at every subsequent IPPNW World Congress. In the remainder of this section, we briefly describe the contexts of each Congress and the ways in which we adapted the workshop for each setting. We report a few findings from each meeting to give a sense of the type of information that surfaces in the workshops.[8]

Moscow, 1987. In the spring of 1987, *glasnost* was just emerging, and Gorbachev's "new thinking" had begun to enter political discourse. Little progress had been made, however, in reducing the nuclear arsenals of the superpowers. The cold war was thawing slightly, but the political world was still intensely bipolar. The IPPNW World Congress in Moscow drew a large international group of participants. Forty-two Congress participants chose to attend the workshop on stereotyping.

Richard Chasin and a Soviet psychiatrist, Dr. Marat Vartanyan, introduced the workshop as an opportunity for participants to gain experiential knowledge of the mistaken assumptions and distorted perceptions that were fueling the arms race. They set one ground rule: Those who felt reticent about participating in any particular exercise were encouraged to "pass" (Lee, 1981) and become an observer for that moment. Then they broke the full group, which included representatives from 15 countries, into five subgroups: Americans, Soviets, American allies, Soviet allies, and representatives of nonaligned countries.[9] Each subgroup met separately to list six negative stereotypes believed to be held about Americans and Soviets that "could be fueling the arms race." The Soviet group and the group of Soviet allies were each asked to list six stereotypes they felt Americans held of Soviets; the American group and the group of American allies each listed six stereotypes they felt Soviets held of Americans; representatives of nonaligned countries performed both tasks. Of the six stereotypes, two were to pertain to personal, social, or cultural qualities, characteristics, or values; two to national (internal) goals or intentions; and two to international goals or intentions.

The lists generated by the five groups were reported to the full group. Later the stereotypes were condensed into two lists, one about Americans and one about Soviets, each list including 16 stereotypes.[10] Each of the five groups then performed a second task. The Soviets and their allies were each invited to disavow as inaccurate four of the 16 stereotypes that they and their allies thought others held of Soviets. The Americans and their allies were each invited to disavow four stereotypes on the list about Americans. The nonaligned group members could disavow two stereotypes from each list. After all the disavowals were reported to the full group, Soviet and American participants were invited to choose one especially offensive stereotype that they thought others held about them and tell the full group why that one was particularly slanderous or injurious.

The Soviets and their allies most frequently disavowed the stereotypes (again, ones that they believed Americans and their allies ascribed to them) that Soviets seek to dominate the world by force and that Soviet peace initiatives are propaganda ploys. One Soviet woman offered a heartfelt disavowal of the latter assumption:

> The Soviet people know what war is. We lost 20 million people [in World War II] and many were crippled, they are invalids. They still have nightmares. My generation can still feel the war pain. It even hurts to bring up the subject.

The Americans and their allies most frequently disavowed the attribute (one that they assumed Soviets and their allies ascribed to them) that Americans believe a nuclear war can be won. The second most frequently disavowed assumption, but the one disavowed with the greatest emotion, was that a moral gulf exists between the peace-loving people and the aggressive government of the United States. The Americans held to their basic belief in democracy: If the government is bad, the people are to blame.

Sincere disavowals of negative attributes (e.g., perceived readiness to pull the nuclear trigger) can reduce tensions by calming the other side's worst fears. Choosing *not* to disavow certain stereotypes can also ease tensions: When one's opponents, in effect, own up to negative attributes, one is relieved of the burden of accusing them. For example, it was refreshing and even disarming when the Soviets did not disavow their human rights violations, and the Americans did not disavow their arrogance and materialism.

The workshop offered Soviets, Americans, and their respective allies an experience of avoiding the usual escalating disputes that typified Soviet/American exchanges at that time and of collaborating to examine some of the stereotypes that were increasing the paranoia of the arms race. It inspired hope at a time when the world was still hostage to the extraordinary build-up of weapons of mass destruction.

Montreal, 1988. We modified the workshop design for the IPPNW World Congress in Montreal as follows:[11]

1. We grouped people by country, rather than by superpower alliance. This change reflected the reality of a world that was rapidly becoming less politically bipolar.
2. The central task was revised as follows and distributed to participants in written form:

> Many people from (name of an adversary country) assume that many people from my country have the following *personal or cultural characteristics or values*, which, if true of us, could fuel the arms race and/or retard the progress of developing nations.
>
> Many people from (name of an adversary country) assume that the leadership of my country has the following *policies, goals, or intentions*, which, if true, could fuel the arms race and/or retard the progress of developing nations.

The *adversary country* did not have to be a nation with which one's own country had overtly hostile relations. Included with the written task was a cartoon (Fig. 8-1) providing examples of circular questions.

3. Each subgroup was instructed to choose a facilitator and a recorder from among its own members. After each subgroup completed the central task, its members also chose a reporter to give a 3-minute report to the full group.

4. To perform the disavowal task, participants reviewed their own lists of assumptions and put colored stickers on those that they judged to be most inaccurate or insulting. This yielded a colorful display of "hot spots" in international relations.[12]

Eighty people attended the workshop.[13] As in Moscow, the American and Soviet groups each thought that they were viewed as aggressive and desirous of domination, images they believed were exaggerated. In addition, Americans thought that they were seen as ethnocentric, greedy, materialistic, and arrogant, whereas Soviets thought that they were regarded as suspicious, unsophisticated, corrupt, inflexible, oppressive, and dogmatic. The Americans painted their gloomy self-portrait with ease; self-flagellation seemed to come naturally to them. The Soviets developed theirs with a sense of excitement and novelty.

The Americans disavowed relatively few stereotypes. No Soviet disavowed the assumption of inefficiency; the assumptions that Soviets are suspicious, corrupt, and dogmatic were only weakly disavowed. The Soviets most strongly disavowed the assumptions that they are treacherous, inflexible, oppressive, and

Figure 8-1

Drawing by Ellen Grabiner, 1987.

unsophisticated.[14] One Soviet explained his heartfelt disavowal of the assumption that Soviets are treacherous by saying that this assumption is the most dangerously provocative, possibly leading an adversary to prepare for a first nuclear strike.

The information generated in the workshop created an image of a world in which countries are seen as being either "pushy" or "pushovers." Representatives of the "pushy" countries tended to list arrogance and ethnocentrism as assumed attributes. The British were even more willing than the Americans to "own up" to such negative images as "arrogant, prejudiced, and imperialistic." The West Germans listed as assumptions the ideas that they are eager to participate in the political and military power of the United States and France (which they did not disavow) and that they are "revanchistic" (desirous of lost territory) and have "tendencies toward racism and feelings of superiority." They strongly disavowed revanchism, racism, and feelings of superiority, but they did say that a small minority of Germans are "fascistic."

The "pushover" countries communicated a sense of being in a silent middle. Some thought that they were viewed as lacking identity and moral commitment. For example, the Canadians thought that they were automatically grouped by others (and sometimes by themselves) with the United States, as if they were indistinguishable clones or younger siblings, with no identity of their own. Some Canadians reported initial difficulty in trying to think of damaging attributes that others might ascribe to their docile and seemingly harmless country. They came to recognize, however, that being a docile follower may not be an entirely benign role.[15]

The Scandinavians felt caught in the crossfire of an ideological battle. For example, the Norwegians thought that they were perceived by the Soviets as being misinformed by the Western press and "in the pocket of NATO," an assumption they strongly disavowed. They said that Americans see them as "unreliable socialists." The Swedish and Finnish participants felt similarly criticized by the West as being "too close to Communism," an assumption they disavowed.

The atmosphere in the workshop was one of self-examination, learning, and excitement. The Canadians seemed to appreciate the opportunity to explore and communicate their sense of identity. The Soviets seemed thrilled to be in a setting in which it was appropriate to experiment with their recently achieved freedom of candid self-disclosure. Attack and debate, still present in conventional international discussions, were virtually absent.

Hiroshima, 1989. The IPPNW World Congress in Hiroshima presented several new challenges. The cold war was ending. The stereotypes shaping global relations derived less from ideological animosity and nuclear terror than from cultural unfamiliarity and the disquieting uncertainties that surface in times of major power shifts. The global situation was less like a family locked in chronic conflict and more like a highly disengaged extended family in which each branch has embraced widely different lifestyles. In such families (and in groups of strange bedfellows at brainstorming meetings), understanding and collaboration are enhanced when the rapport-building[16] phase fosters in all members a respectful appreciation of one another, particularly of their differing areas of strength and pride and of their wishes and fears for the future.[17]

The design of the workshop in Hiroshima was modified as follows:[18]

1. We added a "warm-up" task in which participants were asked to list three components of a hoped-for global future, three components of a feared future, and one or two strengths or resources that they thought their own country could offer to help avoid the feared future and bring about the hoped-for future. This task was added to establish bonds in the full group (based on common hopes and fears), to heighten appreciation of differing perspectives (based on differences among lists), and to give participants an opportunity to put forward some of their most positive national qualities before being asked to reveal what they feared others thought were their worst qualities. This was one of the ways in which we addressed the problem of the workshop design being too "Western," in that it requires strangers to discuss conflicts openly and to put forward negative views of their own culture. These activities are at odds with Japanese culture, in which the boundaries between private and public are strong, and social harmony and "face saving" are highly valued. We also addressed this cultural difference by acknowledging in our introductory remarks how "American" the workshop design was and by apologizing in advance for any awkwardness it might create. (As in previous workshops, the "pass rule" was proposed and agreed on by all.)
2. We printed task forms in English and Japanese and arranged through our Japanese co-leader to have Japanese interpreters present.
3. We gave participants three options for the disavowal portion of the task. They could categorize stereotypes as: untrue, for the most part; true; or largely untrue but understandable. In recognition of the importance of gift giving in Japanese hospitality, we framed each of these choices as a type of gift: Categorizing a negative stereotype as untrue was characterized as a gift of reassurance; categorizing a negative stereotype as mostly true was seen as a gift of acknowledgment; and categorizing a negative stereotype as largely untrue but understandable was seen as a gift of understanding.
4. To discourage not only complete disavowal, but also casual self-castigation, we asked participants to assign each stereotype on their list to one of the three categories (untrue for the most part, largely untrue but understandable, or true), then to review their list to see if any of the three categories was not represented. If so, they were encouraged to add a stereotype to their list that would fit the missing category.

The workshop in Hiroshima attracted the most culturally diverse group of the four IPPNW workshops that we have implemented. As expected, the lists of hopes and fears that the national groups generated revealed much commonality, as most descriptions of a hoped-for global future included references to disarmament, cross-cultural understanding, protection of the environment, and equitable distribution of wealth. Some differences were interesting. Participants from some of the more developed nations included hopes for "quality time" with family and friends and for finding meaning and value in one's activities. Some fears were somewhat surprising: Some Japanese participants listed fear of starvation, and some Americans listed fear of poverty, whereas participants from very poor nations (Zambia and Nepal) expressed fears about moral crisis, loss of native culture, and westernization. It appears that both developed and undeveloped nations feared losing what they had (wealth or spirituality) and worried about becoming like their image of the other (spiritually or materially impoverished) as they took up life in a "global family."

The participants from the United States and Europe generated long lists of stereotypes, many of which they acknowledged as either true or mostly untrue but understandable. The reporters from the less developed countries used the task to educate the full group about their countries, which they felt were little known or understood.

The Japanese group was so large that the co-leaders invited them to divide into two subgroups. Interestingly, they chose to divide by generation. The younger group listed the stereotype that the Japanese are "a barbarous people, wild to kill animals like whales." They disavowed "barbarism," explaining that eating whale meat is a part of Japanese culture. This stereotype, they said, is the result of a "difference in culture." The reporter from the older group listed as the stereotype that the Japanese have a "flat character." He said with a grin, "My face may be flat, but my character is not."

In the closing discussion, formal evaluations, and subsequent correspondence, we learned that many participants appreciated the opportunity to learn and laugh together with people of different cultures. Our emphasis on rapport building seemed to pay off. One American reported: "We thought that they [the Japanese] were all the same, hard working and serious, but they were having as much fun as anybody, laughing at themselves and joining in the fun. What a revelation!" A Japanese participant commented that it was good to talk about problems in a friendly way.

Stockholm, 1991. We made only one significant change in the workshop design for the Stockholm Congress. Participants were asked in the first task (concerning hopes, fears, and strengths) to say something about a source of identity other than their nationality. This was to pave the way for some non-national groups to form for the second task (stereotype listing). We made this change because we thought that in 1991 some of the hottest conflicts in the world were between groups defined not by national borders but by religion, race, or ethnicity. As it turned out, the participating group was relatively small and not very culturally diverse. Fewer than half of the participants grouped themselves geographically; their reports were similar to reports given at previous workshops. The other participants grouped themselves as men, women, world citizens, and family therapists.

The participants clearly enjoyed working within these subgroups and listening to the reports of others. In their closing comments, many affirmed the value of small, cross-cultural discussion groups at large international conferences. We suspect, however, that the option of non-national grouping, intended to permit grouping by the religious and ethnic characteristics over which wars were being fought,[19] had permitted a glossing over of some of the differences that create international tension. Even though the participants found the workshop satisfying, we believe that the information generated was less rich than it might have been had they broken into national and regional groups. If we offer the workshop again, especially in a setting concerned with war prevention, we will take more responsibility for deciding which types of grouping will most enhance learning about damaging misperceptions.[20]

A Systemic Intervention with Peace Activists and Defense Analysts

In the mid-1980s, the Center for Psychological Studies in the Nuclear Age (CPSNA) and the Center for Science and International Affairs (CSIA) at Harvard's Kennedy School of Government shared concerns about the arms race. Members of each group had considerable access to the media, were widely published, and had an indirect impact on governmental decision makers. Leaders of the two groups had made some attempts to sponsor events and discussions among their members jointly, but the ideological divide between these "peace activists" and "defense analysts" at times seemed as wide as that between Soviets and Americans. In the spring of 1988, Richard Chasin made an unusual proposal to Australian therapist Michael White, who was coming to the Family Institute of Cambridge (FIC) to present his clinical work. Chasin asked White to have a *systemic conversation* with representatives of CPSNA and CSIA, while a small group of therapists, mostly from FIC, served as a *reflecting team* behind a one-way mirror.

White is known in family therapy circles for *externalizing* problems, highlighting exceptions to *problem-saturated* descriptions, and promoting examination of self-descriptions that are imposed by prevailing social discourse[21] (White, 1984, 1986). He used similar techniques in his interview with two defense analysts from CSIA and three peace activists from CPSNA (also known as "nuclear psychologists"). The defense analysts had shown little interest in the psychological perspective offered by those at CPSNA. The "real problems" of the nuclear age, they had argued, were political and strategic, not psychological. They thought that when psychological factors were relevant at all they played a minor, and usually unpredictable, role. The psychologists had argued that the *technostrategic approach* was dangerously narrow and, in fact, incapable of framing crucial questions about human values and capabilities; it failed to move beyond a Hobbesian stereotype of human nature. These differences were at the center of the problematic conversation in which White was asked to intervene. He would seek to *externalize the problem,* help the participants *become aware of how it oppressed them,* search out *exceptions* to the problem-saturated description, use these exceptions to launch and nurture a *new description,* and then help the participants begin to develop *new ideas about themselves and their future.*

White began the interview with the question, "What are the advantages of your having conversations with each other?" Representatives from both groups explained that they were interested in "broadening their horizons." Yet they were often unreceptive to each other. For example, the defense analysts' model of the international situation, one psychologist said, "leaves out a million things about human knowledge and interactions." One defense analyst said that he had a difficult time intellectually with the sort of "distortions of fact" that he had heard from physician-activist Helen Caldicott. The styles of thinking of each group (or at least the stereotypes of it) were distasteful to the other.

Such negative exchanges, however, did not typify the conversation that White facilitated. Once the discussion began, an "exception" occurred almost immediately—an exception to the problem-saturated description of the two groups, each believing their own model to be adequate and the other's model to be inadequate. As the groups explored reasons to converse, the defense analysts critiqued their own approach as narrow and "likely to miss something." They portrayed it as inappropriately emulating the hard sciences, as if human interactions could be described with the theoretical simplicity of physics. They did *not* say, however, that the psychologists were helpful in correcting this tendency. In fact, they questioned the *practical applicability* of psychology to issues of national security. Perhaps because of this rebuff, one of the psychologists failed to hear the analysts' own self-criticism and said that they needed someone from "outside" to point out the limitations of their approach. The psychologist, in effect, resumed the problematic behavior by stating that the analysts were in need of the "correct" view of the psychologists. Another psychologist heard the defense analysts' self-criticism as an "exception."[22] In White's terms, the analyst had "refused to cooperate with the problem" by becoming self-critical.

One psychologist raised the question of power: "You may feel at times insecure and limited," she said, "but in fact you defense analysts have the power. The Pentagon turns to you for consultants, not to our Center." The idea that they were "in power" was a surprise to the analysts, who felt powerlessness, on the one hand, in contrast to the "official" power of those in the current Republican administration, and, on the other hand, in contrast to the "popular" power of "new thinkers" like those at CPSNA. The group later speculated that only a few people probably consider themselves to be "in power." Most of us see ourselves as "passengers on the train."

In the first half of the interview, White discouraged references to the respective official heads of the two groups, both absent from the meeting. Instead he asked participants to focus on their own ideas and experiences. This instruction seemed to free the participants to express thoughts that were not defined by their institutional roles as representatives of the two groups. The ensuing departure from these roles allowed the participants, in White's terms, to recognize their *subjugation to specifications,* in this case, professionally defined roles and ways of thinking. The participants appreciated the potential power and range of a *conversation among individuals,* as contrasted with *a debate between two groups* in the presence of the group leaders, seated at opposite ends of a table.

Midway through the interview, White asked his reflecting team[23] to come into the consulting room, and he invited the interviewees to observe the reflecting team's discussion from behind the one-way mirror. In our opinion, one of the most powerful observations made by the reflecting team came from White's wife, Cheryl, who spoke about the common responsibility of all Americans as citizens of a nuclear superpower. In Australia, she said, "we must live or die with the possible consequences of nuclear war," and while she recognized it as a global problem, she thought that the Americans were "exceptionally *burdened* with the weight of responsibility." Most Americans, being citizens of a nuclear power, are prepared to hear blame and criticism. Cheryl White's empathy for the plight of Americans was stunning.

When the participants returned to the consulting room, they continued to discuss the degree to which they felt shaped by their institutional contexts. When one of the defense analysts described this pressure as something that "happened" to him, one of the psychologists said, "but you're not *given* the role and the organization, you *choose* it." This led to a discussion of life choices and goals. One defense analyst admitted that he did make a deliberate choice to be on the "inside" at this time in his life, and he added the opinion that activists can play an important role on the "outside." He commented, "You can move from being an insider to being an outsider, but you can't lie on the railroad tracks [as a war protest], then expect to become Secretary of State." He made it clear that he didn't assume (as he felt peace activists did) that people on the inside, even those who design nuclear weapons, are "warmongers." He also reported, however, an unnerving personal observation he had made of a group of scientists at a weapons laboratory. He said it was "depressing" to him to witness the degree to which the ideology of the scientists' profession had constrained their thinking.

One psychologist said that she felt a lack of openness and vulnerability on the part of the analysts. White took this opportunity to note a striking exception to the problem-saturated description of the two groups. He said, "In this interview it has been my experience that X (the analyst referred to above) took the first step in expressing insecurity, and that he located it for us in a depressing experience. It is a bit paradoxical, isn't it, that X has shared his own personal experience with us a bit more complexly than the rest of us." This observation flew in the face of a stereotypic attitude about analysts.

Such challenges to stereotypes often bring a new type of question into a stale dialogue: questions of curiosity. It was only in the second half of the interview that such questions were asked. A psychologist asked an analyst, "What was it like for you to sit in that meeting at the Kennedy School?" Curiosity questions typically stimulate further challenges to previously unexamined stereotypes and assumptions. Once this process is set in motion, ritualistic debates can be disassembled and new forms of dialogue fashioned.

All participants seemed to agree that the context of the White interview improved their conversation and that their usual institutional contexts, which foster a *we/they* mentality, tended to obstruct dialogue. The dilemma of thinking independently while still being loyal to narrowly defined institutions was not resolved in this meeting nor were issues about the nuclear threat. But specific ideas for promoting dialogue were generated and discussed. Among them was the suggestion to meet under conditions that minimize "group" behavior and maximize the sharing of individual ideas and personal experiences.

One psychologist noted that it had been helpful to converse about conversing: "You begin to think about it as *your* conversation." This is what White had in mind when he designed his opening question. He sought to externalize the problem, inviting participants to reflect on what it did to them and what they could do to it. Externalizing the stuck interaction allowed the participants to view it as something they could reshape. Under White's guidance, the participants were able to identify and appreciate exceptions to the problem-saturated description of their interactions. They also became aware of the institutional forces that were imposing *we/they* attitudes and discouraging the exploration of new and enriching approaches and ideas.

SYSTEMIC INTERVENTIONS BY THE PUBLIC CONVERSATIONS PROJECT

These days, the American public frequently witnesses heated debates on abortion, in which *pro-life* leaders talk about the fundamental value of unborn children, and *pro-choice* leaders talk about the fundamental right of women to control their bodies. Usually neither side seems moved by the other's concerns. By putting forward simple messages to potential constituents, leaders on both sides typically intensify the negative stereotypes of the other side (and often of themselves). As a consequence, pro-life people may become convinced that pro-choice people think nothing is sacred except their own pleasure and convenience, whereas pro-choice people may come to believe that pro-life people are patriarchal religious tyrants who offer women only two options: abstinence or breeding. Those lined up on each side of the issue tend to suppress any ambiguities they experience, for fear of sliding toward compromise and ultimately allowing the devastating loss of life or fundamental rights. Those who are not comfortable with either party line are sometimes turned off by the controversy and exclude themselves from the public conversation.

Beginning in September 1990, the Public Conversations Project developed a model for promoting *dialogue,* as opposed to *debate,* among people who have opposing perspectives on the abortion issue. Our definitions of the differences between debate and dialogue are presented in Table 8-4. As of November 1992, we have conducted 18 dialogue sessions with matched numbers of pro-choice and pro-life participants. Most sessions have had four, six, or eight participants, usually six. The model we describe here[24] has evolved over the course of our work and is still evolving. Each time we conduct a session and talk to participants in follow-up calls, we learn more about the power and limits of our general approach and our specific techniques.

TABLE 8-4   Distinguishing Polarized Debate from Dialogue*

Polarized Debate	Dialogue
Premeeting communication between sponsors and participants is minimal and seen as largely irrelevant to what follows	Premeeting contacts and preparation of participants are essential elements of the full process
Participants tend to be leaders known for propounding a carefully crafted position. The personas displayed in the debate are usually already familiar to the public. The behavior of the participants tends to conform to stereotypes	Those chosen to participate are not necessarily outspoken "leaders." Whoever they are, they speak as individuals whose own unique experiences differ in some respect from others on their "side." Their behavior is likely to vary in some degree and along some dimensions from stereotypic images others may hold of them
The atmosphere is threatening; attacks and interruptions are expected by participants and are usually permitted by moderators	The atmosphere is one of safety; facilitators propose, get agreement on, and enforce clear ground rules to enhance safety and promote respectful exchange
Participants speak as representatives of groups	Participants speak as individuals, from their own unique experiences
Participants speak to their own constituents and, perhaps, to the undecided middle	Participants speak to each other
Differences within "sides" are denied or minimized.	Differences among participants on the same "side" are revealed, as individual and personal foundations of beliefs and values are explored.
Participants express unswerving commitment to a point of view, approach, or idea.	Participants express uncertainties as well as deeply held beliefs.
Participants listen to refute the other side's data and to expose faulty logic in their arguments. Questions are asked from a position of certainty. These questions are often rhetorical challenges or disguised statements.	Participants listen to understand and gain insight into the beliefs and concerns of the others. Questions are asked from a position of curiosity.
Statements are predictable and offer little new information.	New information surfaces.

TABLE 8-4 *(continued)*

Polarized Debate	Dialogue
Success requires simple impassioned statements.	Success requires exploration of the complexities of the issue being discussed.
Debates operate within the constraints of the dominant public discourse. (The discourse defines the problem and the options for resolution. It assumes that fundamental needs and values are already clearly understood).	Participants are encouraged to question the dominant public discourse, that is, to express fundamental needs that may or may not be reflected in the discourse and to explore various options for problem definition and resolution. Participants may discover inadequacies in the usual language and concepts used in the public debate.

Copyright 1991, the Public Conversations Project of the Family Institute of Cambridge, 51 Kondazian Street, Watertown, MA 02172.

Our Process

Potential participants are identified by word of mouth and through organizations such as Planned Parenthood and Massachusetts Citizens for Life. In an initial telephone call, they learn of our project's dual purpose: (1) to provide people who care deeply about the abortion issue but who have different perspectives an opportunity to discuss it in a format designed to enhance safety and respectful exchange and (2) to provide us with an opportunity to learn how dialogue can be promoted on "hot" sociopolitical issues. Those contacted usually respond with some interest. They are sometimes cautious, sometimes intrigued. Some people are enthusiastic about the project. Only a handful of people (on both sides) have rejected the basic premise that "there's something to talk about." Those who decline to become involved generally do so because of scheduling problems. Many people are attracted by the possibility that they can become known to someone on the other side as more than a stereotype.

Those who agree to attend a session receive a written invitation that establishes our role as facilitators and reinforces the distinction between dialogue and debate.[25] The invitation encourages participants to prepare for the session by examining their certainties *and uncertainties* about the issues surrounding abortion and by considering what they might like to learn about a perspective other than their own. They are asked to come to the session "as an individual with a unique set of experiences and perspectives." They are assured that they will not be asked to represent a political group and can decline to respond to any question.[26]

During a light buffet dinner before the dialogue session, the participants and the project members are each invited to say something about who they are "so that we can all know each other as someone other than the holder of a particular view about abortion or a facilitator of a process." At this point, no participant knows which "side" the others are on. The end of the dinner is marked by the signing of provisional video release forms, which limit the use of the tapes to our research team and its consultants.

After dinner, two members of our team go to the dialogue room to serve as facilitators, and the others enter the viewing room. The facilitators suggest that the group make several agreements about their conduct toward one another. These usually include maintaining confidentiality about what others say, not interrupting ("listening until each person has completed what he or she has to say"), using "pro-choice" and "pro-life" rather than "anti" terms to refer to the positions of others,[27] and being free to "pass" if one is not ready or willing to respond to a question—no explanation required.

After outlining the structure of the evening, the facilitators remind participants about the purpose of the gathering. "This dialogue session," they explain, "offers you an opportunity to be with people who have different perspectives and to ask questions that arise from your genuine curiosity." Participants are reminded to speak as unique individuals, not as representatives of a group, about their thoughts and feelings and about what they struggle with in dealing with the abortion issue. The facilitators then share an observation made in previous dialogue sessions: that there is much more variation within each of the two groups (pro-choice and pro-life) than the public debate reveals. This observation leads to the first of two questions that each participant is asked to answer:

> We would like you to say something about your own life experiences in relation to the issue of abortion. For example, can you say something about your personal history with the issue, how you got interested in it, what your involvement has been, what experiences you have had that relate to your views on the subject?

The second question is:

> What is at the heart of the matter, for you as an individual?

A third question is framed as follows:

> A large number of the people we have talked to in these sessions have told us that, within their general approach to this issue, they find some gray areas, some dilemmas about their own beliefs, or even some conflicts within themselves. Sometimes the gray areas are revealed when people consider hard cases—circumstances in which a pro-life individual might want to allow an abortion, or in which a pro-choice person might not want to permit an abortion. Or, in a very different way, sometimes an individual feels that his or her own views on abortion come into conflict with other important values and beliefs. We have found that it's been very productive and helpful when people share whatever dilemmas, struggles, and conflicts they have within their main view. We invite you to mention any pockets of uncertainty, or lesser certainty, value conflict, or mixed feelings that you may be aware of and willing to share.

After each of the three opening questions has been posed, participants are encouraged to take a moment to reflect before answering. Participants are invited to respond to the first two questions in the order in which they are seated. They answer the third question "popcorn style," not in a "go-round"; that is, the question is posed to the full group, and participants may respond in any order they wish.

In the middle phase of the session, participants are invited to ask one another *questions arising from curiosity.* In introducing this phase, the facilitators emphasize the difference between questions of curiosity and rhetorical questions. A question arising from genuine curiosity indicates that one does not understand something about another perspective and is open to learning something new. Unlike a rhetorical question, it is *not* a statement in disguise. The facilitators recommend that the questions relate to the thoughts and experiences of those present, rather than to people or groups outside the room.

In the last phase of the session, the facilitators once again become the questioners. They usually ask what themes the group would find "productive and satisfying" to explore if they had more time. Then the participants are invited to reflect on their process ("What have you done or not done to make this conversation go as it has gone?") and to make a closing comment. Finally, participants are given an opportunity to revise their agreements about confidentiality and videotape use, and they are asked if they are willing to accept a follow-up telephone call from a member of the Project.

Follow-up calls are made about a week or two after the session. During the call, we express interest in learning how the participants experienced the session, and we ask if they have any ideas about improving the process. Other questions we commonly ask are: "Did anything surprise you about your own participation?"; "Does anything stand out in your memory about the format, the ideas, or the people?"; and "What was the most uncomfortable moment for you?" When a specific discomfort is mentioned, the participant is asked whether the facilitators could have done anything to help at that moment. Each follow-up call ends with questions about specific elements of the process, for example, the initial call, the letter, the dinner, taping, observation, physical setting, ground rules, opening questions, and closure. What we learn in follow-up calls has been vitally important to the revision and improvement of our model.

Observations

The following comments on each phase of the dialogue session are informed by follow-up information from participants and by the team's observations and analyses of the sessions.

Many participants have told us that during the dinner they privately tried to guess who was on which "side." When their guesses were proved wrong, they had to confront stereotypes that they did not realize they held. Some have said that they were relieved to discover that "the other side" was not as unusual or threatening as they had imagined.

The first of the opening questions (about life experiences in relation to the abortion issue) grounds the dialogue in personal experience. Some participants have spoken about abortions they have had. One pro-life woman said that when she had an abortion at age 16, she was led to believe that the abortion would terminate not only the pregnancy, but also "my relationship to that life event, which I found to be fundamentally untrue." When she had another unwanted pregnancy at age 19, she gave the baby up for adoption, which was, for her, a better experience. An older woman said that she was pro-choice because she had had an illegal abortion and "it was a terrifying experience. I'm still bearing the scars." In follow-up calls, participants have said that listening to answers to question one and formulating their own answers helped them see how beliefs are influenced by subjective experience of life events.

The second question (What is at the heart of the matter for you?) allows participants to bring their most fundamental concerns into the room without fear of rebuttal. One pro-life woman said, "It would frighten me to think that my life is contingent upon the fact that someone wants me." She said that "wantedness" should not be a factor in survival at any stage of life. A pro-choice woman said that at the heart of the matter for her was respect for the "moral maturity of women." Some participants use the rights-oriented language of the public debate in their answers to this question, but they usually express their concerns about rights in a highly engaging and personal manner.

Having had the opportunity to speak about their heartfelt certainties, participants can respond with a sense of integrity to the third question about the uncertainties, conflicts, or gray areas that they may have within their own beliefs. Answers to the third question often begin to dissolve stereotypes. For example, many pro-choice people say that *some* abortions are not morally justifiable, such as abortions in the third trimester, and abortions when used as birth control or for sex selection; many pro-life people have said that *some* abortions may be morally justifiable, such as in cases involving rape, incest, or danger to the mother's life. Some participants feel certain about their basic position but are troubled by conflicts between that position and other values they have. For example, a pro-choice woman said that abortion is a private issue, but she also felt that some prenatal events are of general concern to the society, citing the rising rates of "crack baby" births. A pro-life man said that his belief in pluralism conflicts with his stand against abortion. A pro-life woman said that her beliefs are firm when she considers abortion in the abstract, but she wavers when a friend confides that she is considering ending an unplanned pregnancy. Her concern for the unborn comes into conflict with her desire to respond with compassion to specific women who are suffering.

When participants start questioning one another, some have needed help in avoiding rhetorical questions, but many have shown genuine curiosity. For example, a Jewish pro-choice woman asked a pro-life woman to explain the process of ensoulment, according to her beliefs as a Catholic. A pro-life woman asked a pro-choice woman why the latter felt less willing to have an abortion after having given birth to a daughter than she had felt before. A pro-choice woman asked a pro-life woman if the latter felt hostility toward women who have had abortions.

A pro-life man asked a pro-choice woman who had had an abortion to describe the thinking that went into her decision.

When asked what they would like to discuss if they had more time, many participants have suggested exploring areas of agreement, such as promoting responsible sexual behavior; reducing the rate of unintended pregnancy; providing social support for families who choose to continue unplanned pregnancies; and supporting sex education, prenatal care, family leave, and day care. Some have suggested exploring different personal and societal attitudes toward sexuality. Some have wanted to explore differences among participants' fundamental assumptions about human nature. Some have said that they would like to address the role of men in reproductive responsibilities and decision making.

Closing comments often compare the atmosphere of the session with that of most debates on this issue. One pro-life man noted that he and his fellow participants were able to speak to one another as people, not positions. He said he was not sure that the people "leading the charge on both sides" could engage in such a discussion. A pro-choice woman responded: "They [the leaders] dominate the discussion, but they are in the minority, I think." She speculated that "there are an awful lot of the four of us out there." One pro-choice woman was surprised that she was able to resist the temptation to try to persuade others to agree with her views. "That was a personal victory," she said. Another pro-choice woman said, "It's very easy to talk about your experience with people you know, who you know are sympathetic to you and your political positions. It's much more difficult to share with people who you know are opposing you on an ideological level. But this is, in my mind, how human community is formed and deepens. We do not change the world by staying on two sides of the fence and yelling at each other."

During follow-up calls, some participants have indicated that they found the experience to be not only enriching, but also personally transformative. One pro-choice man said of a pro-life man, "I was so impressed with his interest in my concerns and his flexibility. It made me wonder why I hold so rigidly to my ideas. This is something I want to work on in my personal life as well as in my politics." When participants tell us what surprised them most, it is often the realization that people on the "other side" are motivated by genuine compassion and by compelling concerns and ideals.

As we continue to review our facilitator role, we have learned that presenting and repeatedly reinforcing the "alternative frame" of dialogue (as opposed to debate) is crucial to creating new conversations about abortion. We have also seen the value of clearly stated and consistently enforced ground rules and guidelines.[28] The aphorism, "an ounce of prevention is worth a pound of cure," certainly applies to dialogue promotion; that is, it is better to risk boring the participants with statements about the special opportunity they have to do something different and with detailed suggestions for how to make that happen than to try to recreate a dialogic atmosphere after the conversation has slipped into argument (even polite argument).

At this point in our work, it appears that, in their hearts, most people on both sides of the abortion controversy seem attracted to the idea of a world in which freedom is balanced by responsibility. In the political world, the opposing movements have created stereotypes of each other, with pro-life people portrayed as being uninterested in the freedom of women and pro-choice people portrayed as not valuing sexual responsibility or the unborn. The moral energies of each side are pitted against each other, rather than joined to discover ways in which *both* sides can work to create a society in which people exercise responsibility and enjoy freedom.

BRAINSTORMING MEETINGS WITH STRANGE BEDFELLOWS

Background

The idea behind the brainstorming retreats listed in Table 8-3 can be traced to March 1983, when Richard Chasin and psychiatrist John E. Mack convened a working conference entitled, "An Exploratory Meeting on the Nuclear Deadlock." The conference brought together 40 individuals from a wide range of professions: academics; activists; religious leaders; psychologists; White House staff; and individuals who had once been weapons designers, military officers, officials of the CIA, or National Security Council staff. The goal of the meeting was to explore the underlying forces propelling the nuclear arms race and the obstacles to its deceleration. The conference went well, but it occurred to Chasin that the traditional format (with lectures and some small group discussions) had not allowed the event to achieve the potential one might have hoped for, given the diversity, energy, and talent of the participants.

In response, he created a new design for a three-day meeting that was held during the summer of 1985, the goal of which was to brainstorm strategies for making peace a more interesting and captivating concept to the general public. Convened in collaboration with a Hollywood activist, Norman Fleishman, and hosted by Richard Chasin and Laura Chasin at a private home on Chappaquiddick Island (Martha's Vineyard, MA), the conference brought together a number of strange bedfellows, including West Coast writers and film producers and East Coast activists, intellectuals, and foundation representatives. The meeting format was carefully designed to heighten creativity and learning among people who share some fundamental concerns and interests but whose professional lives effectively separate them and discourage productive dialogue and collaboration. Since 1985, Laura Chasin and Richard Chasin, along with their friends, colleagues, and adult children,[29] have conducted six other brainstorming meetings (see Table 8-3).[30]

Phases in the Process

Planning. Participants are selected with an eye toward creating an interesting and productive blend of perspectives, skills, fields of knowledge, and arenas of influence. Typically the participants include political leaders (such as governors or members of Congress), people who occupy influential positions in print and broadcast media, leaders in social theory and policy, religious leaders, activists, and writers. Participants are told that they are being invited as individuals not as representatives of organizations. About one month before the meeting, participants receive reading materials, some "warm-up" questions, and information about the format of the meeting. For a group of 30 to 35 "resource" participants, the conveners usually enlist the help of three or four other "process" participants (often therapists) to form a facilitation team, along with four or five assistants to handle logistics and serve as recorders. The facilitation team meets at least once before the event and arrives at the meeting site one day early.

Phase 1: Contracts and Acquaintances. The meeting begins with some brief welcoming remarks by the conveners. Then ground rules for the meeting are presented by the facilitators, most notably, the "pass rule." The issue of confidentiality is raised, and some preliminary group decisions are made about it. If the meeting is being audiotaped, participants are told that they can request that the tape recorder be turned off at any time. They can also ask at a later time to have anything they have said erased from the tape.

The first session of the meeting (usually held on a Friday evening) begins with an introductory "go-round," which gives each participant 2 or 3 minutes to say something about the resources (experiences, talents, and so on) that he or she brings to the tasks at hand and perhaps something about his or her personal sources of inspiration, commitment, or confusion regarding the topic of the meeting. Then the facilitators present a brief overview of brainstorming techniques.[31] They suggest guidelines for the idea-generating phase of brainstorming (refraining from "editing" one's own "impractical" ideas, keeping statements brief, withholding criticism, and others).[32] They explain that the idea-generating phase is followed by an idea-refinement phase, in which participants use their analytic and critical skills to select some particularly promising ideas and organize them thematically.

The agenda for the first night sometimes includes a structured exercise other than the introductory "go-round," but the opening session is always adjourned early enough to allow participants to get a good night's sleep, in preparation for the demanding schedule of the rest of the meeting.

Phase 2: Defining and Advancing Subjects of Interest. During its first morning together, the group is provided with a common stimulus for discussion, usually a brief talk by one or more of the resource participants. Then the full group (usually 25 to 45 people) is broken into three to five subgroups to which members are preassigned to ensure diversity. Each subgroup, assisted by one facilitator and one recorder, meets separately to discuss the same broadly framed topic. The recorder writes all of the ideas generated on a large newsprint pad and tapes each sheet of newsprint to the wall, creating a "group memory," which frees the resource participants from the task of taking notes. At the end of the given time period, usually 60 to 90 minutes, the subgroup selects a member to present its work to the full group. Reports are always given by resource participants, not by facilitators or recorders.[33]

When the full group reconvenes, each reporter gives a report on his or her subgroup discussion, after which members of that group are given the opportunity to correct significant omissions or offer clarification. Then members of the full group may ask questions but only questions of clarification. Full group discussion is permitted only after all reports have been given, and the discussion is kept brief. Participants are assured that they will be given time later on to express thoughts stirred by the reports and the full group discussion.

After the first round of subgroup discussions and reports to the full group, the resource participants are usually each asked to write on a 3" × 5" card a topic or two that each would like to serve as the focus of the next subgroup discussion they attend. The facilitators use these cards to guide them in designing the next session. Usually the topics listed on the cards cluster around three to five general topics, which are then proposed to the full group as potential topics for the next round of subgroup discussions. This time participants are not assigned to subgroups; instead they choose the subgroup topic that is of greatest interest to them. Thus, while the facilitation team provides a clear structure for the meeting, the topics for subgroup discussion are chosen by the resource participants.

Phase 3: Hot Issues Surface.   After two rounds of subgroup sessions and reports to the full group, the facilitation team may decide to continue with a third or fourth iteration of this process. After two or three rounds of subgroup meetings and limited full group discussions, however, some key dilemmas, conflicts, or potential group projects have almost always become salient and compelling for the whole group. This shapes the third phase, which is the least predictable and most emotional part of the meeting. Three examples of dilemmas or conflicts are:

1. At the first brainstorming meeting on abortion, discussions of "litmus tests" for political candidates on women's issues raised sensitive issues of race. An African-American candidate for governor had not been endorsed by some women's groups because he had been noncommittal on the particular aspect of the pro-choice agenda pertaining to parental consent for minors. This angered some of the African-American participants, who thought that endorsements should reflect a broad examination of what a candidate represents. Passions ran high on the topics of race and "single-issue politics." The next day, the full group decided to commit its final morning together to an examination of this issue.

2. At the meeting of conflict resolution scholars and practitioners, gender became a hot issue when the female participants observed that some male participants had framed a group exercise—to conduct a "case" discussion by those with experience in the Soviet Union—in a way that effectively excluded all of the women and "their kind of expertise." The women suggested expanding the frame to include women who had had related experiences, including the

application of communication and collaboration techniques that were fostered by the women's movement. Their suggestion brought to the surface a gender conflict that might otherwise have been a hidden and destructive undercurrent.

3. When a number of hot dichotomies surfaced in the second brainstorming meeting on abortion, the facilitators decided to create a structured exercise through which the genuine needs of various groups could be expressed in a focused manner, without fear of rebuttal. The facilitators asked for volunteers to role-play representatives of various groups (including feminists, political consultants, advocates for the poor, minorities, legislators, professionals working with families, state activists, national activists, and men). The volunteers were to be individuals who could "represent their role with authenticity." Sitting in a circle in the middle of the room, the volunteers were asked to speak in role for a few minutes about ways in which they felt "not adequately understood" or about a source of passion for their work. After each one spoke, he or she entertained questions from the other role-players. For example, the professional working with families defined himself as a "family" and said: "I am misunderstood. . . . If I am a poor family. . . . I don't have a choice in any case. If I am pregnant, I will have another child, and my other two or three children will accommodate. . . . We know how to survive. And, at some point, somebody will decide something about my children. . . . I will not choose. I am excluded from that middle-class discussion. When you say pro-choice, what are you talking about?" The volunteer playing "national activist for choice" asked the "family," "Is the pro-choice movement irrelevant or antagonistic to you?" He replied, "It is not antagonistic. It doesn't have energy."[34]

It is impossible to predict which hot issues will surface during the meeting, but the facilitators have come to expect that *some* sort of group "crisis" will arise, requiring an intervention that will promote understanding of the conflict, generate ideas for resolution, and restore solidarity to the group. The intervention may involve no more than helping the group change its agenda—as in the first two cases. Or, as described in the third example, it may involve designing and implementing a structured exercise.

Phase 4: Resolution and (Possible) Product. The nature of the activities undertaken in this phase depends on the needs of the group. In some cases, the subgroup format is used, particularly when some participants are eager to create "products." For example, at the end of the Entertainment Summit Retreat, some group members developed a plan for establishing a new organization, the Soviet-American Film Initiative, which was formed in the months subsequent to that retreat. Other group members met to write a press release. In other cases, the fourth phase involves a full group activity. Regardless, at the end of every meeting, the full group convenes to discuss products and follow-up activities (if there are any) and to say good-bye.

It is important to note that the model described here does not lead the process toward (or away from) a product orientation. Rather the model uses an *emergent design*[35] to help the group identify and meet its own needs, as they emerge, whatever they may be.

Evaluation and Follow-up. Feedback is elicited from participants about various aspects of the meeting, including the group size and composition, the relative time spent in small or large groups, and the facilitation techniques. Evaluation forms are given to participants as they leave, and the completed forms are mailed back to the conveners over the course of the next month or two. Participant feedback has proved useful in planning new meetings.

Many participants use the evaluation form to reflect on their personal learning experiences. For example, one person wrote that the weekend helped him to be "more aware of alternative paths to effecting social change, more humble about my own path, and more aware of interconnections and interdependencies." Some participants mention new acquaintances they made or actions they have taken or plan to take as a consequence of the meeting. Some of these actions have been quite significant. For example, the ideas discussed at one meeting shaped the writing of a network television show; a discussion at another meeting led to a political candidate in a close race winning support from powerful organizations that had not previously supported him. Several participants have sent us their later publications, indicating that the brainstorming meeting had catalyzed new ideas and directions. The final sessions of some meetings have led to the establishment of new activist and professional groups.

GUIDELINES FOR PLANNING AND CONDUCTING SYSTEMIC INTERVENTIONS IN THE SOCIOPOLITICAL ARENA

Each of the interventions we have described is but one step in a learning process that is very much in progress. As we attempt to review and summarize our learning to date, we are acutely aware of its limitations: We have worked in a relatively small number of specific contexts on specific topics. Yet in the course of our own work and in interaction with other dialogue facilitators, we have been able to develop several guidelines and principles that we hope will help others who wish to plan and conduct systemic interventions. In this section, we focus on work with groups in conflict. Most of our comments pertaining to meetings with strange bedfellows appear in footnotes.

Planning and Preparation

Setting Goals and Learning about the Conflict. In each of our systemic interventions with groups in conflict, our general goal has been to block old, ritualized patterns of interaction and to create openings that allow new information to emerge and productive patterns of interaction to take shape.[36] We believe that coherent, effective work with groups in conflict requires the initial formulation of a general goal. This is hardly enough, however, particularly when one is working with sociopolitical conflicts that are volatile and potentially dangerous. Uninformed facilitators have no place in a sociopolitical minefield; they can do more harm than good. Even interventions that appear to be benignly ineffective may demoralize the participants and discourage them from partaking in future dialogue initiatives. Thus a crucial phase in planning an intervention is the gathering of a team of experienced facilitators who collectively have or can develop an informed grasp of the conflict.

If old patterns of interaction are to be interrupted and new ones encouraged, dialogue facilitators must be equipped with knowledge of the old patterns. Some questions that may guide the accumulation of such knowledge are: How does the ritualized conflict go? Where are the predictable dead ends? Which arguments in the debate are most incendiary? Which arguments invite a predictable counterattack? What stereotypes do the groups hold of each other? Which of those stereotypes are most offensive? What historical or current behaviors sustain such stereotypes? What are the hopes, fears, and grievances of each group, and in what ways are they trivialized by the other group? What is it about the ideological or cultural differences between the groups that either blinds each group to the concerns of the other or justifies each group's dismissal of those concerns? In what ways do people minimize the differences among those on their own side? How and why do they silence misgivings they may feel about the official position of their own side? Who is in "the middle," how do they see themselves, and how do the major adversaries see them in relation to the conflict? Which options for resolution of the conflict have been proposed and rejected? Were the grounds for rejection pragmatic, philosophical, or symbolic?

A potential facilitator should also determine who the key players are, both in public and behind the scenes, and who else participates in the larger system of conflict. Some guiding questions are: Who are the leaders on each side? What are the political, institutional, or cultural constraints on their interactions with the other side? What are the real or imagined consequences of their expressing any reservations about their own avowed position? Who advises or otherwise influences the leaders? Who gives them the most power and support and for what reasons? Where do various segments of the public stand on the issues debated by their leaders? Which segments of the public are well represented by the leaders? Which are not? Whose life experiences and concerns seem to be irrelevant, trivialized, or denigrated? Whose voices are absent? Who is most harmed by the perpetuation of the conflict? Who benefits from the perpetuation of the conflict? Are there forces that sustain the conflict that are not usually considered part of the conflict?

Obviously, generating comprehensive answers to such questions may require years of study. We do not intend to suggest that facilitators must become scholarly experts on the conflict (although they may wish to consult such experts). Rather, we urge that facilitators become acquainted with the fundamental aspects of the conflict before planning an intervention.

Selecting Participants and Choosing a General Format.   Many dialogue facilitators seek to bring together representatives of groups in conflict who have significant influence with leaders or the public but whose political or institutional roles are less constraining than those of the official public leaders, whose political roles may keep them from behaving in novel ways. This approach is an example of *track two diplomacy.* With the help of a third-party facilitator, influential people from each of the groups develop (1) a working relationship, (2) an understanding of each other's perspectives, and (3) some ideas for resolving the conflict. Participants in track two diplomacy bring their new perceptions and ideas back to the official track one leaders, who can privately consider new ideas in conversation with an ally but may not be able to discuss those ideas with an adversary.[37] Many of the participants in our IPPNW workshops can be thought of as track two diplomats, as they have considerable influence in their home countries and, in some cases, easy access to leaders or the media.

Some efforts in dialogue facilitation use a grassroots approach. For example, some of the participants in our ongoing dialogue sessions on abortion are concerned citizens with opposing views but no special political influence. If one works with large enough numbers of such people, however, shifts in the political landscape may be promoted.

Some activities (sometimes grouped under the name *citizen diplomacy*) bring together people who share a common professional, philosophical, or religious interest, even though their home cultures or countries are antagonistic to one another. Such activities require an approach that blends interruption of old patterns (as in our systemic interventions into conflict) and promotion of collaborative and creative work (as in our brainstorming meetings with strange bedfellows). An example of a meeting using such a blended approach was the Entertainment Summit Retreat, which brought together Soviet and American filmmakers. Such gatherings may not require facilitation to avoid overt hostility, but we believe they benefit from careful structuring and informed facilitators who can steer participants away from pseudomutuality.[38] Even brainstorming meetings with participants who do not come from adversarial groups require structure, not so much to prevent conflict but to enhance shared creativity and action.

Inviting and Preparing Participants: Building Trust and Setting Expectations. At the first moment of contact with a potential participant, the intervention begins. The facilitator begins to build trust, communicate goals, and set expectations.[39] For example, when participants are invited in a telephone call to attend a dialogue session on abortion, their immediate thoughts and concerns are treated with care and respect. The *alternative frame* of dialogue (as opposed to debate) is introduced at the time of invitation and further elaborated and reinforced throughout the intervention.[40]

All significant expectations that the facilitators have of the participants should be communicated at the time of invitation (e.g., regarding voluntary participation, confidentiality, and taping of the event). The roles of the participants and the facilitators should be defined; that is, the participants should understand that the *content* of the conversation will be determined by the participants alone. (The participants' "ownership" of the conversation enhances their enthusiasm and sense of responsibility for it.) The role of the facilitators is to create a *structure* and manage a *process* that allows the participants to generate and explore the content safely and productively. We recommend that those who agree to participate in a meeting all receive an identical letter confirming the invitation and reiterating goals and expectations.[41]

The Meeting: Structure and Facilitation

Structuring the Meeting. We have found it helpful to view the meeting as involving the following five phases:

1. Entry: Getting to Know Others as People. During this phase, participants are given a chance to get to know each other and the facilitators as individuals. Even during this "social" phase, the facilitators shape the process to enhance safety and respect. Each person is given an opportunity to introduce himself or herself and say something positive and personal. This reinforces the image of the event as people talking to people, not as a contest between two sides. In our dialogue sessions on abortion, we find it helpful to restrict introductions so they do not pertain to the subject at hand.

2. Agreements, Ground Rules, and Suggestions.[42] This is the time to flesh out agreements made provisionally during the invitation phase. The "pass rule" is virtually always proposed and agreed on in our interventions. We recommend that agreements about confidentiality, audiotaping, and videotaping be made in two phases. Before the session, participants agree to a "draft" proposal on these issues; after the session, they can make a final agreement. At this stage, the facilitators may propose additional agreements (e.g., about participants not interrupting each other), and they may ask participants if they would like to make any other agreements with each other or if they would like to articulate any concerns about trust and safety before proceeding.

The facilitators then offer guidelines for enhancing discussion during the meeting. For example, they may suggest that participants speak from their own experience and avoid making attributions to people outside of the room. This prevents the displacement of the conflict onto people "out there," and reinforces the idea that the definition of the conflict and its earnest exploration are the responsibility of the people in the room.

3. Opening Questions. The opening questions or tasks in an intervention generate a shared pool of information about who is in the room and what their sincere concerns and interests are. The questions are designed to block rebuttal and minimize reactivity. Their goal is to make participants more comfortable with self-disclosure and to enhance their curiosity to learn more about each other. Examples of opening questions are the hopes and fears task at IPPNW workshops and the set of three questions posed by facilitators in dialogue sessions on abortion. In both cases, the content is heartfelt, and the structure blocks rebuttal.

4. *The Middle Phase.* What is done during the middle phase of the meeting is so dependent on the nature of the meeting (i.e., the specific goals and expectations, the participants, the historical context, the dynamics of the conflict, and so on) that it is difficult to offer guidance beyond what we offer here as general guidelines. The facilitation team should have a plan for this phase, but they should be ready to revise it in accordance with the interests, concerns, and needs that arise from the group.

5. *Closure.* At the end of an intensely involving structured event, participants usually appreciate an opportunity to speak briefly about what they have learned or to express something they have not yet had a chance to express. To provide this opportunity, the facilitators may ask, for example, "Is there any comment that you would like to make, or question that you would like to bring into the room— knowing there is not time for discussion and answers—that will help you to bring your participation to a satisfying close?"

Facilitating the Meeting. The first three guidelines listed apply to all phases of virtually any intervention into conflict (including planning and follow-up). The others may be more or less relevant, depending on the nature of the meeting.

1. *Maintain Role Clarity and Avoid Bias.* If the facilitators do not confine themselves to designing and monitoring the process (that is, if they contribute to content), role clarity is lost, and the facilitators become vulnerable to power struggles with participants about procedure. If facilitators show bias with respect to content, the participants' trust in them will be undermined; if participants no longer trust the facilitators, they are likely to retreat to the familiar self-protective conversation. Absence of bias is in the eye of the beholder. This is one reason why facilitator knowledge of the culture(s), language(s), and history of the conflict being discussed is vitally important. In our view, bias is avoided not through detachment from the belief systems in the room, but through *multidirected partiality*—respectful attention to all beliefs (Grunebaum, 1990). When facilitators listen to all participants with care and empathy, they not only earn trust, but also they model behavior that contributes to dialogic interactions and creative problem solving.

2. *Be Specific about Process Expectations.* If the facilitators would like participants to respond to a question in a specific order, that should be stated. (The pass rule is always in effect; if someone passes, they can "pass for now" and respond when others have finished.) If a "popcorn" format is acceptable or desired (i.e., whoever is ready to speak, speaks), that should be made clear. If answers to questions should take no longer than, say, 3 minutes, participants should know that. (In such cases, the facilitators might wish to alert respondents when their time is almost up, so they can conclude their answer.) This level of control sometimes

feels "unnatural." Therefore the facilitators may wish to explain ahead of time that some of the structures and restrictions will feel strange, but they help to prevent slippage into patterns of interaction that are old, familiar, "natural," and useless. For example, political combatants may find it "natural" to interrupt and make offensive attributions about each other. Thus, a dialogue session conducted using our suggested ground rules is likely to feel "unnatural" to them.

Similarly, strange bedfellows may begin a meeting with the expectation that certain types of participants will "naturally" dominate the discussion. A structured introductory task, in which each participant has an equal (and strictly monitored) amount of time to introduce himself or herself, may set a less "natural" tone, as it suggests that equal value is placed on diverse skills and experiences. It also discourages hierarchical positioning and grandstanding.

3. Enforce Ground Rules Consistently. If anyone violates a ground rule or guideline, the facilitators should intervene to make it clear that the group's agreements are being taken seriously. For example, interchanges among participants must be blocked if the time has not yet come for such discussion. If a change in the ground rules or format seems appropriate to the facilitators, they should suggest and get agreement on such a change, rather than simply allowing the change to occur.[43]

4. Encourage Participants to Speak from Personal Experience. For example, people on opposite sides in the battle over abortion, who typically learn little or nothing from each other's pronouncements about "the most important" values held by each side, learn much more when they see the rich mixture of beliefs and experiences on the other side and when they hear how the beliefs and values of those on the other side are related to life experiences that are not subject to debate.

5. Discourage Attributions to Others. If participants tend to attack or accuse the "other side," they should be encouraged to rephrase their contributions as expressions of their own values or concerns or to ask a question of someone on the other side. The following dialogue is an example. Participant: "You pro-choice [or pro-life] people only care about your own convenience [or the unborn, not about children]." Facilitator: "Would you like to ask the pro-choice [or pro-life] people here in the room what they care about?" Leaving out "they" and "them" enhances participant responsibility for the conversation. Helping participants transform untested attributions into questions fosters curiosity and learning.

6. Highlight Exceptions to Old, Useless Patterns of Interaction. For example, in his facilitated conversation, Michael White noted an exception to a stereotype that the peace activists held of the defense analysts. In dialogue sessions on abortion, we ask participants to reflect on what they have done or not done to make the conversation go as it has. In response, participants sometimes remark on new learning or behavior (such as their willingness to share uncertainties, reveal differences they have with people on "their side," or resist the urge to persuade).

7. Make Use of Other Team Members. In situations in which some members of the facilitation team are actively facilitating while others are observing, breaks should be scheduled so that the entire team can share observations and design any required midcourse corrections. For instance, every dialogue session on abortion includes a break during which the interviewers consult with other team members. At brainstorming meetings, the facilitation team works together intensely during every meal break.[44]

Follow-up

Evaluations and follow-up calls communicate the facilitators' continuing concern about the individual participants, their thoughts, and their vulnerabilities, and they provide invaluable opportunities for learning. Follow-up is vitally important when the stakes are high. In the meeting we conducted with practitioners of dialogue facilitation, many of whom work in international hot spots, several practitioners spoke about the need in their own work to promote safe and effective "re-entry" of dialogue participants to their home communities. Only through follow-up can re-entry be tracked and lessons be learned about how it can best be achieved.

In our work, many design revisions have been inspired by feedback from participants. Our follow-up procedures sometimes benefit participants as well; they promote reflection on the experience and solidify the learning that has occurred. For example, after attending the workshop on stereotyping in Hiroshima, a Japanese medical student wrote to us to share two thoughts that were stirred in him by his experience in the workshop. The first was that foreigners must be approached as individuals. He wrote, "There are so many different people in one country. I said in my report that the Japanese are definitely not a barbarous people. But some people in Japan are barbarous, so we must observe the individual." His second thought was that we must resist anger when we encounter a person who seems "bad." He explained, "There surely was a reason why he became such a person. We must observe him . . . (to see) what made his life such a miserable one." Almost two years later, we read a *Boston Globe* article (Nickerson, 1991) in which a Greenpeace activist was quoted as calling whaling a "barbaric deed" and the Japanese people "greedy ecological pirates." Would the Greenpeace activist have used such language if she had had an opportunity to explore this issue in a "cool" atmosphere, where listening and learning are as important as citing grievances?

Through our efforts to date, we have come to appreciate the discrepancy between the kind of interactions we promote and those that typify political exchanges. We have marveled at how much people can learn when they are able to express themselves with authenticity and without fear of attack, when they listen respectfully to people who hold perspectives that differ from their own, and when they take responsibility for the quality of their exchanges with one another. In a diverse and divisive world, such conversations are much more than pleasant exercises. They may be crucial to ending cycles of hatred and violence.

CONCLUDING REMARKS ON DIALOGUE AND DEMOCRACY

For the dream of democracy to be realized, we need more than voting booths and a free press. We also need a revitalized process of public discussion. We need to hear not only from experts and leaders, who are given equal time to present polarized speeches, but also from the ordinary people in the next house, the next town, and the next continent. We need to hear not only pointed arguments, but also stories about complex human experiences. We need not only constraint from impinging on the rights of others, but also the compassion to understand threats to their dignity. We need not only the freedom to speak, but also the curiosity to listen. The personal is political, and the political is personal. As politics embraces the personal—as authentic dialogue finds a place in public exchange—democracy becomes a living and breathing organism, not a machine or a formula. Family therapists can make a major contribution to enriching democracy through dialogue.

NOTES

1. This is not to suggest that family therapists have been completely inactive or silent. During the 1980s, family therapists participated in workshops and panel discussions on the nuclear threat at professional conferences, including those of the American Family Therapy Association, the American Association of Marriage and Family Therapy, the American Orthopsychiatric Association, and International Physicians for the Prevention of Nuclear War. Some of these organizations formed task forces similar to the one that led to the publication of this book. When Reusser and Murphy (1990) reviewed the activities that family therapists had undertaken to address the nuclear threat, however, they found few examples of systemic analysis on an international level, and they cited only our work in their section on intervention.

2. For example, political psychologists have called attention to projective mechanisms that seem to operate when whole nations turn both strangers and former allies into enemies so frightful that mass murder seems justifiable and even noble (Frank, 1967; Volkan, 1988). Lifton (1986) has attributed psychic numbing to the Nazis and to cold warriors. Mack (1983, 1988) has located the roots of nationalism in basic processes of identity formation. For an excellent collection of essays on the psychodynamics of international conflict, see Volkan, Julius, and Montville (1990a).

3. The Center for Psychological Studies in the Nuclear Age (now called The Center for Psychology and Social Change) is a research center founded in 1983 to address the psychosocial forces that fuel threats to global survival. It publishes a newsletter, *Center Review,* to which we have contributed regularly. Some of the descriptions of our work that appear in this chapter first appeared in articles in *Center Review.* Those articles and others are available from the Center in a compendium of reports (Gutlove, Herzig, & Chasin, 1991). The Family Institute of Cambridge is a center for training and research in applied systems theory.

4. The ad hoc brainstorming meetings were convened by Laura Chasin and Richard Chasin, with the help of various colleagues and funders (see Table 8-3).

5. Margaret Herzig was then a social science writer and editor who had worked for several years on research projects in developmental psychology, cross-cultural psychology, and family policy. Paula Gutlove, D.M.D., was then Executive Director of the Center for Psychological Studies in the Nuclear Age and was former Executive Director of Greater Boston Physicians for Social Responsibility. Gutlove was asked to direct the project in 1989. Chasin became Project Advisor, and Herzig became Associate Director.

6. In the first phase of the Project, the working team consisted of Carol Becker, Laura Chasin, Richard Chasin, Terry Real, Sallyann Roth, and Kathy Weingarten, all of whom are faculty members at the Family Institute of Cambridge (MA); Peter Cook, a public television producer; and Margaret Herzig. In the second phase, the working team consisted of Becker, Chasin, Chasin, Herzig, and Roth. An outside consultant was Jay King, a psychologist from the Boston College School of Education. Mary Hess and Eliza Vaillant have served ably as research assistants.

7. See Selvini-Palazzoli, Boscolo, Cecchin, & Prata (1980) and Tomm (1987) on circular questions in family therapy.

8. For more detailed information, see Chasin and Herzig (1988b, 1988d, 1988e); Chasin and Vartanyan (1987); Gutlove, Chasin, and Herzig (1990); and Herzig, Gutlove, and Chasin (1991).

9. The Soviet subgroup was facilitated by Dr. Vartanyan; the Soviet allies by Dr. A. Yablonsky (a World Health Organization official from Bulgaria); the Americans by Dr. Chasin; the American allies by Dr. Gutlove; and the nonaligned group by Dr. Gordon Thompson, Gutlove's husband and a physicist originally from Australia. Other facilitators included Nikolai Popov, a Soviet sociologist from the USA–Canada Institute who now heads the Political Surveys Department at the Soviet Center for Public Opinion, and Laura Chasin and her daughter, Jessica Case.

10. We had expected that the workshop would be completed in one afternoon session, but participant involvement was intense, and the group asked to extend the workshop to the next day in order to complete the second task. The condensation of lists was performed by the facilitation team between the two sessions.

11. The workshop was co-led by Drs. Chasin and Vartanyan, with the help of Margaret Herzig. Volunteers included Margaret Herzig's husband, Jim Herzig; Dr. Chasin's wife, Laura Chasin, and son, Dana Chasin; a Canadian psychiatrist, Alan Weiss; and two IPPNW activists, David Kreger and the late Gale Warner.

12. Participants used green stickers to mark what they believed were untrue assumptions. Each could put stickers on up to half of the assumptions listed. Each participant was offered one orange sticker to mark the most injurious assumption.

13. This was the largest group we have worked with at an IPPNW Congress. Seventy-one attended the workshop in Hiroshima. The workshops in Moscow and Stockholm attracted 42 and 40 participants, respectively. To ensure participant diversity in Montreal, we closed the workshop to American and Canadian participants after the first 40 had signed up.

14. During the discussion period at the end of the workshop, a British woman broke the spirit of self-examination when she challenged the Soviets because they appeared not to think that East Europeans held negative stereotypes about them. A Soviet man responded, "We listed as adversaries 'the West' . . . all that is west of our border." A Western participant, mindful of the Soviets' disavowals, commented, "Not unsophisticated!" A moment of tension, uncharacteristic of the workshop experience, was thus dissolved with humor.

15. One Canadian woman reported that she was most distressed by the assumption that Canada is culturally dependent on the United States. This, she said, "is not simply an issue of magazines and television. It has to do with self-expression, and somewhere in my heart I know that [lack of] self-expression is very much tied up in the problems of the world." She may have been suggesting that those conspicuously absent from the world stage do not always carry a sense of global responsibility and do not bring their cultural resources and understanding to bear on efforts to achieve international peace and well-being.

16. In family therapy, the opening phase of a session is often called *joining* because the therapist "joins" the family to form a new unit. We are using the older phrase *rapport building* because it better conveys our intent.

17. See Chasin, Roth, and Bograd (1989) for presentation of an interview format for couple therapy that uses enactments of an ideal future.

18. Planning for the workshop was done by us and Paula Gutlove, along with two consultants with special knowledge of Japan: family therapist Cathy Colman and sociologist Merry White. The workshop was co-led by Gutlove, Herzig, and Japanese psychiatrist Shoichi Takizawa.

19. When Gutlove and Herzig arrived in Stockholm to co-lead this workshop, they were told that Palestinians and Israelis would attend the workshop. When the workshop convened, however, those delegates were racing against the clock to write a joint statement to be presented to the full Congress the next day. (The clock won.)

20. We do not intend to suggest that cross-cultural contact is of *no* value in preventing war. Citizen diplomacy can be a highly effective means of inspiring and sustaining peace initiatives in the face of powerful cultural and institutional forces that sustain suspicion and conflict. The emphasis on common visions of peace and brotherhood can, however, encourage pseudomutuality and discourage discussion of deeply rooted conflicts.

21. In addressing professional peers (White, 1988), White presented several clinical cases; vignettes from two follow: (1) An adolescent with a habit of lying and stealing sits between his worried parents. His self-description is problem-saturated. He is in deep trouble, with a grim future. White poses numerous questions to the boy to help him stand back from his problems and consider the impact of those problems on his life. White helps externalize the problem by asking not about how and why the boy misbehaves but about how the boy's problems oppress him in daily life and limit his future. White is also on the lookout for exceptions to the boy's troubled behavior—occasions when the boy might have misbehaved, but did not. By the end of the session, the boy has begun to take responsibility for his conduct. He and his parents see exceptions to the problem-saturated description with which they began, not the least of which is the boy's honesty with the therapist. (2) A young housewife feels inadequate and depressed. She cannot perform her drudgery with a smile. Michael White helps her to see her strengths—exceptions to her self-description—and to understand that she has been "subjugated to cultural specifications for personhood," specifications that include oppressive roles for women. She no longer feels inadequate and instead joins the battle against this subjugation and begins to experience victory.

22. An unexpected exception, such as the defense analysts' self-criticism, is like a small ripple in a stream; it can be easily overwhelmed by the larger ripple of long-standing patterns of behavior. The creative task is to maintain and amplify the small ripples.

23. The reflecting team consisted of Richard Chasin, Laura Chasin, Terry Real, Sallyann Roth, Kathy Weingarten, and Cheryl White.

24. See Chasin, Chasin, Herzig, Roth, and Becker (1991); Becker, Chasin, Chasin, Herzig, and Roth (1992); Roth, Becker, Chasin, Chasin, and Herzig (1992); and Chasin, Chasin, Roth, Herzig, and Becker (1992) for more detailed presentations of the model.

25. We have begun to include a slightly modified version of Table 8-4 with the letter of invitation.

26. The letter also provides some information about our procedures (e.g., with regard to videotaping and observation by our team members) and indicates that participants will receive a $25 participant fee for their expenses and trouble. All sessions are held at the Family Institute of Cambridge on weekday evenings, from about 6:00 to 9:30 P.M.

27. The facilitators say, "We suggest that you refer to each other's perspectives using the language that the other group would use. Generally, we've found that people prefer positive terms like 'pro-life' and 'pro-choice' over terms beginning with 'anti.' Over the next couple of hours, we expect that you will come to see each other's views as being more unique and complex than any one label can do justice to, but to start, shall we agree to set aside 'anti' labels?"

28. In sessions in which the facilitators have had to enforce ground rules, the feedback from participants has been variable. Some participants have felt overcontrolled and some underprotected. Overall, the sessions in which ground rules have been followed (with and without the need for enforcement by the facilitators) have been the most satisfying for participants.

29. Several collaborators in these meetings are acknowledged in Table 8-1. Caroline Marvin, a family therapist, and Ira Hirschfield, a leader in the field of philanthropy, have been particularly steady partners in these efforts; their facilitation is always insightful, creative, and energetic. Excellent staff assistance for most conferences has been provided by the Chasin's children: Matt, Jessica, and Peter Case, and Alex and Dana Chasin.

30. For reports on the two brainstorming meetings conducted by the Project on Promoting Effective Dialogue, see Chasin and Herzig (1988b); Herzig (1987); and Gutlove (1990). Reports on three of the other meetings exist, but they are circulated in a limited fashion that is based on agreements made by the participants.

31. For more on brainstorming, see Adams (1986); deBono (1970); and von Oech (1990).

32. At one meeting, the facilitators and their assistants presented a humorous role-play of undesirable behaviors: criticism, filibustering, making pronouncements, prefacing points with lengthy anecdotes, self-aggrandizement, and silence motivated by excessive self-editing or insecurity.

33. See Doyle & Strauss (1976) for role descriptions of facilitators, recorders, and resource participants and an explanation of how people in each of these roles monitors the behavior of those in other roles.

34. People in the family therapy field may be interested to know that "the family" was played by Salvador Minuchin, who assented to having his name associated with his contribution to this structured exercise.

35. *Emergent design* is a phrase used by Charles Verge and Caroline Marvin, co-directors of the Family Institute of Cambridge, to describe the way in which they organize family therapy training programs.

36. In contrast to our goal with groups in conflict, the goal of a brainstorming meeting is to foster creativity and learning about an issue of common interest among people who

are unfamiliar with each other. Unfamiliarity is not as great an obstacle to collaboration as the enmity found in conflict, but it may lead some participants to feel insecure, particularly if they are accustomed to working in an environment with an unchanging conceptual scheme, discourse, and power structure.

37. Joseph Montville, who coined the term *track two diplomacy,* writes: " . . . track two activity is designed to assist official leaders by compensating for the constraints imposed upon them by the understandable need for leaders to be—or at least to be seen to be—strong, wary, and indomitable in the face of the enemy. If there is great tension in a political conflict, a leader who takes risks for peace without his constituents being prepared for it could lose his political base or, as has happened in more than just a few cases around the world, his life" (Montville, 1990, pp. 162–163).

38. To the extent that IPPNW delegates are influential members of antagonistic countries, exploring their differences, they can be considered track two diplomats. To the extent that they are peace activists whose differences are minimal, they are more like citizen diplomats. The workshop in Stockholm was closer to citizen diplomacy than the other workshops because some of the subgroupings highlighted commonalities across national and cultural borders.

39. Third-party facilitators, in Herbert Kelman's terms, serve as the "common repository of trust" for groups with a history of mistrust. This "enables the participants to proceed with the assurance that their interests will be protected, that their sensitivities will be respected, and that their confidences will not be violated" (Kelman, 1986, p. 304). See also Kelman (1990, p. 154).

40. When participants are invited to a brainstorming meeting, they should be told about the goals of the meeting and about any special expectations that the conveners have of them. Although much of the "frame-setting" in a brainstorming meeting can occur in the early phase of the meeting (when detailed instructions are given about brainstorming), the invitation should give a general sense of how the format and atmosphere will differ from that of traditional conferences. As for the development of trust, the stakes are clearly lower in brainstorming meetings than in interventions in conflict, and the earning of trust before the meeting is less important and challenging. To accept the invitation, however, those invited (who tend to have many demands on their time) will need to believe that the conveners will run a fruitful meeting.

41. When prior contact with participants is not possible, as in our IPPNW workshops on stereotyping, a clear statement of goals and expectations at the beginning of the meeting is essential.

42. In brainstorming meetings, because participants are free to comment on the subject of the meeting during their introductions, ground rules are established before introductions are given. The central ground rules are the pass rule and provisional confidentiality. The guidelines that are offered pertain to the spirit and method of brainstorming.

43. The need for strict monitoring of the process became evident at the IPPNW workshop in Montreal. When the facilitator allowed a generous comment to be made that did not conform to the task, this paved the way for liberties to be taken by another participant, who made an accusation (see note 14).

44. It is helpful to tell participants at the start that the facilitators will be meeting separately to do their work (not to be unsociable). Other staff should be available to provide adequate "hosting" of the participant group during such meetings.

BIBLIOGRAPHY

Adams, J. (1986). *Conceptual blockbusting: A guide to better ideas.* Reading, MA: Addison Wesley.

Author Mordecai Richler fondly describes Canada's ambivalent view of itself. (1988, July 15). *Psychiatric News,* p. 16.

Becker, C., Chasin, L., Chasin, R., Herzig, M., & Roth, S. (1992). Fostering dialogue on abortion: A report from the Public Conversations Project. *Conscience, 13* (3), 2–9.

Chasin, L., Chasin, R., Herzig, M., Roth, S., & Becker, C. (1991, Winter). The citizen clinician: The family therapist in the public forum. *American Family Therapy Association Newsletter,* 36–42.

Chasin, L., Chasin, R., Roth, S., Herzig, M., & Becker, C. (1992, Autumn). *The Public Conversations Project: Applying family therapy skills to polarized public controversies.* Plenary presentation at the Fiftieth Anniversary Conference of the American Association for Marriage and Family Therapy, Miami Beach, FL.

Chasin, R. (1988, Spring). Family therapy and international relations. *Dulwich Centre Newsletter* (Australia), 41–48.

Chasin, R., & Herzig, M. (1988a). Breaking the peace activist-defense analyst impasse . . . with a little help from down under. *Center Review, 2*(2), 2–3.

Chasin, R., & Herzig, M. (1988b). Correcting misperceptions in Soviet-American relations. *Journal of Humanistic Psychology, 28* (3), 88–97.

Chasin, R., & Herzig, M. (1988c, July). *Family systems therapy and Soviet-American relations: Modes of analysis and intervention.* Paper presented at the Eleventh Annual Meeting of the International Society of Political Psychology, Secaucus, NJ.

Chasin, R., & Herzig, M. (1988d). Living under the superpower shadows. *Center Review, 2*(3/4), 7–8.

Chasin, R., & Herzig, M. (1988e). Mind-reading in Soviet-American dialogue. *Center Review, 2*(1), 1.

Chasin, R., & Roth, S. (1990). Future perfect, past perfect: A positive approach to opening couple therapy. In R. Chasin, J. Grunebaum, & M. Herzig (Eds.), *One Couple, Four Realities: Multiple Perspectives on Couple Therapy.* New York: Guilford.

Chasin, R., Roth, S., & Bograd, M. (1989). Action methods in systemic therapy: Dramatizing ideal futures and reformed pasts with couples. *Family Process, 28,* 121–136.

Chasin, R., & Vartanyan, M. (1987). *The Workshop on Assumptions and Perceptions that Fuel the Arms Race: Introductions, tasks, and raw data.* Unpublished report available from Richard Chasin, 2 Appleton Street, Cambridge, MA, 02138.

de Bono, E. (1970). *Lateral thinking: Creativity step by step.* New York: Harper & Row.

Doyle, M., & Strauss, D. (1976). *How to make meetings work.* New York: Jove Books.

Frank, J. (1967). *Sanity and Survival: Psychological aspects of war and peace.* New York: Random House.

Grunebaum, J. (1990). From discourse to dialogue: The power of fairness in therapy with couples. In R. Chasin, J. Grunebaum, & M. Herzig (Eds.), *One Couple, Four Realities: Multiple Perspectives on Couple Therapy.* New York: Guilford.

Gutlove, P. (1990). *Facilitating dialogue across ideological divides: Techniques, strategies and future directions.* Cambridge, MA: Center for Psychological Studies in the Nuclear Age.

Gutlove, P., Chasin, R., & Herzig, M. (1990). The global family faces the future. *Center Review,* 4(1), 8.

Gutlove, P., Herzig, M., & Chasin, R. (1991). *The Project on Promoting Effective Dialogue Across Ideologies: Compendium of project reports, 1987–1991.* Cambridge, MA: Center for Psychological Studies in the Nuclear Age.

Herzig, M. (1987). *A report on the entertainment summit retreat.* Cambridge, MA: Center for Psychological Studies in the Nuclear Age.

Herzig, M., Gutlove, P., & Chasin, R. (1990). Facilitating the facilitators: Defining and advancing the field of dialogue facilitation. *Center Review, 4*(2), 8.

Herzig, M., Gutlove, P., & Chasin, R. (1991). Connections and divisions in the global community. *Center Review, 5*(2), 6.

Kelman, H. (1986). Interactive problem solving: A social-psychological approach to conflict resolution. In W. Klassen (Ed.), *Dialogue toward interfaith understanding.* Jerusalem: Tantur.

Kelman, H. (1990). Interactive problem solving: The uses and limits of a therapeutic model for the resolution of international conflicts. In V. Volkan, J. Montville, & D. Julius (Eds.), *The psychodynamics of international relationships.* Lexington, MA: Lexington Books.

Lee, R. (1981). Video as adjunct to psychodrama and roleplaying. *Videotherapy and Mental Health.* Springfield, IL: Charles C. Thomas.

Lifton, R. J. (1986). *The Nazi doctors.* New York: Basic Books.

Mack, J. E. (1983). Nationalism and the self. *The Psychohistory Review, Spring, 2* (2–3), 47–69.

Mack, J. E. (1988). The enemy system. *The Lancet, January,* 385–387.

Montville, J. (1989). Psychoanalytic enlightenment and the greening of diplomacy. *Journal of the American Psychoanalytic Association, 37*(2), 297–318.

Montville, J. (1990). The arrow and the olive branch: A case for track two diplomacy. In V. Volkan, J. Montville, & D. Julius (Eds.), *The psychodynamics of international relationships.* Lexington, MA: Lexington Books.

Nickerson, C. (1991, June 21). Saving whales means losing a life style. *Boston Globe,* p. 1.

Penn, P. (1982). Circular questioning. *Family Process, 21,* 267–280.

Penn, P. (1985). Feed-forward: Future questioning, future maps. *Family Process, 24* (3), 299–310.

Reusser, J., & Murphy, B. (1990). Family therapy in the nuclear age: From clinical to global. In M. P. Mirkin (Ed.), *The social and political contexts of family therapy.* Needham, MA: Allyn & Bacon.

Roth, S. (1992). Speaking the unspoken: A work-group consultation to reopen dialogue. In E. Imber-Black (Ed.), *Secrets in families and family therapy.* New York: Norton.

Roth, S., Becker, C., Chasin, L., Chasin, R., & Herzig, M. (1992, August). *Fostering dialogue on abortion: Systemic approaches to chronic political conflict.* Presentation at the Centennial Convention of the American Psychological Association, Washington, D.C.

Selvini-Palazzoli, M., Boscolo, L., Cecchin, G., & Prata, G. (1980). Hypothesizing-circularity-neutrality: Three guidelines for the conductor of the session. *Family Process, 19,* 3–12.

Tomm, K. M. (1987). Interventive interviewing, part II: Reflexive questioning as a means to enable self-healing. *Family Process, 26*(2), 167–183.

Tomm, K. (1988). Interventive interviewing, part III: Intending to ask circular, strategic, or reflexive questions. *Family Process, 27*(1), 1–16.

Volkan, V. (1988). *The need to have enemies and allies: From clinical practice to international relationships.* Northvale, NJ: Jason Aronson.

Volkan, V., Julius, D., & Montville, J. (1990a). *The psychodynamics of international relationships: Volume I, concepts and theories.* Lexington, MA: Lexington Books.

Volkan, V., Julius, D., & Montville, J. (1990b). *The psychodynamics of international relationships: Volume II, unofficial diplomacy at work.* Lexington, MA: Lexington Books.

von Oech, R. (1990). *A whack on the side of the head: How you can be more creative.* New York: Warner Books.

Watzlawick, P., Beavin, J., & Jackson, D. (1967). *Pragmatics of human communication: A study of interactional patterns, pathologies, and paradoxes.* New York: W. W. Norton.

White, M. (1984). Pseudo-encopresis: From avalanche to victory, from vicious to virtuous cycles. *Family Systems Medicine, 2*(2), 150–160.

White, M. (1986). Negative explanation, restraint and double description: A template for family therapy. *Family Process, 25*(2), 169–184.

White, M. (1988). *Playful intervention in a systemic frame: Strangeness as a stimulus to change.* Conference presentation sponsored by The Family Institute of Cambridge, Watertown, MA.

Chapter 9

Teaching Family Theory and Therapy in the former Soviet Union: A Continuing Experiment in Citizen Diplomacy*

Katharine Gratwick Baker

I am sitting in a small, barren office on the first floor of the Polyklinika in Vilnius, Lithuania. The gray stone floor, chipped yellow paint, and erratic heating system are typical of the decor in this aging building, built in Soviet style perhaps 20 or 30 years ago, but rapidly deteriorating. The room's one window at my back offers light and a view of other crumbling buildings. The 20 young Lithuanian psychologists and psychiatrists crowding the room, seated on small, straight-backed chairs, bending over their notebooks, bring their own energy to our meeting. They have come from all over Lithuania to attend a two-day seminar presented by American family therapists, and I have volunteered to lead the discussion with "beginners," those who have had no previous family therapy training with visiting Americans. After introductions and a discussion of initial concepts, halfway into the morning I find myself talking about the idea of *multigenerational family process* from Bowen theory. Rather pedantically, I explain that patterns of emotional relationship across generations can be affected not only by internal family factors, but also by external societal factors. Then trying hard to find the commonalities across cultures, I ask how this concept might be relevant for Lithuanian families. After a moment of silence, a

---

*The body of work reported in this chapter took place before the ending of the Soviet Union as a political entity. Throughout the text, the term *Soviet* is used to refer to the Soviet political and socioeconomic system that existed from 1917 to 1991. Colleagues and friends are identified by nationality, i.e., Russians and Lithuanians.

young bearded psychologist sighs, "Of course we must talk about the deportations." Hesitantly, feeling the weight of my ignorance, I ask, "What deportations?" Over the next day and a half I learn in harrowing detail of more than 300,000 Lithuanians wrenched from their families and sent to eastern Siberia in unheated freight trains, where they lived and died over a 15 year period, starting at the time of the Soviet takeover of Lithuania in 1940 and ending after Stalin's death during the liberalization of the Khrushchev regime. Their recounting has the quality of a lamentation, as they pour forth stories shrouded in secrecy and shame until the spring of 1989. No one in the room has escaped the deportation of a family member. For every family *multigenerational family process* is a concept layered with political, societal, economic, and emotional implication.[1]

In this brief seminar, I began as a teacher and swiftly became a learner. The experience repeated itself again and again as I was invited to return to what was then the Soviet Union to present ideas about the development of family therapy as a theory and clinical approach in the United States. Soviet mental health professionals were interested in learning about family therapy, as they were interested in a broad range of Western ideas not available to them during the years of intellectual and professional isolation imposed by state socialism. My personal goals, however, reached far beyond presentation of seminars, as I sought to broaden my understanding of a fascinating society in transition, to learn about the commonalities of the human family in different cultural settings, and to develop relationships with thoughtful colleagues from the many republics of the former Soviet Union.

This chapter weaves back and forth between the subjective and the objective, between my personal experience of teaching in the former Soviet Union and more objective descriptions of such societal processes as citizen diplomacy, the politicizing of Soviet psychology, the emergence of clinical practice in the former Soviet Union, and creating a context there for family therapy through Bowen Family Systems Theory. The chapter concludes with some personal observations, again through a Bowen theory lens, of the transitional process experienced by Soviet refugees and immigrants when they move to the United States.

CITIZEN DIPLOMACY

Just a few months before a handful of Communist Party conservatives attempted and then failed to achieve a political takeover in Moscow in August 1991, Warner (1991) wrote of Soviet citizens who had worked informally and unofficially through the 1980s to make connections with the world beyond their sealed borders. She spoke of the "individuals and groups [who] are attempting to prod their communities and nation into behavior based on the understanding that we all belong to a diverse global family living on a small and vulnerable planet. Such a movement is not unique to the Soviet Union, of course, but it has special meaning in a country that historically has been cut off from communicating with the rest of the world and that is still suffering today from a legacy of xenophobia, kneejerk militarism, and bitter nationalistic disputes" (p. 3).

Conceptual Origins

This informal, nongovernmental movement came to be called *citizen diplomacy* or *track two diplomacy*. The concept was first articulated by W. Davidson and Joseph Montville, a former Foreign Service officer, in an article in *Foreign Policy* in 1981–1982 (Winter). Montville described two diplomatic tracks: track one, the official diplomatic connections between governments, and track two, the "unofficial, nonstructured interactions" between nonofficial citizens. Montville emphasized that the underlying assumption of track two diplomacy is "that actual or potential conflict can be resolved or eased by appealing to good will and reasonableness" (p. 155). After Montville's article was published, institutionalized track two diplomacy, such as regular scientific and cultural exchange and the Dartmouth Conferences organized by Norman Cousins, took on a formidable power with profound impact on U.S.–Soviet relations. Even more informal connections such as mine between American, Russian, and Lithuanian friends and colleagues were sometimes described as track three citizen diplomacy. Track three is noninstitutional and occurs at an informal level of common individual professional and personal involvement. It is open to anyone with energy and interest to participate.

Track Three Citizen Diplomacy

My own experience as a track three diplomat led me to relationships with a variety of professional colleagues with open minds and a desire for dialogue. As we moved from the professional to the personal, we became friends. We ate together, stayed in each others' homes in Moscow and Washington, and continually corresponded, despite difficulties with their postal system (most letters were hand-carried by friends). I wrote articles for Soviet journals and encouraged distribution of Russian professional writing in the United States, presented papers to American professionals on Soviet mental health systems, spoke to American community and professional groups on the Russian family, arranged lectures by Russian and Lithuanian psychologists visiting the United States, and connected with the rapidly growing Soviet refugee community here in the United States. This personal participation in Russian–American reciprocity broadened my life, work, and understanding of the global human family.

Warner (1991) quotes Gandhi's statement that "what each of us does may seem insignificant at the time, but it is terribly important that we do it" (p. 5). In describing her own experience with Soviet "peace creators" or "social innovators," she writes: "We strengthen and empower each other, pull each other through the hard times, refuse to believe in the borders others see. When our voices blend, something powerful and previously unspoken is heard. The threads between us shimmer and hum with hope" (p. 242).

The connections between family therapists here and there often seemed tentative, perhaps overly academic, didactic, laden with the idea that our way was right, and that they had to learn from us. Yet to the extent that the learning, the openness, went both ways, the threads between us too began to "shimmer and hum" with increased understanding of what it means to be part of the human family, regardless of the vicissitudes of domestic or world politics.

Writing before the abortive 1991 Soviet coup attempt, in a world locked in cold war, Carl Sagan (1987) noted that, "just as war is too important to be left to the generals, so the relation between the superpowers is too critical to be left to the bureaucrats." According to Sagan, it was up to ordinary people to mediate a "moral credibility" between the United States and the Soviet Union, as "every bilateral exchange of opinion, every shared nonbureaucratic experience brings the quarrelsome nation states closer together" (pp. x–xii). During the polarized cold war period, being a track three citizen diplomat meant attempting to take some personal responsibility for mediating the connections.

In the post–cold war world, as a broader range of possibilities for connection opened up, participation in that connection continued to be a responsible personal choice. In fact, this type of informal diplomacy has remained critical in keeping communication open between the two countries, thus helping to avoid the misunderstanding, isolation, polarization, and stereotyping that inevitably evolve when people do not "know" each other.

MY PERSONAL EXPERIENCE AND BACKGROUND

Becoming involved in track three citizen diplomacy was an expression of my own multigenerational process. While I was a child, my mother told me lively tales of her adventures as a young actress participating in a neorealist theater festival outside Moscow in the early 1930s. I often wondered who I would have been if she had accepted the marriage proposal of an Uzbek chieftain who asked her to become first among his 30 wives and move with him to Tashkent. My father, the man whose proposal she did accept several years later, was principal of a New York City independent day school and established one of the first teacher-student exchange programs between an American and a Soviet high school in the late 1950s. Although my own ethnic background is English and Scotch-Irish, I loved Russian literature, history, and music for their drama, beauty, and intensity.

In 1962, I took my first short trip to the Soviet Union before enrolling in a master's program in Russian history and starting to work for for Radio Liberty in New York. The Russian language radio station served as a free voice of political and cultural commentary on internal Soviet affairs during the darkest years of the cold war. Like Radio Free Europe, Radio Liberty was established in the early 1950s and continues to the present. Vigorously jammed by the Soviets until the late 1980s, its offices were staffed by Russian émigré intellectuals who dreamed of returning to their country as free journalists in the post-Soviet period. In the 1960s, that time seemed far away, but their dream was intense and contagious, and their programming, when it got through, was eagerly listened to by Soviet citizens.

While working at Radio Liberty, I dreamed of eventually finding some employment that would use my Russian training and give me the opportunity to travel back and forth between the United States and the Soviet Union, hoping to participate on a personal level in softening the barriers between our countries.

In 1965, I married John Baker, an American Foreign Service officer who had specialized in Russian affairs. In 1958, as a junior political officer, John had been requested by the Soviet government to leave his assignment at the American Embassy in Moscow, in a Soviet reciprocal response to our expelling a Soviet diplomat from Washington. As a *persona non grata* in the Soviet Union, John (and his family) could not return there as long as he worked for the State Department. He changed his specialty to East European and United Nations affairs, I changed my specialty to social work and family therapy, forgot Russian, and we spent the next 21 years in New York, Prague, Washington, and Rome.

After John left the State Department in 1986, we decided to test his *persona non grata* status indirectly. In the new period of glasnost and perestroika, there appeared to be more flexibility in obtaining visas to the Soviet Union. We searched for a way that I could travel there professionally, with John accompanying me as a tourist member of a professional group. In May 1989, we joined eight American family therapists and conflict negotiators who had been invited to present workshops in the Soviet Union under the auspices of the Association of Humanistic Psychology (AHP). AHP had begun a Soviet Exchange Project in 1983, sending more than 150 North American psychologists, psychotherapists, and educators to the USSR in a seven-year period (Hassard, 1990). The small group I joined presented a series of two-day workshops on family therapy, family business, and conflict negotiation in Moscow and Vilnius, with a brief visit to the Bekhterev Institute in Leningrad.

The following year I worked hard at reactivating my Russian and was invited to return to Moscow to present a four-day seminar on Bowen Family Systems Theory at Moscow State University's Department of Psychology, which led to additional invitations, friendships, and publication of articles as well as connections in Washington with former Soviet citizens who had emigrated to the United States. What began as an adventure in testing my husband's ability to obtain a visa turned into a personal odyssey, linking my professional life as a family therapist with my long dormant personal fascination with Russia and the Soviet Union.

SOVIET PSYCHOLOGY: BACKGROUND

Before returning to the Soviet Union in 1989, I reactivated my interest in Russian and Soviet history through learning all I could about the field of psychology during the Soviet period. This approach is congruent with Bowen theory in attempting to understand the complex evolution of societal process through a focus on a special area of interest.

Not unexpectedly, I found that psychology was deeply enmeshed in the Soviet political process, particularly after Stalin had consolidated his power in the early 1930s. Psychology in prerevolutionary Russia and during the early years of the Soviet period had been lively and well connected to the developing field in Western Europe. The highly creative work of Pavlov (1849–1936), Bekhterev (1857–1927), and Vygotsky (1896–1934) dominated the field.

During the 1920s, political influences on psychological research were minimal. During the early 1930s, however, the Communist Party began to crack down. Western psychological theories were discouraged, and Soviet psychologists were encouraged to develop approaches more congruent with Marxism. In 1936, the Central Committee of the Communist Party issued a decree that outlawed all forms of psychological testing, henceforth defined as a "worthless, harmful, bourgeois hoax" and a "pedagogical perversion." Western psychological theory ran counter to Marxist teachings, which emphasized that humans are formed by their socioeconomic environment. Psychologists were politically pressured to develop a theory of human behavior that supported this ideology. As a result, many psychology journals discontinued publication, and the field in general spiraled into a period of decline.

In the late 1940s, after World War II, Stalin again attempted to galvanize psychology in service of politics through his rediscovery of Pavlov (Tucker, 1971). This led to a revolution in the behavioral sciences, with a distortion of Pavlov's concept of the conditioned reflex central to creation of a *New Soviet Man*, responsive to Marxist theory and molded by the influences of the Communist Party.

Following Stalin's death in March 1953, some shifts took place in the field of psychology. The Stalinist commitment to total environmental determinism softened somewhat, and new views sanctioning the concept of the individual psyche began to be expressed. In 1955, a new Soviet journal, *Problems of Psychology,* began to publish some of these divergent views. The predominant orientation of Soviet psychology continued to be fundamentally Pavlovian, supporting the political concept that through propaganda and other forces of state pressure, individuals will become more compliant to the political purposes of the state.

The academic field of psychology had been decimated in the 1930s, but research psychology began to re-emerge as a subspecialty under the protective umbrella of some university departments of history and philosophy in the mid-1960s. Clinical practice was virtually unknown in the Soviet Union until the 1980s except as a minor adjunct to psychiatric inpatient treatment. Child-focused counseling existed in a school context but usually did not include family systems dynamics or parental involvement, unless specifically related to psychosomatic or other dysfunctions of the child.

Decades of state terrorism and chronic political intimidation following Stalin's death made Soviet citizens highly resistant to clinical approaches that would ask them to reveal their innermost thoughts, feelings, and family secrets. Fear of the consequences, from losing a job to psychiatric hospitalization to imprisonment, kept their mouths closed. Only in the later years of glasnost did this resistance begin to ease.

Soviet psychiatrists usually worked in inpatient psychiatric hospitals and clinics with highly disturbed patients, and their treatment emphasized medication management. Sophisticated Western psychotropic medication was rarely in adequate supply. In addition, Soviet psychiatric diagnostic categories did not parallel those used in Western Europe and the United States and became as highly politicized as psychology had been during the Stalin period.

For many years, diagnoses of "sluggish schizophrenia" and "desire to emigrate" were used to implement control and punishment of political dissidents. As a result of outraged international response to reports of these human rights abuses, the Soviet Society of Psychiatrists and Narcologists withdrew from the World Psychiatry Association (WPA) in January 1983 and had difficulty being reinstated over the following five years because of continuing abuses.

In its October 1989 meeting, the WPA accepted the Independent Psychiatric Association (IPA) of the Soviet Union as an organizational member without conditions. This small nongovernmental association had been founded in early 1989 for the purpose of rehabilitating victims of the political abuse of psychiatry and preventing the abuse of psychiatric patients in the future. The vast majority of Soviet psychiatrists, although not members of the IPA, did not participate in the psychiatric abuse of political dissidents and worked as responsible professionals under difficult physical conditions in hospitals and within the constraints of continuing isolation from Western colleagues, research findings, and medication.

DEVELOPMENT OF CLINICAL PRACTICE IN THE SOVIET UNION

In the 1980s, a few psychologists and psychiatrists working on their own began to explore clinical treatment concepts through reading Western psychological and family therapy literature. Some experimented with abbreviated collegial psychoanalysis and then began tentatively to initiate informal clinical practice. An Association of "Practical" Psychology was established in the mid-1980s, as was a small Center for Marital and Family Therapy in Moscow. This center offered training to interested psychologists and psychiatrists as well as clinical treatment to couples and families. Several other small "psychology cooperatives" were set up in which groups of colleagues practiced and consulted together.

Regular contacts with American mental health professionals began in 1983, when yearly delegations of the Association of Humanistic Psychology (AHP) met with Soviet psychologists in Moscow, Leningrad, Tbilisi, and Vilnius. Early connections had also been established through the Esalen Institute (Anderson, 1983, p. 306), which eventually established an Esalen Soviet-American Exchange Project with a psychology component.

Connections with American clinicians led to increasing efforts to establish clinical programs and services in the Soviet Union. The major problems facing these early clinical efforts were (1) a deeply entrenched societal suspicion of revealing the intimacies of personal and family thought, feeling, and experience to outsiders; (2) resistance from a large bureaucratic national health system, which did not recognize clinical psychology as medical treatment and "problems with relationships and daily life" as legitimate health concerns; payment, there-fore, had to come directly from clients; and (3) lack of adequate training for practitioners. Even during the perestroika period of the late 1980s, clinical psy-chology was not a financially viable profession.

Despite these impediments to practice, many psychologists and a few psy-chiatrists became interested in what they read about clinical psychology and family therapy in Western Europe and the United States. They began to attend professional conferences in Europe and the United States. When American and Western European practitioners spoke to Soviet professional groups, they noted the avid attention with which they were listened to and their words inscribed. Having been cut off from any substantive intellectual, practical, and personal contact with Western colleagues since early in Stalin's regime, Soviet psycholo-gists were madly trying to catch up.

At least 60 years of political manipulation and repression had left psychology with few nonideological institutional supports or intellectual channels for expres-sion. With the new openness of glasnost in the 1980s, however, many energetic, imaginative young people in the field scrambled to make connections with West-ern colleagues and become respected participants in the ongoing development of a common body of knowledge, including family therapy.

FIRST EXPERIENCE AS A TRACK THREE CITIZEN DIPLOMAT

My first opportunity to discuss family therapy with Russian mental health professionals came in mid-May 1989, when, as part of the small AHP clinical delegation, I was scheduled to give a lecture in a large auditorium at Moscow State University. I had observed other American professionals earlier in the week presenting concepts through consecutive interpretation in hot, overcrowded classrooms. The presentations ranged from an explanation of genograms, to fam-ily systems concepts used in family businesses, to management techniques, to a sophisticated explanation of individual personality theory. The Russian listeners appeared to write down everything that was said and asked few questions, although some presenters divided audiences into small discussion groups and encouraged participation. This teaching style was clearly unfamiliar to Russian learners, and although they chatted among themselves, they did not really use the opportunity for self-expression and exploration of new ideas. Reactions ranged from obsessive note-taking to disinterest.

In my lecture, I made the same mistakes. I had prepared a half-hour talk in which I hoped to present the ideas of Murray Bowen, one of the pioneers of the family therapy movement in the United States. I planned to explain some of the key concepts from his theory—differentiation of self, triangles, sibling position, multigenerational process, cut off, and societal emotional process. I hoped my lecture would generate interesting questions and a discussion of the implications of the theory in the context of Soviet experience. Wishing to bridge the distance and formality imposed by consecutive translation, I introduced myself and spoke for about 5 minutes in halting, rusty Russian but then fell back on the able bilingual psychology graduate student who had helped the other American presenters explain their ideas.

The experience of speaking through consecutive translation rapidly reduced me to communication in "sound bytes." I made a statement, and the interpreter restated it in Russian. I made a second statement, and he restated it. My comments became increasingly simplistic, with little linguistic flow or intellectual continuity. By the end of the lecture, I had lost at least half the audience, and the other half (the obsessive note-taking half) asked me a few questions relating to minutiae buried within the presentation. When my time was up, the crowd clapped dutifully, presented me with a bouquet of flowers, and trotted me out of the auditorium, to make way for the next American speaker, a psychiatrist scheduled to talk about hospital programs for acting-out adolescents.

A Personal Connection

One middle-aged psychologist, a faculty member, followed me out of the lecture hall and asked if he could have a cup of tea with me, so we could discuss the concepts in my lecture in more detail. When we sat down together in a cafeteria the following afternoon, he wanted to tell me about his own family. He had been raised in a Jewish family in Kiev, had come to Moscow to study, and had married a Russian woman. He and their children had taken his wife's Russian family name because his "wife's older brother had died young and her father wanted the family name to continue." He denied that fear of anti-Semitism had played a part in the decision, but during glasnost he had taken back his own Jewish family name to honor his father who had recently died. Should he impose this name on the children?

Sitting in the crowded cafeteria, speaking a mixture of Russian and English, we drew his family diagram on a napkin, noting the deaths of all his grandparents and uncles in the Stalin purges of 1937 and his cut-off relationship with his younger sister and aging mother, both still living in Kiev. As we explored the need for reconnection and pride in this family, he became tearful, expressing confusion about who he was and who he could be for his children. "Can family systems theory be a guide to me in this dilemma?" he asked. I told him there were no easy answers to his question because it was so complex, involving his relationships with his wife, his children, his parents-in-law, and his own family as well as societal and political attitudes, but that he needed to start with himself, clarifying what was important to him. As family systems theory takes note of the impact of prior generational events and relationships on present-day life situations, it also values the position a responsible individual must take in relation to them. I agreed to send him some helpful articles from the United States and to correspond with him about his dilemma, which I continued to do for several years.

CREATING A CONTEXT FOR FAMILY THERAPY

Many American clinicians visiting the former Soviet Union have observed that members of the audience are frequently more interested in personal therapy than in theoretical concepts. Beyond the sterile formality of the lecture hall, I found this personal contact with a colleague lively and challenging, as abstract ideas from family theory became more real through a brief discussion across cultures. But I had serious concerns about the teaching/learning process I was engaged in with Russian professionals. I saw that a context was necessary for explaining to our Russian colleagues where various American professionals were coming from in the materials they presented. In any given month in Moscow, Russian psychologists might be offered lectures on Virginia Satir, Carl Rogers, strategic/structural family therapy, or Bowen theory as well as psychosynthesis, self psychology, and materials from EST. How did we all fit together in the minds of Russian colleagues and in their notebooks? How could this diversity become integrated in their developing training programs?

Through a Russian psychologist friend, Dr. Vladimir Ageev, I obtained an introduction to Dr. Ekaterina Shchedrina, the editor of *Problems of Psychology*, the journal founded in 1955 during the post-Stalin period and published bimonthly by the Moscow State University Department of Psychology. Dr. Ageev took me to her tiny dark office, piled high with old manuscripts and half-completed articles. Over cups of hot tea, Dr. Shchedrina told me that she had been editor for 14 years. It had always been difficult for her to combine her own postdoctoral research with some of the challenges of her editorial work—evaluating manuscripts and often translating them from other languages as well as negotiating with state paper and glue supply sources and physically putting the journal together. With the increasing economic instability of the perestroika period, these efforts had become all-consuming. She was interested, however, in my writing an article for the journal that would explain the many practical unknowns of the mental health professions in the United States: required training, different degree levels, licensing and certification as well as a discussion of theoretical and philosophical orientations toward clinical practice. During 1990, I prepared this article for her, and it was published in the December 1990 issue of the journal (Baker, 1990).

A key aspect of the article was its discussion of family therapy as a subspeciality of the major professions, with its own professional organizations, literature, training programs, degrees, licensing, certification, and clinical approaches. I described the origins of family therapy in the 1950s, when practitioners and researchers in different parts of the United States began to differentiate themselves from traditional psychoanalytic clinical practice and experiment with observing and treating family groups. I also explained the origins and adaptations of systems theory as they applied to human family and other emotional groups. The article included a brief explanation of the variety of clinical approaches that had evolved in the field of family therapy, focusing specifically on strategic, structural, and Bowen models of theory and treatment. I ended the article with the observation that "family theory and therapy must continue to be studied and tested in other cultural settings before they can take a position of leadership in the field of mental health" (p. 62).

INTRODUCING BOWEN THEORY

Although Soviet psychology from 1936 to 1990 was dominated by Pavlovian, linguistic, and behaviorist models, with a strong emphasis on environmental determinism, ideas from family systems theory struck a congenial chord among those who were interested in developing clinical skills. As in all human cultures, the family was clearly the core emotional unit in Soviet society, but understanding the wider complex of relationship systems within the community or "collective" could also be enhanced through concepts from family systems. The relevance of family systems thinking was expressed to me in letters to the editor that were forwarded to me and conversations I had with other Soviet readers of my article. They were interested in family theory and therapy as providing not only new techniques for clinical practice, but also as a broad theoretical base for thinking about human behavioral and emotional phenomena. For this latter purpose, the work of Bowen (Bowen, 1978; Kerr & Bowen, 1988) was the most useful starting point. Ekaterina Shchedrina translated and then published a second article I wrote for *Problems of Psychology* (Baker, 1991) that focused on Bowen theory. My family therapy seminars in the former Soviet Union used Bowen theory as a starting point for connecting the field of family therapy with Soviet psychology. They also stimulated Russian psychologists to think about societal issues through the prism of systems theory. My own postgraduate training with Bowen at the Georgetown Family Center in Washington, D.C., made his theory a natural starting point for me. Bowen's efforts to link family systems theory to the natural sciences provided a reasonable intellectual link for Russian psychologists with a science-based approach to the study of human functioning on individual, family, and societal levels.

In presenting Bowen theory, I emphasized that Bowen did not intend to create techniques for the practice of psychotherapy but rather to develop a broader understanding of human behavior based on scientific principles. I also pointed out that, as American therapists began to study Bowen theory and develop this broader understanding, they found their therapeutic work improved. Russian psychologists were interested to learn that therapists trained in Bowen theory did not function as experts but rather as consultants or "coaches" in their work with individuals and families. They were also interested to learn that Bowen-trained therapists were encouraged to address their personal anxiety and emotional reactivity in the relationships in their own lives that were the most problematic (their own families, schools, and work systems). As therapists learned to participate in these relationships more calmly and thoughtfully, they were then theoretically able to be more useful to the individuals and families they worked with professionally, encouraging their clients to find their own solutions to life's dilemmas. This approach seemed to make sense to Russian psychologists and permitted more latitude in the development of individual clinical styles than did specific instruction in techniques of intervention.

Setting Training Goals for Teaching Bowen Theory

Before returning to the Soviet Union to present a four-day seminar on Bowen theory at Moscow State University's Department of Psychology in August 1990, I reviewed some materials on training. Learning Bowen family systems theory is usually a long-term undertaking. As described by Papero, Training Director of the Georgetown Family Center (1990), "the goal for the [Bowen theory] learner is to move toward greater differentiation of self. In this process, both parties [learner and instructor] are in fact learning. Each challenges the other to think for him- or herself. . . . A necessary quality in both teacher and learner is a curiosity about the nature of human behavior and the problems families face" (pp. 102–103). Training in Bowen theory "is not easily measured in terms of time spent in a particular training program. . . . People learn differently. . . . Many [trainees] continue their contact with the Family Center for several years beyond the completion of their initial training" (p. 105). He continues, "Training within the framework of Bowen theory attempts to be as consistent as possible with the directions suggested by the theory itself. . . . At its best [it] allows the individual to press ahead into the unknown, guided by theory and thought, toward the promise of a new science" (pp. 108–109). Given the necessity for a long-term time frame in teaching Bowen theory and traditional Soviet teaching/learning styles, which do not include student participation, I wondered if it would be realistic to present ideas from Bowen theory in a short seminar, but I was willing to give it a try.

A Moscow Seminar: Narrative of One Teaching Experience

About 40 students filed into the university classroom early on a Monday morning in late August 1990, helping themselves to small bottles of mineral water set up on a table in a corner of the room and settling into a long row of desks that faced the blackboard in a semicircle. I asked them each to introduce themselves and tell me where they were from.

Participants came from all over the Soviet Union: many from Moscow and Leningrad, a contingent of four from Lithuania (who had been in my workshop in Vilnius the previous year), one young psychologist from Vladivostok in the far east, six from a psychiatric hospital staff in Krasnoyarsk in central Siberia, two psychiatrists from a hospital near Chernobyl in the Ukraine, and two from Kazan. They stood up behind their desks and introduced themselves rather formally, welcoming me to Moscow. There were at least six Natashas and almost as many Tamaras. Perhaps a third were men. All seemed to be between about 30 and 45 years old. I took notes rapidly, trying to attach a name and hometown to each.

I explained my plan for the four days we would be together, outlining time for lunch breaks and smoking breaks (large numbers of young people in the

Soviet Union were smokers) and encouraging them to interrupt me, ask questions, and offer opinions. I said I would be particularly interested in aspects of Bowen theory that might be relevant to their own family life and clinical experience. I also said I would be asking for volunteers to present their own families and interesting case families they might be working with. There was an obedient air of dutiful scholarship in the classroom as I launched into an explanation of Bowen, his background, the origins of the theory, and some of its basic terms and concepts.

As the four days progressed, we got comfortable with each other. I was able to dispense with my helpful young translator during much of the conversational question and answer periods. We struggled with recalcitrant ceiling fans, stuck windows, and inadequate lighting. We walked out into the cold muddy streets of Moscow for lunch, searching for places to eat in a city whose food distribution systems had practically ground to a halt. Often we found no more than a roll and a cup of tea at a stand-up bar crowded with workers in dirty overalls, but the conversation was cheerfully energetic. I was most fascinated hearing tales of life in Krasnoyarsk in central Siberia where the Yenisei River flows north to the Arctic Ocean through solitary wilderness, and the pine trees grow 100 feet tall.

As I taught them how to draw family diagrams, many participants presented their own families to the group, almost all of them indicating a complete loss of the grandparent generation because of collectivization, the political purges of the 1930s, and massive numbers of Soviet World War II casualties. Many of them lived as adults with their elderly parents (because of acute urban housing shortages) and described their difficulties functioning as adults in those intensely close living situations. Others had been divorced but continued to live in the same apartment with their ex-spouses, again because of apartment shortages. Differentiation of self, establishment of autonomy without emotional distancing or cut-off, proved to be the most challenging Bowen concept throughout the seminar.

Those professionals who lived and worked in Siberia described a community of people without roots, with little connection to the past, as many of the parent and grandparent generations there had been sent to Siberian concentration camps from other parts of the country and then had perished because of tortuous living conditions. Their descendents had a toughness and wildness, a lack of family connection, and often an antisocial quality that challenged the concepts of family systems theory. To start with defining a responsible professional self in a chaotic, often primitive environment meant giving up Pavlovian theories of environmental determinism and looking within for strength and understanding.

On the third morning, the participants asked me to conduct a live interview with a mother and her 14-year-old son, so they could see how one "did" family therapy. Although I do not usually like the idea of the grandstanding involved in a one-time family therapy interview, I agreed to have a half-hour conversation with this family. The mother, a technical writer, had had some traditional individual therapy focusing on her anxiety and unhappiness. She had not discussed her concerns about her son with her therapist, but it turned out that he was not doing well in school. They had recently moved to Moscow from Kazan, where all their relatives lived, and her husband traveled frequently for weeks at a time. The boy was a cheerful, relaxed, large, but rather immature-looking adolescent who said his major energies were going into friend-making and socializing. He was interested in his mother's concern, which she had not articulated to him directly before. The mother described her own adolescence as anxious and pressured, as she strove to please her critical, demanding parents. Her husband (with whom she had gone to high school) had been more athletic, less academic, and in fact quite disinterested in his studies.

As I asked the mother and son questions that elicited family information, I established a calm, reflective atmosphere with them, and the session ended as I asked them to think about what personal directions they would like to work on in relation to "the problem" and in their lives in general. In a discussion with the entire seminar group (including the mother and son) following this "demonstration," the mother and son were able to maintain a reflective tone in evaluating their experience of talking with me. The seminar participants, when asked for their impressions, initially began to give the mother advice about how she ought to handle her son. She answered that she appreciated their input but had begun to make some new connections in her mind and thought she might find the answers to their family situation for herself. The boy wandered off in search of a bottle of mineral water.

Later that afternoon, the psychiatrists from the Chernobyl region began to describe the immense depression and hopelessness of patients who came to their clinic. As parents watched their children sicken from radiation exposure or perhaps become genetically compromised while the parents themselves developed symptoms from radiation exposure, many lost their ability to function as effective adults. What could family systems theory offer to these people? Would there be a way to act responsibly for children, family, and community in a society so deteriorated that it had ceased to offer safeguards to its citizens and in fact actively damaged them? Could responsible adults find a way to band together to challenge the enormity of the state during a time of personal tragedy?

These were some of the questions we discussed as the seminar took up Bowen's final concept, societal emotional process. I asked them what they considered to be the characteristics of effective societal and political leadership. They proposed objectivity, balance, tolerance, dedication to principles, decisiveness, respect for subordinates, competence, ability to take initiative, flexibility, humanism, separation of personal from societal goals, the ability to take calm action without being swayed by the emotions of others, and the ability to cooperate and work with others toward common goals.

The discussion of leadership was challenged by one participant who commented that responsible citizenship was as important as leadership and included the same characteristics, all of which would define individual functioning at the high end of the scale of differentiation of self.

When I asked the participants to give their own ideas about the impact of the events of the past 73 years on their generation in the Soviet Union, some of them made the following comments:

"We had a new society after the Revolution. It was very savage and there was no pity. As we have learned about it, we have come to hate our grandfathers, our fathers, and ourselves."

"The Revolution cut all our roots and ties with the past. We have no connections across generations, no traditions, no sacred places."

"People are still afraid of being honest with each other. There is an element of secrecy even in the closest relationships."

"We carry our pain inside ourselves."

"The present tragedy of our society is that we have been artificially selected. All the people at the higher levels of differentiation were systematically eliminated during the 1930s. Many of those who survived function at a lower level based on self-preservation, accommodation, and moral irresponsibility . . ."

"Because of their own losses and focus on survival, our parents can't teach us how to be responsible citizens. We have to teach ourselves. This is the most serious problem of our generation. We must learn how to take responsibility for our own future."

In the final segment of the training session at Moscow State University, I asked participants to commit themselves to personal action plans, to integrate the ideas we had discussed into their work and family relationships. They met in small groups with others who came from the same part of the country and committed themselves to meeting regularly to discuss theory, continuing to read in the area of family systems theory, working on relationships within their own families, and most importantly to develop their own new ideas based on observation and thinking.

Although I know that training in Bowen theory is a long-term process, I believe that we made a good start in a thoughtful direction during those four days in Moscow. I learned much from my own participation in the seminar, enriching my understanding of the complexities of Russian society and working on my ability to communicate ideas clearly. I also learned much about the resiliency of human experience even under the most stressful circumstances and the capacity of many members of the younger generation to regenerate high levels of adaptive functioning, although the interpersonal connection with parents and grandparents may have been lost. Somehow the strength of those who were "systematically eliminated during the 1930s" lives on in their descendants.

CONNECTIONS IN THE UNITED STATES

I corresponded with some of the Moscow seminar participants and, in fact, returned to Russia after the failed coup to continue our discussions in 1991 and 1992. But these personal and professional training experiences in the Soviet Union and then Russia also led me in a related direction after I returned to the United States. I became interested in Soviet Jewish refugee resettlement in the United States after meeting several Soviet Jewish refugees who were among the many hundreds who had recently arrived in the Washington area. Clearly they had come from a multigenerational life experience that was similar in many ways to that of my colleagues in Moscow.

In the United States, faced with the new stressors of cross-cultural adjustment and personal choice, they manifested a predictable range of functioning, from highly anxious and symptomatic to flexible, calm, and imaginative. Bowen theory was a useful lens for understanding this variability in individual and family reactions to immigration (Bunting, 1985). The variability seemed to correlate with Bowen's concept of differentiation, the ability to function autonomously while still emotionally connected to significant others. Those refugees who functioned best in the United States had either come with many family members or maintained a regular connection with those left behind. They also felt in control of the choice to emigrate and described themselves as moving positively "toward" a new life. Those who were most symptomatic tended to be emotionally cut off from significant family relationships. They also took a helpless stance toward the emigration and felt they were trying to "get away" from an unhappy life in the old country.

An organization founded by a group of Russian psychologists in Moscow in June 1991 planned to help Russian emigrants and refugees before they left home, so they could anticipate and prepare for the predictable adjustment difficulties of moving to a new country. With the benefit of Bowen's ideas about differentiation, societal process, and emotional cut-off, I planned to consult with the psychologists in Moscow and with new arrivals in the United States to help enhance the adjustment process.

My connection with Russian refugees and immigrants in the United States and with Russian colleagues in Moscow has been a continuation of track three citizen diplomacy on a microsystemic level. In attempting to function as a responsible citizen, I have worked to promote intercultural understanding on three levels: (1) personal friendship, (2) shared professional work with colleagues, and (3) adjustment in moving from one culture to another. My interest in Soviet/Russian-American relations on all three levels has evolved as opportunities evolved. I believe I am just at the beginning.

The small group of Communist Party conservatives who attempted to turn the clock back in August 1991, to shut down glasnost, turn off perestroika, unplug the vast emerging technology of electronic connection, and slam shut the windows of interpersonal relationship between the Soviet Union and the rest of the world, were too few, too late, and too half-hearted. Just four and a half months later, the 74-year-old Soviet Union came to an end, and a new, initially somewhat shaky Commonwealth of Independent States was born. In 1992, tracks one, two, and three diplomacy moved on determinedly in the direction of increased openness and connection between Americans and former Soviets. Track three may offer the greatest flexibility and opportunity for developing interpersonal understanding between the two countries. It also continues to provide a path to adventure and personal growth for all who are interested, even (or maybe especially) in the post-Soviet period.

NOTE

1. This training experience is explored in greater detail in Baker, K. G. (1991). Family systems in Lithuania. *Lithuanus: The Lithuanian Quarterly 37* (1), 29–38.

BIBLIOGRAPHY

Anderson, W. T. (1983). *The upstart spring: Esalen and the American awakening.* Reading, MA: Addison-Wesley.

Baker, K. G. (1990). The mental health professions, family theory and therapy in the United States: A short review. *Vosprosi Psichologi, December,* 53–63.

Baker, K. G. (1991). Bowen family systems theory. *Vosprosi Psichologi, December,* 55–65.

Bowen, M. (1978). *Family therapy in clinical practice.* Northvale, NJ: Northvale.

Bunting, A. (1985). *Immigration and emotional cut off.* Paper delivered at Georgetown Family Center, Washington, D.C.

Carlson, D., & Comstock, C. (1986). *Citizen summitry.* Los Angeles: Tarcher.

Cole, M., & Maltzman, I. (Eds.) (1969). *Handbook of contemporary Soviet psychology.* New York: Basic Books.

Davidson, W. D., & Montville, J. V. (1981–82). Foreign policy according to Freud. *Foreign Policy, 45,* 145–157.

Farrand, R. W. (1991). Speaking out: Privacy and the 'right' to know. *Foreign Service Journal, August,* 12–16.

Hassard, J. (1990, Summer). The AHP Soviet exchange project: 1983–1990 and beyond. *Journal of Humanistic Psychology, 30*(3), 6–51.

Kerr, M., & Bowen, M. (1988). *Family evaluation: An approach based on Bowen theory.* New York: W. W. Norton.

Mercer, E. (1991). *Summary of American Psychiatric Association activities related to the use of psychiatry for political purposes in the Soviet Union.* Washington: APA Report.

Papero, D. V. (1990). *Bowen family systems theory.* Boston: Allyn & Bacon.

Sagan, C. (1987). Unlocking the deadly embrace. In G. Warner & M. Shuman (Eds.), *Citizen diplomats,* pp. ix–xii. New York: Continuum.

Tucker, R. C. (1971). *The Soviet political mind: Stalinism and post-Stalin change.* New York: W. W. Norton.

Warner, G. (1991). *The invisible threads.* Washington, D.C.: Seven Locks Press.

Warner, G., & Shuman, M. (1987). *Citizen diplomats.* New York: Continuum.

Chapter 10

From the Outside In:
The Human Side of Crisis Management

Benina Berger Gould*

Four conditions which give rise to a psychological enemy system: the surrender of responsibility to a governing authority; dehumanization or deionization of the "other"; projection of responsibility onto others; and adherence to political ideologies which offer simplified solutions to complex problems and thereby sustain polarized views.

—*Mack, 1991*

EMBRACING THE ENEMY

A true practitioner considers his/her enemy to be his greatest friend, because only he can help you develop patience and compassion. (Tenzin Gyatso the Fourteenth Dalai Lama, 1992)

Many people in the field of family therapy have thought about war. Although only some shared their views publicly, most therapists at some time or another

* I gratefully acknowledge my former colleagues at the Center for Science and International Affairs and support to the Carnegie Foundation for an Avoiding Nuclear War fellowship; to David McGill, Ph.D., of Cambridge, MA, for listening to and helping me clarify my observations; and to Susan Moon, Marsha Pravder Mirkin, Pamela Pomerance Steiner, and Donna Hilleboe DeMuth for sensitive and helpful editing. The Center for Psychology and Social Change in Cambridge always provided a haven for stimulation and coherence. This chapter is adapted from a talk presented at University of California, Davis, Women's Resource and Research Center, March 6, 1991, as part of the "Women and War" series honoring Women's History Month.

are compelled to try to make sense of war. Belief systems and mythologies get reviewed and clarified in this process. For some of us, the need to speak out about war and world crisis has become paramount in our work. This happened for me when my awareness of the threat of nuclear war became a reality, and I became concerned with the question of how to deal with children in the family and in the classroom after an international crisis had brought the possibility of war into the forefront of public attention.

Making sense of war can be done by walking many paths. For the last 10 years, ever since I became concerned with children's fear of nuclear war, I have taken the peace route, placing myself squarely in the community of peace activists and peace researchers. Recently I have taken a more academic direction, trying to understand war by placing myself in the belly of a predominantly male, arms control think tank. Allowing myself to be fully inducted into each of these arenas, yet aware that I was also studying them as an anthropologist surveys new cultures, I have been grateful for my experience with family systems theory in a very special way. Not only could I view the system from a relatively objective standpoint, but also I was able to see my own participation in it and, in the case of the arms control think tank, to discuss the process with a group of therapists outside the system who served as an informal reflective team.[1] When I got stuck, they helped me move and to begin again the cycle of observing, questioning, losing my objectivity, and then talking to the team. Now in addition to studying the "nuclear club," I am also taking a hard look at how I personally make sense of war and violence. This chapter primarily addresses my involvement in the community of strategic defense specialists and international affairs academics.

When I entered the Kennedy School of Government at Harvard University's Center for Science and International Affairs in 1988 for three years of research, I was "embracing the enemy." I was an Avoiding Nuclear War Research Fellow funded by the Carnegie Foundation for two years. My area of research was nuclear psychology, Khrushchev, and the Berlin Wall Crisis of 1961. The methodology used was an oral history of that period of time. Key government officials as well as historians, journalists, and scientists were interviewed about the crisis. Transcripts from the meetings provided material I am using for my inquiry. For a third year, I was an adjunct research fellow and continued my work at the Center for Slavic and East European Studies at the University of California, Berkeley.

In taking these steps, I had to leave political judgments and feminist theory on the doorstep. I wanted to know how men relate to weapon systems, to know more about the lack of integration between politics and psychology, and I wanted to continue my own research in the nuclear psychology of international crisis. For these reasons, I entered the world of nuclear strategic specialists who were constantly going to Washington to build policy for a stronger, more "nuclear safe" country. Not only was I an outsider to this world as a woman and nonscientist, but also I had never been outside of the world of psychology for my entire professional career. I was influenced by Cohen's brave work on *deconstructing male defense language*. Cohen (1989) was concerned with the "strain of feminist theory that takes as its object of scrutiny discourses produced by men . . . and how these discourses work and how they exert their dominance." Glendinning (1990) was concerned with how technology wounds us on an emotional as well as physical level. Where I differ is that my work is not concerned so much with an antimale, antitechnology paradigm but with new ways to observe and report male war and crisis discourse.

My purpose was to understand the male world of "nuclear strategy" by placing "myself" in the middle of it, as participant observer. My only association with the field of military technology up to that time was very peripheral as a family therapy consultant at Letterman Army Base in San Francisco. I wanted to bring a woman's perspective to the theory of crisis management and prevention, and I was excited by the opportunity to observe and evaluate a system to which few had access. Perhaps I could discover how to suggest some interventions that would bring politics and psychology closer together. I tried to approach this new world as a cultural anthropologist. Like other family therapists, I believed I could learn a lot from working as an anthropologist. From this stance, Gregory Bateson had shown us how to study the inner workings of families and other systems.

The group I joined consisted of about 30 men and women. In the first year, there was only one other senior fellow like myself. She was there for three months. There were also five women getting their masters or doctorate degrees in government. During the second year, I was the only female senior fellow. There was one sociologist, one philosopher, and one lawyer, and the rest were mainly former government employees or scientists. The "village" was not in New Guinea but on the second floor of a renowned School of Government, with quiet offices, state-of-the-art electronic equipment, a private library, and dining room. I was struck by the efficiency and privacy of the center and by the isolation, which I found both comforting and frightening.

I shared an office with a physicist, and my responsibilities were simply to hand in two planning papers a year called "milestone reports" and to attend weekly Fellows' Seminars. In addition, I needed to produce a final book or article. I went to a monthly *avoiding nuclear war* seminar and to the *nuclear crisis group*, whose project was an oral history of the Berlin Wall. I also had the opportunity to go to frequent "high-level" dinners with National Security Council speakers, defense leaders, authorities on nuclear proliferation, visiting diplomats, and scientists involved in strategic planning. What follows are the observations of a systems psychologist in an international security world.

Illusion of Power

Deterrence Theory.   Because of the cold war, nuclear weapons have proliferated on an international scale. These weapons provide one way for small countries to gain power in the world. This concept of power is related to the belief in deterrence theory. In fact, the actual stockpile of weapons belonging to any given nation is less important than the level of arsenal that others perceive to be owned by or accessible to that nation. For example, in the recent Gulf War, one of the questions asked throughout the war and which continues to be a mystery is the issue of whether Iraq has a nuclear arsenal. Saddam Hussein, through secrecy and international gamesmanship, has succeeded in being powerful not only because of his supply of oil, but also because of the fact that he has everyone thinking his country has a huge nuclear arsenal.

> Objective reality, whatever that may be, is simply irrelevant; only the subjective phenomena of perception and value-judgment count . . . prestige effects deriving from the possessions of strategic weapons are psychologically by far the most impressive of all instruments of power . . . with informed public opinion the world over there is definite awareness that one side or the other has more and more is widely regarded as implying greater power. (Kull, 1990)
>   The player's concern with his own prestige plays an important role in this phenomenon. (Glad & Rosenberg, 1990)

Six countries are known to have nuclear weapons (former U.S.S.R., United States, France, Great Britain, Israel, and China), and three more almost certainly do (South Africa, India, and Pakistan). Proliferation means expansion. Where once the buildup of weapons in the United States and the U.S.S.R. was the most extreme, the expansion of nuclear weapons to many nations has become the issue of greatest concern to those in the arms control world today. Proliferation is the "unconscious" issue of our times, and our denial of it is creating a deeper entrenchment of the *genocidal mentality*. As Lifton and Markusen (1988) state, "mentality, the willingness, under certain conditions, to take steps that could kill hundreds of millions of people has become both an everyday matter and part of the various structure of society both routinized and institutionalized." The concept of the "illusion" or false state has created our present-day nuclear normality, which allows us to live with the "bomb," at the same time fearing and despising it. In the think tank, illusions and grandiosity are paramount.

To have power, it is essential to sound powerful and to speak with authority. People in the National Security Council (NSC) or covert operations must not reveal the true nature of the government's military power, and so bluffing is the name of the game. When you listen carefully to these power people, you begin to see the paucity of information that is actually being shared. We tend to assume that the "power people" have more knowledge than they really do. In the think tank, we see an exaggeration of the whole society's habit of acting "as if" we know, of denying our ignorance and uncertainty.

Japan and Germany are countries that do not have significant nuclear weapons. Because of their past experience with war, they have gained power through economic means. This is a second way for nations to be powerful in the world. A third way has been through the drug trade. All these are negative ways of gaining power and serve to endanger people rather than to protect them. They do not give people the security that is possible through nonviolence and through the potential of conflict resolution and negotiation. In the Middle East war and in the cold war, "bluffing" was one of the illusionary techniques used to give a sense of power to a country.

Disillusionment of Power. In our world today, which is bottoming out on consumerism and greed, we need to make our illusions of power conscious and to put an end to bluffing on all levels if we are to retain our integrity as a nation and people. We may no longer be able to fool our neighbors with grandiosity and image making when our streets are filled with homeless, the unemployment problem hits almost every family, and the violence in our communities makes everyone feel isolated and alone.

With the election of November 1992, the end of the cold war was clearly felt. The Gulf War, which occurred two years ago, is distant in everyone's mind. Although more women than ever ran for office, there still was no sign of a female president or vice-president. Our social consciousness seems rooted in local politics and domestic issues. The lack of research money for acquired immunodeficiency syndrome (AIDS), the lack of housing for the homeless, and the violence in the streets are no longer connected to the ravages of the cold war and accompanying nuclear mentality. The rise of "hate crimes" with much silence surrounding them is disturbing.

Perhaps the proliferation of weapons makes countries feel powerful in the same way that the proliferation of hate crimes makes people feel powerful. This, however, is an illusion. It creates a sense of false power. The United States has been called narcissistic (Bellah et al., 1985). As we see evidence of the bottom falling out economically in the 1990s after a decade of overspending and greed, one cannot argue with this point. The United States is now suffering from a process parallel to that of the narcissistic person who experiences the deep emptiness of a faulty self. Instead of being strong and proud of its democratic heritage, we are basing our strength on institutions that are not working, foreign policy that does not create peace, and a fear of the future.

> Most of us really know that, just behind the bravado of the assertion that our lives are completely in our own hands is a fear that our future will be determined by forces beyond our control. Focusing on what is close at hand, then, may be as much an expression of fatalism as of self-confidence. (Bellah et al., 1991)

The Powerful Club. You are not a man if you do not demonstrate your superiority over others. This male induction went on constantly for the younger members of the center. Many times I felt like I was part of a football game or fraternity initiation when I observed the senior professors making fun of and otherwise showing their supremacy to their younger colleagues in a combative manner. During these fencing matches, I experienced myself to be the most "outside" the Center both because I am a woman and because I abhorred being a bystander to violence and inhumanity. At the same time, this aberrant behavior made me want to delve deeper into the minds of the people I worked with to understand more fully the roots of this evil and violent behavior. Had this kind of behavior contributed to the need for nuclear weapons in some way? This question was always on my mind. Unfortunately, much of the illusion of power gained by this jostling depends on "being a victor over others." Women were not exempt from expressing this superior attitude, although they tended to make fun of other men and not their female colleagues. The way nonsupport was shown for their female colleagues was through silence, much the way a woman becomes silent in a marriage that is not working. I suspect that the women's behavior, that is, mocking men and being combative and silence toward other women, resulted in a less than full voice for both sexes and left out much of the creative, deviant thinking that would have enriched the conversations and perhaps led to new ways of thinking. This victimization of others as an acceptable model of behavior both in the think tank and in the larger world reinforced the basic belief system of *the natural aggression of man* and Waltz's (1959) belief that "wars result from selfishness, from misdirected aggressive impulses, from stupidity." I found many women as well as men in the arm's control world were "mirror images of their victimizers" (Fields, 1991).

As time went on, so as not to be on the outside looking in, I joined the culture in some way. Although I did not overtly express the same aggressive impulses, I began to enjoy the sadism and laugh with the others at inappropriate behavior. To defend myself against being more isolated and alien than I already was by my profession and gender, I put on the armor that gave me the kind of thick skin needed to be morally inhumane and socially uncaring. This armor was also enhanced by the isolation of the powerful club and its emphasis on elitism and power as supreme virtues. What I experienced happening to myself was a shrinking of my creative potential and an increase of my cognitive skills. The rational mind had taken over and with that a belief that male reason was superior and the feminine intuition a failing.

> The male is more complete, more dominant than the female, closer akin to causal activity, for the female is incomplete and in subjection and belongs to the category of the passive rather than the active. So too with the two ingredients which constitute our life-principle, the rational and the irrational; the rational which belongs to mind and reason is of the masculine gender, the irrational, the province of sense, is of the feminine. Mind belongs to a genus wholly superior to sense as man is to woman. (Colson & Whitaker, 1929)

The seemingly reasonable exterior that I adopted was a defense against the disgust I experienced as I watched people abuse each other and themselves. In more analytic terms, I was identifying with the aggressor, the power people. In family systems thinking, I was placing myself closer to the hierarchy. I experienced this position as safer and more protected, since the closer you were to the people in charge, the less chance you had of being attacked.

The powerful club was indeed powerful but lacked creativity and humanity. As time went on, I began to long for those qualities that I was used to in my other associations. I watched as my potential allies (the sociologist and philosopher in the group) and I became inducted into the society. It was a frightening time. It all but paralyzed my original intent of coming to the center to do research. Ironically I was living out my research questions, exploring further the relationship of psychology to politics and technology.

Groupthink/Induction. This induction through identification with the aggressor and posturing with the hierarchy was also created by a powerful force in groups called *groupthink*. I expect that my colleagues at the center would have used this more political explanation of their behavior to describe the locker room atmosphere.

> Whenever a group develops a strong "we feeling" and manifests a high degree of solidarity, there are powerful internal as well as external pressures to conform to the group's norms. We can surmise from studies of work teams, social clubs, and informal friendship groups that such constraints arise at least partly because each member comes to rely upon the group to provide him with emotional support for coping with the stresses of decision-making. (Janis, 1971)

Nuclear strategists are naturally invested in nuclear weapons and strategy. Their powerful careers are dependent on the continuing development of new weapons or "modernization of weapons" and decisions that affect added military planning. They, like many of us, are afraid to change professions and leave positions they have worked hard to attain. Instead they turn their back on values and morality, believing that deterrence will keep us out of war. At the same time, they are creating a defense system that is far beyond what is necessary to keep the peace and a *nuclear professionalism* that is based on "overabstraction, scientism, numerology, and technical jargon." This mode of thinking invites a kind of dissociation. It creates a world for arms control strategists that "maintains a radical separation between thought and feeling and enables one to make analytic calculations while remaining numbed to their consequences in pain, suffering, and death" (Lifton, 1990).

I asked myself, what is wrong with belief systems that construct a sense of reality detached from human experience? I answer, it is wrong to allow people to live in a microworld that encourages weapons to be built that endanger our species. In this world, feelings of fear, anxiety, omnipotence, and threat are split off, detached, and dissociated and renamed protection, courage, heroism, and creation. Alternate paradigms of global security, track II diplomacy (people to people), or a search for a new way of thinking do not enter the minds of these people except as the voice of a deviant like myself that is heard from time to time.

As Cohen (1989) has said, "it is a powerful club." I feel fortunate that I got out because as I saw myself caught in the web more and more of the groupthink, I knew it was getting more and more difficult to return to normal life where power, dominance, and competitiveness were not the acceptable modes of acting.

Belief Systems

The Natural Aggression of Man Hypothesis. Freudian thinking has assumed the following:

> The instinct that thus disturbs man's relations with man and requires society to rise as the implacable dispenser of justice is, of course, the death instinct, here identified with the primordial hostility of man toward man. Man's natural aggressive instinct, the hostility of each against all and of all against each, opposes this program of civilization. This aggressive instinct is the derivative and the main representative of the death instinct which we have found alongside of Eros and which shares world dominion with it. . . . It must present the struggle between Eros and Death, between the instinct of life and the instinct of destruction, as it works itself out in the human species. (Ricoeur, 1970)

Nuclear strategists have different *belief systems* than the people I am familiar with in the more liberal world of peace activists. (Since I did not interview my colleagues about this, the following section is conjecture only.) The strategists work from theories that are more akin to Hobbes's view that "everyman is obsessed with the appetite for power" and that a "despotic, tyrannical mentality pervades the structure of all men" (Dietz, 1990). While most observers do not attribute the waging of war to one single cause, many do perceive a basic motive for war in man's innate aggressiveness and pugnacity. For them, the important causes of war result "from selfishness, from misdirected aggressive impulses, from stupidity" (Clesse, 1987, p. 259).

> According to Durbin and Bowlby, war is due to the expression in and through group life of the aggressiveness of individuals. There are only two ways, he thought, to reduce war in its frequency and violence: a slow, curative and peaceful one, a new type of emotional education to remove the ultimate causes of war in human character, and an immediate, coercive one, aimed at symptoms, namely the restraint of the aggressor by force. (Clesse, 1987, p. 259)

Many psychologists support the first peaceful means to change, and most political scientists and physicists uphold the second way.

Many feminist theorists consider "heroism" to be the goal of war. According to Hartsock, "heroism requires a heroic action. And heroic action in itself is a complex construction that consists of deliberately facing the cessation of existence, a flirtation with death. A man cannot do great deeds without acting in a situation so dangerous that it threatens his continued existence" (Cohen, 1989, p. 141). Becker argues "that our central calling, our main task on this planet is heroic and that heroism is first and foremost a reflex of the terror of death since we admire most the courage of those who face their own extinction. This is the greatest victory we can imagine" (Cohen, 1989, p. 2).

Heroism requires that men put the lives of others above that of their own. It is about being courageous as well as about feeling omnipotent. The concept of heroism has become an adaptive belief system for those working in the arms control industry. It allows these men to deny their fear of death by placing themselves above the normal anxiety and fear we all experience in relation to our own death and with which we struggle all our lives. This also allows dissociation, denial, and detachment to become normalized by calling these feeling states "courage." I understand now that the "holier than thou" attitude I experienced in this world is interpreted as courage. It permits weapons to be built that put every human being at risk. It creates a world of elitism and male dominant thinking that is impermeable not only for a woman, but also for anyone not interested in building or working on a weapon system.

Men are doing a job. People who think about, plan or commit acts of war almost always say that you cannot let yourself feel anything about the possibility of civilian or "enemy" casualties, about suffering human bodies. They believe those feelings get in the way of rational analysis and action. To let such feelings influence you is seen as unprofessional. Thus, implicit in describing oneself as a professional doing a job is an injunction against thinking about and feeling for the people who suffer and die in war. This is the most dangerous aspect of this "doing a job" usage (Cohen, 1991, p. 15). For most, doing this particular job grew out of a desire to keep people alive and de-escalate the possibility of war. They, too, however, grew to put feeling aside and see the intuitive or irrational sense of emotions as interference rather than as a guiding force.

Along with the belief system that man is naturally aggressive and heroic by virtue of courage is the conviction that war is caused by emotions that have gotten out of control. Hitler, Stalin, and now Saddam Hussein are illustrations of this. The narrative goes something like this: Technology will overcome emotions, precision will defeat chaos, and strategic planning will control weapon systems, "personality cults," and even war itself.

The belief system that man is naturally aggressive and that war is caused by emotions is adaptive to the lives of people in the nuclear weapons industry. These beliefs support the notion that emotions are destabilizers, and only nonhuman forces such as institutions and technology can secure our world from aggression. Abstraction and disassociation enable men to forget that smart bombs kill real people and to speak instead of "collateral damage," and "friendly weapons."

The Creation Myth

> Take, for instance, a twig and a pillar, or the ugly person and the great beauty, and all the strange and monstrous transformations. These are all leveled together by Tao. Division is the same as destruction. (Chuaug-Tzu, 369–286 B.C., in Yutang, 1942)

The notions of heroism and of the supremacy of technology over emotions lead to what many people refer to as the *creation myth*. The men I worked with always challenged me to be like them and to be as excited about and in awe of the inventive new weapons as they were. The implication, to me, was that you are not a man if you do not work on a weapon system. Whenever I asked a friend how he dissociated so well from the destructive capabilities of nuclear weapons, he replied "What is the matter, Benina? Aren't you into doom, death, and destruction? Can't you be like me and get off on the purely scientific, creative potential of building technically difficult and challenging weapon systems?" He would ask me this over and over again with a chuckle. His black humor made my skin crawl.

> Stopping the destruction requires not just regulating or eliminating individual items like pesticides or military weapons. It requires new ways of thinking about humanity and new ways of relating to life. It requires a new worldview. (Mander, 1991)

The Einstein world view that requires a new way of thinking view is seen as negative in the think tank. It is the view I went in with and is the groupthink of the psychological world.

Burden of Responsibility Hypothesis

I came out of the experience more humble, less blaming, and more understanding of the human drives that motivate the arms control world. I now believe that "living with the bomb" is a burden of responsibility for my colleagues that imposes superhuman stress on the psyche. This responsibility creates what looks like a syndrome of *detachment, dissociation, and denial.* In fact, what we may be seeing is more akin either to post-traumatic stress syndrome or to truly heroic courage. The calmness of the people may be a function of controlling fear, not denying it.

This area is not explored but is worthy of research and further study. We on the psychology side need to be more tolerant and open to the stories these defense intellectuals tell. We need to find creative ways to "get into their minds" as in the work of Kull, who found that generals experience the nuclear weaponry still as conventional weapons (Kull, 1990). Doing this requires much dedication on our part and a participant observer stance that is centered in the political world rather than our own.

> A policy-relevant psychology of avoiding nuclear war must begin there, where the policymakers begin, deep within the international system and situation as it presently exists. . . . A nuclear psychology of the real must be psychologically real to those who inhabit the world where nuclear decision making occurs. (Blight, 1988)

Psychology and the Trash Bin Phenomenon

In this world of the academic defense intellectuals that I joined for three years, I experienced a phenomenon that at first left me perplexed. I noticed that anything that does not fit or is unmanageable from an analytic perspective (cannot be put into boxes, or Schelling's game theory) is called psychological or counterfactual and thrown away (Schelling & Ferguson, 1988). I call this the *trash bin phenomenon* because I am so struck by the trivializing of anything that is considered emotional or nonscientific.

There are a number of reasons I believe that the trash bin phenomenon exists:

1. One derives from the previously discussed belief system that man is naturally aggressive, despotic, and so forth. This leads to a major distrust of emotions and psychology, which is assumed to support a different, "softer" belief system. Thus, there is a rational reason for throwing psychological concepts away.
2. Another reason is that the desire to understand the psychological underpinnings of war is missing. Coupled with this lack of desire is that think tank professionals are unfamiliar with psychological thinking. This can lead to distrust, in the same way that many peace activists are lacking in understanding and respect for political and scientific thinking (this can be a political trash bin phenomenon). I believe people construct reality from the stories and narratives they share with friends, lovers, and colleagues. If the peace activists' world was also within the arms control think tank and the Pentagon or CIA, we also would not give as much meaning to feelings as they do.

> Social construction theory posits an evolving set of meanings that emerge unendingly from the interactions between people. These meanings are not skull-bound and may not exist inside what we think of as an individual "mind." They are part of a general flow of constantly changing narratives. Thus, the theory bypasses the fixity of the

model of biologically based cognition, claiming instead that the development of concepts is a fluid process, socially derived. (Hoffman, 1990)

3. The trash bin phenomenon may be a protection against hidden fears. It is difficult for me to imagine a world in which experiencing feelings does not intrude in everyone's lives in some way. I hypothesize that in the world of the defense analysts the "burden of responsibility" that is experienced through the immediacy of living with the bomb in a technological way is frightening. We psychologists might say that the veneer of calmness that is evident is a defense against the fear these analysts experience and that this is the *hidden emotion*. We are equally one-sided when we remain "stuck in our emotions" and unconscious of the political dynamic of proliferation and all its manifestations. Fear may also be the hidden emotion for us, but I expect *helplessness and powerlessness* is more to the point.

4. Another reason for defense analysts to throw out the psychological is that they see emotions as a hindrance rather than as a help in a difficult, if not impossible, situation. For example, when I actually saw the triggers on a submarine that would set off missiles, I was calm. I experienced a detachment that was overwhelming. The triggers seemed like a part of a video game. Afterward I was shaken terribly by this, making the abstract experience concrete. If I worked with this technology day in and day out, I would need to habituate to fear and anxiety or I could not continue with the work.

5. The question then becomes, "What was the original motivation that drove these scientists and political people into the arms control world?" As mentioned, I experienced the notion that feelings are destabilizers. Leaders like Hitler, Kadafy, and Hussein are creatures of their emotions, and this is what causes war. Unfortunately, the reaction to this phenomenon has been too extreme. The result has been a separation between psychological and political thinking. If psychology and politics operated together, the two modes of thinking could perhaps hold the events (crisis, war) and the feelings (fear, anxiety) in a more systemic model. This way, as McGuinness (1987) has said, could bring about "a new type of emotional education which would remove the ultimate causes of war in human character." Unfortunately, the polarization between the two groups keeps one too centered on the event and the other too preoccupied with feelings. Both, however, share an interest in the motivations of war. This may be a common ground.

We had some experience of this when President Bush used the psychological profile of Saddam Hussein (Post, 1991) as groundwork for basing his wartime strategies. There was much in this profile, however, that did not pan out. For example, Bush predicted that if Hussein was pushed to the wall, he would retreat. In following this lead, Bush had to look as if he were preparing for war, which he did, fully expecting Hussein to back down, which he did not do, proving again that human beings are volatile, particularly in stress situations. As a psychologist, I understand the fear of the psychological because of the strong belief the strategists have that "feelings destabilize a system and emotions would interfere with the task of looking and acting powerful."

Importance of the Event

Social construction theory posits an evolving set of meanings that emerge unendingly from the interactions between people. These meanings are a part of a general flow of constantly changing narrative (Hoffman, 1990). This denies the importance of the event and further scares the bomb builder into thinking that we are at the mercy of our emotions.

A good example of this is the recent admission of George Bush after the cease fire in the Gulf that he was moved to tears many times during the Gulf War but would not show this emotion because it might make us look like "wimps."

Defense intellectuals seem unable to differentiate psychological process from psychological warfare or *brainwashing*. Most technical weapons strategists were most familiar with psychology through CIA attempts to understand "how one could gain control of another human being and, in addition protect oneself against such control" (Weinstein, 1990, p. 189). The brainwashing methodology developed by Edward Hunter, the CIA, and the military blended well "with the Cold War fears of Chinese and Russian abilities to influence attitudes and behavior" (Weinstein, 1990, p. 132).

Closet Psychology: Positive Aspects

There is a curious mix between fear of the unknown and an excitement about the unfamiliar. For this reason, there does seem to be a positive place for psychological insights and sharing in the political think tank, if they remain discreet, hidden, and secretive.

On the positive side, when I was in a relaxed situation like a dinner party or in my office, people would often feel permission to give me their psychological insights. I called this closet psychology. Men who were impersonal in formal meetings would stand in my doorway telling me their problems and sharing their thoughts. At a dinner at the Faculty Club, a former appointee of Richard Nixon expressed the view that Nixon was the greatest intellectual of our time, but that he was so insecure about this that he recklessly refused to destroy the Watergate tapes because he wanted his words to go down in history. Whether this is true or not is not the point. When I identified myself as a psychologist with a neutral position, this sort of response was elicited.

Policymakers consider another useful application of psychology to be the study of public opinion and how to win an election. Otherwise, psychology is dismissed as "intuitive" or nonfactual.

Understanding the Psychological Metaphors of Defense Language

ARMS Control is literally Arms Control, physical and mental. It is also a sexual metaphor as well as a term used about controlling nuclear weapons in this world. I experienced it as a way for men to control their "arms" from reaching out in any way toward the opposite sex. There was the impression at all times in the center that everything was in control. The underlying belief system was that if you can control your body, there will not be trouble between men and women in this sexy, fast-paced, high-powered world of international relations. Thus everything will be balanced. Rosenthal (1990), who studied the daily lives of scientists, engineers, and technicians at Los Alamo and Sandia National Laboratories, also found "everything under control" among the men and women who worked in these weapons laboratories.

In other words, people and countries would stay out of trouble if there were not two sexes. Conflict on some level is seen as primitively the "battle of the sexes." The ways in which this thinking is applied to crisis is worth much more expansion and research. Perhaps family therapists who know a great deal about marital conflict are drawn to this world because they also can understand international relations from the perspective of the "couple." Psychologists are especially astute at understanding gender differences and how these differences create tension and volatility.

Political scientists gave *nations* and *institutions* human qualities. Nations and institutions could "learn," be "educated," and change their "behaviors," all qualities usually given to human beings. In the following quotes, Nye uses emotional and behavioral terms to describe a territory and to discuss power. "Moreover, the superpowers will need the cooperation of small weak states, which often cannot manage their own problems alone" (Nye, 1989, p. 43). "Proof of power lies not in resources but in the ability to change the behavior of states" (Nye, 1990, p. 155).

"When the analyst refers to the opposing state as 'he' or the 'other guy,' the image evoked is that of an individual man, a unitary male actor. But states are not unitary and unified. They are not capable of changing or of having human emotions or nuclear learning. People do these things. This anthropomorphizing of states, institutions, and nations may serve to help analysts keep their distance from the more emotionally evocative issue. That is, that nations, states, and so on are large groups of people like themselves who can be killed by nuclear weapons and their strategic plans" (Cohen, 1991).

Role of Women in the Arms Control World

The time that I spent living in the Pentagonese world of "collateral damage" and "smart bombs" has made it difficult for me to return to the real world, where each morning newspaper and television reports bring bleak despair from a human point of view. I believe more than ever that serious dangers face us as a world filled with nuclear weapons. I recognize that in this arena, everyone feels out of control. The inability to control technology has replaced the inability to control the aggressive nature of man. I appreciate the predicament the nuclear strategists have gotten themselves into and the difficulty they have either in making weapons safe or in removing them from use.

In some ways, I have been silenced by "men," who dismissed what I have to say as unimportant. At the same time, I've been given the message that my presence is important. I choose to translate this double message into "Listen, and then formulate your question or comment in a way that is comprehensible to them, but which does not give up your point of view."[2]

The role of women in an arms control center or in the world of international security is marginal because women are thought to be "soft and intuitive" and because there are so few of us who stay in that world. Only the woman who sounds like a man is acceptable. Women have two choices: either to hide their vulnerability and act like the men or to be dismissed.

The price of hiding, however, can be high. For women who collude with the abstractions and denial of emotions, the pain of hiding can become unbearable. The nuclear club is strong and seductive, and to be accepted into it, women give up their subjectivity. It is difficult, if not impossible, to stay in touch with one's feelings and vulnerability in a totally male arena. The group dynamics of the think tank are at the opposite extreme from the feminist approach to dialogue.

> From a social constructionist perspective of intimacy, what people talk about or share is less important than whether each person feels included in the interaction. (Weingarten, 1991)

The gender distinctions I have just described may have a lot to do with the burden of responsibility that nuclear weapons bring as well as men's history and carrying the responsibility of the "public world" so exclusively. I will never again be glib in my estimate of the people working in this difficult, if not impossible, area. I think the effects of this "burden of responsibility" are worthy of research.

As my colleague Pam Steiner states, the nuclear strategists "are caught in a terrible bind because of their superhuman responsibilities. The rest of us can and will make mistakes, and the situation for which they bear great responsibility is only partly in their control." They are in an impossible situation, which society demands (Pomerance-Steiner, 1989).

FROM THE OUTSIDE LOOKING IN

Integrating the personal, professional, and political in my life is a stretch for me. Having "embraced the enemy" and my personal observations of the nuclear club, I am ready to move on to the next phase of "making sense of war." This concerns women's place in the military.

The observations I have made about my experience in the international security world are preliminary. Women in the military world is a complex issue that deserves much more attention from those of us interested in gender and war issues. Because there is no theory of war written by women, the task is the more difficult and challenging. Women have written about war, as Barbara Tuchman did in *Guns of August* and Antonia Fraser did in *Warrior Queen*, but none to my knowledge have espoused an academic argument for war. Tuchman's work, however, may have in fact been politically effective. Theorists argue that "President Kennedy's skillful management of the Cuban missile crisis was influenced by reading Tuchman's (1962) account of the outbreak of World War I which emphasized the dangers of miscalculation and policy rigidities in a crisis" (Blight & Nye, 1987).

With women being more actively involved in the Gulf War both on the front-line and at home, it is time to find out more about why women enter the service and why they believe in war. I hope my research will lead to understanding the process by which our society constantly reframes war as "normal," even though the traditional feminine instinct has been seen to perceive it as abnormal.

According to Mary Catherine Bateson, Gregory Bateson "used to speak of the clarity that a state of war brings as a great relief, of the temptation in any society to resolve ambiguity and hard decisions by turning to warfare" (Bateson, 1984). This certainly was something that seemed important when I and others dropped almost everything else during the Gulf War of 1991. It was not a question of whether I or my friends and colleagues supported the war or not, it illustrated dramatically the focus war brings and the clarity that Bateson speaks of. Steinham states "in peacetime men lack a way to prove they are men" (Lloyd, 1987). For me the period just before the Gulf War illustrates the ultimate induction I was party to, having been in an arm of the military establishment for three years. Before the war broke out, the meaning of social issues seemed dim and unfocused. The greed of the 1980s had taken over, and the anticipated return of social responsibility in the 1990s seemed overpowered by the domestic violence and health issues facing us as a nation. I had given up hope of the United States attending to its own problems and out of despair identified with the aggressor, by taking some pride in the technology of the Gulf War. I now consider it more usual to be at war than at peace. The state of war rather than peace has also been the political context of most of my life. Since I was born, there has been the end of World War II, the Korean War, the Vietnam War, the cold war, and now the Gulf War, with many small wars in between.

> At issue here is a set of attitudes and assumptions that can be grouped around the concept of "normality" or nuclear "normality," and by nuclear "normality" I do not mean a fleeting image or a temporary psychological tone, but rather a lasting constel-lation of ideas and judgments concerning ways that are deemed appropriate to one's behavior and feelings in relation to nuclear weapons. (Lifton, 1987)

In the next phase of my work about women and the military, I expect the area of nonviolence to go hand in hand and that this will illuminate much needed understanding of positive peace. As a group of people, we have relied on negative peace as the context for much of the investigation.

THERAPEUTIC CONTEXT OF WOMAN AND WAR

Some of what I learned from being an outsider on the inside I brought back to my clinical work. I have observed that therapists have always been concerned with the general importance of culture and political structure in relationship to clinical work, but the importance of the specific event or crisis, be it the Holocaust, the Vietnam War, or the Gulf War, has received less attention. When war breaks out between countries and imposes itself on families, it has an impact on every individual as well as on the family system. When I walked into my office the day after the United States began bombing Iraq and a scud missile had just hit Israel, I brought my own feelings with me. I encountered the feelings of another therapist in my office building, who with her client, was sitting with a radio to her ear in the waiting room. They both looked at me when I walked in and asked, "Should we go on with therapy, when this is happening, as if nothing out of the ordinary has occurred? Or should we go home and listen to the radio?" I asked the obvious question, "What do you want to do in face of this crisis?" Both my colleague and her client answered, "Go home."

I found myself asking clients at the beginning of each hour how the war was affecting them and sharing openly my feelings. Sometimes the whole hour was spent on this.

When I paid attention to the "event" of the war, my clients began to pay more attention to the catastrophic happenings in their own lives, too. For example, one client, Jill, had entered the University of California, Berkeley, just before the riots of the 1960s broke out. Not only had the course of her school years been affected by the significant political demonstrations during the Vietnam War, but also she had become afraid of being involved with any political movement. She feared the return of the bloodshed of the 1960s and associated all political activity with these riots. No one was placing on her any expectation that she be involved, but nevertheless she berated herself for this lack. Jill eventually realized by looking at these riots that not all socially responsible or political activity was violent and that there were many other avenues that she could take to express her empathy toward people and caring about the world. She is now involved in a homeless shelter in her very affluent neighborhood and sponsors many people through Alcoholics Anonymous. She is working on limiting the energy she extends to the world so she does not burn out and so her commitments can be longstanding and sincere.

Although work has traditionally been the way most people "lay claim" to their place in the world, many people also have an expectation that they will be politically involved and socially responsible. This interface between the individual and society gives meaning and purpose to many people's lives. When one is able to find a way to integrate one's sociopolitical self with a professional career, a sense of deep self-worth is possible. A sense of purpose grows from believing that the "inner and outer processes are in fact continuously interacting and affecting each other, the outside world being shaped by what goes on in our inner spaces bother consciously and unconsciously. Whenever we focus unduly on one world to the exclusion of the other we obtain an unbalanced view of reality . . ." (Nichols, 1987).

> Family therapists recognize that people are embedded in a social context, and thus corrected the psychology of separateness. But each of us is both separate and embedded. Neither a psychology of separateness nor one of embeddedness alone is fully adequate to explain human behavior or to serve as a guide for clinical practice.

Although it is not possible to understand people without taking into account their social context, notably the family, it is misleading to limit the focus to the surface of interactions to social behavior divorced from inner experience. Personal relationships exist in the intersubjective experience of the participants, an experience shaped as much by memory and desire as by contemporary facts. The people we relate to are made of flesh and blood, but we filter our experience of them through cloudy images of expectation. (Nichols, 1987, p. 7)

Something about war compels me more than most people. I am against it and a pacifist, yet I navigate toward war at any opportunity. The "boys" at Harvard were right in daring me to work with them and not become captivated by weapon systems. I look at the targeting bases in the newspapers, hungry to know more about the defense systems that protect us and at the same time create such an impossible and preposterous world situation. I refuse to feel guilty for this fascination. Still, I wonder, "what can I do and remain the nonviolent pacifist I believe I am?"

I wish I had the answer; I wish I could make sense of war, but the burden of that responsibility in the context of the world we live in and the position I play as "messenger" keeps me asking the questions that tell the story each time I am brave enough to do something, even if it is just a small turn on the wheel. This is a challenge to me, and one that I see clearly.

NOTES

1. American Family Therapy members of the study group Family Systems Thinking and the Nuclear Dilemma were Faye Snider, Steve Zeitlin, David McGill, Donna Hilleboe DeMuth, and Marsha Pravder Mirkin.
2. This is a difficult task, but, fortunately, to a family therapist it is not a new skill. All family therapists share in their work a common imperative to learn the new family's language and speak from this tongue.

BIBLIOGRAPHY

Bateson, M. C. (1984). *With a daughter's eye: A memoir of Margaret Mead and Gregory Bateson* (p. 23). New York: W. Morrow.

Bellah, R., et al. (1985). *The genocidal mentality, Nazi holocaust, and nuclear threat.* New York: Basic Books.

Bellah, R., et al. (1991). *The Good Society* (p. 19). New York: Alfred A. Knopf.

Blight, J. (1988). Can psychology help reduce the risk of nuclear war? Reflections of a "little drummer boy" of nuclear psychology. *Journal of Humanistic Psychology, 28*(2), 7–58.

Blight, J., & Nye, J. (1987). The Cuban missile revisited. *Foreign Affairs, 66*(1), 171.

Clesse, A. (1987). Nuclear weapons and the control of aggression. In D. McGuiness (Ed.), *Dominance, aggression and war* (p. 258). New York: Paragon House Publishers.

Cohen, C. (1989). America's linguistic deterrent. In A. Harris & Y. King (Eds.), *Rocking the ship of state toward a feminist peace politics* (p. 155). Boulder, CO: Westview Press.

Cohen, C. (1991). The language of the Gulf War. In *Center Review* (p. 14). Cambridge, MA: Center for Psychological Studies in the Nuclear Age.

Dietz, M. (Ed.) (1990). *Thomas Hobbes and political theory* (p. 26). Lawrence, Kansas: University of Kansas Press.

Fields, R. (1991). *The code of the warrior* (p. 259). New York: Harper Collins.

Glad, B., & Rosenberg, P. (1990). Bargaining under fire: Limit setting and maintenance during the Korean War. In B. Glad (Ed.), *Psychological dimensions of war* (p. 195). Newbury Park, CA: Sage Publications.

Glendinning, C. (1990). *When technology wounds: Human consequences of progress.* New York: Morrow.

Hoffman, L. (1990). Constructing realities: An art of lenses. *Family Process, 29*(1), 1–12.

Janis, I. (1971). Groupthink among policy makers. In N. Sanford & C. Comstock (Eds.), *Sanctions for evil* (pp. 71–89). San Francisco: Jossey-Bass, Inc.

Kull, S. (1988). *Minds at war: Nuclear reality and the inner conflicts of defense policy makers.* New York: Basic Books.

Kull, S. (1990). The role of perceptions in the nuclear arms race. In B. Glad (Ed.), *Psychological dimensions of war* (pp. 295–309). Newbury Park, CA: Sage Publications.

Lifton, R. J. (1987). *Nuclear 'normality': The ethics of annihilation.* Conference hosted by the Center on Violence and Human Survival, New York: Center on Violence and Human Survival.

Lifton, R. J., & Markusen, E. (1990). *The genocidal mentality, Nazi holocaust, and nuclear threat.* New York: Basic Books.

Lloyd, B. (1984). *The man of reason, "male" and "female" in Western philosophy* (p. 27). Minneapolis: University of Minnesota Press.

Lloyd, G. (1987). Selfhood, war and masculinity. In C. Pateman & E. Gross (Eds.), *Feminist challenges* (pp. 63–76). Boston: Northeastern University Press.

Mack, J. (1991). The language of the Gulf War. *Center Review* (p. 14). Cambridge, MA: Center for Psychological Studies in the Nuclear Age.

Mander, J. (1991). *In the absence of the sacred: the failure of technology and the survival of the Indian nations* (pp. 37–38). San Francisco: Sierra Club Books.

McGuinness, D. (1987). *Dominance, aggression and war.* New York: Paragon House.

Nichols, M. (1987). *The self in the system: Expanding the limits of family therapy.* New York: Brunner/Mazel.

Nye, S. J., Jr. (1989, Winter) Arms control after the cold war. *Foreign Affairs, 68*(5), 43.

Nye, S. J., Jr. (1990, Fall) Soft power. *Foreign Policy,* (80), 155.

Pomerance-Steiner, P. (1989, December) In collusion with the nation: A case study of group dynamics at a strategic nuclear policy making meeting. *Political Psychology, 10*(4), 647–673.

Post, J. M. (1991). Hussein, Saddam of Iraq—A political psychology profile. *Political Psychology, 12*(2), 279–289.

Ricoeur, P. (1970). *Freud and philosophy: An essay on interpretation* (p. 305). London: Yale University Press.

Rosenthal, D. (1990). *At the heart of the bomb: The dangerous allure of weapons work.* Reading, MA: Addison-Wesley.

Schelling, T., & Ferguson, A. (1988). *Nuclear crisis project, Center for Science and International Affairs, Kennedy School of Government, Harvard University.* Unpublished manuscript.

Tenzin Gyatso the Fourteenth Dalai Lama (1992). *The global community and the need for universal responsibility.* Boston: Wisdom Publications.

Waltz, K. N. (1959). *Man, the state, and war: A theoretical analysis.* New York: Columbia University Press.

Weingarten, K. (1991). The discourses of intimacy: Adding a social constructionist feminist view. *Family Process, 30*(3), 285–305.

Weinstein, H. (1990). *Psychiatry and the CIA: Victims of mind control* (p. 189). Washington, D.C.: American Psychiatric Press.

Yutang, L. (1942). *Wisdom of China and India.* Canada: Random House.

Chapter 11

Scenes from a Revolution: Reflections of a North American Family Therapist

Hinda Winawer*

My affiliation with Nicaragua, which began during the incumbency of the Sandinista government, was at the outset intended to be professional. As I learned about the objectives of the Sandinistas (who had overthrown the dictator, Anastasio Somoza) and about the attempts of my government to disable their revolution, however, it became impossible to avoid engagement in the political dimension. In the United States, the relative silence about the deaths of men, women, and children killed in an undeclared war, waged by a "contra" insurgency trained and financed by my government, compelled me to bear witness personally. The changing political conditions, which I observed during the course of three visits, served as contexts for a personal evolution. Although I had previously considered human service delivery in its relationship to social, political, and economic events, the experiences in Nicaragua affirmed the importance of the connection among these phenomena. Gradually the subtext of my involvement with Nicaragua became an attempt to integrate three arenas of my life: the professional, the political, and the personal.

The initial objectives of my trips were compatible with concepts previously cited by family therapists who have explored connections between the political and the professional: (1) citizen diplomacy, based on the assumption that we can

---

*Dedicated to the Nicaraguan Mothers of Heroes and Martyrs who live each day with the memories of their children's tortures, deaths, and disappearances.

interrupt cycles of violence through understanding and dialogue (Berger-Gould, 1985); (2) the need to educate ourselves and our fellow citizens to another image of the "enemy" (Keen, 1988); and (3) our vulnerability to induction into a collusion of silence about dangerous and unconscionable acts against humanity (Wetzel & Winawer, 1986).

In Nicaragua, I observed deprivation I had known existed in the Third World. Here, however, in contrast to a prevailing sense of despair in areas of poverty and strife, even in the face of war, there was also a creative mobilization of human resources inspired by the ideals of the revolution. Most impressive was the story of a people's rise from oppression, a government's attempt to serve its most needy constituents, and ecosystemic consumer-relevant models of human service delivery.

The following are selected vignettes (scenes), embellished by personal and political reflections of a systemic nature:

Scene: San Francisco

AN INVITATION

My first invitation to Nicaragua was as a family therapist. At the annual meeting of the American Orthopsychiatric Association, the Director of the School of Psychology of the Central American University (UCA) in Managua asked me if I would come to Nicaragua to teach.

Later that year, after ascertaining how safe, and indeed popular, travel to Nicaragua was, I joined a delegation of Princeton community and university women whose focus was to study the changing role of women in Nicaragua. I had planned to conduct workshops at UCA, but my contact was reduced to brief consultations because my letter of confirmation had never arrived at the University in Managua (an early lesson about the inconveniences that regularly challenge life and work in the Third World).

Reflection. Nicaragua was immediately engaging. Dotted with lakes and volcanoes, the air, laced with the scent of wood fires for cooking, is my Proustian sensory memory. I particularly remember masses of humanity on the sides of roads, driving ox carts, riding horses, or walking to and from work in the darkness of early morning and evening.

As a nation, they were involved in an attempt to build a new society. In contrast to years of brutal dictatorship, since 1979, there had been steady progress toward elections and a constitutional democracy. Local communities were formally organized, and public services were conceptualized as inalienable rights.

Social foundations had undergone second-order change: from oppression to empowerment, from elitism to grassroots organization and prioritization of the needs of the poor, and from dictatorial centrality of power to not only representative, but also participatory democracy (Ruchwarger, 1987). Many previously rigid social patterns had been disturbed; some were, at the very least, challenged.

JANUARY 1989, THE FIRST TRIP

Toward Second-Order Change for Second-Class Citizens:
The Women of Nicaragua

It is not surprising that I would choose a female-oriented construction for my first exploration of the Nicaraguan revolution. Issues concerning the development of women in relation to the progress of the revolution provided a good personal and ideological fit. In the company of women, visiting women's organizations, feminist ideology commingled with my family therapy perspective.

Scene: Granada

A MOTHER

Our last night in Granada we went to an outdoor dance cafe on Lake Nicaragua. A woman, attractive, in her early forties, was dancing with unmistakable gusto. She swigged beer between dance numbers. During a break, she came to our table to say hello to the pediatric surgeon from the Granada hospital.

She then turned and looked me straight in the eye and said, "Yo te conozco, norteamericana (I know you North American). You were at the meeting of the Mothers of Heroes and Martyrs. I saw your tears!"

The tone of her voice and expression in her eyes were rage. I could hardly look at her directly. I nodded in response with some contortion of my mouth that knew it shouldn't form a smile. By the time she'd danced the next number and drank some more beer, I regained my balance and got in touch with what must have been a very small part of her pain. It seemed that to ignore her anguish would have been disrespectful, a rejection of her passionate overture. I somehow expected another encounter. My impression was confirmed; she came back to our table.

"You lost a child," I said.

"Yes," she said, still glaring.

"How old was he?"

"He was 22 years old, my first-born, beautiful, handsome, strong, full of life, in the flower of life, and he went to the front with the Contras and that was the end of his beautiful life!"

She shed tears that must belong to the mourning for a child. By the time she finished talking, I found that we were holding hands. Touching just happened in Nicaragua. This was pain that couldn't be soothed. As a therapist and as a woman I knew not to try to calm a mother's anguish for her child. That pain belonged to her. One of my sons was 22. I didn't say that. I said some words that were inadequate about honoring her son's life by speaking out against the war. And we sat.

Reflection. There is also, of course, a historical basis for this woman's rage. Like other Latin American countries, Nicaragua, "... has specialized in losing ever since those remote times when Renaissance Europeans ventured across the ocean and buried their teeth in the throats of the Indian civilizations" (Galeano, 1984, p. 11). In recent history, the dominant presence of U.S. intervention is a consistent aspect of Nicaragua's experience and of its collective memory as a nation: In 1850, the United States and Great Britain decided, without asking Nicaragua, that there should be a trans-Nicaraguan canal; in 1855, U.S. adventurer William Walker declared himself president of Nicaragua, and the first of nine U.S. invasions occurred in 1912, followed by 25 years of occupation by U.S. marines. The United States withdrew only after the infamous Guardia, the Nicaraguan National Guard under Anastasio Somoza Garcia, was in place. One of Somoza's early interventions was the clandestine execution of the dominant inspiration for Nicaraguan resistance, the now legendary Augusto Sandino. Somoza and his sons ruled Nicaragua consecutively until 1979.

The U.S. attitude toward this despot and his progeny is reflected in Franklin Delano Roosevelt's well-known description of Somoza: "He may be a son-of-a-bitch, but he's *our* son-of-a-bitch." The policy of the United States toward Nicaragua has been described as a *guerra santa*, a holy war, based on the presumptions of Manifest Destiny and the Monroe Doctrine (Ramirez, 1985, p. 111). Indeed, the trademark of the Reagan administration was the infamous support for the insurgent right-wing "contras" in pursuit of the president's expressed goal to make Nicaragua "cry uncle."

There are many stories similar to those of this mother who seems to dance and drink to have the strength to remember her pain. As of 1988, 20,000 people had died in the Contra war; thousands more were maimed, crippled, or kidnapped (Gilbert, 1988), a direct result of the U.S. policy of intervention and aggression against Nicaragua. I had not originally thought of it also as violence against women.

Scene: an AMNLAE[1] Women's Center

CONSCIOUSNESS RAISING AND EMPOWERMENT

That Martha,[2] the woman who described the center, had been tortured by Somoza's Guardia distracted me from the first part of her talk. As we listened, a woman brought out a tray of cool drinks decorated with fresh fruit and served in worn but colorful plastic cups. We had intended to avoid drinking the water, for fear of bacteria. We drank it nevertheless, not because of the heat, but to honor their generosity.

Martha described the activities of the center: work for legal changes to increase women's rights with regard to abortion, divorce, adultery, and rape. In March, there will be a meeting at the National Assembly. Eighteen-hundred women from all over the country will attend: factory workers, campesinas and military women.

To educate community women about rape, sexuality, and family planning, the center regularly offers workshops. Since the revolution, women have become not only technically, but also culturally trained, the latter primarily through consciousness raising. One teaching method elicits discussion by using a video illustrating a couple in a destructive interaction, that is, one in which a man is mistreating a woman. The major focus of the educational component is consciousness raising about domestic violence and relevant women's rights.

Reflection. The Sandinista revolution, its errors notwithstanding,[3] constituted second-order change with respect to social, political, and economic organization. Accordingly, improvements in women's status and the transformation of the society in which they rose can be seen as intertwined. Gender relations are rarely unproblematic anywhere. In Nicaragua, however, before the revolution, public conversations endorsing women's rights were unusual.

The oppression of women is universal. Even in developed countries, the feminization of poverty (and the lack of proportionate access to power) has been clearly established (Gelpi, Harstock, Novak, & Strober, 1986). If women's rights are the last to change, we may contemplate a converse assumption: If the condition of women has begun to improve, the general level of human rights in the society as a whole is likely to be improving. Second-order change for women can provide a lens, therefore, through which to view the entire social structure. By way of example, women's plight under Somoza and their engagement in the resistance can be seen as a reflection of the plight of the Nicaraguan people as a whole. A brief examination of their experiences in war may enhance our understanding of the challenges and importance of the women's movement to human services in Nicaragua.

Women lost their sons and their daughters during the insurrection before Somoza's overthrow in 1979 and during the Contra war. In the city of Masaya at the museum of Heroes and Martyrs, two women guided us through the gallery of photographs. One had lost a son during the insurrection; the other had lost two sons and a daughter. Showing us the exhibit, photographs of men and women, most in their teens and twenties, the women retold, in images that haunt the memory, how the youth of their town had died at the hands of Somoza's men. The National Guard's mission was to intimidate and terrorize; they not only murdered, they mutilated.

But the women fought back. Many young mothers fought against Somoza's Guard, often leaving their own mothers to care for their children. Thirty percent of the fighting force against Somoza were women. In 1978, women constituted 40% of the armed population. They not only fought in direct combat, but also they served as nurses, participated in guerrilla activities, ran meetings, made explosives, hid combatants in safe houses, and sent food to others. Some, like Dora Maria Telez, became commandantes. Others, like our speaker, Martha, were tortured (Randall, 1981).

Women's participation in the insurrection and in the Contra war was double-edged: It involved struggle and loss but also engendered a sense of strength and empowerment. Fighting for their children and for their country became as well a metaphor for the struggle for their own rights.

The history of women's oppression is addressed in the women's center workshops, in which domestic violence is described and clearly labeled in a supportive group setting. Although such consciousness raising has been practiced in more static societies, here women's involvement and success in the revolution and their developing understanding of their country's history contributed to a sense of hope and entitlement. Awareness of the revolutionary struggle, therefore, can be seen as supporting Nicaraguan women's emergence from isolation, from views of domestic violence as rooted in personal deviance, and from beliefs about rigid gender roles. This cultural education enables them to begin to recount their personal histories of oppression in a context that validates their experiences. The practices in this center highlight how understanding of and participation in the sociopolitical arena can have a direct impact on the delivery of human services.

Scene: Granada, Bernardino Diaz Ochoa Hospital

WOMEN AND HEALTH CARE

As we walked through the interior garden, Dr. Torres pointed to a double door in a crumbling wall: "Before the revolution that section was for the wealthier patients."

The building was clean but practically in shambles. Supplies were short. There were no sheets on the beds as there were no washing machines. On the obstetrical ward, postpartem women were lying on the leatherette mattresses with their babies.

In the pediatric section, virtually all the staff were women. Many patients were very thin babies suffering from dehydration. Mothers, or fathers, stood or sat next to the beds of their sick children, partly because there were not enough nurses. Dr. Lopez showed us through the ward. She was the only pediatric surgeon. During this visit, I was living in her home. She had one phone and personally responded to every emergency call, often leaving the house during the night.

In another section of the hospital, the wards were in tents, as was at least one operating room, because other areas were uninhabitable. As I was going from tent to tent, a woman asked if I would make a Polaroid of her with her baby, as I had done for her friend outside the pediatric ward. I agreed and was soon facing a long line of mothers and babies. The very poor did not usually have photographs of their children. Many of the infants looked weak and gravely ill. Someone said the photo would be the only concrete memento of their children.

Reflections. During the Somoza regime, mothers had little hope of proper health care for their children. Living conditions bred disease: Eighty percent of the population had no running water; 47% had no sanitary facilities. There were epidemics of malaria, polio, tuberculosis, typhoid, and gastroenteritis. In the last year of Somoza's power, more than 100 babies out of every 1,000 died. Six in 10 deaths were from curable infectious diseases. Fifty percent of the nation's deaths were of children younger than 14 years old. There was an elitist health care system. Service to the poor and to the productive population was at the lowest levels.

In 1979, the new government developed a comprehensive health care delivery system that constitutionally mandated that medical services be the duty of the state and the right of the people. The Sandinistas expanded health care to 589 centers throughout the country, the geographical size of Virginia. The emphasis shifted to prevention. Polio was eradicated, and the infant mortality rate was halved, from 121 to 62 per 1,000 (Zapata, 1989).

The rapid expansion of services and facilities, however, did not immediately or completely reverse chronic health care problems. The actual number of hospitals did not increase, and those that stood were often in disrepair. The revolution was always in serious economic difficulties. One major source of problems was U.S. opposition to the Sandinista government, operationalized in the support of an armed opposition force and in the imposition of a comprehensive trade embargo. The Sandinistas' need to maintain a military resistance diverted crucial economic resources from health care and other domestic survival and development needs. Similarly, the embargo, imposed in 1985, undermined the goal of achieving adequate care for the children. Seventy percent of the hospital equipment in Nicaragua had been made in the United States. Consequently there were often no spare parts available for critical care. There were never enough supplies. I saw plastic surgical gloves, which had been washed and disinfected, hanging on a wooden clothes dryer. Incubators stood in hallways, unserviceable because there were no replacement parts, harsh reminders of the relationship between politics and health services.

Here too we see how the development of women may be seen as isomorphic to the triumph of the revolution, that there are parallels between class and gender struggle. In other words, if women are doing better, perhaps it is a sign that the society has improved. It is reasonable to assume that ". . . women's oppression is inextricably bound up with a world system of exploitation. To analyze the status of women in order to change it, is to analyze the need and possibility of the most fundamental social transformation" (Leacock, 1979, p. 7.). This relationship can be seen in this most basic life and death issue, that is, changing medical services for women.

Scene: Granada, Regional AMNLAE Legal offices

WOMEN'S LAWS AND MEN'S POWERS

On the wall hung a brightly colored poster with the words: "In the name of God, stop the oppression!" (a phrase attributed to slain Salvadoran Archbishop Romero). In this narrow room bordering a sparsely planted inner courtyard, we discussed the legal status of women with the staff of the center. Also included were law students for whom 200 hours of social service were required as part of their training. We talked in general:

"Women, in Nicaragua," one young attorney explained, "still do not understand their rights."

"One of the major goals of our center," another added, "is education. Most women have not developed a concept of themselves as having rights. Many are still physically and psychologically abused."

We continued the dialogue between our two groups:

North American: Why do women come to a lawyer rather than to a social worker?

Nicaraguan: Women and children are second-class citizens. Men have all the rights; they go out when they want, spend the money. More than anything, the central issue is a question of basic rights. Men impose their power over women. Women are subjected to double exploitation, at work and in the home. The man doesn't help. Often, if a woman is resting or enjoying herself, a man will find something for her to do, or there will be violence. It's a question of abuse and discrimination that brings women here. Men are raised to subjugate women. We believe that men here are educated to violence against women and that the men are a product of their society and of their system.

Reflection. Change is countered by the stabilizing force of machismo, the Latin version of the universal concept of male chauvinism. Women's quest for power, as reflected in new laws, the creation of women's centers, the women's movement, the new government, and an unprecedented public dialogue on women's issues in Nicaraguan society, suggests, on one level, second-order change. On the level of daily existence, however, the more assertive the women, the more likely a reactionary response from the men. All this occurs in the context of generations of machismo. As in other countries, the society is still male dominated. In the revolutionary government, women hold seats in the national assembly and head ministries in numbers that well exceeded levels of female representation in our own national government. The greatest power, however, is still with the men. Although women have unprecedented access to psychological and legal counseling, laws regarding rape and other domestic violence are still inadequate and difficult to enforce. Abortion, although not prosecuted, is still illegal. Can this be understood because of Catholicism? Machismo? Or is it a revolutionary policy which is unwilling to risk a diminution of popular support during wartime by aggressively pursuing socially divisive issues. Although lobbying continues, the daily oppression of women persists, as the poster had alerted.

Scene: Granada, With the Mothers of Heroes and Martyrs

GRIEVING COMMUNALLY

In the evening, we went to a small building, to an inner patio. All attendees held white paper doves mounted on the top of sticks. Rodrigo Perez, a Sandinista representative to the National Assembly from Granada, played his accordion, and his comrade accompanied him on the guitar. They played selections from the Missa Campesina, the peasant mass now used as part of the Liberation Theology liturgy.

Then the room fell silent. One by one, the women, some alone, some accompanied by their husbands, stood and told the story of the death or disappearance of their children. Julia stood. I could hardly see her face in the darkness. She spoke. Her son got involved in the struggle when he was 14 years old. He was in maneuvers for three years. He received the highest medal of honor. Although she still feels the pain of his death, she is proud to have had a son like him.

A second woman spoke. "Every morning we go to the house of Cardinal Obando y Bravo [considered antagonistic to the Sandinistas] to be recognized, to get answers, to get some Christian response, to ask him to be a mediator. He has never received us. We were received at the peace talks by president Arias [of Costa Rica] and did get some hope. The question of the disappeared and kidnapped will be addressed at their next meeting."

Another woman testified. She is the mother of a fallen soldier and of another who will complete his military service on the 28th of this month. "We put flowers on the graves of the fallen heroes and do things that make us feel better about our children. As mothers of martyrs, we know where our children are. There is some comfort. It is harder for those of the disappeared and kidnapped."

Reflection. Formally incorporated into the organization of this new society, the National Commission of the Mothers of Heroes and Martyrs (a government endorsement of an organization, similar to grassroots mothers' groups in other Latin American countries) is a structure that validates loss and supports the national expression of grief. As a family therapist, I looked for intergenerational dialogue about loss and fear related to war. If it existed, I found strikingly little. The government-supported Mothers of Heroes and Martyrs, however, provides mental health services, in a nontraditional format, which not only supports grieving families directly, but also channels their energy into constructive work for its members and society.

Scene: Managua, A Women's Wellness Clinic

ECOSYSTEMIC HEALTH CARE

This center was new but simple. On the wall behind the reception desk, there was a straw woven mat (tapiseta) of a woman. The waiting area had unusually comfortable chairs. The director spoke:

"This is a wellness clinic, not a center for sick women. We give more than traditional services. Treatment by women of women is different. If a woman comes to another woman, her problem is my problem. We offer three kinds of services: (1) health; (2) reproductive health, to avoid cervical cancer; and (3) prevention of the death of women through disease or unwanted pregnancy. Our primary means to deliver these services is a Pap smear and sex education. We also help women with regard to divorce. We educate them; women know little about the divorce process.

We also offer a combination of services to victims of rape: (1) medical treatment of bruises, a tetanus shot, a "morning after pill," or the insertion of an

intrauterine device (IUD); (2) psychological assistance with the emotional reper-
cussions, which are often very serious; and (3) legal advice. The kind of legal help
women generally get in other settings can be another form of rape.

"We are now developing an outreach campaign so that women can come to
the center without fear. One of the problems of women," she continued, "is that
we undervalue ourselves, give everything out of love and don't work hard to be
recognized."

Political activism in support of women's issues is an integral part of their
work. Last December, for example, five women from the center attended the first
International Congress of Latin American Lesbian Women. We were told that,
although lesbian women personally have difficulty proclaiming their sexual orientation, the revolutionary government was supportive.

Reflection. Here is one of the many examples of an ecosystemic concept that seems
to be an aspect of many women's services, in general, and which appears particularly prevalent in Nicaragua. The sociopolitical context is immediately seen as
interacting with individual or domestic problems. Not only the understanding,
but also the work is more than interdisciplinary. They appear to have truly
integrated health, law, psychology, and political action in their concept and execution of human service delivery.

Reflection on the Women's Centers. These are women's ways: Power gained is power
shared. The shared feature of the women's organizations was that they were
organized by and for women in women's styles. Instead of using power competi-
tively and hierarchically as might happen in a capitalistic patriarchal society,
many women's organizations and services emerged that de-emphasize patriarchal, hierarchical, and competitive values. They are instead characterized by
collaboration, affiliation, and empowerment of other women as peers.

Scene: Monimbó, A Barrio of Masaya

MEN'S WAYS OF MOURNING?

Here we saw only men. At five o'clock, the sun was low in the sky. We
crowded into an old schoolhouse. The only light came through two small windows. We sat on benches that ringed the room. Facing us, standing were what
seemed to be the all-male council of elders of Monimbó. A man, who looked about
60 years old, spoke to us softly. It was the most gray, motionless of all the meetings
we attended. The speaker described their activities.

"We arise at 3:00 A.M., take care of our cemetery, pave our roads, and then go
to work." This was his refrain. His story digressed to other subjects but always

came back to the early morning tasks. His speech, uncharacteristic of anything I had heard in Nicaragua, was unanimated, without that lilting intonation, almost without affect. When we left, a member of our delegation was critical about the all-male composition of the group. "There was something different here," I responded.

Reflection. I had seen depression. I had heard recurrent themes. For me, women's oppression is axiomatic. But the question here was not whether feminism is the preferred model for understanding the human condition. Later, on my departure from Nicaragua, I was listening to a song by a popular female vocalist, Norma Gadea, whom I had met earlier. The song was "Pajarita de la Paz," little bird of peace. At the end, the lyrics list a number of countries as birds of peace—El Salvador, Guatemala, and so on—and includes with them, "pajarita Monimbó." Why did she especially include Monimbó, a barrio, in her list of countries that were suffering and struggling?

Monimbó, I later learned, was the site of a spontaneous uprising in early 1978 after Somoza's guardsmen had tear-gassed a memorial mass for Pedro Joachim Chamorro, the slain La Prensa newspaper publisher who had opposed Somoza. An estimated 200 residents died in the fighting (Gilbert, 1988). For this small barrio, the killings had constituted a massacre.

Scene: Managua, Iglesia Santa Maria de los Angeles

RELIGION AND THE REVOLUTION

After a weekend on the beach at Pochomil, I arrived in Managua just in time for the Liberation Theology Mass. The celebrant, Father Ramirez, was flanked by Methodist Bishops visiting from the United States. On a platform behind him were three folk musicians performing the "Peasant Mass" (Missa Campesina). The congregants filled the church to capacity. We sang a popular Nicaraguan song about war and peace. It was the art in the church, however, that most powerfully joined Catholicism and the people. The stations of the cross depicted the history of the struggles of the Nicaraguan people against oppression. In a style I would describe as an unlikely combination of Chagall and Soviet Realism, there was the traditional crucifixion of Jesus in the person of the new revolutionary man. On the lower right, in the position generally reserved for Mary, was a crowd of supplicant Mothers of Heroes and Martyrs bearing before them the photographs of their missing children.

Reflection. A more extensive consideration of culture and history (beyond the scope of this discussion), as with families in treatment, would illuminate the present struggles of the Nicaraguan people. Similarly, religion, central to Nicaraguan life, can be only mentioned here, particularly liberation theology, which is intimately associated with the revolution.

The formal origins of liberation theology are attributed to the Second Council of Latin American Bishops in Medellin, Colombia, in 1968. In response to the underdevelopment of their region, the Bishops sought to create a church inextricably associated with the plight of the poor (Dodson & O'Shaughnessy, 1990). An outgrowth was the concept of Christian base communities among the indigent, emphasizing empowerment, peace, and social justice. In these settings, "Jesus is within reach of the people—definitely not put up off on a pedestal somewhere."(Heyward, 1987, p. 50). Liberation theology, in Nicaragua, is an ecumenical phenomenon that encompasses feminist theology as well. The political history of the people and their travails is understood in terms of the Gospel. It is a new construction for an old story.

The split between the official Catholic Church and the Popular People's Church is a crucial dimension of the Nicaraguan Revolution. The conflict is best described for me in an image, a popular photograph that I saw at the Val de Viezo Ecumenical Center in Managua. Ernesto Cardenal, national poet,[4] Sandinista, Minister of Culture, and an ordained priest, genuflects before Pope John Paul II on the pontiff's visit to Nicaragua. The papal response is to wield a castigating finger over the head of the kneeling priest.

JANUARY 1990, THE SECOND TRIP

Occam's Razor Third World Style: The Context of Limitations
is the Context of Possibilities

On this trip I was back in the familiar role of the lone traveling family therapy consultant. I was finally to teach a course for the School of Psychology of UCA and another for a nationwide program. The unusual elements of bringing material donations, struggling in another language, and working in another culture, one of poverty and revolution, in a country for so long dominated by my own, added unfamiliar dimensions to the teaching experience. All of this was set against the atmosphere of a Nicaragua pervaded with the energy of a presidential campaign.

What impressed me on this trip was that, although you could expect everything to break down, so many people seemed creatively adaptive. I often found myself in the company of people who could spin straw into gold or, at least, into something functional: Someone would invariably transform a situation replete with disadvantage into an opportunity for resourcefulness and ingenuity. If you were lucky enough to have a car and afford gasoline, igniting and keeping that machine going seemed to be one of life's daily triumphs (Coburn & Flores, 1991).

Scene: On the Road to Managua

LIFE ON THE EDGE *to* A CITY WITHOUT A CENTER

One morning, after a breakfast of "gallo pinto" (rice and beans), we headed in the bright morning sun back to Managua for my first workshop with the Multiplicadores. I was thinking how much I delighted in this road; it abounded in human activity and splendid landscape. Momotombo, the Managua volcano, had just come into view. We were riding behind one of the many open trucks, overloaded with people and produce, probably going to one of the markets in Managua. I had been noticing the women's muscular calves, straining to keep a balance while standing in the open truck. The truck veered onto the shoulder, tipped, and went over on its side. Within seconds, there were screams and cries. People were all over the ground. We got out of our cars to see how we could help. One woman's face was streaked with blood. She was pointing to a younger woman who was lying motionless. Others stopped as well. The unconscious woman revived. There was ample assistance from passersby, helping people to their feet, comforting them, eventually collecting the scattered fruits and vegetables and righting the truck. I thought these accidents must happen more often, that there are many people riding and living precariously on the edge in Nicaragua.

A Reflection on Entering Managua. Each time I drive through Managua, I am struck that it has no center. The earthquake of December 23, 1972, the worst natural disaster in the history of Nicaragua, killed more than 10,000 people. One hundred thousand were dislocated. Somoza's response to the devastation was to divert the emergency foreign aid to his private enterprises. The capitol was never rebuilt. "Managua," Salman Rushdie (1987, p. 16) wrote on his visit in 1987, "... sprawled around its own corpse."

Scene: Managua, National School for the Sandinista Youth

MENTAL HEALTH MULTIPLIERS

Here in this center, borrowed from the Managua training center for Sandinista Youth, in the lounge area, I met some of the 48 women and men, ranging in age from early twenties to about 50, of the Multiplicadores (multipliers) who had traveled from all parts of Nicaragua (some by boat) for this two-day workshop.

I did not have much to set up. The course materials had not arrived on the plane with me. It had consisted of workshop folders, pens, pads, handouts in

Spanish, and articles as well as videotapes donated by colleagues in the United States.[5] "The articles are in the maletas" (suitcases) was to be a humorous refrain over these next two days.

The group is called the Multiplicadores (multipliers). They are part of a project, as Tortorici, its director describes, which was designed to multiply the availability of human services. The project is co-sponsored by the Nicaraguan Ministry of Health, the House of Support to Combatants, and INSSBI (the welfare department) and is financed by the Swedish organization Radda Barnen. The project's central activity is the training of mental health multipliers who in turn train promoters in the geographical departments (Tortorici, 1989).

As part of their training, Multiplicadores are given periodic workshops as well as ongoing supervision by a psychiatrist and a doctoral-level psychologist. Some have been previously trained in their particular discipline: psychologists, social workers, teachers, community workers. Most are actively involved in work with children or families. Additionally, the Multipliers themselves give training sessions for promoters (paraprofessionals) in their respective regions: church leaders, community activists, traditional healers, students, Mothers of Heroes and Martyrs. The Multipliers' teaching is in the presence of the two supervisors.

The project has spread around the country, to war-affected areas, that is, the Atlantic Coast and the northern and southern borders. Six months after the project's inception, there were 200 promoters in this country of 3.2 million.

I conducted a workshop and was able to visit a number of their local training sites and observe Multipliers incorporate their learning into the teaching of promoters. During one of the breaks in the workshop, a social worker asked what Minuchin might do in a particular interview. Her question included possible micro-moves and reflected a familiarity with Minuchin's work. I asked if she had seen him interview in person or on video. She said that she hadn't but that she had read *Families and Family Therapy* (Minuchin, 1974) five times.

Reflection. Was Occam's razor a practical imperative here? It seemed as though a parsimony of resources was the condition for new formulations for living and thinking. For me, in revolutionary Nicaragua, through the creative use of material and human resources, the context of limitations, this Third World economy under stress, had become a context of possibilities.

On February 15, 1990, the Sandinista presidential candidate, Daniel Ortega, was defeated by the U.S.-backed UNO coalition candidate, Violetta Chamorro. The Sandinistas got 40% of the vote and remained, nonetheless, the largest single party in the National Assembly. Some say the 60% voted with their stomachs in the hope that the war would end, the embargo would be lifted, and U.S. aid would relieve their hunger.

JUNE 1991, THE THIRD TRIP

After the Elections: The Context of Ambiguity

Traveling to Nicaragua is different since the election of Violetta Chamorro. I do miss the ambiance of flying with the Honduran airlines and the intimate atmosphere of that leg of the journey. I remember walking from the plane to the small terminal in Tegulcigalpa. The sudden abundance of humanity flowing from the deck of the terminal was my cultural transition: a contrast to those monuments to Pittsburgh Plate Glass and U.S. Steel, our airports. Now with the success of the U.S.-backed presidential candidate, the presence of the United States has returned. Air traffic is direct and more efficient.

On the flight, I read about scattered violence in Nicaragua. There were also peaceful takeovers by the Sandinistas of Mayors' offices in some cities in response to an attempt by the UNO coalition in the National Assembly to repeal Sandinista-sponsored property laws for the poor (Nicaragua Network, 1991). Unlike past trips, people on this flight to whom I spoke seemed more ambiguous about their political persuasion.

I am traveling with an historian friend who is writing about the postelection influence of the AID, the U.S. Agency for International Development in Nicaragua. Our candid conversation, revealing continued support for the Sandinistas, is overheard by a high-ranking UNO official, who comments angrily: "There is no danger. They are finished. They have no power!" My colleague and I remind each other that we have to be more discrete.

After that, it often seemed difficult to discern individuals' political positions. Impressed by the ambiguity of the politics and by the continued struggle of the Nicaraguan people, my reflections took the form more often of questions rather than of observations and statements.

Scene: Managua

VARIED TEACHING: DIFFERENT IMPRESSIONS

On this trip, I taught a two-day seminar organized by the Ministry of Mental Health. I also conducted consultation seminars for the psychology faculty and the students of the UCA. Additionally, I consulted to two faculty treatment teams at the University. I was in contact with many professionals with a variety of perspectives. Drug addiction as a clinical problem had become a major concern. The "huele pegas," the school-age glue-sniffing children (some five or six years old), roamed the streets and markets of Managua tragically intoxicated.

Conversations had a different shape. It seemed that those who opposed the Sandinistas were vague, whereas opinions on the left were uttered sotto voce. Several psychologists whispered to me that the organizational relationship between mental health professionals and the barrio communities had deteriorated. During the revolutionary administration, "responsables," community leaders, had been pivotal in the relationship between psychologists and the people, often facilitating contact between individuals or families and therapists. Now the present administration does not organize the communities.

A similar exchange occurred when a co-presenter included in her farewells that her nephew had been killed in a coffee brigade in Nicaragua in the 1980s. As participants embraced her, some whispered to her that they were "glad she was one of us."

Reflection. The new political atmosphere, that is, the changes in government since the election, has already created a context so different that communication takes on new meanings, and people are unwilling to commit themselves. In this shifting political context, what will be the organization of human services under an administration beset by increased financial strain and less oriented toward a model of collaboration with grass roots leaders?

Scene: Granada, Olga Sanchez' home

COMPOSING A LIFE (Bateson, 1989) "NICARAGUAN STYLE"

On the weekend, I went to Granada, as part of liaison work in the program that partners my hometown with this Nicaraguan city. I lived with Olga Sanchez and her extended family. Olga manages her home, works at the women's center, and is active in the Sandinista-sponsored Movimiento Communal (the communal movement). As do many Nicaraguans, she also has a small food business in her home. At breakfast Sunday morning, she expressed her anger about the changes since the election. At Olga's invitation, I looked through her granddaughter Rosita's new edition of a second-grade school book. In the history section, there was no mention of Sandino.

Scene: Granada, Barrio Caracolitas

COMMUNITY CONTINUES

I met several women who run the Comedor Infantil, a children's dining hall. They serve lunch to more than 100 children from the barrio. The center is also used for classes in karate for men and women, for dance, and for sewing instruction. Most of the time, the building is a day care center for preschoolers. This one-story, two-room house also serves as a health station for the physician who comes twice a week and writes prescriptions, which can never be filled because there are not enough medications in the country. The women tell me that they are now conducting parenting classes for very young mothers and fathers; the center workers consider this service long-term drug abuse prevention. The greatest obstacles to running the center optimally are lack of supplies and an inadequate diet for the children; there is only rice and beans daily and a half-pint of milk per week for each child. I thought of the dry milk shipments some solidarity groups had sent. A Nicaraguan friend suggested that a cow would be better.

Reflection. Do the lives of these women illustrate the new evolutionary feedback in Nicaragua? Have some gains of the revolution been retained (i.e., women's centers, ingenuity, community organization, women's leadership)? Is change then now associated with the return of the values of the previous regime? Are the changes I see related to a lack of resources or to a radical change in government priorities?

Scene: A Visit to an Orphanage

The organization that financed this trip was embarking on a program to improve orphanages. They asked me to visit this particularly poor one. I thought, why orphanages? Why not strengthen families? Why raise children in institutions? Many of these children had a parent whom they saw monthly and at Christmas. Developing orphanages was criticized by revolutionary activists; it was not seen as empowering. I had spoken with a hacienda owner the day before. He was very critical of the Sandinistas. The work of the padre who had founded the orphanage, he thought, was wonderful. So many children are otherwise unsupervised, living on the streets and sniffing glue.

Reflection. AID has returned to Nicaragua (Quant, 1991). They are interested not only in economic development, but also in these kinds of programs, orphanages. Is there a reciprocal relationship between the return of the charity model and disempowerment, or are my formulations blind to the realities of poverty and of cost-benefit analysis? The return of official U.S. influence reminded me of my position as an outsider. I remembered that, as with families, one cannot totally comprehend a nation's experiences.

SUMMARY

My encounters with Nicaragua provided a lesson in intersubjectivity: Learning from others and teaching others about one's experiences are rooted in the relational process of empathic, mutual understanding with the partners in the encounter. The personal, the professional, and the political aspects of this process are inseparably interwoven.

Given the contexts of my trips, one could assume that I operated from an objective position as an observer, interviewer, visitor, teacher, or consultant. On my return, educating various communities in the United States was designed to correct the misinformation about Nicaragua as portrayed in the mainstream media. Like the Physicians for Social Responsibility in their education about the dangers of nuclear armaments, I assumed that here too information alone could make a difference. Yet that was a linear, unidimensional understanding. In reality, the experiences in Nicaragua changed me in ways that influence my personal, professional, and political behaviors. Solidarity became an integral part of the process.

Information as Intervention

As a teacher in Nicaragua, I shared thinking and imparted skills in applications of the family systems paradigm pioneered by others (Maldonado, 1990). My presence also represented the interest of concerned U.S. citizens and the collegiality of family therapists who directly or indirectly had supported my trip. Discussions of continued contact to bring more North American family therapists to Nicaragua and to find ways for Nicaraguans to train in the United States helped build the connections between our countries.

After the women's delegation returned to Princeton in 1989, the "Sister City Project" organized a series of public relations events. Like a small information brigade, the group gave presentations at the University; to community organizations; and in radio, television, and press interviews. A speakers' bureau was formed to respond to opportunities to speak about women in Nicaragua. The objective was to educate and to engender curiosity and dialogue where disinformation about Nicaragua predominated.

As a family therapist, I recounted the observations of my first trip in the *Ackerman Newsletter* (Winawer, 1990). I also gave a talk for the institute's faculty and presented at the annual meeting of the Association for Women in Psychology and at other conferences.

Solidarity

Knowledge of the other is an essential step in the process of creating solidarity among people. I went to Nicaragua because I wanted to meet the people against whom my country was waging war. My motivation had less to do with

Christian theology or feminism, with which solidarity is often conceptually associated. My personal imperative was more relevant to my identification as a Jew. The horror of the Holocaust had been compounded by the silence of an entire people, of governments, churches, and the people of other countries. As a U.S. citizen, I considered it my civic responsibility; as a Jew, I felt an imperative rooted in recent history to speak out against injustices ordered by my government and to challenge the collusion of silence among citizens in my country. The force of my own heritage, of Nicaragua's history, and of the ideas and people to which I was exposed created a context of solidarity in which we could teach and learn from one another on many levels.

Solidarity is mutual. It is a process. I went to teach marriage and family therapy to colleagues and returned with a deepened awareness about alternative approaches to human services. As a result, my work as a family therapist has changed conceptually and in practice. A project conducted with colleagues (at the Ackerman Institute) from 1988–1991 focused on developing a model for treating families who, as a result of child abuse charges, are caught in a web of adversarial legal and social service agencies. The family/interagency interface was central to understanding the family's behavior in the therapeutic context (Ackerman, Colapinto, Scharf, Weinshel, & Winawer, 1991). Here and in my work in general the sociopolitical context of therapeutic services has become increasingly central.

Hunger and Change

On the third trip, I saw graffiti that read: "If the war is over, why are we still hungry?" Nothing could encapsulate the present situation in Nicaragua more succinctly. I later learned that 70% of Nicaraguans live in poverty. In fact, food consumption for the nation has declined 31% over two years (Vickers & Spence, 1992). I myself had noticed a greater diversity of political behaviors. I had caught a glimpse of the ambiguity and complexities of survival in a society that lacked the essentials for living. I appreciated that I, coming from an affluent society, on many levels, know little about life in Nicaragua.

My relationship with Nicaragua continues to be instructive and has renewed my commitment to actualizing solidarity with Third World citizens of my own country. In the words of the young social worker at INSSBI (the Nicaraguan welfare department), however, "Society has to be ready for a change." In revolutionary Nicaragua, social justice seemed achievable. The revolutionary government's design and goals can serve as a model for governments truly interested in serving their people.

Thinking about family therapy is no longer possible for me without taking up the challenge to integrate the political dimension. Change within the confines of therapy cannot be isolated from stagnation, repression, and deprivation in society. What then is the meaning of political action for the field of family therapy?

NOTES

1. AMNLAE: Asociacion de Mujeres Nicaraguenses Luisa Amanda Espinosa (Association of Nicaraguan Women Luisa Amanda Espinosa), the name used for the women's movement during the decade of the revolutionary government, named for the first FSLN (Sandinista National Liberation Front) woman to die fighting for the revolution. Luisa Amanda was 21 years old and was killed by the National Guard on April 3, 1970 (Randall, 1981).
2. The "scenes" are descriptions of my experiences with real people. I have attempted to represent their stories accurately. The names, however, of people in the "scenes" section (other than historical figures, i.e., Somoza) are fictitious.
3. It is not within the scope of this chapter to present a critical discussion of the complexities of the Sandinista revolution. It is my view that their achievements have been misrepresented in the mainstream U.S. media. Analyses of the revolution are numerous. For more specifically developed perspectives, the reader may wish to consult works about the literacy crusade (Hirshon, 1983), North American volunteerism in Nicaragua (Jones, 1986), agrarian reform (Collins, 1986), recent history (Leiken & Rubin, 1987), human rights (Pax Christi International, 1988), or another therapist's personal reflections (Covel, 1988) in addition to references cited for this chapter.
4. Cardenal is perhaps the most widely acclaimed Nicaraguan poet. His work is rich in the images of his country and its revolution (Cardenal, 1988). Nicaragua, however, has a wealth of poets, painters, musicians, and other artists.
5. In 1989 and 1990, Salvador Minuchin generously donated numerous copies of his family therapy texts in Spanish as well as several videos. The 1989 trip and teaching materials were subsidized, in part, by individuals on the faculty of the Ackerman Institute for Family Therapy. The 1991 trip was funded by Partners of the Americas.

BIBLIOGRAPHY

Ackerman, F., Colapinto, J. A., Scharf, C. N., Weinshel, M., & Winawer, H. (1991). The involuntary client: Avoiding "pretend therapy." *Family Systems Medicine, 9*, 261–266.

Bateson, M. C. (1989). *Composing a life.* New York: Atlantic Monthly Press.

Berger Gould, B. (1985). Large systems and peace. *Journal of Strategic and Systemic Therapies, 4*, 64–69.

Cardenal, E. (1988). *Nicaraguan new time* (D. Livingstone, Trans.). London: Journeyman.

Coburn, F., & Flores, R. S. (Illustrator) (1991). *My car in Managua.* Austin: University of Texas Press.

Collins, J. (1986). *Nicaragua: What difference could a revolution make?* New York: A Food First Book, Grove Press.

Covel, J. (1988). *In Nicaragua.* London: Free Association Books.

Dodson, M., & O'Shaughnessy, L. N. (1990). *Nicaragua's other revolution.* Chapel Hill: University of North Carolina Press.

Galeano, E. (1984). *Open veins of Latin America.* New York: Monthly Review Press.

Gelpi, B. C., Harstock, N. C. M., Novak, C. C., & Strober, M. H. (Eds.) (1986). *Women and poverty.* Chicago: University of Chicago Press.

Gilbert, D. (1988). *Sandinistas.* New York: Basil Blackwell.

Hirshon, S. L. (1983). *And also teach them to read.* Westport, CT: Lawrence Hill & Company.

Heyward, C. (1987). *Revolutionary forgiveness.* Maryknoll, NY: Orbis Books.

Jones, J. (Ed.) (1986). *Brigadista: Harvest and war in Nicaragua.* New York: Praeger Publishers.

Keen, S. (1988). *Faces of the enemy.* San Francisco: Harper.

Leacock, E. (1979). Women, development and anthropological facts and fictions. In *Women in Latin America.* Riverside, CA: Latin American Perspectives.

Leiken, R. S., & Rubin, B. (Eds.) (1987). *Central American crisis reader.* New York: Summit Books.

Maldonado, I. M. (1990). Mental health: The history of an internationalist cooperation with Nicaragua. *Family Systems Medicine, 8,* 327–337.

Minuchin, S. (1974). *Families and family therapy.* Cambridge, MA: Harvard University Press.

Nicaragua Network. (1991). New York: Peacenet Computer Bulletin.

Pax Christi International (1988). *Human rights in Central America.* Antwerp, Belgium: Pax Christi International.

Quant, M. (1991). U.S. aid to Nicaragua: Funding the right. *Z Magazine, August.*

Ramirez, S. (1985). *Seguimos de Frente.* Caracas: Escritos Sobre La Revolucion.

Randall, M. (1981). *Sandino's daughters.* Vancouver: New Star Books.

Ruchwarger, G. (1987). *People in power.* South Hadley, MA: Bergin & Garvey.

Rushdie, S. (1987). *The jaguar smile.* New York: Viking.

Tortorici, J. M. (1989). Mental health care in Nicaragua: The challenge of reconstruction. Presented to the Convention of the World Association for Psychosocial Rehabilitation, Barcelona, Spain.

Vickers, G., & Spence, J. (1992). Nicaragua: Two years after the fall. *World Policy Journal, 9,* 533–561.

Wetzel, N., & Winawer, H. (1986). The psychosocial consequences of the nuclear threat from a family systems perspective. *International Journal of Mental Health, 15,* 298–313.

Winawer, H. (1990). Patterns that connect: Peace activism and family systems therapy. *Ackerman Newsletter, Winter, 3.*

Zapata, J. (1989). *Health care in revolutionary Nicaragua.* Address to Princeton Women's Delegation, National Ministry of Health, Managua.

The Inner Voice of the Global Family Therapist

Here Faye Snider and Benina Berger Gould move deeply into their internal reactions to global threats, as they present two chapters in which the personal and the political are strongly intertwined.

Faye entitles Chapter 12 *Poetry: A Way to Bear Witness.* She finds her voice in writing poetry and illustrates a personal journey of working therapeutically with survivors of the Holocaust and of other violent acts. Thus, she is able to deal with her own intense reactions to horrifying material, giving hope to all who do work with people who have survived enormous trauma. She talks about finding a private voice and a unique form to be heard and to bear witness for future generations.

Benina focuses, in Chapter 13, on *Personal Reflections on Women and War.* She finds the personal journey to be the best way to chronicle the pain and confusion she experienced during the Gulf War of 1991. As she and her clients experience the war together, she uses personal awareness to inform the political and political awareness to stabilize the personal, so she and her clients do not feel as isolated and fragmented as the global situation could otherwise dictate.

Chapter 12
Poetry: A Way to Bear Witness
Faye L. Snider

Why poetry? Why this chapter on the emergence of the writing of poetry as a form of bearing witness? I am drawn to an image by the poet Rainer Maria Rilke, quoted in the August, 1991, "Noted With Pleasure" *New York Times Book Review* column: "our lives are like rooms—but too often, rooms we have yet to explore or settle comfortably into." In contrast, the Russian poet Anna Akhmatova distinctly saw her role as poet in the context of remembering and bearing witness. John Bayley, also in the *New York Times Book Review*, quotes Akhmatova: "to forget was to commit a mortal sin. Memory has become a moral category: one remembers one's misdeeds, atones, and achieves redemptions" (1992). It is surprising, is it not, that in more than 30 years of listening to the stories of clients and their families, I had no conscious awareness that memory had, in fact, become a moral imperative. It took the presence of Holocaust imagery in the lives of young Jewish-American couples to confront this internal dilemma—that is, of the choice of denial and avoidance and fragmentation, on the one hand, or of confrontation and bearing witness, on the other.

In December, 1987, I was close to burnout. Clearly, the aftermath of emotional contagion had some relationship to the chronic fatigue and intractable series of viruses I struggled with. Because my caseload had profoundly shifted to a large number of second-generation Holocaust children, I found myself immersed in an exploration of the effects of silencing on relationships and family life. The effect of the Holocaust had become very real as I listened to these young adults who had no permission to discuss fear openly. Further, I was struck by how a profound sense of unsafety had triggered symptoms of anxiety that intruded and limited choice in the present. It seemed ironic that for some Holocaust parents, living in the United States meant to bury the past. The children understood, as if by osmosis, that to be afraid in the United States was somehow wrong. I remember my own horror the first time I sat with a mother and her daughter and laid out a genogram where I crossed out square after square and circle after circle. Both the mother and father's family had been wiped out in concentration camps. In their early twenties, they had met and married only a few months after the camps had been evacuated. With all my "understanding," I had never borne witness to the moral weight of all those absent lives. I went silent, my mind a blank. The mother, familiar with this response, graciously carried on the conversation while I composed myself. In that moment, I came to comprehend more fully the meaning of Lifton's (1979) explication of "death imprint and related death anxiety" and the term *survivor.*

In a chapter entitled "Holocaust Trauma and Imagery: The Systemic Transmission into the Second Generation" (Snider, 1990), I wrote the following:

> Therapists who treat victims of the Nazi Holocaust need to be aware of the possibility of the intergenerational transmission of the trauma response. At any point, we can be sitting in our office and come upon a genogram in which a generation of a family has been wiped out by being within the boundaries of the Nazi death machine. Our ability to explore, comprehend, integrate, and manage the fact of that experience with the family will depend upon our own pattern of adaptation and response, as well as how this level of trauma and loss affects the individual and those immediately involved. (p. 309)

The repetition of genograms and their stories increased my awareness that a generation of children had not, in fact, totally escaped. The process of focusing on transgenerational issues seemed useful and healing. Further, I was surprised at how meaningful it was to explicate and share with colleagues the struggle to know and sit with the pain of those historical events, for I was clearly searching for a way to encourage collegiality in this process of bearing witness.

> For those of us who were fortunate enough to be in another place during the Nazi onslaught, the ability to comprehend and respond to death imagery requires a leap into the unknown. To respond to the underlying symbols and pictures, one must confront one's own anticipatory trauma anxiety. I have found that facing Holocaust imagery means facing my own sense of vulnerability and helplessness. (Snider, 1990, p. 319)

Along the way, I developed a highly refined sensitivity to clients with symptoms of trauma; so it was a logical next step to translate what I had learned to discussions with other silenced survivors. Enlarging on Rilke's metaphor, I had not only entered and explored rooms and their closets, but also I was now entering caverns and deep caves and bearing witness to the unspeakable terror hovering in those spaces. This experience with trauma imagery and the stories led me to appreciate the fact that hidden trauma had a language of its own, often in the expression of physiological responses and dissociative reactions. It seemed a natural transition that I would develop an affinity for clients who had experienced early sexual abuse, another population replete with hidden histories of atrocities. Over time, the accumulated effects of working with this imagery, of being so close-in, penetrated my very core. Indeed, I was bearing witness; beyond that, I was engaging in the stories so as to enable clients to create new endings. The work was both compelling and highly rewarding. Ironically, however, the context—that of the privileged sanctuary of the professional relationship and the implicit value on confidentiality—reinforced the possibility of contagion and inhibited the possibility of releasing the stories or the pain I felt in them. The acts of bearing witness alone and my internal experience of how it was for me in those lonely, dark moments sat dormant, and, as I came to understand later, merged with my own transgenerational issues and the hidden stories and feelings from my childhood.

I knew that I needed to write. Indeed, I tried to write. I made a commitment and cleared my schedule, experimenting with various permutations of time. Sometimes a poem would emerge as a "poetry attack," a bursting of imagery straight out of the context of a session with a client. I did not take these efforts seriously and put them aside as a kind of release. During those times when I sat with myself in a more planned way, when I wanted to write and could not, I experienced a sense of anxiety and silence. It seemed as if no matter how much effort I made, time got away from me. The disinclination to write was so pervasive that I engaged an individual therapist with a strong orientation to self-in-relation theory. In retrospect, I am struck by the isomorphism of my need to engage a witness in the exploration of my lost voice. In the presence of an empathic listener, I discovered my own silenced story. It had been hidden behind my father's (who at age six lost his mother to nearly 30 years in a mental hospital) and my mother's (from whom I had felt emotionally detached at age 13 when my brain-damaged brother was born). I realized that I had been raised to respect my family's values of privacy, and even though the holding of these stories blocked major pathways of creativity and expression, I held an implicit pledge to protect my parents from exposure to the shamebound feelings of those out of control events.

I learned from my therapy that I needed to know and explore my own stories more fully, and I needed to dare to try to tell them. A month after terminating therapy, I decided to start a novel. I spent hours on an outline of the story, not dissimilar to themes of my own experiences. I wrote fruitfully at first. After several chapters, I came upon a character in a mental hospital, a woman who could not talk, not surprisingly, a character based on my paternal grandmother of whom my father never spoke and therefore to whom I could give no words. I went silent again. This silence lasted for a week. One night, I awoke at 2:05 A.M. with a line in my head. "We travel on the dice of the mind." I told myself to remember the line and went back to sleep. At 3:05 A.M., I awoke again with the same line and repeated the injunction to sleep. When I awoke again at 4:05 A.M. with the exact same line, I found myself muttering into space: "all right . . . all right" as I went to the computer. Once there, it seemed as if a part of me jumped out onto the screen. Line after line tumbled out into the following poem (revised), which I now understand to be about fragmentation.

The Crapshoot

We travel, as the die are cast—
the mind flip
flops,
as if the solidity
of a throw
could be
reality.
Deuce, seven, eleven—
a chance
to win the game;
as if a number
were a sign,
a release
from pain.

Alone, we are alone
no matter
how the dice
settle—
they represent
what is
a resolve to know
as the hand
firmly settles
on the next throw.

Each morning thereafter, I wrote poetry. Mind you, I knew nothing about poetry, its form or its structure. I only knew that this form freed me to write. I wrote steadily for six weeks; then when I saw page after page, I understood that I had entered another room, a commitment into a realm of expression that I needed to explore more fully. Mark Strand, the former poet laureate of the United States comments:

> . . . the context of a poem is likely to be only the poet's voice: a voice speaking to no one in particular and unsupported by a situation or character, as in a work of fiction. A sense of itself is what the poet sponsors, and not a sense of the world. It invents itself. Its necessity, its urgency, its tone, its mixture of meaning and sound are in the poet's voice. In such isolation, the poem engenders its authority. (Strand, 1991, p. 36)

The leap to writing poetry and the possibility of a new identity as a *poet* was both frightening and exhilarating. I knew no poets, and so I had no mentor or models. Fortuitously, I had the ritual of reading the *New York Times Book Review*. It was there that I saw a notice about the summer poetry workshops at Bennington College. I proceeded to sign up and had the good fortune to choose a female teacher, Mary Oliver, who offered a course on the form and structure of poetry writing.

It is the custom in the world of poetry writing to submit one's work to careful scrutiny, line by line (not unlike the beginning process in my social work training, when I sat with my supervisor and went over process recording line by line). When I came to my first conference and saw the large, old-fashioned desk strewn with 12 pages of my poetry, each line scribbled and commented on, I realized that this teacher, a Pulitzer prize poet, was taking me seriously. She understood both my excitement and my anxiety, had read those beginning lines of poetry, and appreciated that there was a voice struggling to be heard. She did not judge but encouraged me to write and, in fact, showed me how to rewrite, for I had believed that poetry was 90% inspiration. She encouraged me to adopt a discipline of sitting with myself and working the words to evoke imagery; from this discipline, my voice, in its own form, would evolve.

Two years later, I have come to a form, a narrative style that holds and structures my voice. David St. John, writing in the *Antioch Review* about "Poetry, Hope, and the Language of Possibility" (1990), expresses well the dilemma of having and expressing one's voice in the late 20th century.

> In many ways, the lessons of the twentieth century have been ones of fragmentation and disjunction; as experience itself seems to be accelerated, we've been faced with a truly kaleidoscopic display. Think of the breathtaking variety of events and experiences we're faced with in a single day; and though our experience is disjunctive and fragmentary, our experience *of* it must necessarily remain fluid, or else that sense of fragmentation and breakdown that is external will be taken in, and become our own.
>   One of the things that poetry allows us is a way to understand how these jagged, fragmented, and potentially harmful pieces of experiences that make up our lives can be held and supported by what is fluid and fluent in consciousness. (p. 269)

It seems that writing poetry offers a sense of possibility. In the process of giving myself over to the experience of the poem, it becomes a moving into, a moving through to, completion. All along, I am guided by the knowledge that the form and its words are a journey to shape and share with others, if and when I choose. There is a sense of mastery, of some control of a subject matter often fraught with a sense of being out of control. For a while, this process was selfishly my own and highly personal. I felt shy, even awkward that I had turned in a direction so different from my everyday world and struggled to understand where I would be going on such a course. When the budget cuts hit Massachusetts in the spring of 1990 and I listened to the pain of my colleagues, I started to write about social and political issues. My passion and outrage were strong. When the poem *Orwell Got it Right Afterall* emerged, I felt compelled to find a way to share it and called on an American Family Therapy Academy (AFTA) colleague, Ethan Harris, who edited the local *Society for Family Therapy and Research Newsletter.*[1] He was both intrigued and welcoming of my efforts. The first time a colleague gave me feedback, it was in response to the Orwell poem. A 20-year veteran of a targeted mental health clinic, she said: "I've put the poem on the bulletin board so everyone, clients and staff, can see it. Thank you for writing what we all feel and could not articulate." I felt surprise at her words and began to understand that bearing witness through poetry had the possibility of creating a rippling effect, a way to bring the images and metaphors back from the context of isolation into a shared experience.

Donna Hilleboe DeMuth and Benina Berger Gould must have had a sense of that for they stayed closely in touch with me for a good part of this journey. Having committed myself to writing a prose chapter and then backing off, I am grateful that they offered me the option to write the chapter to include poetry. In the next section, I offer several poems and explicate their themes.

POEMS

Theme: State Budget Cuts

In the spring of 1990, state budget cuts hit the mental health system in Massachusetts and threatened to unglue the bonds of mental health professionals and their clients. The therapist for many mental health professionals, I sat with the pain of their helplessness as I realized that structures and jobs that reinforced and guaranteed dedication and loyalty to public service were being dismantled. The first poem emerged shortly after Governor Dukakis proposed budget cuts in his televised "fireside" chats. The second poem was written in the spring of 1991, when the then new Governor Weld offered privatization as a Band-Aid, and my colleagues were desperately trying to raise funds to keep the private community mental health system afloat without benefit of state funds.

Orwell Got it Right Afterall*

In 1955, I read Orwell's 1984.
I was scared to death
by the image of Big Brother watching
and judging my every move.
In 1985, I read it again;
and breathed a sigh of relief.
It is now November, 1990.

A man I do not know died yesterday.
Like an old, well-cared-for dog,
they put him out on the street,
his home of twelve years torn away.
The Commissioner says it's nothing personal—
that, in fact, he likes dogs.
It's just policy.

Another man I'll never know has survived
ten years outside a state hospital.
He cowers with fear,
and merely needs a steadying hand.

Twice a week, he visited with Bill,
a clinic social worker, who got cut.
The Commissioner said these lay offs
weren't personal—
simply a matter of economics.

Rich is a World War II veteran,
a paraplegic, who lives in a residence
with other shattered vets.
It took a long time before Rich trusted
their faithful counselor, a state employee,
who came weekly.
The Commissioner cut that position, too.
He sent a replacement from three towns over
who hasn't yet arrived.

For the third time in a year,
the Governor appears on the screen.
His stoney face clips the sparse words:
"We have to make sacrifices for the state,
and cut deep to the bone."
Faceless bond dealers on Madison Avenue
with their spread sheets hover
like devils slicked up in shining silk,
advising to pay up or suffer the doom
of purgatory junk.

The Governor ends with speak-words:
"Believe me, it hurts to dig so deep,"
and the screen fades to gray
as he walks away with the ease
of one who thrives on the fast gait
of two sturdy legs going home
where the familiar lays in wait.

Nice Folks Don't Win*

Budget crisis—
Withdrawal of funds,
Priority decisions,
Privatization,
It's all the same—
A bitter chorus, wrenching farewells
will echo and resonate
throughout the state,
all the coming days
when social workers and psychologists,

psychiatrists as well,
will say "good-bye"
to men and women, boys and girls
they have long cared for.

"I am sorry I will no longer be able
to provide service—we are closing."
(*God help me, I'm abandoning you.*)

"I am sorry but the rules have changed—
I now must charge a fee of $25.00."
(*and I know you can't afford that.*)

"I am sorry I have to leave,
and you will be placed on a wait list."
(*If and when there will be a replacement.*)

What does it mean
when a trained and ready cadre
of caregivers cannot stay
and attend to support and sustain
mothers, fathers, their children
and grandchildren, because . . .
(*God help me, I'm only a poet—
Isn't there anyone to answer
up there on the Hill?*)

Theme: Gulf War

In January of 1991 when the Gulf War broke out, every poem I wrote held themes of war. I went on vacation to Sanibel Island, Florida, the last week in January and wanted to focus on images of sand and surf and shells. I wrote on the plane going down about the fear of terrorist bombs and, once there, of shelling in Israel and downed American pilots. I could not leave the war behind. Some of the following poems emerged there.

We Got the Message

The worn and bruised faces
of three American flyers stare out
from the front page
of this January Times.
I recoil from the sight
of three pairs of eyes,
raw with pain—
and I want to look away.

It's obvious that Saddam
wants me to tremble,
to recoil
at their battered sight.
I will not.
In fact, I cannot but look all the harder—
for pictures do not lie,
nor do men who hold their pride
in the curl of a lip, the set of a jaw,
or the firm fix of a shoulder.

A Bird in Hand

I wonder at the miseries
of this Gulf war
where Holocaust survivors
and their children
again wait
in dark and sealed places
while masters of technology
promise safe passage
via the magical eye
of the Patriot missile.

On the third day of the war,
an Iraqi scud somehow slipped by.
It blasted a Tel-Aviv neighborhood,
and ninety-eight citizens were injured.
Three more died of heart attacks—
a synonym, for too much fright.

Daily, Russian cast-aways
pour into the wide-open port.
With joy, they touch soil,
rising up to greet the issue
of a charcoal filtered gas mask,
a practical gift
from their Holocaust cousins.

Myopia*

1.

On the twenty-second of February
in nighttime pitch,
men in green tinted goggles,
turreted in treaded rolling tanks,
crawl in the splattered dust
like desert snakes

with transparent caps
that fix eyes open
round the clock.

2.

I awaken with a recent memory
of an after dinner walk
in downtown San Francisco
where a streetlight spotted
two wide-eyed girls
digging the dirt
of an empty jardiniere,
while their mother
spread sleep-quilts
along the sloped brick
of an alley hideaway.

3.

They say it costs $2300
to purchase one pair
of infra-red goggles.
Perhaps, when this war ends,
the military will re-cycle
the surplus
to night dwellers
on the concrete desert
here, at home.

Parade Rest*

I cry at parades—
small ones, big ones.
The minute I hear the brass band
and see the marshall strut
with his baton overhead,
I dissolve.

The Monday after the Gulf War,
there was the grandest parade ever—
with confetti and ticker tape and flags
and yellow ribbons
and I couldn't go and I couldn't watch.

Across the river,
some mourners gathered
to follow a lonely drum beat.
It was steadfast and somber—
a dirge I resonate
since that first memorial parade,

yellow balloon in hand
and close to the curb,
a lone and frail World War I veteran
stopped in salute, and turned
his eyes, bleeding
onto me.

Theme: the Homeless

In the fall of 1989, a week after the earthquake had hit, I went to a conference in San Francisco. On a break between sessions, I encountered my first experience with the homeless.

San Francisco, 1989

Who are these people
drifting,
hovering at store entries,
carrying their stories
on crayoned signs,
their cups beckoning
as I trot to Macy's
all dressed-up
to shop.

I notice a young woman,
my daughter's age.
She says she has no job.
I hesitate, put five dollars
in her cup
and pass a man
cross-kneed, reading a book
as if alone in a park
on a sunny day.

My eyes move to the sight
of a stately woman, her arms
wrapped tight
around a gaunt toddler.
I mirror her shy caution.
Her words, polite,
are an invitation
for our eyes to connect.

The Macy's sign just overhead,
I move inside

where perfumed fumes swirl my senses
and clerks with shined mouths dazzle—
their smiles, surreal.
The oddity of a makeover
propels me. I back out
to the sidewalk,
to the bare faces,
to the stories that linger.

Theme: Trauma

Finally and perhaps most importantly to my own sense of what is "myself,"
I have written poems about trauma. In these, I have begun to find a way to
express some of the responses and dilemmas of holding privileged communication while expressing the essence or meaning of these painful stories. Often I
would shrink back from the imagery that evolved. Sometimes it evoked a retrau-
matization and reliving of affect. Those times were the hardest. Yet I learned that
once I have completed this type of poem, what emerges is often a startling
awareness at a different level of meaning—as in the poem *In The Devil's Lair*,
where the image of exorcism seemed right. As a way of maintaining absolute
integrity around the issue of confidentiality in the poems that follow, I have asked
each client for permission to use any semblance of his or her story before publication.

No Matter How Hard You Try
Not to Let It Get to You, It Does.
(And Why Shouldn't It?)

I go down a dark hall
to a room jammed and full
with splinters of memory—
arms and legs,
a backbone bent carelessly
with that pain called disdain.
I hear her voice: *Shut the door,*
lock it up,
for it will spill over
and fill your every orifice,
as it has done my own.

I smell the stink
from the wasting of that child waif
who wandered into the devil's cavern,
suffered the sin of sacrifice,
her body privates mutilated

and hung for display
where she understood
there would be more,
for the telling.

She became a brave soldier
and buried that time,
masking the throbbing within
with surliness towards the parent
who dressed her sweetly
and who, oddly—
seemed not to notice
the sudden and peculiar
drying up
of a spring
that once bubbled
with abandon.

In the Devil's Lair

The face of pain, frozen—
is everywhere in this space
as I sit in my chair,
attuned to voices grasping
for release from the grip
of spirits still hovering,
still able to cause harm.

Not quite fixed in time,
they float—
as invisible smoke
igniting in the eyes,
curling in the gut,
searing the legs, an arm—
It is the face of the devil
dressed in fiery-red
and burning lust.

With his pitchfork, he probes
and pokes the child.
She is tied, belly-down—
She is braced, legs-bound.
Her mouth is locked,
and she is caught
in a corridor,
in the loft of a barn,
in the clearing of a vacation wood.

I spar with him.
He hisses
at the show of care, my sadness,
for their wounds are palpable.
He hates any face
where the flicker of rawness
filters in the eyes.
He disdains my hand,
and threatens to cut it off.

In defense, I grab the arms
of my chair to feel
the nub soothe.
I want to recoil but must not,
for evil thrives on terror
and the fanning of that fire fuels.
I call my breath to slow;
and in release, I wonder—
Is this casting off of beasts at prey
a veritable ritual of healing,
or a mere refinement
of a little understood practice,
called exorcism?

The Need for Decorum, No Matter What*

We meet, the second Tuesday at noon—
four women healers,
to say out loud
what we otherwise would not—
this time, a sexually driven man
frequenting the combat zone
worries, disgusts us;
a woman, blinded by pride
dispensing hurt upon her child,
angers us;
a couple, clawing
like caged cougars,
alarms us.

The mood is somber
when Jan bursts in with a story—
that very morning, in the midst
of a client's tears, she noticed
a roach creeping above her client's head.
When it leapt onto the woman's shoulder,

moving straight for her bare neck,
she acted with the ease
of one brushing a speck off velvet,
standing up and slipping
the creature into a paisley hanky—
and the client went right on.

It seemed a relief to laugh.
It seemed odd.

CONCLUSION

We live in a world filled with the potential for violence and trauma. Last night, the television showed a 2-minute clip of three big cops billy-clubbing one man. After 3 seconds, I had had enough. I saw the clip five times in 24 hours. I knew to turn my head. I knew to switch the dial. I knew if I didn't, I would carry those images into my dreams, perhaps into my behavior—and that was only a clip. It seems that the potential for arousal and hyperarousal is everywhere. All the issues written about in this book are about real and painful experiences. As clinicians, we are faced with the fallout of irritability, anger, detachment, a sense of depression, anxiety, headaches, stiffness, pain as well as chemical and physiological changes (van der Kolk, 1987, p. 63).

Poetry is a significant form of language capable of expressing the layering of these human dilemmas. It offers both the possibility of new metaphors and images and the potential for healing imagery with a reduction in the arousal response. I would like to call on the words of Stanley Kunitz, an American poet now in his eighties, who writes in an essay (1975):

> The words of a poem are language surprised in the act of changing into meaning. The poem is always becoming meaning, but is not meaning itself. Language overwhelms the poet in a shapeless rush. It's a montage, an overlapping of imagery, feelings, thoughts, sounds, sensations, which has not yet submitted to regimentation. Part of the freshness of the poem comes from leaving some of the primordial dew on it, not polishing the language down to the point where it becomes something made, not something born. (p. 305)
>
> Language comes to you with certain preordained conditions—it has, for example, syntax; it has vocabulary; it has symbolic meaning. Nobody owns it. When you touch language, you touch the evolution of consciousness and the history of the tribe. You reach for a tool, a common tool, and you find to your surprise that it has a cuneiform inscription on the handle. (p. 300)

The possibility of newness, of transformation, is what continues to motivate me to write and read poetry. The completion of a poem offers the perspective of a linguistic reordering of meaning, a spiraling of images, and, perhaps most of all, the opportunity to illuminate the layering of meanings. It seems fitting that I offer the following poem of Mary Oliver as an example of one poet's belief that a poem should "elevate, to energize, to give a seed."[2]

Spring

Somewhere
  a black bear
    has just risen from sleep
     and is staring

down the mountain.
  All night
    in the brisk and shallow restlessness
     of early spring

I think of her,
  her four black fists
    flicking the gravel,
     her tongue

like a red fire
  touching the grass,
    the cold water.
     There is only one question:

how to love this world.
  I think of her
    rising
     like a black and leafy ledge

to sharpen her claws against
  the silence
    of the trees.
     Whatever else

my life is
  with its poems
    and its music
     and its glass cities,

it is also this dazzling darkness
  coming
    down the mountain,
     breathing and tasting;

all day I think of her—
  her white teeth,
    her wordlessness,
     her perfect love.

Notice your response. For me, there is a slowing down, a sense of coming into a new place. As soon as my eyes hit the line "there is only one question: how to love this world," I experience an enormous sense of relief; following with "I think of her rising like a dark and leafy ledge to sharpen her claws against the silence," I want to know more, to tumble along with her. By the end of the poem, I am wrapped in the bear's being.

As therapists, it is no surprise to us that language has the potential, in rhythms, intonations, and symbols, to be a tool with a capacity to click in and unlock door after door of consciousness. Clearly it is a tool we use everyday in our verbal exchange with clients. Marge Piercy elaborates on this subject in the introduction of her book *Circles on the Water* (1982):

> We have few rituals that function for us in the ordinary chaos of our lives. . . . Poetry is too important to keep to ourselves. One of the oldest habits of our species, poetry is powerful in aligning the psyche. A poem can momentarily integrate the different kinds of knowing in our different and often warring levels of brain, from the reptilian part that recognizes rhythms and responds to them up through the mammalian centers of the emotions, from symbolic knowing as in dreams to analytical thinking, through rhythms and sounds and imagery as well as overt meaning. A poem can momentarily heal not only the alienation of thought and feeling . . . but can fuse the different kinds of knowing and for at least some instants weld back mind into body seamlessly." (p. xii)

I have begun to offer poetry and other writings to my clients. At times, I read aloud or xerox poems (to be handed out) with specific themes that match what I experience as their issues (Piercy, 1982; Yevtushenko, 1991). I try to select poets that hold a sense of vision, a sense of hope (Kunitz, 1975; Oliver, 1990). I pay close attention to clients who speak of their longings to know their writing voices—several (no surprise) poets, a biographer, a journal writer, and a cartoonist with powerful messages have emerged. Those sessions, in which there is the expression of hidden voices, are very meaningful. As one trauma survivor stated, "It is in the poetry that all my voices can be heard and expressed without conflict."

In ending, I offer a small bouquet of poems, a grouping of images and experiences—the choice of which one, if any, that pleases is yours.

A Special Kind of Trip

When I read a good poem,
I traverse that distance
where dreams and fantasies merge,
a kaleidoscopic transmission
when I am born away
from sameness.

Re-Entry

The first days
after vacation
are the hardest.
I sit in the chair,
curious
as to how I earn a living.

Odd is it not
that tears and fears,
pain and shame
put bread on my table,
that people pay me
to listen.

Oh, I listen—
perhaps, too well.
Some days, the pain is endless.
It stays,
following me
through the night.
Mornings after,
I fantasize
about "normal" work—
like running a boutique,
an inn,
becoming a poet
in Vermont.

The Visitor

The first time I noticed,
she was perched on the long, log fence
facing the front of the house.
She looked to be the length
of a full-grown crow
with broad, sturdy shoulders
only colored all mottled brown and beige.
I marveled at the eagle shaped head
tilted in solitary reflection,
and wondered: *Can she be lost?*

I practiced stillness
as she soared
on wide, brown and tan striated wings.
I thought: *She could be a sister
of the Florida osprey,*
and noticed a curious unease.

Her presence changed the order;
her difference, so evident
from her suburban cousins—
the genteel, red capped cardinal couple,
the darting chickadees, the steadfast doves—
all tamed by the ready seed
at the back yard feeder.

I don't know where or what she ate.
Her strength of wing and wary watchfulness
seemed to belong to the sweep of grasses,
the untethered rivers and streams.
She visited three full days.

I found her story in my guidebook—
"The burino, a hawk-like bird sometimes
frequenting Southern Maine."
Sometime on the fourth day,
she flew away—
and at the sight of that empty space,
I was grateful, for she had taken me
to places I had not known.

It is my hope that this chapter took you to places you have not known and
that it offers inspiration and encouragement for leaps of daring and courage to
express that which you may not yet know lies within you.

NOTES

1. An asterisk denotes that a poem has been previously published in *The Society for Family
   Therapy and Research Newsletter.* Reprinted with permission.
2. From Oliver, M. (1990). *House of Light.* Boston: Beacon Press. Copyright 1990 by Mary
   Oliver. Used by permission of the Molly Malone Cook Literary Agency.

BIBLIOGRAPHY

Bayley, J. (1992, May 13). The sheer necessity for poetry. *The New York Times Book Review,*
    p. 9.
Kunitz, S. (1975). *A kind of order, a kind of folly. Essays and conversation.* Boston: Little, Brown.
Lifton, R. J. (1979). *The broken connection.* New York: Simon & Schuster.
Mitchell, S. (1991). *The enlightened mind: An anthology of sacred prose.* New York: Harper
    Collins.
Oliver, M. (1990). *House of light.* Boston: Beacon.
Piercy, M. (1982). *Circles on the water.* New York: Alfred A. Knopf.
Reeder, R. (1991). *The complete poems of Anna Akhmmatova* (J. Hemschemeyer, Trans.).
    Somerville, MA: Zephyr Press.
Snider, F. (1990). Holocaust trauma and imagery: The systemic transmission into the
    second generation. In M. Mirkin (Ed.), *The social and political contexts of family therapy.*
    Boston: Allyn & Bacon, pp. 307–329.
Strand, M. (1991, Sept. 15). Slow down for poetry. *The New York Times Book Review,* p. 36.
St. John, D. (1990). Poetry, hope, and the language of possibility. *The Antioch Review, 48*(3),
    269.
van der Kolk, B. A. (1987). *Psychological trauma.* Washington, D.C.: American Psychiatric
    Press, Inc.
Yevtushenko, Y. (1991). *The collected poems, 1952–1990.* New York: Henry Holt & Co.

Chapter 13

Personal Reflections on Women and War*†

Benina Berger Gould

When the Gulf War broke out in January, 1991, I found myself completely opened once again to the horrors of the threat of nuclear war. I had so neatly tucked away these feelings, sublimating myself both in my private practice and in the "business of war." This "business of war" concerned my spending two years in an arms control think tank at Harvard University. I had entered this male-dominated system to learn more about the integration of psychology, politics, and technology (see Chapter 10).

Since 1983, when I had become chairperson of the American Family Therapy Academy (AFTA) study group on Family Systems Thinking and the Nuclear Dilemma, I had joined many people who wanted to do something about the technological buildup of nuclear weapons during the cold war era. Many of us were anxious, living in the shadow of nuclear war. We were also guilt ridden by our part in the legacy of silence that accompanied the proliferation of nuclear weapons since 1945.

When I found myself inducted into the arms control think tank, my feelings and emotions went underground. I was more than surprised when my shell was

*Acknowledgments to Michelle Klaven Ritterman, Susan Moon, Marsha Pravder Mirkin, and Donna Hilleboe DeMuth for constant support and editing. I also wish to thank the Slavic and Eastern European Studies for an office of my own.

†Presented in part at the Women's Institute of the American Family Therapy Association, June 21, 1991, San Diego, California.

cracked by the Gulf War, and I was once again open to the feelings that accompany my more intuitive side.

My only purpose in sharing these excerpts is to stimulate in all of us a story that must be told only in conversation with each other.

September 30, 1914

Cold, cloudy autumnal weather. The grave mood that comes over one when one knows: there is war, and one cannot hold on to any illusions any more. Nothing is real but the frightfulness of this state, which we almost grow used to. In such times it seems so stupid that the boys must go to war. The whole thing is so ghastly and insane. Occasionally there comes the foolish thought: how can they possibly take part in such madness? and at once the cold shower: they must, must! All is leveled by death; down with all the youth! Then one is ready to despair.

Only one state of mind makes it all bearable: to receive the sacrifice into one's will. But how can one maintain such a state? (Kollwitz, 1975, p. 241)

EXCERPTS FROM MY JOURNAL ON WAR

January 16, 1991

War broke out in the Gulf at 7 P.M. on January 16, the day of my mother-in-law's seventieth birthday. We were at dinner, having taken a break from the blaring news of the T.V.—the minute-to-minute, second-to-second news coverage that was so compelling and so loud that nothing could compete above the blaring. We sat close as a family, having felt the need of connection during these times of fear and violence.

Like many people, I had slept few hours the previous week. In fact, I had not slept well since August 2, 1990, when the Iraq government invaded Kuwait. I am one of those people with nuclear anxiety. I have trouble dissociating from the horrors of the threat of war or impending international crisis. I am glad of that fact, even if it keeps me in a state of heightened sensibilities. This time around, I am particularly empathetic with the mothers and fathers of children in the Gulf. My son is 25. He is climbing among the Mung people of Thailand, safe in the cocoon of the primitive. Our family has supported his evading the draft, and even my mother-in-law threatened to live in Canada if he was ever caught.

It is a frightening time as we await war. I am very scared and preoccupied. I feel fragile and insignificant. I can't stand the thought of sons and daughters, mothers and fathers, men and women, being killed, maimed, and injured in war. I don't care which country is at fault. It is horrible. I am a pacifist. I don't believe in war under any circumstance. I can't come to grips with Hitler or my confusing feelings about the protection of Israel through violence. I admit defeat.

I want peace. My mind is in disarray with the tension that is around everywhere. I do nothing, paralyzed by the fear, in awe of what is going on. The only thing that matters to me now is hearing Congress struggle with decisions about the Gulf. I want to cry out to everyone, "They will drown in their own fluid if chemical weapons are used," but I say nothing. I am frozen by disempowerment, choked by disgust, silenced by anger, and made incompetent by Desert Shield.

How strange! I know so much about war and peace. I have spent the last seven years engrossed in research about war. Today it all feels new. I must learn about peace. I need to know what it takes for countries to feel secure enough to negotiate and to use diplomatic channels when there are differences.

I feel like Anne Frank, upstairs in her annex, looking out. That is how I sense the world from my bed tonight. I lose sleep, I cry out, I cry in, but the words do not come out. I have only questions, shared with thousands of others, "Why are we there?"; "What can I do?"; "When will there be quiet again?" I think of Greenham Common, the bright lights, brighter than anything I have ever seen, scanning the fields from the reactors, from the village set up by the weapons industry to scare the women. I can almost smell the cold and feel the fog, I see the women I met, the colors of their hair, dyed in the quiet hours in rebellion to the status quo. Yes, war has quiet times, too, when there is not shooting, real or metaphoric. What are those women thinking now? They were so brave. Will I ever have the passion, energy, and stamina to fight again like I did that night in Greenham Common? I had joined my friends from around the world, gone on trip after trip into the unknown. I was connected to a global village that shuns war, that hates gunfire, but, above all, knows the overwhelming odds we play with a world full of nuclear weapons, ready to go, wanting to be sold.

"Where is there sanity?" I ask myself. I call out with this question to Anne Frank and Hannah Arendt. Must we die not knowing the answer? Must we live disassociated from ourselves because the odds are so overwhelming? Do men fight wars as a way to escape their fears and women fear war as a way to protect themselves from stopping it?

It is getting more frightening by the minute with about six hours until war is supposed to start. Everything now runs right on schedule, even war. I have finally imaged the Israelis being killed, our own men and women maimed, gassed, and blown up. All are minorities, the Iraqis, the people of Kuwait, the Israelites, the Saudis, the blacks, the Hispanics and the women. This is our testimony to the troops. We keep posted, using our big Sonys, while they are in the desert poised to shoot, fire, and kill. I feel that everyone around me will be killed in this war.

Friends, family, and animals are not safe when this war breaks out. I do really comprehend war now. In the Vietnam War, I was protected because I had a newborn daughter and a small son. I repress a great deal about that war because I am too frightened today to remember its horrors.

Like so many others, I have felt numb, sad, helpless, and confused since war broke out. I want to do something, even go to the front to talk to our boys and girls. Last night I saw myself as Cherry Ames, flight nurse. Something about war compels me, despite being so strongly opposed to it. When I was an Avoiding Nuclear War Research Fellow, the boys at the Center for International Affairs at Harvard dared me to work with them and still remain disenchanted by weapon systems. For a time during this war, they succeeded. Now I look at the newspapers, hungry to know more about the defense systems that protect us and at the same time create such an impossible and preposterous world situation. I struggle not to feel guilty for this fascination. Yet how can I remain the nonviolent pacifist I believe I am? Do I delude myself? Maybe wiping out other weapon systems is far removed from killing people. But I know that civilians do get killed and injured in the process, although meant to be purely technical and mechanical.

There is no answer. The search is what makes life worth living and interesting to me.

January 24, 1991

It continues to get worse. There are more bombings of Israel. There is a huge oil slick in the Gulf, from the bombing of the pipeline in Kuwait. There are new words everyday: theater, patriots, scuds, surgical strikes, collateral damage, gas masks, smart bombs. It goes on and on, the bombing, the threats. The world feels smaller as we all engage in soul searching. We are trying to figure out what would stop the war. There is no answer coming forth. "Confused Jews against the war is about as far as I can think." We shouldn't be there, and yet we are there. Is this the end, or is this the beginning? Are people stocking up on food and gas masks in the United States because they are crazy, or am I crazy not having a gas mask? Should I go to Israel now and share my expertise on war anxiety?

I remember that my son is in Thailand. There is no escaping the horrors of chemical warfare and black clouds. I counsel others and try to help as many as possible. I stay in touch with my friends, the political women who have found some solace in connection.

January 29, 1991

This is all a prelude to my first half century birthday tomorrow. Since I was born, several wars have been fought, World War II, the Korean War, the Vietnam War, and the cold war. Now we have the Gulf War, with many small wars in between. No wonder I dedicate half of each week to trying to understand war. There is no longer any reason to ask myself the question "why?" I know that this is as much my work as is the hands-on seeing of clients and building my family.

Yesterday when I watered the grass and saw the flowers blooming I realized that if one does not enjoy life, one does not have to worry about war.

March 3, 1991: Postwar Exhaustion

This is a somber story. I am sure it is brought back more vividly by the cease fire in the Gulf. I realize today that my body is so weary, my bones so achy, and my heart so sad, hurting again from the knowledge that we had killed tens of thousands of innocent people in this war. Nobody talks about the Iraqis killed.

We all celebrate the fact that so few Americans were killed. Nobody talks about the Israelis who are scared for a lifetime because of fears that remain after living for 100 days within reach of a gas mask and sealed room.

The stories we have heard for days on CNN are yet a bad dream for most people. But I believe for most women and children, and for some men, the scars remain. The wounds will not close, no matter how many analysts project a mighty future, no matter how many leaders forecast peace in the Middle East, no matter how many newspapers read "Cease fire." Many people are experiencing the shared pain that our nation is afraid to talk about. Are we traumatized by the looks of the Iraqis that we see surrendering? Their words ring in my head. They had no food, no water. The bombs flew overhead moment after moment, 3,000 sorties in 100 days. I find this knowledge unimaginable.

The more integrated our vision of the world, the more responsible we feel for the planet as a whole, the more involved we become, and the more clearly we perceive the connection between inner and outer processes (Phipps, 1991, p. 4).

June 18, 1991: The Fighting Is Over, But Not the War

I am only now realizing how much the Gulf War threw me into a state of despair, such complete abhorrence for men and power that I have considered giving up my work in the area of women and war. Since 1983, I have tried to integrate the professional, political, and personal parts of my life. Now I find myself wanting to separate these things.

But I know that this way of thinking is a move of desperation, not a full-blown belief system. I cannot easily return to an old way of thinking. For me, the metaphor for this war was "five men and a war" (Bush, Schwarzkopf, Powell, Scowcroft, and Cheney). This image evokes the constant sense I felt of having been out of control of all decision making. I was not represented by any women in the government. On every level, things that women cherish were abused. We were "privileged" to see children and mothers unnecessarily dying, to view children and mothers locked up in rooms with gas masks, to be aware that the environment was going up in flames and that toxic gases were spreading over all of the world. We were subjected to a disinformation campaign of great magnitude.

In addition, we were numbed by the constant violence we watched. At first, this made this war compelling and addictive. Then we were abused by being told almost nothing. In the final days, we were "allowed" news that reported only patriotic and positive views of the war. The newsmakers marginalized the women who went to war by describing their participation only in relation to whether they left their children home unattended. The women who went to war never had a chance to say something about why they were risking their lives on the battle-field.

To say the least, the Gulf War was disempowering for all women, including myself.

June 21, 1991: Making Sense of War

It is becoming easier to integrate the political, professional, and personal. It is like a Buddhist prayer that repeats itself over and over again and like the Jewish sabbath that comes each week no matter what the days have brought. Spirituality serves as the link for my bringing other women close to their wall of fear about war. As for men, I try to help them to see that they do not always have to be in charge and that the burden of responsibility has created their wall of fear.

> She with her prayers
> He with many armed men
> Juan Del Encina on Ferdinand and Isabella of Spain
> (Fraser, 1990, p. 182)

March 23, 1992: A Year Later

As the next election approaches, the Gulf War now seems very distant. However, the basic troubles of our world remain. Although more women than ever are running for political office, there still is no sign of a female presidential or vice-presidential candidate. Our social consciousness seems to be rooted in local politics and in domestic issues. The lack of funding for AIDS research, for housing for the homeless, and for halting violence in the streets is no longer connected to the ravages of the cold war and the accompanying nuclear mentality.

We still fight wars of aggression, manifested in "hate crimes," here on our own territory. I am disturbed by the rise of hate crimes, particularly the Japanese bashing I experience in the Bay Area. A Japanese-American client I have says "I feel like I could be sent to a camp any minute like my parents were." He lives like a refugee in his own country. I share similar feelings, having been raised in a Russian family that escaped the pogroms.

Perhaps weapons provide nations what violence and racism provide individuals, a perceived security and sense of power through the ability to damage or destruct human life. My personal rejection of this destruction was most recently realized when my husband and I adopted a precocious and beautiful two-year-old Tibetan girl, Tenzin Lhadon Gould, a victim of a holocaust going on today that most are unaware of.

BIBLIOGRAPHY

Fraser, A. (1990). *The warrior queens: The legends and the lives of the women who have led their nations in war.* New York: Vintage Books.

Kollwitz, K. (1975). Excerpts from her diary. In M. J. Moffat & C. Painter (Eds.), *Revelations diaries of women.* New York: Vintage Books. 241.

Phipps, J. (1991). *The politics of inner experience.* London: Greenprint.

Conclusions: Toward a Theory of Global Family Therapy

Benina Berger Gould

My aim is not to tie loose ends together but to untie knots*

This is a book about the invisible and distant threats to our physical and mental health. It defines normal reactions to the pathological situation of living in a world that exposes us to toxins we cannot see or feel that endanger our physical health. We also live in a world where the threat of nuclear annihilation weighs on our psyche. We are victims and we are perpetrators of these dangers. For many of us, the role of bearing witness to these global survival issues is the best answer we have. To remain silent only encourages the victim and perpetrator position. To blame accomplishes nothing but angry-outpouring and alienation. So the road is to tell the truth as we experience it. We must test our truths every day through our observations in the therapy arena, through our research, through our advocacy role, and through our constantly questioning our position vis-à-vis these issues.

In this book, we all struggle with what it means to take an outspoken position. Perhaps the main thing we all agree on is that silence is evil. Our only hope against silence is through our individual desires to make sense and meaning of the catastrophic situation we are in and to share these with everyone.

This is a book about how each of us has made meaning and how this process has given us hope and energy to continue on this path. We are not living in denial

---

*Berberova, N. (1991). *The italics are mine.* New York: Alfred A. Knopf, Inc.

or with *psychic numbness.* We are doing the best we can in a troubled world that poses problems that are out of control and overwhelming.

More specifically, this is a book about how a group of professionals deal with their personal and political responses to the threat of nuclear war, to the cold war mentality, and to environmental toxins on a personal, political, and professional level. Ultimately it is about the fear and hope we have experienced as people working in the global context, whether the form was theory building, research, direct intervention, or finding one's voice in relation to the issue of global survival. It is also a book about truth, the truth about the serious threats we face from environmental contamination, nuclear annihilation, and the moral degeneration of our culture and society.

This book is not meant to be self-righteous. It does not say that we have the answers or that those who did not participate in the study group or have opposing views are wrong. It is just that some of us could not bear the anxiety, toxic stress, impotence, and physical pain related to working on an issue as threatening as the possibility of our annihilation, so we joined together in a study group in 1982 sponsored by the American Family Therapy Association called "Family Systems Thinking and the Nuclear Dilemma." We learned to live in a community that met year after year to try to record our progress, our frustrations, and our achievements, to provide a container for our outspokenness. The book reflects this process and attempts to show how a collective of people with similar professional backgrounds have worked together in the hopes of making some changes on this earth, despite the discomfort, the toxicity of the subject matter, and the length of time this endeavor has taken us. It is difficult to work on this material alone. Yet we have proven that it is possible by "writing," a very lonely act.

What most distinguishes this book from others that speak out about our shared fate is that the family is the focus point. We took as our task the redefinition of family systems thinking to include the global context. We also tried through pilot research projects to understand best how families interact around these emotionally charged issues. We included the therapist in this system and recognized that the referring person is as much a part of the system as the patient. Very rarely does a patient or family get referred to therapy because they are suffering from their worries about global survival. Nor do families easily volunteer to talk about these issues. The issues are almost always invisible. Since there has not been a nuclear bomb detonated on our soil and since most people do not develop diseases from environmental contamination, we, as therapists who care about people, are faced with making "the referral."

The book moves from an attempt to develop a philosophy and epistemology of global family therapy to applied research, to interventions, and finally to examples of individuals' specific responses to living under the threat of nuclear war.

It has been a most difficult task to formulate a new "stance" and philosophy toward global survival issues because the position of the therapist in the traditional setting is questioned. Many of the authors suggest new approaches. Some of them include the therapist and the client/family recognizing together their shared fate on this earth as part of the ongoing therapy; the therapist being openly involved in the problems of the world, as these impinge directly on the clients; and the therapist being an advocate for the client/family in the larger system through research as well as activism.

There is no one way to work on the global level to make this a better world for the next generation. The experiments that are reported in this book reflect both the newness of the subject matter and the enormity of the context. Each author took a different form to try to make a contribution to global survival. These forms reflect each person's personal style and particular work modality. Although the forms are varied and different, they have as an underlying theme the need to question how we do therapy in a world where social and political ills prevail and violence is the number one issue of our time.

The writers stretched themselves so that working on the international level or in their professional community did not just mirror old styles of interacting with families and colleagues. We took chances with our individual therapy practices because not all people agree that the public and private should be integrated. The work we did by and large was not supported by federal or public grants, so many of us went into debt. But we believed strongly that silence is the real death of our culture and society. So by giving voice to the dialogues, conversations, stories, and facts about this particular issue, we took a chance that "breaking of the silence" would further our civilization.

We also wanted to bring the issues to our colleagues and trainees so they would incorporate the challenges of our particular political and global situation into their practices and conversations. There is no one in the darkness of the night to assure us that life will continue on this planet. We try as ordinary people to insure a safer future for the next generation by speaking out against Hiroshima, Nagasaki, the Holocaust, the Vietnam War, the Gulf War, and the present proliferation of weapons to so many nations. This is the act itself.

There are problems, too. In reference to the first section, theory building is just beginning and sometimes gets mixed with proselytizing. Yet this best illustrates the blend of the personal, professional, and political, and we have no other language to do this.

In reference to the section on families' reaction, it is clear that a methodology is not in place to measure ongoing exposure to the threat of nuclear war or the effects of environmental contamination on our emotional well-being. Longitudinal studies would help. In addition, we need more sensitive measurement techniques. Finally, the invisibility of the problem and the vulnerability of the examiner make the process of long-term research in this area a complicated task. Along with this, all researchers face lack of institutional backing, enough volunteer subjects, limited if any funding, and risk being ostracized in their community for this kind of work.

The following are some ideas for future directions for global family therapists:

1. To develop a comprehensive global family therapy theory, we have to define what is the optimal family style and developmental stage for dealing with the nuclear issue and other threats to global survival.
2. Suggestions have been made for furthering our research into areas that tell us more about why some families are activists and others are not. Who are the people who can hold the long-range issues of possible natural and international disaster so they can tolerate both the anxiety of these issues and the work it takes to try to live with this knowledge? There is hope that the new literature on resiliency will shed some awareness on people's ability both to hold the concept of global awareness and to live a normal life.
3. Although I am optimistic that we can understand from the beginning research more about the place of discussion in families of emotionally charged issues, further research is still needed to illustrate that discussing "difficult issues" in the family about survival on this planet should be viewed as a normal process.
4. My personal next step would focus on the questions we need to ask about individual and family political and social activism histories. How can we incorporate individual and family political and social activism histories and pockets of social consciousness in our assessments so the questions are as natural as "How many brothers and sisters do you have?" Can we become comfortable with confessional forms of dealing with difficult issues in therapy as normal, not pathological? How to do this and how to encourage families to be an active part in the democratic process are unclear. If the political was taken as a normal part of our family history taking, we could possibly shed light on client/family reluctance to be more active or on their need to be overactive, in some cases taking too much time away from everyday living and enjoyment.

A therapy that concentrates on meaning rather than techniques or structures is in order, but how to define that in the context of family systems thinking is a challenge. As Katharine Baker states in Chapter 9 in this book, "we must learn how to take responsibility for our own future."

People are in charge now more than ever. This is exemplified by people's participation in the events in Eastern Europe, in gender issues, and in stopping violence. Empowerment is the issue. We hope this book will illustrate how a few of us took responsibility. We all have the capacity if we recognize our common existence on this earth and our shared journey.

Afterword

When the work on which this volume is based began in 1982, the world political situation was dominated by the fearsome competitive struggle of the two nuclear superpowers. They were overarmed beyond belief, trigger-happy, and easily destabilized. Institutionalized paranoia was cultivated as fuel for the ever-expanding arms war. One did not know which to fear more, the Soviet Union with its combination of gross ineptitude and bureaucratic layering that could mindlessly lead to such disasters as the shooting down of the unarmed Korean airliner or the dangerous adventuristic dreams of Western politicians and militarists.

In that climate, many professional groups were asking what they could add to the pitifully weak struggle to "give peace a chance." The effort of family therapists and systems thinkers to give voice to their concerns and to use what tools they had available led to a number of activities, many of which have been chronicled in this book. The international family therapy community joined with others in direct political action; we tried through research and clinical activities to be spokespeople for the anxieties being experienced by families with whom we worked and for the anxieties of our own families.

We undertook to help build bridges across the chasms separating the adversary nations; this led to the joint-venturing of several East-West family therapy conferences. A bridging series of conferences began in Prague, Czechoslovakia, in May of 1987 and continued in Budapest, Hungary, in July of 1989 and Krakow, Poland, in September of 1990. They were exciting beyond belief; information about our differences and similarities flowed like wine, and we were all giddy with imbibing it.

It would be cosmic chutzpah to suggest that these bridging conferences catalyzed the stupendous social and political unraveling of the Eastern Bloc, but it is, I think, close to the truth to suggest that some of the links, professional and personal, that were established in the course of those years had political consequences. It is certainly true that the contacts heartened our trapped colleagues and that, in turn, their bravery and clarity of purpose spurred us on. Those connections have persisted and are even stronger now.

Family therapists are a persistent lot: The persistence is about the relevance to global concerns of two ideas, *family* and *systems*. To the degree that family therapy is the expression in action of a systemic epistemology, we continue to be interested in how its principles might apply to macro level problems. An excellent case can be made, in my view, that the relevance has increased rather than lessened.

The proliferation of international family therapy organizations continues, for example, the recently formed European Family Therapy Association, and no corner of the world seems to be without its international conference. I should like to describe briefly some organizational work going on in the international family therapy field both for its intrinsic interest and as an exemplar of systemic thinking at work on the organizational level.

Since its origins, family therapy has had a dual identity: as systemic epistemology and as intervention technology. These are the tectonic plates of our continent. When one stands safely in the middle of one, there is no sense of continental drift or of shear at the fault line. It is only at the margins that the ground falls out from under our feet as we step, in Auerswald's phrase, to the edge of the paradigm. Professional organizations, in this respect, are centered around owning and protecting an intervention technology. These activities tend to be seen as necessary evils with differing emphasis on the necessary or the evil. A recent current effort will illustrate: A nonbureaucratic, nonterritorial organization in the international family therapy field has been established that attempts, in its structures, to follow an ecosystemic design. The International Network of Family Therapists (the Network) is being set up to respond to the *communicational* needs of therapists, researchers, and teachers in the field. Unlike other organizations, it will *not* concern itself with such matters as establishing training standards or running or authorizing international conferences.

The Network will maintain a database with appropriate information permitting members to be in touch with each other, set up interest groups, and arrange for visits. Electronic communication will be used wherever possible. On an ad hoc basis, organizations sponsoring international meetings will be asked to include time and space in their programs for a meeting of those Network Associates who are present. In effect, the tools will be provided for the international community of family therapist clinicians, scholars, and researchers to be easily in touch with each other.

Management is to be kept to a minimum because the principal needs are for *facilitators* rather than decision makers. The most important feature of this design is that it is deliberately *powerless;* specifically it is the gatekeeper to nothing. The design is *organismic* and can exist only in dialogue with bureaucratic organizations. In this respect, it is reminiscent of the family therapy approaches of Boscolo and Ceccin, Lynn Hoffman, Peggy Penn, and Goolishian and Anderson, all of which depend, in my view, on the possibility of dialogue with rigid, power-oriented, family structures. Initial responses have been enthusiastic, and there is cautious optimism about its future.

Other similar efforts of family therapists to take systemic thinking into the political arena are underway. The work of Laura and Richard Chasin of Cambridge should be mentioned as an instance of devising a social form to temper and modify highly polarized, conflict-ridden discourse around such issues as abortion. They and their colleagues have developed a structured group discussion that effectively promotes dialogue and understanding even under conditions that would seem highly unpromising.

What issues should be addressed by global family therapists in the future? I will list a few of the major topical areas that must concern family therapists as world citizens and that seem relevant to our twin defining paradigms: systemic thinking and family.

Racism and tribalism must be at the top of the list of our concerns. Readers of this volume need no introduction to the scope and dangerous virulence of these social patterns. Sadly the examples are everywhere: for example, the re-introduction of anti-Semitism as a political force in Germany and the emergence of tribal warfare in South Africa, Belfast, and Los Angeles. In all of these patterns, family is implicated; it seems clear that there are important connections between the bonds that tie us to each other in our primary groups and the violent strictures of racism and tribalism. We need to be a part of work groups of social scientists to unriddle these dilemmas.

Gender issues may be mentioned in the same spirit. The forces in the family that lead to violence against women are the same as those that prevent children from being protected and nurtured adequately. Family work is uniquely capable of informing the discussion about these issues, although once again it is properly viewed as part of a social science array that must be assembled to continue work on this delicate issue.

Privilege and elitism grow in the bosom of the family and are closely connected to those protective and stimulating interactions that fortunate parents conduct with their children from infancy onward. Again we are faced with a paradox: the close linkage of positive elements of family interaction with the most dangerous forces in human society.

Regarding families at risk, we deal with issues of families devastated by warfare, forced migration, political oppression, and rapid social and economic change. How can we protect these families? What can be learned from successful efforts in this direction?

Thus, there are problems enough that fall properly within our area of interest. Indeed, there are far too many, given our slim resources. One might indeed despair of making any headway toward solutions. We are obliged to try, however. It is worth pointing out that, by dealing at the clinical level with issues of gender, war, and violence and at the organizational level with bridge-building to isolated societies, we have already enriched our theory and practice, to say nothing of our personal lives.

I might end by recalling the observation that children who were anxious about the possibility of nuclear war were comforted by knowing that their parents were working as hard as they could to see that it did not happen. That is hardly the worst reason for doing this kind of work. The best reason is the opportunity to be associated with the others who are doing the work, many of whom are represented in this volume.

Donald A. Bloch, M.D.
October 23, 1992

About the Authors

Benina Berger Gould, M.S.W., Ph.D.

Benina Berger Gould is adjunct faculty in psychology at Saybrook Institute in San Francisco and in private practice in Berkeley. She received the Fielding Institute of Psychology Social Justice Award in 1987. Dr. Berger Gould was a Carnegie Avoiding Nuclear War Fellow at the Center for Science and International Affairs at Harvard University's John F. Kennedy School of Government and is research associate at the University of California at Berkeley's Center for Slavic and East European Studies. She also has taught family therapy for many years at the California Graduate School of Family Therapy and at the Cambridge Family Institute, where she trained in family therapy. Dr. Berger Gould is nationally and internationally known for her research on children and the trauma of international crisis, and has published in the areas of gender and war, children, the threat of nuclear war after an international crisis, and Soviet psychology. Her first book was *Growing up Scared? The Psychological Threat of Nuclear War on Children.* Her present research focuses on "A Transitional Psychology in the Former Soviet Union" and "The Controversy Surrounding Women and Combat Duty." Her current clinical interest is in issues of cross-cultural parenting.

Donna Hilleboe DeMuth, M.S.W.

Donna DeMuth is a clinical social worker who has extensive experience working with individuals, families, and groups. Currently, she consults with agencies that serve culturally vulnerable youth and adults, having been a pioneer in extending the practice of family therapy beyond the clinical setting. She serves as adjunct faculty at the School of Social Work of the University of New England. She is the Child and Family Advocate for Head Start Centers in Oxford County, in southwestern, rural Maine. Since 1982, Ms. DeMuth has studied, taught, conducted research, and written extensively on the subject of children, families, and global survival issues. She is now investigating the relevance of resilience concepts to therapeutic work with children and families.

Contributors

Katharine Gratwick Baker, D.S.W.

Katharine Gratwick Baker is a practicing family therapist in Washington, DC. She teaches family therapy at the National Catholic School for Social Service and travels frequently to the former Soviet Union.

Donald A. Bloch, M.D.

Dr. Bloch is a physician, psychoanalyst, and former editor of *Family Process and Family Systems Medicine*. He was the first Chair of the AFTA Task Force on nuclear issues. He recently retired as Executive Director of the Ackerman Institute in New York City.

Richard Chasin, M.D.

Richard Chasin is Co-Director of the Family Institute of Cambridge and Associate Clinical Professor of Psychiatry, Harvard Medical School at Cambridge Hospital. He and John Mack were the founding directors of the Center for Psychology and Social Change (formerly called the Center for Psychological Studies in the Nuclear Age). Dr. Chasin is currently President-Elect of the AFTA.

Priscilla Ellis, Ph.D.

Priscilla Ellis is a clinical psychologist with Newton Psychotherapy Associates, and Co-Founder and Co-Director of Social Research Institute of New England and the Atomic Veterans Family Project.

Sarah Greenberg, Ed.D., M.S.W.

Sarah Greenberg is Assistant Professor, Salem State College of Social Work, Co-Director of Social Research Institute of New England and the Atomic Veterans Family Project, and a private practitioner and consultant in Newton, Massachusetts.

Margaret Herzig

Margaret Herzig is a writer, editor, and researcher in psychology. She is Executive Director of the Public Conversations Project at the Family Institute of Cambridge (Watertown, Massachusetts) and Associate Director of the Project on Promoting Effective Dialogue Across Ideologies at the Center for Psychology and Social Change at Cambridge Hospital, an affiliate of Harvard Medical School.

Evan Imber-Black, Ph.D.

Evan Imber-Black is Director of Family and Group Studies and Professor, Department of Psychiatry, Albert Einstein College of Medicine, Bronx, New York. She has lectured internationally and published widely in the areas of family therapy training and supervision, creative interventions (especially rituals), the uses of collaborative therapy teams, women's issues in family therapy, and families and larger systems. Her most recent publication is *Rituals for Our Times: Celebrating, Healing and Changing Our Lives and Our Relationships*, HarperCollins, 1992 (with Janine Roberts).

Evan is the recipient of the American Family Therapy Association's 1990 award for "Outstanding Contribution to Family Therapy Theory and Practice."

Bianca Cody Murphy, Ed.D.

Bianca Cody Murphy is Assistant Professor of Psychology at Wheaton College, a counseling psychologist in private practice, and Co-Director of the Atomic Veterans Family Project, a research project on the psychological effects of exposure to nuclear radiation. Her publications include book chapters and articles on teaching about nuclear issues, working with families exposed to environmental contaminants, and the application of family systems thinking to nuclear issues. In addition, she has written about lesbian couples and training clinicians to work with gay and lesbian clients. Dr. Murphy is the past Co-Chair of the Nuclear Issues Study Group of the American Orthopsychiatric Association (ORTHO), a founding member of the Division of Peace Psychology of the American Psychological Association, and an active member of Psychologists for Social Responsibility.

Jonathan Reusser, A.C.S.W., B.C.D.

Jonathan Reusser has studied the effects on families of the threat of nuclear war as well as the responses of the families of Atomic Veterans to the aftermath of exposure to ionizing radiation during nuclear weapons testing. In addition, he collaborates on designing "coming-of-age" experiences for 13- and 14-year-old children in a church setting. Mr. Reusser maintains a family therapy practice in Lexington and teaches family therapy at the University of Massachusetts. He is interested in exploring the uses of play in therapy, parenting, and life.

Jules Riskin, M.D.

Jules Riskin is a Senior Research Fellow, Mental Research Institute, and Clinical Associate Professor of Psychiatry, Stanford University School of Medicine. His private practice is in Palo Alto.

Faye L. Snider, M.S.W.

Faye Snider, clinical social worker, family therapist, and teacher, came to writing poetry from the context of her work with survivors of trauma and childhood sexual abuse. She is a charter member of the AFTA and has published on Holocaust transgenerational issues and mind control.

Erika Waechter, M.S.W., M.F.C.

Erika Waechter is on the faculty of the Eugene Family Institute/Center for Family Development and is in private practice in Eugene, Oregon. She has formerly worked at the Children's Health Council of the Mid-Peninsula in Palo Alto, California, and at the Philadelphia Child Guidance Clinic. Her experience in giving family therapy training includes teaching in Israel, Germany, Philadelphia, California, and Oregon. She is a member of NASW and a charter member of the AFTA.

Norbert A. Wetzel, Th.D.

Norbert Wetzel is a professor at the Graduate School of Applied and Professional Psychology, Rutgers University, and has lectured and published nationally and internationally on the psychological aspects of the nuclear threat.

Hinda Winawer, M.S.W.

Hinda Winawer is a faculty member, Ackerman Institute, New York; a founding member of the AFTA Study Group on Global Survival; past chair, Study Group on Nuclear Issues, American Orthopsychiatric Association; and co-author (with Norbert Wetzel) of "The Psychological Consequences of the Nuclear Threat from a Family Systems Perspective" and other publications.